MW01492777

A Brain for Speech

Francisco Aboitiz

A Brain for Speech

A View from Evolutionary Neuroanatomy

Francisco Aboitiz
Department of Psychiatry, Medical School,
and Interdisciplinary Center for Neuroscience
Pontificia Universidad Católica de Chile
Santiago, Chile

ISBN 978-1-137-54059-1   ISBN 978-1-137-54060-7 (eBook)
DOI 10.1057/978-1-137-54060-7

Library of Congress Control Number: 2017938913

Cover illustration © Isabel Guerrero

Printed on acid-free paper

This Palgrave Macmillan imprint is published by Springer Nature
The registered company is Macmillan Publishers Ltd.
The registered company address is: The Campus, 4 Crinan Street, London, N1 9XW, United Kingdom

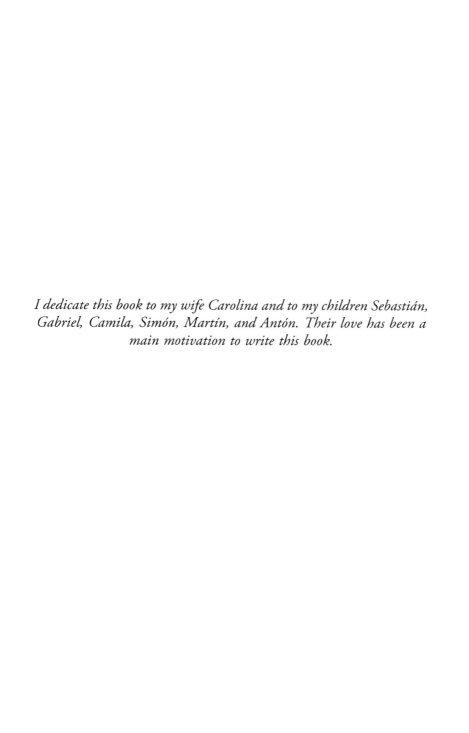

I dedicate this book to my wife Carolina and to my children Sebastián, Gabriel, Camila, Simón, Martín, and Antón. Their love has been a main motivation to write this book.

Acknowledgments

I am most grateful to all those who used their time to read preliminary versions of this book: Michael Arbib, Conrado Bosman, Barbara Finlay, Ximena Carrasco, Pablo Fuentealba, Ricardo García, Giorgio Innocenti, Leonie Kausel, Juan Montiel, Marcela Peña, David Poeppel, and José Zamorano-Abramson. Their insightful comments, criticisms, and ideas were fundamental for making the final version. Nonetheless, any errors or pitfalls in the book are my exclusive responsibility. I am also grateful to George Montgomery for his help in editing the final English version and to Isabel Guerrero for her help with the illustrations, including the book cover. I also have to mention the Pontificia Universidad Católica de Chile, which provided constant support to this project and granted me a sabbatical year to finish it. Special thanks to Claudia Andrade, Pablo Fuentealba and Paty Opazo, who covered my administrative duties and allowed me to focus on this book. I also need to thank all the students I have had over my career, as they have been a source of ideas and enthusiasm that have contributed to inspiring the proposals in this work. Finally, I extend my most sincere gratitude to my wife Carolina, for her love, inspiration, and especially her patience.

Before Reading This Book

This is a book on brain evolution that focuses on the human brain and the origin of speech and language, which as will be seen in the book, are not exactly the same. It is primarily directed to graduate and undergraduate students of areas related to neuroscience, psychology, linguistics, and biology and to anybody interested in the evolution of the brain and language. The book has a strong neuroanatomical content, as this has been my personal field of interest throughout my career. In addition, historical issues permeate practically all chapters, in three different dimensions. One of these is biological evolution, which explains how we came to be as we are. Like any historical process, evolution does not follow a predetermined path, but is full of accidents and contingent situations that make the process much less smooth and more intricate than we could imagine at first consideration. Nonetheless, evolution is usually a gradual process, and therefore many times it is possible to find evidences of intermediate stages in the acquisition of different features, including language. A long linguistic tradition has maintained that language is so different from any other form of animal communication that it must have appeared all at once. Here, I will argue for a continuous transformation of the brain and its circuits in human evolution, which led to a brain capable of speaking and using language. I will look through the lens of comparative neuroanatomy, where evidence for continuity is, in my view, quite strong.

The second historical dimension is that of science. Science, and especially evolutionary theory, advances through controversies, sometimes very agitated. I have tried here to provide a glimpse of the discussions that have taken place in the search for human and language origins to illustrate that many of the arguments in which we are presently engaged have their roots in our deep history. Controversies in science are not supposed to be resolved by brilliant arguments, but rather by straight evidence. Unfortunately, in many cases, this evidence has been hard to find, and this has fueled intense research programs that, although providing much knowledge, in many cases have not provided clear-cut answers to really important questions. Many current ideas are shaped by much of the earlier thoughts of brilliant researchers that have been left to oblivion. As a prestigious journal editor once mentioned to me, sometimes people seem to believe that the field they work in did not exist before Internet.

Finally, the third perspective is my personal history. Throughout this book, I discuss the topics that have been of my own interest and in which my students and I have contributed with data and hypotheses. As I said, the main thread in this history is evolution, particularly of the human brain. Being anthropocentric, language can be seen as the epitome of biological evolution, and its origins deserve study. This is reflected in my early research in the laboratories of Humberto Maturana and Francisco Varela in Chile, then Albert Galaburda in Boston, and finally Eran Zaidel and Arne Scheibel in Los Angeles, California, where I did my doctoral thesis studying the neuroanatomical aspects of brain asymmetry and interhemispheric communication. Besides this, I became interested in other aspects of brain evolution, like the acquisition of a large brain size and the origin of the cerebral cortex, a character found only in mammals. In several chapters, I discuss my own work on these lines, attempting to provide a deep evolutionary perspective to the human brain, which I hope may provide useful insights into our self-knowledge.

The book is divided into two parts. The first, "A Special Brain", covers some characteristics of the human brain like the language-specific network (Chapter 2), the size of the human brain (Chapter 3), its lateralization of functions (Chapter 4), and interhemispheric integration

(Chapter 5), and a cognitive capacity called working memory, especially a circuit termed the "phonological loop" that I argue was a key innovation in human evolution (Chapter 6). In the second part, "Before Speech", I discuss the neuroanatomy of the monkey brain, trying to find the ancestry of the language networks (Chapter 7). Next, I critically discuss research on mirror neurons, which have been proposed to account for language origins in humans (Chapter 8); and on songbirds and vocal learning birds like parrots, which are used as models for human speech acquisition (Chapter 9). After this, I address emergent evidence of vocal learning capacities in mammals, which are phylogenetically closer to humans (Chapter 10), and the ecological and social context in which speech evolved in our early ancestors (Chapter 11), in order to provide a coherent picture of language and the evolution of other aspects of human behavior. I hope this book will motivate young researchers to pursue work and develop further testable hypotheses along these lines, which in my opinion represent the most fundamental questions of our own existence among the seemingly endless variety of life forms on this planet.

Contents

List of Abbreviations

A	auditory area
AC	anterior cingulate cortex
AI	anterior insula
AIP	area intraparietalis
AF	arcuate fasciculus
AM	amygdala
ATL	anterior temporal lobe
B	Broca's area
CC	corpus callosum
CP	cortical plate
C-R	Cajal-Retzius cells
CX	cerebral cortex
CVC	consonant-vowel-consonant
DLM	dorsal lateral nucleus of the medial thalamus
DLPF	dorsolateral prefrontal cortex
DMN	default mode network
DTI	diffusion tensor imaging
EC	extreme capsule
EEG	electroencephalography
EQ	encephalization quotient
ERP	event-related potentials or evoked potentials
FAT	frontal aslant tract
fMRI	functional magnetic resonance imaging

He	cortical hem
HM	Henry Molaison
HP	hippocampus
Hy	hyperpallium
HVC	Nucleus HVC of the songbird brain
ICo	nucleus intercollicularis
ILF	inferior longitudinal fasciculus
IZ	intermediate zone
L	field L of the songbird brain
LC	laryngeal cortex
LGN	lateral geniculate nucleus
LMAN	nucleus LMAN of the songbird brain
M	mesopallium
MGE	medial ganglionic eminence
MLF	middle longitudinal fasciculus
MPF	medial prefrontal cortex
M	motor cortex
MRI	magnetic resonance imaging
MT	area MT
M1	primary motor cortex
N	nidopallium
NA	nucleus accumbens
nXIII	XIII cranial nucleus
OF	orbitofrontal cortex
Ol	olfactory cortex
PAG	periaqueductal gray
PAR	parietal lobe
PC	posterior cingulate cortex
PET	positron emission tomography
PFG	area PFG of the inferior parietal lobe
PP	planum parietale
PS	pial surface
PT	planum temporale
Q	optic chiasm
RA	nucleus robustus archistriatum of the songbird brain
RG	radial glia
SLF	superior longitudinal fasciculus
SLF I	dorsal superior longitudinal fasciculus

SLF II	middle superior longitudinal fasciculus
SLF III	ventral superior longitudinal fasciculus
SMG	supramarginal gyrus
SP	subpallium
SPECT	single photon emission tomography
STS	superior temporal sulcus
SVZ	subventricular zone
TC	tectal commissure
TE	visual area TE
TMS	transcranial magnetic stimulation
Tpt	area Tpt in the planum temporale
UF	uncinate fasciculus
VE	ventricular epithelium
VLPF	ventrolateral prefrontal cortex
VM	ventromedial cortex
VOF	vertical occipital fasciculus
VZ	ventricular zone
V1	primary visual area
V2	secondary visual area
W	Wernicke's area
X	area X of the songbird brain

List of Figures

1

Introduction: The Beginning of Words

If alien visitors were to come to earth, there is little doubt that we would be the first species they noticed as they approached from space. After all, we are the only animals that have managed to leave our planet and adventure into outer space, sending robots to other planets and placing a probe on the surface of a nearby comet. Few if any changes in the history of life have been as radical as the ones we are imposing with our technological capacity, changing the shape of the biosphere in a geological instant. Thus, there is no doubt that our species is vastly different from all others in the ability to alter the environment for our immediate benefit. Furthermore, this is largely due to our unique ability to communicate through language. Language enables a mental or semantic space that we share with others and helps us to coordinate our behavior, anticipate the future, describe the world around us, imagine utopic scenarios, and manipulate our surroundings. Language is expressed in a variety of forms, the most obvious being speech, but we also use language for reading and writing, and some use sign language. Some claim that language first arose in the form of hand gestures that were later overtaken by the elaboration of speech, while others, including myself, are more comfortable with the notion that speech was the first

© The Author(s) 2017
F. Aboitiz, *A Brain for Speech*,
DOI 10.1057/978-1-137-54060-7_1

way to express modern language. In any case, our capacity to communicate has made us perhaps the most successful animal species, which is the signature of biological adaptation. Our present nature is inseparable from our language. How our ancestors came to acquire language is therefore a fundamental evolutionary and social question that touches on our very nature and, as I believe, can give us useful information on how to survive as a species.

This book is concerned with the key neurobiological steps that allowed us to start the language explosion that changed our lives forever, which for all we know does not show signs of having ended. It is commonly said that we are genetically 98.6% similar to our closest relative, the chimpanzee, so this extraordinary impulse must have been caused by only a few mutations that reorganized our brains and our capacity to understand the world, to communicate with others, and to manipulate our environment. These changes may have been caused by classical genetic mutations, possibly in so-called regulatory genes that work as master organizers of large-scale developmental processes. Mutations in these genes may have been important in producing rapid changes in the overall structure of neural networks or in rapidly increasing brain size. One example of these genes may be FOXP2, whose mutations have been associated with certain forms of speech disorders. In addition, recent research has called attention to epigenetic modifications that are acquired but lasting alterations in the patterns of expression of some genes. At the behavioral level there are cultural modifications that can influence the plastic development of the brain, producing connectional rearrangements in ways we do not yet completely understand, and which may have contributed to rewiring our brains for language. One intriguing possibility is whether epigenetic mechanisms are influenced by cultural transmission. Although research on these lines is fundamental, one problem with genetic studies of language capacity is that they do not tell us what the phenotype is, or precisely which anatomical and functional characteristics allowed us to develop speech, and eventually language. In my opinion, this is the most critical question of language origins, and all others, including genetic, cultural or linguistic accounts, will eventually have to be subordinated to an explanation of how our brains construct language.

Before continuing this discussion, it will be useful to clarify some basic definitions, so that we can agree about the terms I will use. First, what is language? Human language differs from other forms of animal and human communication in its internal structure, which is organized in several components. Human language has syntax or grammar, a lexicon or set of words, and semantics or meaning. For modern linguists and other specialists, language is not equivalent to speech. Speech is a particular way to express language, as there are also sign and written languages. Furthermore, spoken language has phonology, which refers to the articulation of different sounds (phonemes) to make up larger meaningful units (morphemes, that are words or parts of words), and prosody, which relates to the intonation patterns and emotional contents we transmit during speech. Other forms of language, like sign language, have an equivalent of phonology and prosody, while written language relies on auditory representations that contain phonological and some prosodic features. Finally, associated with language are other elements like its pragmatics, or the social context in which language operates, and related cognitive abilities like mathematics and of course music, which Charles Darwin said was closely related to speech in its origins.

While the more abstract notion of language has been the subject of interest for most linguists and some biologists, in this book I will focus rather on speech. The latter is an observable behavior that includes clear functional and morphological adaptations, making it more amenable to a biological approach. Furthermore, in recent years there has been a tendency (with some notable exceptions) to downplay the importance of speech in language origins in favor of hypotheses that consider speech as a secondary achievement. Throughout this book, I will speak of language when referring to more abstract aspects of human communication, and to speech when referring to the specific sensorimotor system involved in speech production. Sometimes, I will refer to language and speech to emphasize that I am speaking of both the vocal-sensorimotor and the abstract components of language. My interest in this book is to highlight speech as a fundamental element in the origin of modern language and to depict an educated scenario for the evolution of the neural circuits involved in its generation. For this purpose, I will explore the evolutionary history of our brain to understand from where these networks originate.

Darwin, Broca and the Human Brain

Perhaps the most basic assumption we need to make before continuing is that the human brain is the product of biological evolution and that the origin of language is inevitably related to the evolution of the human brain. In the mid to late nineteenth century, Charles Darwin's ideas on evolution sparked intense debate, not only with the church, but also within science. Darwin first published his *Origin of Species* in 1859, and in 1871 he published the *Descent of Man*, in which he argued that humans and apes had a common ancestry, and also proposed a biological origin of human language (Darwin 1859, 1871). On this point he dissented from the co-founder of the theory of evolution, Alfred Russell Wallace, and with the main linguistic tendency of the time, which viewed language and the human mind as attributes unique to the human species. Darwin proposed three stages in the acquisition of human speech or language, first a general increase in intelligence that permitted more complex social behavior and a primitive kind of thought, which was followed by the development of complex vocal control in the form of primitive melodies, a "musical protolanguage" as termed by Tecumseh Fitch (Fitch 2010). Subsequently, these melodies achieved meaning by imitating natural sounds, aided by signs and gestures.

However, Darwin never directly addressed the issue of brain evolution, or whether the human brain evolved gradually from that of non-human primates. On the other hand, Richard Owen (Owen 1837; Desmond 1984), Darwin's main scientific opponent and arguably the most brilliant anatomist of his time, pointed to apparent key differences between the human brain and that of non-human primates. Instead of believing in a historical transformation of species, Owen believed in an ideal, abstract world where forms or species existed immutably. Owen was also a strong defender of man's privileged place in nature and published several works highlighting the uniqueness of the human brain. In 1857, two years before Darwin's *Origin*, Owen published an article indicating characters apparently unique to the human brain, namely the so-called calcar avis or hippocampus minor, which is a small groove in the posterior horn of the lateral ventricle (now known to be associated with the development of the calcarine fissure, which contains the primary visual area) (Gross 1993). In addition, the development of the posterior lobe of the brain, associated with the enlargement of the posterior horn of the lateral ventricle, was also considered to be a uniquely human attribute. Both features endowed humans with their supreme power over all other animals and creation. Owen illustrated this point by comparing the brains of a gorilla and a "negro", the former supposedly lacking these characteristics. While Darwin made only mild commentaries on Owen's statements, his close follower Thomas Henry Huxley (nicknamed "Mr. Darwin's bulldog") defended him against Owen and the church's opposing creationism. On this particular issue, Huxley demolished Owen by quoting other authors that showed the presence of a calcar avis in several animals including non-human primates (Gross 1993). This pointed to a gradual transformation of the brain from apes to humans. Still, the question remained, what was in our brains, and not in those of apes, that made us speak?

Another character of relevance for our purposes is Pierre Paul Broca, a brilliant physician, surgeon, and anthropologist contemporaneous to Huxley (Broca was only 1 year older), who embraced the notion of human evolution (Schiller 1992). He has been quoted as saying that he preferred being an evolved ape than Adam's degenerate descendant. However, although he agreed that it was a splendid hypothesis, he insisted on the lack of evidence to support the theory of evolution by natural selection. In 1859, Broca founded the Society of Anthropology of Paris, which was dedicated to the study of the human races, their origins, and their evolution. Two years later, Broca presented the case of a patient with a localized lesion in the brain that had lost the ability to speak, a crucial finding that initiated the study of the neural basis of language and established that speech was the product of specialized structures in the human brain (see Chapter 2). In addition, Broca made important contributions to physical anthropology, analyzing the cranial shapes of different European groups and attempting to trace European – and French – ancestry. The first formal paper from the Society of Anthropology was of his authorship, in which he argued that the French were in fact a mixture of peoples, at odds with the widespread notion that the French were a single race derived from the Celts. An important part of his anthropological work consisted of a craniometric analysis of Basque skulls, as compared with skulls from northern France. Although Broca believed in a separate origin of the human races, he also firmly argued that the mixing of races was not detrimental to their vigor or intelligence, which challenged the contemporaneous notion of the superiority of "pure races" like the Celts or Aryans. Broca also did some paleoanthropological work, notably describing the skull and skeleton of the Cro-Magnon man found in the region of Les Eyzies in southern France, and the study of ancient trephined Peruvian skulls.

Did Language Evolve?

While the notion of human evolution was slow to be accepted, ideas about the origin of language and speech were debated long before Darwin's evolutionary theory. However, it was only after him that these traits began to be considered a biological issue. In *The Descent of Man*, Darwin asserted that speech owes its origin to the capacity to imitate and modify natural sounds, as well as the voices of other humans and other species (Richards 1989). He emphasized the coevolution of music and language, arguing that the earliest languages were musical, and claimed that language evolution was closely aided by the development of communicative gestures. With his characteristic insight, he went on to propose that the process of speech acquisition was not much different from the mechanism of song learning in songbirds. However, Darwin was not alone in his interest in the genesis of speech. Nearly contemporaneous to the publication of Darwin's work, there was an avalanche of ideas on the origin of language, including proposals of imitation capacity, emotional exclamations, rhythmic behavior, and gestural communication. Among the most influential of these theories was that of Gottfried Herder (Herder 1800), who proposed that the first words were imitations of natural sounds, like the onomatopoeias of modern languages (words that recall natural sounds like "oink", "meow", "buzz", etc.). Another theory was that innate calls like crying or laughing served as the substrate for the origin of words, as these calls convey socially important emotional information. Grunts and other calls gradually transformed into primitive words, or proto-words as they are called. In a similar line, James Burnet proposed that innate cries became varied by musical tones before becoming articulated words. This hypothesis implied that speech derived from music, which was considered to be a more primitive form of expression. However, the neurological findings at the time, showing dissociation between speech capacity and emotional expression, were used as firm evidence against this hypothesis. Finally, the prestigious philosopher Étienne de Condillac supported the notion that language originated as gestural communication, akin to the sign communication used by the hearing impaired (Richards 1989; Fitch 2010).

All these theories had one thing common: none had a single bit of evidence in their support. They were all speculations about our early history. In 1866, the *Societé de Linguistique de Paris* decided to ban this sterile discussion from academic contexts, producing a long eclipse in research about language evolution. Fitch asserts that the linguist Friederich Max Müller was perhaps the most radical opponent to theories of speech origins (Fitch 2010). He rejected the most well-known theory of onomatopoeia on the grounds that most words are not strict imitations of sounds. However, this imperfect imitation can be sufficient for others to match the vocalized sound to the natural sound it refers to. It does not need to be perfect to communicate its meaning. Müller acknowledged that humans could have evolved from other species, but in agreement with the Book of Genesis, he believed language to be a gift from God, who gave humans a single language that diversified into all extant languages. Müller's research focused on the reconstruction of the original human language, a subject on which he had been a pioneer, and in this respect considered himself to have been a "Darwinian before Darwin". However, the original language was to him an abstract entity, a machine for thought, not a concrete system of sounds. On this, he joined the idealist tradition that has continued into modern linguistics.

Even if at first sight the arguments proposed at that time sound naïve, all these proposals remain important in the literature of language acquisition and evolution. To be fair, although we have acquired tremendous knowledge of linguistics, biology, anthropology, and psychology, the main question of why we were the only species to acquire language, and the specific process underlying this transformation, remains unsolved. This may not be anyone's fault, given that language and behavior, unlike other biological characters, do not leave fossil traces, and we cannot know directly how our ancestors communicated. Moreover, despite our genetic similarity, non-human primates show nothing remotely similar to language or speech, and there are no living human-like species using a primitive form of communication that would help in tracing the history of language acquisition.

Deep Structures

In the second half of the last century, the extraordinary linguist Noam Chomsky (well known to the general public for his radical anarchistic declarations) and biologists like Richard Lewontin (Chomsky 1957; Lewontin 1975) further contributed to dismissing the evolutionary origins of language by boldly claiming that language was so unique that it was not explainable by evolutionary theory. Excluding notable attempts by a few twentieth-century neurologists and psychologists, scientific enquiry into the origins of language and speech only re-emerged in the last 20 years by virtue of the advent of neural imaging techniques to assess language processing and brain anatomy, and the development of comparative approaches to non-human species that provided insightful models of the development of communication and other behaviors. There has been much research recently on neural networks and the mechanisms underlying language, memory, and motor control, together with exciting comparative studies on the brains of non-human primates and animals like songbirds that are able to learn new vocalizations. All these studies have yielded important evidence that, although still fragmentary, provide a new avenue to thinking about language and its origins.

Apart from this recent influence, linguistics has traditionally been an issue of paper-and-pencil work, attempting to unveil the logical organization of linguistic utterances. Chomsky's revolutionary theory emerged in this context, claiming that despite their superficial differences, all languages share a deep grammatical organization based on the hierarchical organization of phrase structure (broadly referred to as generative grammar). The acquisition of grammar is considered to be innate, as all humans share the capacity (or competence) to master language. Thus, language has a universal structure and we are endowed with the ability to learn it from birth. Furthermore, the structure of language is considered to be unique, having no parallel in either other human cognitive functions or any animal cognitive or communication system. Chomsky strongly emphasized phrase structure as the key element of language, downplaying other elements like lexicon, phonology, or semantics as less relevant to the essence of language. For Chomsky, language consists of a core computational system that, although useful for communication, represents the fundamental structure of the human mind.

Chomsky made a titanic contribution to formal linguistics. He is probably the best syntactician that has ever lived, and imposed a tough, logical approach to the study of grammar. His influence began with the publication of the book *Syntactic Structures* (Chomsky 1957), which was based on his doctoral dissertation. There, he attacked and practically destroyed the then prevalent view that language was acquired by behavioral mechanisms of learning and associativity, proposing instead that language was the result of an innate capacity. In subsequent works, Chomsky engaged in in-depth analysis of syntactic organization, for which he developed a highly intricate logical system that, although clear to him, became increasingly obscure for non-linguists and even many linguists as well (Chomsky 1965). This whole analysis revealed that the grammatical structure of language could become extremely complex, so much that it required a sort of Copernican revolution to make more sense of it. Attempting to simplify his theoretical construct,

Chomsky argued that the essential feature of language is its recursive grammatical structure, which in simple terms is the process of inserting sentences into other sentences, generating an embedded organization where phrase components are hierarchically nested into longer phrases in a potentially infinite branching tree. Recursion, he claimed, is unique to language and is not originally intended for communication, but makes up the architecture of the mind. Going further in this search for simplicity, Chomsky offered "The Minimalist Program", in which he pointed to a minimal operation he called Merge, which consists basically of joining different elements (be they words or phrases) iteratively in a binary tree that is able to generate all syntactic structures (Chomsky 1981). It is interesting to note that in the opinion of the evolutionary linguist Derek Bickerton, Merge may more accurately represent the brain mechanisms involved in language than does recursion, as it refers to the binding and connectivity of lexical items in terms of their semantic significance (Bickerton 1990, 2009, 2014). Furthermore, Bickerton boldly asserted that by creating Merge, Chomsky "assassinated" his own child, recursion. He went on to argue that all recursive structures can be achieved solely by using Merge, with no need for recursion. Thus, it is the lexical properties of words that determine the binding rules and the resulting hierarchies of phrase structure. In Bickerton's view, what is critical for the initial emergence of language is not syntactic structure but a lexicon and its associated semantic representation. He said that this of course is only the basics. Much more is needed to develop modern language, including grammatical elements of inflection, case marking, etc. that are not accounted for by this model.

Chomsky's perspective has been also criticized by linguists like Steven Pinker and Ray Jackendoff, who argued that phonology also shows a unique syntactic organization (but different from phrase structure) and highlighted the relevance of many other aspects of language, including semantics, the lexicon and large-level discourse structure (Pinker 1994; Jackendoff 1999). Pinker and Jackendoff claimed that syntax is actually a mechanism to represent hierarchical cognitive mechanisms in a phonological dimension. In particular, Steve Pinker advocated a more biologically based perspective on language. In line with Charles

Darwin, he saw language evolution as a highly complex adaptive process at all levels, from the remodeling of peripheral vocal structure to the elaboration of instinctive learning mechanisms, very much like the acquisition of birdsong or the development of flight in birds. According to Pinker, language is in fact unique, but so are the elephant's trunk and many other specialized organs in the animal kingdom.

Shared or Unique?

Considering the above, it is not surprising that in relation to language evolution, Chomsky has always been skeptical. In his early years Chomsky claimed that the complexity of language was such that it was impossible to find an organization so intricate in general cognition, even less in animal communication. Furthermore, his view that language is perfect does not admit the possibility of a gradual acquisition of distinct elements. It is either complete, or it is not. However, in later years, coincident with his strategy of simplifying his syntactical theory, Chomsky has become closer to biology and evolutionary theory. He teamed up with evolutionary psychologist Marc Hauser, who up to that point had strongly advocated a gradual Darwinian evolution of language. After what was probably very intense conversations at the beginning of this century, Chomsky and Hauser reached an agreement in which they parceled the study of language into two territories: one amenable to comparative and evolutionary studies (Hauser's domain) and the other reflecting the core elements of language and impenetrable to evolutionary analyses (Chomsky's domain). In 2002, they published a now highly cited paper, together with co-author Tecumseh Fitch, whom we met above, in which they made a clear distinction between what they termed the faculty for language in the broad sense (FLB, Hauser and Fitch's expertise), and the faculty for language in the narrow sense (FLN, Chomsky's expertise) (Hauser et al. 2002). FLB includes all biological traits shared with other species or with non-linguistic cognitive mechanisms, while FLN is a single monolithic and indivisible trait that must have appeared only once (recursion stands out as a prime candidate to be included in FLN).

As an example of FLB, Hauser, Chomsky, and Fitch discussed the case of categorical perception, which consists of the capacity of the auditory system to perceive discrete phonological categories like /ba/ as distinct from /pa/, while in fact there is a continuous transformation of the spectral composition as one goes from one phoneme to another (more on this in Chapter 8). This was first observed in the laboratory of Alvin Liberman in the 1950s and was presumed to be the basis for speech perception (Liberman et al. 1957, 1967; Liberman and Mattingly 1989). Theoretically, Lieberman's hypothesis considered that the acoustic system was somehow framed by the phonological motor apparatus by mapping continuous perceptual categories into discrete motor programs involved in the execution of these phonemes. This hypothesis was based on two assumptions: first that categorical perception is unique to humans and is an adaptation for speech perception; and second that speech perception is highly dependent on motor programs. Neither of these statements survived for long in science. In the seventies and eighties, several articles appeared showing categorical perception in chinchillas (a cute furry South American rodent), monkeys and even birds, none of which are able to speak (see Chapter 10) (Hauser et al. 2002). Thus, the trait is not uniquely human, and categorical perception does not depend on the existence of phonological motor programs, because these are clearly absent in chinchillas, monkeys, and birds. This theory has re-emerged as the now fashionable mirror neuron hypothesis, which I will discuss at more length in Chapter 8. For Hauser, Chomsky, and Fitch, categorical perception is a paradigmatic instance of a trait that fits into FLB. Furthermore, they say that the claim of human uniqueness is difficult to demonstrate as it "must be based on data indicating an absence of the trait in nonhuman animals and, to be taken seriously, requires a substantial body of relevant comparative data" (p. 1572). This example also illustrates some ambiguity in defining FLB, because although they worded their arguments in such a way to give space for evolutionary processes, they also implicitly consider the traits included in FLB as uninteresting and uninformative about language origins. Another arguable point is that Hauser, Chomsky, and Fitch provide examples of species distantly related to humans as instances of shared FLB, denying that this character is absent in non-human primates and must have been acquired during human evolution, independently of whether distant lineages also acquired it in parallel.

FLN should include features that are present only in human language and are not shared with other animals or with other general cognitive abilities. In the article's abstract, they "hypothesize that FLN only includes recursion and is the only uniquely human component" (p. 1569). In the article, however, they emphasize that recursion maps into the sensorimotor (phonological) and conceptual-intentional (semantic) interfaces, and extend their hypothesis for FLN as consisting of "the core computational mechanisms of recursion ... and the mappings of the interfaces" (p. 1573). Thus, FLN may not only consist of recursion but also of any link that connects recursive processes with phonological and cognitive mechanisms. Besides lacking precision, this sentence leaves much in the air. In this extended version, FLN could consist of multiple mechanisms ("the mappings of the interfaces") besides recursion itself, which would make FLN a complex evolutionary acquisition. If this is so, FLN might not be the single monolithic element that was proposed above. Finally, they proposed that FLN (recursion) originated from a domain other than communication (in line with Chomsky's assumption that recursion is not primarily for communication), but then, in what appears to be a concession from Chomsky to his evolutionist partners, they proposed that it may have emerged from computations involved in number processing, navigation skills, or social relations. This is perfectly possible but there is no evidence suggesting that this is the case, as opposed to the alternative of an origin directly related to communication. Furthermore, it contrasts with Chomsky's earlier argument that recursion is produced by a modular, encapsulated computational system that is distinct from those involved in general cognitive mechanisms. Attempts by other authors to observe recursive-like processing in animals have been severely criticized by these authors, who seem to deny this possibility *a priori* while opening the possibility of recursion having its origins in animal capacities. More recently, Chomsky has associated with computational linguist Robert Berwick, insisting on the separation between externalized, sensorimotor elements, and the central properties of language (Berwick and Chomsky 2016). Berwick and Chomsky make special emphasis on stochastic effects in evolution, where few mutations can account for dramatic evolutionary changes (as seen in the descending neural control of vocalization in humans and songbirds), and on the fact that contingent factors like having a very small population size (as it may have happened in human evolution) can yield non-adaptive changes in gene frequencies, driven by chance. While I will get into those issues through the book, now I will focus on the central argument of FLN as the core element of language.

Experiments on Recursion

Although Hauser, Fitch, and Chomsky sometimes defended their notion of FLN as a hypothesis, in subsequent articles, these authors and others assumed that recursion actually represents the core aspect of language and neglected any other approach to language evolution as being totally irrelevant (Hauser et al. 2014). While they asserted that a claim of the uniqueness of a human trait requires "a substantial body of relevant comparative data", they did not apply this criterion to the capacity for recursion. There have been only a handful of experiments assessing the capacity of recursion in non-human animals, and by no means have these been exhaustive. Perhaps the most important experiment in this line was in 2004, when Fitch and Hauser assessed the capacity of tamarin monkeys (a cute, little South American monkey with a complex social life) to process recursive auditory patterns (Fitch and Hauser 2004). To do this, they implemented what is known as an artificial grammar, or a laboratory invented grammar. Two grammatical versions were included, using acoustic stimuli consisting of consonant-vowel syllables like "ba", "pa", "du", etc. These syllables were separated into two classes, those voiced by a female (class "A" syllables) and those voiced by a male (class "B" syllables). They then combined these stimuli into two different patterns, one that ordered the syllables in sequence, like "AB", "ABAB", "ABABAB", representing what they termed a finite-state grammar and dubbed $(AB)^n$. The other pattern consisted of recursively inserting a pair of AB syllables into another AB syllable ("AB", "AABB", "AAABBB"), termed phrase structure grammar and dubbed A^nB^n. Two groups of tamarin monkeys were exposed to repeated playbacks of either the $(AB)^n$ or the A^nB^n grammar, to familiarize them with these patterns. The next day, the monkeys were briefly re-familiarized with the same stimuli and then presented novel stimuli, some that fitted the "grammar" that they had been habituated to, and some that violated this "grammar", for example, a sequence "AABA". Previous studies in human infants and animals had shown that a novel, unexpected stimulus raises the subject's attention and makes him/her look at the stimulus source (the speaker in this case). Fitch and Hauser found that monkeys that had been trained with the non-recursive grammar $(AB)^n$ were surprised when a deviant pattern was presented, while monkeys that were habituated to the recursive structure A^nB^n did not distinguish violations from grammatically correct sentences. For adult humans, it is very easy to distinguish the deviants of both recursive and non-recursive grammar types. Thus, they concluded that tamarin monkeys were unable to process recursive patterns. In 2006, Timothy Gentner and colleagues published a highly controversial paper in which European starlings (a species of songbird) were able to learn recursive A^nB^n grammars (Gentner et al. 2006), but this has been dismissed by several authors that argued the birds were able to predict surface regularities of the different grammars based on probability and memory, and not by making an abstraction of a recursive pattern. We will go further into this discussion in Chapter 9, when discussing songbirds as animal models for speech acquisition.

In 2005, Steven Pinker and Ray Jackendoff published a strong and lengthy critique of Hauser, Chomsky, and Fitch's original article, claiming that language is the result of highly complex and interrelated adaptations (Pinker and Jackendoff 2005). Furthermore, Pinker and Jackendoff highlighted phonological and lexical processes and many other elements of syntax like case marking, agreement, and other grammatical subtleties. These are essential for the main function of language, which is to transmit information of who did what to whom, what is where, and other semantic relations. Pinker and Jackendoff claimed that these issues had been severely neglected by Hauser, Chomsky, and Fitch, in the same way as Chomsky's minimalist program de-emphasizes them. Furthermore, they criticized Fitch and Hauser's experiment on tamarin monkeys on the basis that although language is recursive, the artificial grammar A^nB^n is not a possible human language, and violates basic principles of Chomsky's universal grammar. Finally, they ended by agreeing with Hauser, Chomsky, and Fitch in their statement that recursion may not be unique to language, and assert that the only reason language needs to be recursive is for expressing recursive thoughts. There was a reply from Fitch, Hauser, and Chomsky, and a counter reply from Jackendoff and Pinker, both claiming that the others had not touched their essential points, reaching then a point at which no one cared about or considered the others' arguments (Fitch et al. 2005; Jackendoff and Pinker 2005). Perhaps one issue that deserves further comment is Jackendoff and Pinker's claim that at least human visual processing has an A^nB^n recursive structure. Consider a semi-regular array of pairs of dots, nested in groups of two, four, sixteen, two hundred and fifty six, and so on. This combinatorial process can go on indefinitely and may play a role in visual categorization. However, this is not exactly the same as linguistic recursion, as there are no labels or rules to know which patterns combine with others.

Another less publicized but very important point was raised by Pierre Perruchet and Arnaud Rey in 2005, who showed that humans learning the A^nB^n recursive pattern did so "without exploiting in any way the embedded structure" (Perruchet and Rey 2005). Furthermore, when they modified the conditions and made recursive processing mandatory, human subjects were unable to learn these patterns, just like monkeys. More recently, in 2012, Rey, Perruchet and Joël Fagot showed that baboons were able to process visual stimuli in a center-embedded or recursive pattern (Rey et al. 2012). They trained baboons in an intensive task where the animals had to sequentially touch pairs of visual shapes presented in a screen as in (first, touch figure A1 → then, touch figure B1); (A2 → B2); (A3 → B3), etc. The pairs were sometimes presented together with distractors to be ignored. In the second part of the experiment, (A1) appeared on the screen together with a distractor, and the animal had to press on (A1). Then, (A2) appeared with another distractor and the animal had to press (A2). Afterwards, (B1), (B2) and a third stimulus (that could be a distractor or an unrelated target figure like (B3)) appeared together on the screen, and the baboon had to touch on either of the target stimuli (but not on the distractor) in whatever sequence. Subjects preferred to touch (B2) and then (B1), as (A2) had previously appeared more recently than (A1), making up the embedded sequence (A1 → A2 → B2 → B1). The authors concluded not only that human recursive abilities may be tracked to non-human animals, but more strongly that they rely more on short-term, or working memory capacities than on abstract representation of recursive rules. As in Pinker and Jackendoff's example of visual recursion, the kind of embedding reported by Rey, Perruchet and Fagot is rather different from the recursive mechanisms observed in language, but it does fit the artificial A^nB^n pattern used by Fitch and Hauser with tamarin monkeys.

Regardless of discussions about their linguistic validity, Fitch and Hauser's experiments raise important questions about the real psychological processes used by subjects to solve these tasks. Although the researchers had the abstract property of recursion in mind when they designed the tasks described above, this may not have been the mechanism by which subjects resolved the problem. Rather, they may have relied on clever, but perhaps lower-level tricks based on associativity and short-term memory. A notable example of this is Clever Hans, not the Brothers Grimm fairy tale character, but an actual horse that lived in the early 1900s (Richards 1989; Candland 1995). The horse's owner claimed it could count, add, subtract, and provide correct answers to complex questions. While different answers were presented to the horse, it responded only to the correct one by tapping its forelimb. Wilhelm von Osten, the horse's owner, was a mathematics teacher and was impressed with Darwin's ideas about the evolution of behavior and intelligence. Clever Hans received so much attention that Oskar Pfungst, a psychologist interested in this phenomenon, went to observe the horse's performance. First, he found that the horse responded correctly to anyone, not only to its owner. But it responded correctly only when the questioner also knew the answer. Pfungst went on to conduct many tests, including isolating the animal from the public and blocking its visual contact with the questioner. He found that the body posture and facial expressions of the questioner changed before offering the correct answer. The horse perceived these subtle cues and hoofed its response right away. The extent to which we are dealing with "Clever Hans" phenomena in language or psychology is a major issue today. Are we really grasping at abstract representations of complex stimuli, or are we using subtle unconscious cues to make up an illusion about reality? Moreover, what about children learning to speak, or animals tested in the laboratory? Are they really attending to the deep grammatical or conceptual structures, or do they use subtle perceptual cues to predict complex outcomes? Throughout this book we will see that the Clever Hans issue pervades much of today's human and animal research, including language processing and other theories of human behavior.

Pidgins and Creoles

Besides discussions about whether animals can or cannot master recursive patterns, and whether recursion is indeed unique to language, in my opinion the main problem with the proposal of Chomsky and his colleagues is that strictly speaking, they do not provide any fundamental insight into language evolution. The main ideas in Hauser, Chomsky, and Fitch's article could have been written by a non-evolutionist, highlighting that we have shared features with other species (that are therefore uninteresting), and we have unique characters provided by recursion. This has been in fact the standard classificatory logic even before the advent of Darwin's evolutionary theory. Species are clustered by their shared characters and differ from each other by non-shared characters. The Australian agnostic anti-evolutionist Michael Denton has in fact argued that the entire classificatory method provided by modern biology and genetics points to a hierarchical or nested categorization of different groups, where larger groups share more characters and smaller groups differ from each other in features that are unique to each group. For him, there is no need for an evolutionary theory (Denton 1985).

Derek Bickerton, a well-known evolutionary linguist mentioned above in relation to Chomsky's concept of Merge, has said that the arguments of Hauser, Chomsky, and Fitch provide no clues as to the process by which we acquired language (Bickerton 2009). Bickerton made his reputation by studying creole languages in Hawaii and the Caribbean, which according to him provide cues about the origin of language. Creoles are people of foreign ancestry (usually African) born in European or American colonies. Creole languages consist of a grammatically simplified mixture of ancestral languages and the dominant language of the colony. Creole languages derive from pidgin languages, which are even simpler forms of communication used by the parents of creoles, who were born in a different land and have the ancestral language as their mother tongue. Pidgin is used for trading with the colony owners, as neither Africans nor Europeans understand the other's language. The mother tongue of creoles is, in a way, the pidgin spoken by their parents. Bickerton has proposed that the cues for a universal grammar can be found in the structure of creole languages, whose rudimentary grammar develops spontaneously from language competent children taught in pidgin. In a way, Bickerton embraces Chomsky's conception of universal grammar and the uniqueness of language, but differs radically in his conception of language evolution. He has proposed some hypotheses (admittedly, some of them quite difficult or impossible to refute or verify) about the evolution of language, which in essence represent a sequence similar to the transition from pidgin →creole → established language with full-fledged syntax.

Bickerton, together with other scholars like Terrence Deacon, have strongly emphasized the capacity for symbolic representation as the initial impetus for language evolution (Deacon 1997). Symbolism is the capacity to evoke a mental representation of an object or an event by providing a sensory stimulus not directly related to that object or event. Symbols are the result of consensual agreements among different people and are in essence arbitrary. For Bickerton, a key event in the acquisition of symbolic capacity was related to the ecology of early *Homo*, who constructed an ecological niche for themselves in high-level scavenging, competing with other hyper-carnivores. Early *Homo* species like *H. erectus* developed primitive tools that were used both for cutting up dead animals and for defending themselves from other animals, and established a vague social organization consisting of large, loosely knit groups that assembled and disassembled over time, which may have been optimal for finding carcasses over a wide area. Under these conditions, it was essential to have ways to call one another in an honest manner (that is, providing a signal that the other considers true), as individuals or small groups needed to recruit as many others as possible when they found a good carcass to fend off dangerous scavengers that competed with them. According to Bickerton, this was the key for the acquisition of displacement, that is, providing an alert signal about something that is not there but somewhere else. Most animals communicate using honest signals (there are also "dishonest" ones that provide benefit only to the sender, but this is not our issue at this point). However, as Marc Hauser had already shown some time before his association with Chomsky, animal communication systems provide information about the here and now, and there are only exceptional examples of animals providing signals for events distant in time and space (Hauser 1996). In the 1980s and 90 s, comparative psychologists Robert Seyfarth, Dorothy Cheney and Peter Marler showed exciting evidence of alarm signals produced by vervet monkeys (a mid-sized African monkey) in response to specific predators that differed whether the predator was a snake or an eagle (see Chapter 10) (Seyfarth et al. 1980). But were they saying "eagle" or "snake"? The current interpretation is that this is not likely, as the two calls trigger different escape responses. Monkeys do not call to talk about an eagle or a snake; rather they may be saying, "Danger from above, lets hide in the bushes". On the other hand, bees and ants, although quite different from us, do show the capacity for signal displacement, as seen in the bee's waggle dance. But again, this kind of signal is very hard wired and genetically determined. Instead, early humans achieved signal displacement by conventionalized learning.

The first displacement calls were probably not truly symbolic, but contained some elements reminiscent of the object they referred to, as for example imitations of the sounds made by the living animal whose carcass had been found, made by vocalizations or pantomime. Eventually, these signals became truly symbolic and allowed concepts to emerge. In the first stage of this sequence, early humans must have acquired the ability to imitate the sounds produced by other animals, or the sounds made by natural elements like wind or water. Other species, notably parrots and songbirds, but also marine mammals and elephants, do show imitative vocal capacity, and have been called vocal learners. Humans are also vocal learners, but our common ancestor with the chimpanzee was probably not a vocal learner. Thus, the acquisition of vocal learning must have been a crucial requisite for speech to evolve.

After the acquisition of symbolic representations in long-term memory, humans developed linguistic concepts, claimed to be different from animal concepts as these are "anchored" by a symbol that permits evoking it in different contexts, and keeping it active online in short-term memory. Short-term, or working memory, also allowed combining these symbols in different ways, and messages began to increase in complexity by arranging strings of a few of these primitive words, generating a pidgin-like protolanguage, with few if any rules governing the order of these utterances. Based on the notable conservation and lack of improvement in tools for some 200 million years in early human evolution, Bickerton claimed that the protolanguage stage remained unchanged for all this time. With the appearance of *Homo sapiens* and its cultural revolution some 100,000 years ago, the hierarchical structure of language developed together with the acquisition of Merge, Chomsky's operation that provides rules for assemblies of words into sentences. This was mainly a cultural, rather than a biological innovation. For Bickerton, the crucial event for the development of language was the acquisition of a lexicon in which the semantic component of words determined the possibilities of joining with other words. For this, many auxiliary words began to appear as links between lexical entities and modern grammar was on its way.

The scenario just summarized is, as I said, quite speculative and largely impossible to verify. Nonetheless, there are important considerations that can be used when tracing the evolutionary history of language. The first is that language conveys displaced learned signals, as opposed to animal communication, which shows no displacement although they may communicate with learned signals, particularly vocal ones. The second is that symbolic representations were probably a critical event in language evolution, and these could be stored in long-term memory and manipulated in short-term or working memory. However, Bickerton said little about the nature of these early words, and how we came to develop a rich vocal system that enables us to imitate sounds and generate long strings conveying a theoretically immense number of possible messages. In this line, Ray Jackendoff suggested a similar sequence of events as Bickerton's in the acquisition of language, more focused on syntactic operations, but perhaps more importantly, emphasizing the early development of a phonological system that combined preexisting sounds to form new ones (Jackendoff 1999). The words of protolanguages may have had a rich phonological structure, a point that I will discuss later. Basically, Bickerton did not put much attention on the development of the vocal system, and seemed to take this for granted. But more likely, the protowords that enabled protolanguage may only have been possible with a previous, rich repertoire of learned vocal signals that were used in social contexts, including mother-child behavior, group cohesion, alliances, and other instances. It is also clear, and Bickerton noted this, that gestural communication was an important component of the social life of early humans.

Toward Biology

One thing that Chomsky and Bickerton have in common is their assumption that the human brain must have been "rewired" for the acquisition of modern language, that is, its connectivity must have diverged from the condition of our close ancestors. However, neither of them says anything about the specific neuronal changes that could have brought about this tremendous achievement. In the 1950s and 60s, the cognitive psychologist Eric Lenneberg teamed up with Noam Chomsky, attempting to provide a biological foundation to Chomsky's innateness hypothesis (Lenneberg 1967). At about the same time, the neurophysiologists Wilfer Penfield and Lamar Roberts 1959 first proposed the existence of a critical period of language acquisition, based on the earlier concept of a critical period for the development of innate behaviors coined by the Nobel laureates Konrad Lorenz 1981 and Niko

Tinbergen (Tinbergen 1951; Penfield and Roberts 1959; Lorenz 1981; Burkhardt 2005). The concept of a critical period was neurobiologically supported by the contemporaneous studies of the also Nobel laureates David Hubel and Torsten Wiesel (awarded in 1981), in the development of the visual system of monkeys (Hubel 1977). Hubel and Wiesel demonstrated that alterations in sensory experience could have dramatic effects on the connectivity of the visual cortex, but only during a brief period after birth. After this period, connectivity stabilizes and becomes more resistant to sensory deprivation. The notion of a critical period in language was based on two lines of evidence. One is the fact that the earlier one learns a second language, the less evident is one's accent. A well-known example is the Kissinger brothers Walter and Henry (the latter former US Secretary of State), both German Jews that immigrated to the US when Henry was 12 years old, and Walter only 10. While both learned to speak English fluently, Henry never lost his German accent, while Walter is said to sound like a native English speaker. It is commonly said that this is due to the difference in their ages; with the younger Walter still able to reorganize his language network while the older Henry was not. However, it is also possible that Henry was simply not as good at languages as his brother, at any age. The second line of evidence originates from the few known cases of feral children that apparently grew up isolated from human contact, either in a state of confinement by their parents or other people, or simply living in the wild (Candland 1995). Feral children usually have profound difficulties in getting used to living with humans, are incapable of following basic norms like using a toilet, let alone communicating. Their inability to learn to speak is notable, which has been attributed to their lack of early social stimulation. Nonetheless, these children usually show signs of having been abused and mistreated, and it is not clear whether they suffered neural developmental disorders that may have worsened their condition. Today, the study of critical periods for language acquisition (whether a first or second language) in humans represents an intense research agenda, some of which we will address in Chapter 10.

Lenneberg relied on this evidence and on Alvin Lieberman's motor theory of speech perception mentioned above, to popularize the notion that language is a discrete and separable, species-specific trait, whose biological foundations followed patterns observed in other instinctive behaviors (Steven Pinker's bestselling 1994 book, *The Language Instinct*, is in some aspects a follow-up of these ideas) (Pinker 1994). In the 1970s, when I was doing my undergraduate training in Biological Sciences, I was impressed with all these ideas, embracing animal behavior, neuroscience and human language. I felt particularly motivated with Eric Lenneberg's book *The Biological Foundations of Language*, which at the time represented a brave attempt to conceive language as a biological trait, and it is no exaggeration that reading it was highly significant in my choice to study the evolution of human language.

Contemporary with these developments and a nascent link between linguistics and biology, some scholars began to ask whether language was truly innate in our species. After all, it was known that some bird species like parrots can learn human words even if they do not understand them. Furthermore, at this point there was the widespread notion that apes had a highly developed imitative ability. The first attempt to teach human language to a non-human primate was in the 1940s–1950s by the wife and husband team Catherine and Keith Hayes, who raised a young chimpanzee called Viki (Hayes and Hayes 1952). The Hayes taught Viki to speak by using extensive sessions of speech therapy procedures normally used for children with language disorders. Despite long intense efforts, Vicky was able to voice only four words: "mama", "papa" "up" and "cup", showing that the chimpanzee lacks the vocal motor control necessary to utter human words (however, see Chapter 10). But as noted above, language is not only speech. In the 1960s, the wife and husband team Beatrix and Allen Gardner, both comparative psychologists, followed by their student Francine Patterson in the 1970s and then others, underwent the painstaking task to train apes in hand-sign language commonly used by the deaf (Gardner and Gardner 1969, Patterson and Linden 1985). The Gardners worked with Washoe, a chimpanzee that was 10 months old when the training started, while Patterson worked with Koko, a young gorilla. Their intention was to determine the extent to which apes could acquire linguistic skills, by using a sensorimotor system other than auditory-vocal circuitry. These studies were successful in teaching animals to use signs with humans (after many years, Koko mastered 1,000 hand signs, and understood an even greater number of voiced words). This was, however, the result of very long and intensive training procedures. In comparison, by the age of three, children use around 3,000 words, but these have been learned effort-lessly on the part of themselves and their parents. However, the most striking finding was that in none of these long and tedious experiments, were apes able to produce a simple combination of words in something resembling syntax, which is reminiscent of Bickerton's early stages of protolanguage, where there are words but little or no syntactic rules.

In the 1970s, Kenneth Oakley, and later on in the 1980s, researchers like William Calvin and Michael Corballis proposed that language arose as an evolutionary outgrowth of hand dexterity, which was initially used in shaping and handling tools and throwing objects (Oakley 1972; Calvin 1983; Corballis 1993). From that, communication may have developed using body and manual signs, and was finally transferred to the mouth for reasons that are not completely clear (see Chapter 4). This proposal received very intense support from findings by the neurophy-siologist Giacomo Rizzolatti and collaborators in Parma, Italy. Rizzolatti's team identified an interesting class of premotor neurons in the macaque cerebral cortex, called "mirror neurons", which were acti-vated both during the execution of a motor act and the observation of another performing the same motor act (or so it seemed) (Rizzolatti 1998). Together with Michael Arbib, Rizzolatti proposed that mirror neurons provided the neuroscientific grounds for the origin of a gestural language that was eventually supplanted by vocal speech (Rizzolatti and Craighero 2004). The role of gestures, and the relevance of the mirror neuron hypothesis in language evolution will be the subject of Chapter 8.

In the last 50 years another research tradition has followed Darwin's original line, which is the study of vocal learning in non-human species, mainly songbirds but also other kinds of birds, as well as mammals like dolphins, bats, and elephants (Chapters 9 and 10). Again, this tradition has experienced an explosion in the last 20 years, in which behavioral, electrophysiological, neuroanatomical, and genetic approaches have con-verged to analyze the mechanisms underlying the capacity for vocal imitation. Although these vocal learning species are only distantly related to humans, it is expected that they will serve as models to understanding the neurobiological and genetic mechanisms involved in the acquisition of vocal plasticity. For example, the speech-related gene FOXP2 is mutated in specific regions in humans while it is not in non-vocal learning apes and monkeys. It is also known to participate in vocal learning in songbirds and other species.

Our Family

Finally, before we begin with this book, it is necessary to consider human evolution, early human behavior and the fossil evidence for the evolution of the human brain. I said that language does not fossilize, but fossils and human-made artifacts yield important clues about the behavior and the brain capacity of our ancestors, which allow us to make educated guesses about the evolution of human communication. The human lineage started some 6 million years ago, when our common ancestor with chimpanzees split into two lineages. Possibly the closest we have to the last common ancestor is *Ardipithecus*, which lived in trees but was able to walk on two feet. Australopithecines appeared 4 million years ago, and lived until almost 1 million years ago in Africa. *Ardipithecus* and most Australopithecines were small (4 feet tall) with brains not much larger than 500 cubic centimeters, about the same size as that of chimpanzees. The genus *Homo*, our lineage, makes its debut about 2.5 million years ago in early species like *H. habilis, H. rudolfensis* and *H. naledi*, which are gradually replaced by *Homo ergaster* and *Homo erectus* about 1.8 million years ago (Plummer 2004; Anton et al. 2014; Kimbel and Villmoare 2016; Crompton 2016). Brain size was slightly larger in members of the *Homo* lineage, particularly *Homo erectus*, which lived in Africa and Eurasia, with a brain size ranging from about 700 cubic centimeters in the earliest specimens, to somewhat more than 1,000 cubic centimeters in the latest individuals that lived 200 thousand years ago (Cornélio et al. 2016). The more modern *H. antecessor* and *H. heidelberguensis* had significantly larger brains than the last *H. erectus* specimens. Finally, Neanderthal man (*Homo neanderthalensis,* or *H. sapiens neanderthalensis)* and the closely related Denisovan Man

(*H. sapiens denisova*) appeared about 600,000 years ago, while modern humans (*Homo sapiens*) originated 200 thousand years ago. All these late humans had similar brain sizes of about 1,500 cubic centimeters, comparable to the average size of human brains today. Neanderthals and Denisovans disappeared about 30,000–25,000 years ago, possibly at the hands of our direct ancestors. But they did not become totally extinct, as there was an intense interbreeding between these species (or subspecies, to some), and we have inherited many of their genes. The small-sized and small-brained *H. floresiensis* (with a body and braincase the same size as that of Australopithecines) had a very short appearance, between 50,000 and 10,000 years ago. This is a contentious species, as some authors claim that it was a microcephalic or Down syndrome child of normal modern humans. *H. floresiensis* was found associated with Oldowan-like tools that some argue were made by Australopithecines.

Therefore, three stages can be observed in the evolution of the human brain. First, was the Australopithecine stage, in which brains are no larger than that of other apes. Then, the appearance of the genus *Homo* (especially *H. erectus*) set the brain race in motion, slowly increasing brain size over a period of 1.5 million years (Rightmire 2013; Cornélio et al. 2016). However, the increase in brain size was not accompanied by spectacular cultural advances. Early *Homo* species managed primitive stone tools from the beginning, and there is evidence suggesting that at least some Australopithecines used them too, as the oldest stone tools yet discovered date from about 3.3 million years ago. Early *Homo* made sturdy stone tools referred to as the Oldowan industry. The shape of Oldowan stone tools is very stable over time, with very little change in the design of the cuts to sharpen their edges. More sophisticated hand axes appear some 1.7 million years ago, with the Acheulean industry, which overlaps Oldowan technology. Some anthropologists have assigned Oldowan industry to *H. habilis*, and the Acheulean tools to *H. erectus*, with a larger brain size. In any case, both Oldowan and Acheulean tools remained more or less the same over time, evidencing very little evolution in their design. *H. erectus* also used fire and remains of one-million-year old campfires have recently been unearthed, which may support the cooking hypothesis for brain growth that I discuss in Chapter 3. How the use of fire relates to toolmaking and eventually to language evolution is a highly intriguing question to which unfortunately we have as yet no clues. Fire also changes social dynamics, as individuals begin to join around campfires, which increases food sharing and social interactions, and of course the task of making and maintaining fire, which requires strict cooperation among members of the group.

The last step in increased brain size, occurred first in Neanderthals and the closely related Denisovans (with a brain size comparable to ours), and is associated with the origin of more elaborate stone tools that appeared somewhat later, about 300,000 years ago (Sankararaman et al. 2016). This new technology is referred to as Mousterian industry, characterized by sharp flint tools, used for fine cutting and other tasks. Modern humans, who entered the scene slightly later, are also believed to have used Mousterian tools. From then on, there is an evident increase in cultural artifacts in the archaeological record, slowly initiating the Cultural Revolution that is still taking place among us. Why didn't *H. erectus* go further in its cultural development, despite reaching (in later specimens) brain sizes in the lower range of modern humans? Derek Bickerton termed this two-million-year period in *Homo erectus* history "the long stagnation", given that cultural achievements were slow to develop despite the doubling of brain size. The cultural explosion that began in Neanderthals, and then in modern humans could not have been due solely to brain size, as the brain had already been increasing in volume for a long time. What about language and speech? When did they appear? It is likely that modern speech is a very recent acquisition, which evolved together with cultural innovations. Bickerton claimed that *H. erectus* had a simple communication system, consisting only of a small set of word-like elements used to recruit subjects in the search for food. But in what context did these word-like elements appear? What was the biological difference that made our species able to speak about the world? I will touch on these critical questions throughout the book, but this is an advance for which neither I nor anyone else has a definite explanation

Ideally we could obtain additional information about our ancestors' brains by observing the cranial shape and the impressions the brain leaves in the cranial vault. The study of human brain endocasts (molds of the cranial cavity) has been an important discipline in paleoanthropology, yielding information about brain size, shape and growth trajectories in extinct lineages. Nonetheless, this discipline has also been plagued with controversies, the most well-known being that between Dean Falk and Ralph Holloway, which started as an argument about the presumptive presence of an ape-like sulcus in the occipital endocast of the Taung child, an immature specimen of *Australopithecus africanus*, originally described by Falk (Falk and Clerke 2007, 2012; Folk 2009; Holloway and Broadfield 2012; Holloway et al. 2014). Additional findings have been made by Philipp Gunz and colleagues, who observed that modern humans diverge from chimpanzees and from the Neanderthal man in the shape of the braincase, acquiring a more globular shape (Gunz et al. 2010; Neubauer et al. 2010). Furthermore, this unique globular shape is evident in the human neonate, differing significantly from the more elongated skulls of chimps and Neanderthals. These authors attribute the difference in shape to changes in neural organization to support higher cognition and cultural learning. Dean Falk, Emiliano Bruner, and others have focused on reproducing the sulcal patterns in fossil skulls, based on impressions in the inner surface of the cranial cavity (Falk 2014; Bruner et al. 2014). These and other authors claim to have found evidence for reorganization of Broca's region, the parieto-temporo-occipital region and the prefrontal cortex (which is almost the entire brain), a process that started in the Australopithecine brains when compared to modern apes. These arguments are reminiscent of Franz Gall's phrenology doctrine (see the next chapter), or the aforementioned studies on Basque and French skulls by Paul Broca. Can anything about cognition be reliably concluded from these cranial differences? In my opinion, not much. In general, the study of cranial morphology tells us little about the development of the neural networks involved in cognition. The distinct developmental trajectories in the shape of the cranial vault can be attributed to many factors, ranging from obstetric constraints to general craniofacial development, but there is no strong evidence that braincase geometry has anything to do with cognitive capacities. Nonetheless, I have to say that in a very large sample of human adults and children, Michael Gregory and collaborators recently reported that general cognitive capacity correlated with increased gyrification in the inferior parietal lobe, temporoparietal

junction, insula and prefrontal cortex, all regions that have been associated with language processing (see next chapter) (Gregory et al. 2016).
Whether these differences are reflected in cranial morphology still needs
to be confirmed.

Although there is a full Chapter (Chapter 3) discussing the evolution
of brain size, I want to mention here that achieving a large brain size has
not been easy for humans. The upright posture achieved by
Australopithecines implied profound changes in pelvic structure, providing more support to gluteal muscles and constraining pelvic diameter.
As the brain size increases, a conflict develops between locomotor
adaptation and the development of a larger skull at birth (human newborns are especially large-headed for their body size), which has been
termed "the obstetric dilemma". Humans are very special animals that
require assisted delivery and possibly have the highest rate of obstetrical
complications. This constraint has implied a series of adaptations, like
the rotation of the newborn before birth, so that the head comes out first
(as opposed to what usually occurs in monkeys and apes), and the
development of a circular pelvic canal to facilitate the transition of the
newborn (Trevathan 2015, Huseynof et al. 2016; Ponce de León et al.
2016). Instead, others argue that the solution to the obstetric dilemma is
rather a consequence of the geometry of growth rather than a specific
result of natural selection (Fischer and Mitteroecker 2015; Mitteroecker
and Fischer| 2016). This idea is in line with the now classic notion of
evolutionary "spandrels", by Stephen Jay Gould and Richard Lewontin,
who criticized an overly adaptationist trend in the 1970s that interpreted
practically every observable trait as emerging from specific selective
pressures (Gould and Lewontin 1979). Perhaps the most important
developmental modification associated with the obstetric dilemma consists of delivering the newborn in earlier periods, thus giving birth to
smaller and more immature babies. Steven Piantadosi and Celeste Kidd
used an estimate of brain size as a proxy for measuring intelligence across
species, and reported a strong positive correlation between intelligence
estimates and weaning time across many primate species (Piantadosi and
Kidd 2016). They propose that selection for increasing brain size leads
to progressively immature newborns, which selects back to further
increases in brain size as parents need more intelligence to raise their

young. Although this is an interesting possibility, comparing intelligence across species is a contentious issue, as different species need to solve different kinds of problems to survive. In this line, Stephen Jay Gould and many others noted that humans retain juvenile characters such as a flat face, hairless skin, a thinner skeleton, and a large brain in relation to body size (Gould 1977). Changes in the developmental timing of different biological characters are called heterochronies, and the process of juvenilization, or keeping juvenile characters until the age of reproduction and beyond, is specifically called neoteny. Humans are neotenic primates according to many standards, including some behavioral characters including playfulness and less aggressiveness. Brain maturation rates are similar in humans and other primates, simply more prolonged in humans than chimps than monkeys, such that the human brain increases at rates expected from its size, only for longer times. In Chapter 11 I will take on this issue again.

This Book

A lasting perspective in the study of speech and language, of which I have talked little as yet, comes from neurology and consists of getting directly inside the speaker's brain. This became possible by the early findings by Paul Broca, and continued through most of the twentieth century. I will provide a short historical account of this tradition in Chapter 2. Notably, the linguistic and the neurologic traditions followed largely parallel histories for most of last century, without much communication between the two disciplines. Only recently, with the revolution caused by new brain imaging methodologies, have these two lines begun to converge. In this book, I will focus on the neuronal and connectional changes that made the emergence of language possible. To do this, in several instances I will delve into the biological aspects of human evolution, to which the acquisition of speech and language is necessarily subordinate. As mentioned, I will refer mostly to speech rather than other forms of language, and will not describe in detail the linguistic aspects of syntax, semantics, phonology or lexical structure, although I will make reference to them as they often impinge on neurobiological discussions. I will take into consideration the different perspectives on the evolution of the neural circuits for language, but will propose the novel approach that a key ingredient was the functional consolidation of a particular circuit connecting auditory and vocal regions in the cerebral cortex, termed the phonological loop by the brilliant psychologist Alan Baddeley (Chapter 6) (Baddeley 2007). This circuit largely overlaps with the classical language areas, but here I emphasize its critical role in verbal working memory in the evolution of speech. The activity of the phonological loop enables us to keep linguistic strings in short-term or working memory while we process them and plays a role in the acquisition of vocabulary and speech. Furthermore, it contributes an internal speech domain that facilitates the recognition and visualization of our own mental states, and may also contribute to engaging in long-term reciprocal conversations with others. Amplification of this circuit astronomically propelled our communication capacity compared to an ancestral multimodal (vocal-gestural) communication system, and may have facilitated the development of a complex grammar. Finally, I will argue that speech was the first instance of elaborate language, and that it allowed us to generate a shared semantics, and consequently a shared mind (Chapters 10 and 11).

In following this approach, it is necessary to discuss several features of the human brain, notably its size, functional asymmetry and the necessary exchange of information in both hemispheres in a lateralized brain. Since Darwin, language has been associated with the size of the human brain (Chapter 3). Is this really causal, and if so, do larger brains give rise to language, or vice versa, does language increase brain size? In addition, language is usually localized in the left hemisphere of the brain, incidentally the same side that controls hand dexterity in right-handers. Why is this so? Do we really have one dominant hemisphere? What is the link between language lateralization and hand preference (Chapter 4)? Finally, interrupting the connections between cerebral hemispheres has significantly informed us about the lateralization of functions and the organization of our brains. But what is the role of this huge tract in non-lateralized animals and how does it contribute to a lateralized brain and the origin of lateralized speech (Chapter 5)?

I will develop my argument starting with the history and current interpretations of the neurology of language (Chapter 2), followed by some general attributes of the human brain like its large size (Chapter 3), lateralization (Chapter 4) and the transfer of information between hemispheres (Chapter 5). I will then introduce Baddeley's concept of working memory and its implications for language development in children (Chapter 6). In the second part of the book, I will review possible evolutionary roots of the phonological loop in the non-human primate brain, presenting the main argument of the book outlined above (Chapter 7). After this, I will discuss the argument that language has its origins in hand gestures, which has been championed by exponents of the mirror neuron hypothesis (Chapter 8). I will then provide an overview of some recent findings on mechanisms of vocal plasticity and learning in other animals, showing how these can be used as models for the early stages of human vocal communication (Chapters 9 and 10). In the last chapter, I will discuss how the phonological loop contributed to amplifying a semantic space that led us to a shared mind and the consequent interpretation of the world, with all its cultural consequences (Chapter 11).

References

Antón SC, Potts R, Aiello LC (2014) Evolution of early Homo: an integrated biological perspective. Science 345:1236828

Baddeley A (2007) Working Memory, Thought and Action. Oxford University Press, Oxford

Berwick RC, Chomsky N (2016) Why Only Us: Language and Evolution. MIT Press, Cambridge

Bickerton D (1990) Language and Species. University of Chicago Press, Chicago

Bickerton D (2009) Adam's Tongue. How Humans Made Language, How Language Made Humans. Hill and Wang Press, New York

Bickerton D (2014) More Than Nature Needs. Language, Mind, and Evolution. Harvard University Press, Cambridge

Bruner E, de la Cuétara JM, Masters M, Amano H, Ogihara N (2014) Functional craniology and brain evolution: from paleontology to biomedicine. Front Neuroanat 8:19

Burkhardt RW (2005) Patterns of Behavior: Konrad Lorenz, Niko Tinbergen, and the Founding of Ethology. University of Chicago Press, Chicago

Calvin W (1983) The Throwing Madonna. Mc Graw-Hill Press, New York

Candland DK (1995) Feral Children and Clever Animals. Reflections on Human Nature. Oxford University Press, Oxford

Chomsky N (1957) Syntactic Structures. Mouton de Gruyter, Berlin (2002)

Chomsky N (1965) Aspects of the Theory of Syntax. MIT Press, Cambridge (2014)

Chomsky N (1981) Lectures on Government and Binding. The Pisa Lectures. Mouton de Gruyter, Berlin

Corballis M (1993) The Lopsided Ape. Oxford Univeristy Press, Oxford

Cornélio AM, de Bittencourt-Navarrete RE, de Bittencourt Brum R, Queiroz CM, Costa MR (2016) Human brain expansion during evolution is independent of fire control and cooking. Front Neurosci 10:167

Crompton RH (2016) The hominins: a very conservative tribe? Last common ancestors, plasticity and ecomorphology in Hominidae. Or, What's in a name? J Anat 228:686–699.

Darwin C (1859) On the Origin of Species by Means of Natural Selection, or the Preservation of Favoured Races in the Struggle for Life. Murray Press, London

Darwin C (1871) The Descent of Man, and Selection in Relation to Sex. Murray Press, London

Deacon T (1997) The Symbolic Species. The Co-evolution of Language and the Brain. Norton Press, New York

Denton M (1985) Evolution: a Theory in Crisis. Burnett Books, Sydney

Desmond A (1984) Archetypes and Ancestors. Palaeontology in Victorian London, 1850–1875. University of Chicago Press, Chicago

Falk D (2009) The natural endocast of Taung (Australopithecus africanus): insights from the unpublished papers of Raymond Arthur Dart. Am J Phys Anthropol 140 (Suppl 49):49–65

Falk D (2014) Interpreting sulci on hominin endocasts: old hypotheses and new findings. Front Hum Neurosci 8:134

Falk D, Clarke R (2007) Brief communication: new reconstruction of the Taung endocast. Am J Phys Anthropol 134:529–534

Falk D, Clarke R (2012) Letter to the editor: response to Holloway and Broadfield's critique of our reconstruction of the Taung virtual endocast. Am J Phys Anthropol 148:483–485

Fischer B, Mitteroecker P (2015) Covariation between human pelvis shape, stature, and head size alleviates the obstetric dilemma. Proc Natl Acad Sci USA 112:5655–5660

Fitch T (2010) The Evolution of Language. Cambridge University Press, Cambridge

Fitch WT, Hauser MD (2004) Computational constraints on syntactic processing in a nonhuman primate. Science 303:377–380

Fitch WT, Hauser MD, Chomsky N (2005) The evolution of the language faculty: clarifications and implications. Cognition 97:179–210; discussion 211–225

Gardner RA, Gardner BT (1969) Teaching sign language to a chimpanzee. Science 165:664–672

Gentner TQ, Fenn KM, Margoliash D, Nusbaum HC. (2006) Recursive syntactic pattern learning by songbirds. Nature 440:1204–1207

Gould SJ (1977) Ontogeny and Phylogeny. Belknap Press, Harvard, Cambridge.

Gould SJ, Lewontin RC (1979) The spandrels of San Marco and the Panglossian paradigm: a critique of the adaptationist programme. Proc R Soc Lond B Biol Sci 205:581–598

Gregory MD, Kippenhan JS, Dickinson D, Carrasco J, Mattay VS, Weinberger DR, Berman KF (2016) Regional variations in brain gyrification are associated with general cognitive ability in humans. Curr Biol 26:1301–1305

Gross CG (1993) Huxley versus Owen: the hippocampus minor and evolution. Trends Neurosci 16:493–498

Gunz P, Neubauer S, Maureille B, Hublin JJ (2010) Brain development after birth differs between Neanderthals and modern humans. Curr Biol 20: R921–922

Hauser M (1996) The Evolution of Communication. MIT Press, Cambridge

Hauser MD, Chomsky N, Fitch WT (2002) The faculty of language: what is it, who has it, and how did it evolve? Science 298:1569–1579

Hauser MD, Yang C, Berwick RC, Tattersall I, Ryan MJ, Watumull J, Chomsky N, Lewontin RC (2014) The mystery of language evolution. Front Psychol 5:401

Hayes KJ, Hayes C (1952) Imitation in a home-raised chimpanzee. J Comp Physiol Psychol 45:450–459

Herder G (1800) Outlines of a Philosophy of the History of Man. Bergman Publishers, New York

Holloway RL, Broadfield D (2012) Reply to Falk and Clarke on Taung virtual endocast midline and volume. Am J Phys Anthropol 149:326

Holloway RL, Broadfield DC, Carlson KJ (2014) New high-resolution computed tomography data of the Taung partial cranium and endocast and their bearing on metopism and hominin brain evolution. Proc Natl Acad Sci U S A 111:13022–13027

Hubel DH, Wiesel TN (1977) Ferrier lecture. Functional architecture of macaque monkey visual cortex. Proc R Soc Lond B Biol Sci 198:1–59

Huseynov A, Zollikofer CP, Coudyzer W, Gascho D, Kellenberger C, Hinzpeter R, Ponce de León MS (2016) Developmental evidence for obstetric adaptation of the human female pelvis. Proc Natl Acad Sci U S A 113:5227–5232

Jackendoff R (1999) Possible stages in the evolution of the language capacity. Trends Cogn Sci 3:272–279

Jackendoff R, Pinker S (2005) The nature of the language faculty and its implications for evolution of language (Reply to Fitch, Hauser and Chomsky). Cognition 97:211–225

Kimbel WH, Villmoare B. (2016) From Australopithecus to Homo: the transition that wasn't. Philos Trans R Soc Lond B Biol Sci 371:1698

Lenneberg EH (1967) Biological Foundations of Language. John Wiley Press, New York

Lewontin RC (1975) Genetic aspects of intelligence. Annu Rev Genet 9:387–405

Liberman AM, Mattingly IG (1989) A specialization for speech perception. Science 243:489–494

Liberman AM, Harris KS, Hoffman HS, Griffith BC (1957) The discrimination of speech sounds within and across phoneme boundaries. J Exp Psychol 54:358–368

Liberman AM, Cooper FS, Shankweiler DP, Studdert-Kennedy M (1967) Perception of the speech code. Psychol Rev 74:431–461

Lorenz K (1981) The Foundations of Ethology. Springer Verlag, New York

Mitteroecker P, Fischer B (2016) Adult pelvic shape change is an evolutionary side effect. Proc Natl Acad Sci USA 113:E3596

Neubauer S, Gunz P, Hublin JJ (2010) Endocranial shape changes during growth in chimpanzees and humans: a morphometric analysis of unique and shared aspects. J Hum Evol 59:555–566

Oakley K (1949) Man the Tool-Maker. Bulletin of the British Museum of Natural History, London (1972)

Owen R (1837) The Hunterian lectures in comparative anatomy. University of Chicago Press, Chicago (1992).

Patterson F, Linden E (1985) The Education of Koko. Holt, Rinehart and Winston Press, New York

Penfield W, Roberts L (1959) Speech and Brain Mechanisms. Princeton University Press, Princeton

Perruchet P, Rey A (2005) Does the mastery of center-embedded linguistic structures distinguish humans from nonhuman primates? Psychon Bull Rev 12:307–313

Piantadosi ST, Kidd C (2016) Extraordinary intelligence and the care of infants. Proc Natl Acad Sci U S A 113:6874–6879

Pinker S (1994) The Language Instinct. Penguin Books, London

Pinker S, Jackendoff R (2005) The faculty of language: what's special about it? Cognition 95:201–236

Plummer T (2004) Flaked stones and old bones: biological and cultural evolution at the dawn of technology. Am J Phys Anthropol Suppl 39:118–164

Ponce de León MS, Huseynov A, Zollikofer CP (2016) Reply to Mitteroecker and Fischer: developmental solutions to the obstetrical dilemma are not Gouldian spandrels. Proc Natl Acad Sci U S A 113: E3597–3598

Rey A, Perruchet P, Fagot J (2012) Centre-embedded structures are a by-product of associative learning and working memory constraints: evidence from baboons (Papio Papio). Cognition 123:180–184

Richards RJ (1989) Darwin and the Evolutionary Theories of Mind and Behavior. University of Chicago Press, Chicago

Rightmire GP (2013) Homo erectus and Middle Pleistocene hominins: brain size, skull form, and species recognition. J Hum Evol 65:223–252

Rizzolatti G, Arbib MA (1998) Language within our grasp. Trends Neurosci 21:188–194

Rizzolatti G, Craighero L (2004) The mirror-neuron system. Annu Rev Neurosci 27:169–192

Sankararaman S, Mallick S, Patterson N, Reich D (2016) The combined landscape of Denisovan and Neanderthal ancestry in present-day humans. Curr Biol 26:1241–1247

Schiller F (1992) Paul Broca. Explorer of the Brain. Oxford University Press, Oxford

Seyfarth RM, Cheney DL, Marler P (1980) Monkey responses to three different alarm calls: evidence of predator classification and semantic communication. Science 210:801–803

Tinbergen N (1951) The Study of Instinct. Clarendon Press, New York

Trevathan W (2015) Primate pelvic anatomy and implications for birth. Philos Trans R Soc Lond B Biol Sci 370:20140065

Part I

A Special Brain

2

Pandora's Box

It may seem obvious to many of us that our capacities for reason and language are the product of the activity of interconnected neurons in the brain. However, coming to this interpretation is the result of a long history, starting from early conceptions that interpreted brain matter as little more than a cushion to protect the spirits inside the brain from harm. Furthermore, identifying the brain regions related to speech and language processing became possible only after the postmortem study of language-impaired individuals, a discipline that progressed quite slowly during the late nineteenth and twentieth centuries. Only with the advent of brain imaging techniques in the late twentieth century have we gained more detailed insight into the organization and structure of language-related networks. This chapter provides a historical account of the discovery of the brain as the organ for thought and language, and the different interpretations and controversies that shaped the history of neurolinguistics, many of which are causing sparks to this day.

© The Author(s) 2017
F. Aboitiz, *A Brain for Speech*,
DOI 10.1057/978-1-137-54060-7_2

White Matter, Gray Matter

Modern neuroanatomy probably began with the work of Thomas Willis in Oxford in the mid seventeenth century (Zimmer 2004). Willis was the first to emphasize the difference between gray and white matter, and to pay attention to the cerebral convolutions of the brain. His interest in the minute anatomy of the brain led him to make fundamental contributions to what is now modern neurology (in fact, he and his colleagues coined the term "neurology"). He made elegant descriptions of the cranial nerves, the corpus callosum (then called the mesolobe, and noted that it was composed of fine parallel lines), the corpus striatum (a deep nucleus inside the cerebral hemisphere, so named because of the mixture of gray matter and fiber tracts), the thalamus and other regions, including the circle of Willis, a circle of arteries surrounding the hypothalamus, obviously named after him. Besides these empirical contributions, Willis also came to the conclusion that it is in gray matter that our feelings and thoughts are located. He conceived white matter as a series of channels that convey perceptions and thoughts into the gray matter of the cerebral cortex, which stores them as enduring memories. Willis drew attention to the distinct brain folds and convolutions in different animals, which he believed served to store sensory impressions, and noted that these were less complex in quadrupeds than in apes and humans. Furthermore, he believed that "storms" of atoms in the brain caused mental phenomena, and that mental disorders might be effectively treated with pharmaceutical products.

After Willis, another important step in advancing neurology was the development of phrenology in the early nineteenth century by the German anatomist Franz Joseph Gall. Instead of observing cerebral tissue itself, Gall dedicated himself to analyzing the variability of skull shapes, which according to him represented the development of different parts of the brain in individuals, resulting in outward pressure on the cranium during growth. Thus, he developed an elegant but seriously erroneous map of different mental faculties located in specific parts of the brain, represented by distinct "bumps" on the surface of the skull (Corsi et al. 1991; Steinberg 2009). This discipline is often dismissed as a classic example of pseudoscience, as there was no empirical support for the proposed localizations. This was solidly demonstrated by Pierre Flourens when he sectioned brain regions of animals and observed their behavioral effects. However, the influence of Gall on the subsequent development of neurology was tremendous. Jerry Fodor proposed that Gall set the path for the concept of cerebral localization in which different functions are circumscribed to specific brain regions. Perhaps more fundamentally, he argued for what is called "faculty psychology", that is, the psychological processes like attention, memory, and language are functionally different faculties (Fodor 1983). Furthermore, his notion that the growth of "bumps" on the skull (and the underlying brain) corresponds to the development of different capacities presaged the modern concept of experience-dependent plasticity. We all take these notions for granted now, but Gall's implicit influence on these basic ideas is substantial.

Gall considered that language is localized in the region of the frontal lobes above the eye orbits, which is now called the orbitofrontal cortex. This notion received support in the early nineteenth century from Jean Baptiste Bouillaud, who presented postmortem evidence from lesioned patients that indicated frontal localization of speech functions (Corsi et al. 1991). Bouillaud's work was highly criticized by many, but the point was made that at least one of the frontal lobes was found to be damaged in the autopsied brains of individuals that had lost the capacity for speech, while there were no cases of loss of speech in individuals with intact frontal lobes. Bouillaud distinguished the capacity to produce mental symbols and ideas that are preserved in memory (inner speech, controlled by the frontal lobe gray matter), from the actual articulation of these ideas in concrete words (external speech, controlled by frontal lobe white matter).

The Power of the Microscope

Unlike Gall, Paul Broca (whom we met in Chapter 1) was interested in brain anatomy and the structure of brain convolutions, which were notably conserved in distinct species. By that time, the comparative study of brain gyri was well on its way after the work of Luigi Rolando in the early nineteenth century, who divided the brain into posterior and anterior components, separated by Rolando's fissure (now called the central fissure). Sometime before in the seventeenth century, Franciscus Sylvius described the other main sulcus of the human brain, called the Sylvian or lateral fissure (Zimmer 2004; Schiller 1992). Broca had studied with Jules Baillarguer, who discovered the microscopic six-layered structure of the cerebral cortex, which is conserved across the different gyri but with subtle differences in the thickness of these laminae, as, for example, the bands of Baillarguer, two horizontal stripes of myelinated fibers that are especially prominent in the visual cortex. These findings were precursors to the field of cytoarchitectonics, which consisted of the systematic analysis of the laminar composition of the cerebral cortex across brain regions. Researchers like Theodor Meynert found that the thickness and appearance of the different laminae are not uniform across the cerebral cortex, which could be parcellated into several areas, each being relatively homogeneous in its laminar composition. This provided support to the concept of the cerebral cortex as a mosaic of specialized areas rather than a uniform, homogeneous mantle covering the encephalon (Schiller 1992; Corsi et al. 1991).

Cytoarchitecture received substantial support from the emerging studies of the cellular composition of the nervous system, led by Camillo Golgi and Santiago Ramón y Cajal. Both scientists took advantage of Golgi's discovery of a silver staining method to analyze the fine structure of individual neurons, which permitted observing the immense variety of neuronal types in different regions of the nervous system. Particularly, two main neuronal morphologies were observed in the cerebral cortex, first pyramidal cells with vertically oriented apical dendrites that are organized in columns perpendicular to the cortical laminae, and second smaller granular cells, with star-like dendritic arborizations (so-called stellate cells), of which there are two kinds: spiny (displaying small dendritic "spines" on the surface), and smooth stellate cells. The characteristic laminar distribution of these cell types represented important evidence for the field of cytoarchitectonics. It later turned out that spiny cells and pyramidal neurons are excitatory, while smooth stellate cells are inhibitory. The evidence of a vertical organization of neurons in the cerebral cortex, mainly provided by Cajal, complemented the horizontal laminarity concept of Baillarguer, both of which form the basic scaffolding for the modern conception of cortical anatomy (see Fig. 2.1) (Corsi et al. 1991).

Perhaps the most important exponent of cytoarchitectonics was Korbinian Brodmann, who in 1909 published a comprehensive account of the cerebral cortical areas in different mammals including humans and described more than 50 areas in the human brain (Fig. 2.2) (Brodmann 1909). This map is the most commonly used by contemporary researchers, as several of these areas were found to correspond to different sensory and motor regions in the brain. Subsequent students of cytoarchitectonics that deserve mention are Constantin Von Economo and Georg Koskinas, who made an exhaustive study in 1925 of laminar differentiation of the cerebral cortex (Von Economo and Koskinas 1925). They observed that cytoarchitectonic characteristics did not change abruptly; rather there is a gradient of differentiation along the cerebral cortex. Thus, regions involved in sensory processing display densely packed small (granular) neurons, especially in the middle layer, while motor and limbic areas show large pyramidal neurons, especially in the deep layers. Between these regions, there are extensive areas where granularity decreases with distance from sensory areas and the pyramidal component increases with proximity to motor regions. Another characteristic of these intermediate regions is the enlarged thickness of the superficial layers, considered to be the site for associative connectivity. Von Economo and Koskinas' approach also represented a slight departure from a more phrenologically oriented view of the brain, consisting of discrete areas or modules, to a gradual pattern of functional differentiation along the cerebral cortex (Corsi et al. 1991). Combined approaches including high-resolution cytoarchitectonics, gene and receptor distribution, and new imaging techniques have been used recently to produce high-resolution atlases of the human cerebral cortex (Ding et al. 2016b; Glasser et al. 2016). Although these are promising achievements, their consistency and reliability still needs to be improved.

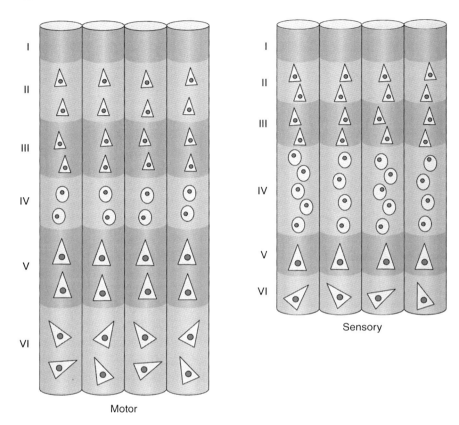

I

II

III

IV

V

VI

Motor

I

II

III

IV

V

VI

Sensory

Fig. 2.1 Cellular organization of the cerebral cortex. The cerebral cortex is organized in horizontal laminae (layers I–VI) and vertical columns crossing each of the laminae. Cytoarchitectonics refers to the parcellation of the cerebral cortex in different areas, based on the relative development of the layers in different regions. As an example, a motor area, with a robust layer V (output layer), is contrasted to a sensory area displaying a thick layer IV (input layer). Morphologically, excitatory cells are of two kinds: pyramidal (triangles), and spiny granular cells (circles), the latter concentrated on layer IV. Inhibitory interneurons (also called smooth granular cells; not shown) are distributed in all layers

(a)

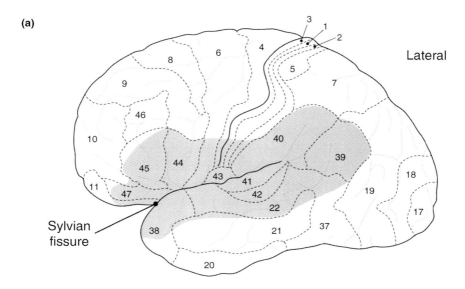

(b)

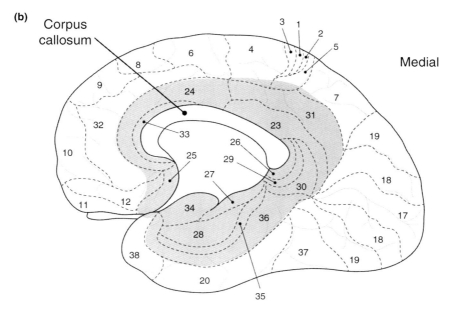

Fig. 2.2 Lateral and medial aspects of the human cerebral hemispheres. Figures depict Brodmann's cortical areas in numbers, and the longitudinal

Broca's Brains

To Broca the evidence above strongly indicated that convolutions supported distinct mental functions. In the following, I will mainly refer to Francis Schiller's lucid biography of Broca, which is probably the main modern reference to his work (Schiller 1992). On April 18, 1861, Broca reported in the *Societé D'Anthropologie* the postmortem brain of his patient Leborgne, who had a lesion of the left third frontal convolution of the left hemisphere. This region is now referred to as the inferior frontal gyrus, or ventrolateral prefrontal cortex (which is to be distinguished from the ventral premotor cortex, located just posteriorly, which codifies complex motor patterns executed by the ventral motor cortex). From now on, I will use the term "ventrolateral prefrontal cortex" to specify the location of Broca's region. Leborgne had a specific impairment to articulate speech (he could only pronounce the word "tan"), while speech comprehension was intact. A few months later, Broca found Lelong, another patient with a similar lesion, whose speech was also impaired, being able to utter only six French words: *oui* (yes), *non* (no), *tois* (*trois*, which meant not only three but any number), *tojours* (always), and *Lelo* (Lelong). Like Leborgne, this patient showed a reasonable capacity to understand what was said to him. Leborgne had a long-lasting, presumably progressive

Fig.2.2 (Continued)
subdivisions specified by Foville in gray. (a) In the lateral aspect, Foville's *circonvolution d'enceinte*, or the Sylvian convolution surrounds the Sylvian fissure. This includes the inferior parietal lobe (areas 39 and 40, angular and supramarginal gyri), the ventrolateral prefrontal cortex (areas 44-pars opercularis, 45-pars triangularis, and 47), and the ventral premotor (area 6), motor (area 4), somatosensory (areas 3, 1, 2) and insular (area 43) regions. In the temporal lobe, areas 22, 41 and 42 make up the superior temporal gyrus, which is separated from the middle and inferior temporal gyri (areas 20, 21 and 37) by the superior temporal sulcus (not shown). The temporal pole corresponds to area 38. (b) The medial aspect of the hemisphere depicts Foville's and Broca's limbic lobe (in gray). The anterior cingulate cortex corresponds to area 24, and areas 23, 26, 29, 30 and 31 behind the corpus callosum make up the posterior cingulate cortex or retrosplenial region. The default mode network involves areas 10 and 32 in the frontal lobe, and the posterior cingulate cortex

condition, as his brain had softened in regions spanning the white matter, the basal ganglia, and nearby cortical regions. Lelong acquired this condition suddenly, likely due to a localized brain hemorrhage in the same left third frontal convolution (the ventrolateral prefrontal cortex). Finally, localization of brain functions was confirmed. Broca called this condition aphemia, and postulated that it was due to the loss of a special kind of memory involved in the procedure used for articulating words (Broca 1865). He was, however, clear in saying that not all cerebral faculties were as circumscribed as this one. It is less known that the neurologist Marc Dax, at Sommières (a small town close to Montpellier), had made similar observations some 25 years before Broca, but instead of specifying the brain region, he emphasized the left hemisphere as the site where lesions produced language disturbances. Dax was largely ignored in his time, presumably due to his early death 1 year after his findings. After Broca's presentation, Dax's son published these observations again, but was unsuccessful in vindicating his father. Broca was late in recognizing the leftward asymmetry of the observed lesions, initially attributing them to chance, but eventually he concluded that there was in fact a clear tendency shown by evidence (Schiller 1992).

Broca was not without his detractors, among them the anti-localizationist Pierre Flourens, who viewed these interpretations as a new form of phrenology. In addition, the eminent Jean Martin Charcot presented a case with undeniable aphemia with a lesion on the upper border of the Sylvian fissure (in modern terms, the gyrus supramarginalis in the inferior parietal lobe). Responding to this, Broca claimed that a single case did not make a tendency, but perhaps more importantly for our purposes, he relied on Louis Foville's anatomical descriptions of brain convolutions, which contrary to Rolando's depiction, subdivided the brain into three major longitudinal lobes (Fig. 2.2). The most medial of these was the convolution of the hem, which includes the cingulate gyrus and the medial temporal lobe. Secondly, there was a large lobe encompassing dorsal frontal, superior parietal, occipital, and inferior temporal areas, and finally there was the convolution around the Sylvian fissure or *circonvolution d'enceinte*, involving all areas surrounding the Sylvian fissure. In modern terms, these are Broca's region, the adjacent premotor and motor cortices and the inferior parietal lobe on the upper side of the

Sylvian fissure, and on the lower side, the superior temporal gyrus where auditory areas and Wernicke's region are located. Broca initially argued that the speech organ was the entire Sylvian convolution, and that there are differences in its organization among individuals, but he later insisted on the third frontal convolution (the ventrolateral prefrontal cortex) as the site of speech (Schiller 1992).

Although little recognized today, Foville's subdivision fits the current notions about the arrangement of major longitudinal tracts of the brain. Broca renamed the hem convolution as the limbic lobe. He published a massive work on the "great limbic lobe" of mammals, surrounding the medial borders of the cerebral hemispheres. Broca also made a thorough analysis of the brains of several mammals, and concluded that the primate brain was divided into regions comparable to the brains of other animals, indicating a conservatism in structure that was not generally agreed on at that time (Broca 2015). The limbic convolution is connected through a tract called the cingulum bundle and other tracts, making up a circuit that was described in the twentieth century by James Papez, and termed the Papez circuit. Foville's large convolution in the middle is the arrangement of the visual system, with one pathway following through the superior parietal and dorsal frontal cortices (as we will see, this is involved in visuomotor coordination), and the other pathway running along the middle and inferior temporal lobe (involved in visual recognition). Finally, all the areas included in the Sylvian convolution have been directly or indirectly associated with language processing. We will come back to this anatomical partition in Chapter 7.

Another antagonist of Broca was Armand Trousseau, who analyzed a large series of brains of speech-impaired individuals. Although he found a clear prevalence of left hemisphere lesions, when looking for the exact location of the lesion in a subset of the subjects he studied he found no strong evidence for Broca's hypothesis. Ironically, Trousseau coined the word "aphasia", which eventually replaced Broca's term aphemia. But perhaps Broca's hardest critics were the neurologists John Hughlings Jackson in England and Pierre Marie in France. Jackson considered language a very complicated faculty and was highly skeptical of the localizationist perspective. He emphasized subcortical regions involved in language, particularly the corpus striatum, which could have been damaged in aphasic patients. In addition, he claimed that damage to one part of the brain could produce effects in distant regions, affecting functions not necessarily located in the damaged site. Jackson also highlighted the case of a patient who had severe difficulties in speaking normally, but was able to swear with complete precision and vigor (York and Steinberg 2011). Pierre Marie had a similar interpretation to Jackson's, arguing that language is one and indivisible, and that Broca's cases only involved the lower motor systems involved in speech production rather than an intellectual impairment. Notably, Marie argued that aphemia or aphasia could be produced not only through lesions of the left third frontal convolution, but also with deeper lesions involving the insula (a portion of the cortex that is buried deep within the Sylvian fissure), or the basal ganglia. The dispute between holists and localizationists went on for over a century, the former providing important theoretical insights, while the latter contributed increasingly detailed anatomical evidence in their support (Schiller 1992; Steinberg 2014).

Comprehending Speech

Broca's observations fell short on the capacity to perceive speech and language. In 1874, at the age of 26, Karl Wernicke proposed the existence of a brain center involved in the storage of speech sounds, located in the posterior superior temporal gyrus (Wernicke 1874). This is now called Wernicke's area, corresponding to the posterior part of Brodmann's area 22, a region now associated with high level auditory processing. This region is dedicated to storing acoustic images of words that are then transferred to Broca's area, controlling speech. Supporting this notion, Wernicke described patients that could hear but had difficulty understanding speech. He distinguished this "word deafness" or sensory aphasia, as opposed to Broca's motor aphasia, from semantic deficits. Thus, he believed that this sensory speech region was responsible for transforming orthographic signals into phonological patterns, and making the generation of inner speech possible (Corsi, 1991; Schiller 1992; Petrides, 2014; Weiller et al. 2011).

Wernicke was greatly influenced by the work of Theodore Meynert, who beside his contribution to cytoarchitectonics, was also the first to propose a systematic subdivision of the fiber tracts in the human brain, with ascending or descending projection fibers, commissural fibers connecting the cerebral hemispheres via the corpus callosum, and association fibers connecting different regions of the cerebral cortex within each hemisphere. Following Meynert, Wernicke postulated a connection between Wernicke's and Broca's areas that made the association of sensory inputs with motor commands possible. In contrast to the localizationist view, Wernicke emphasized the associative nature of these projections, presaging modern concepts of brain connectivity. Lesions in the connectivity between the sensory (Wernicke's) and motor (Broca's) regions resulted in a disconnection syndrome called conduction aphasia, which included paraphasia. This consisted of the generation of erroneous syllables, words or even phrases during speech. Another symptom was impaired writing, although speech was fluent and comprehension preserved. Wernicke attributed the production of paraphasias to the suppression of mental reverberation of acoustic images while speaking, which serves to monitor motor images. However, a cardinal symptom of conduction aphasia was eventually specified as the difficulty to repeat sentences or utterances presented to the patient, something that Wernicke did not originally describe (Corsi et al. 1991; Schiller 1992; Petrides 2014).

It is widely believed that Wernicke's model considered that conduction aphasia was due to disruption of the arcuate fasciculus, a tract of fibers that runs around the Sylvian fissure, deep to the inferior parietal lobe, and connects the posterior superior temporal lobe (Wernicke's area) with Broca's region (Fig. 2.3). However, Cornelius Weiller has recently argued that although Wernicke may have been aware of the existence of this tract, his original diagrams point to a much shorter pathway via the mid-or anterior temporal lobe, which he considered traveled deep to the insula, a buried cortical area located between Wernicke's and Broca's regions

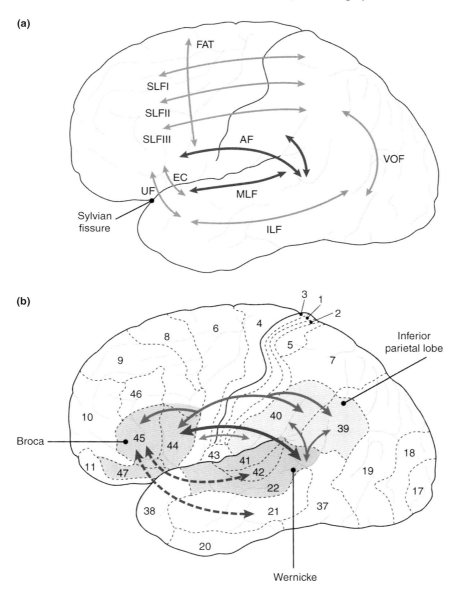

Fig. 2.3   The main cortico-cortical tracts discussed in this book. (a) This schematic is not intended to be anatomically accurate but to reflect the topographical arrangement of these tracts. In addition, these tracts are not

(Weiller et al. 2011). The arcuate fasciculus, named after Karl
Burdach, was first described at the beginning of the eighteenth
century by Johan Cristian Reil as a bundle of fibers running around
the superior border of the Sylvian fissure, encompassing the superior temporal, inferior parietal and inferior frontal areas, beneath
Foville's upper Sylvian convolution (see above). Constantin von
Monakow first postulated that this tract plays a role in aphasia,
and it was only later that Wernicke accepted that it is a main tract
in language pathways, whose disruption produces conduction aphasia (nonetheless, more recent findings have evidenced gray matter
involvement in many cases of conduction aphasia). From then on,
Wernicke's original model of a short language pathway underlying
the insula fell into oblivion, as attention shifted to the arcuate
fasciculus as the main connection between Broca and Wernicke's
areas (Schiller 1992; Catani and Mesulam 2008a; Weiller et al.
2011).

Fig.2.3 (Continued)
discrete bundles but rather overlap in a continuous plexus below the cortical
surface. AF, Arcuate fasciculus; EC, Extreme capsule; FAT, Frontal aslant tract;
ILF, Inferior longitudinal fasciculus; MLF, middle longitudinal fasciculus; SLF I,
II, III, dorsal, middle and ventral components of the superior longitudinal
fasciculus, respectively; UF, Uncinate fasciculus; VOF, Vertical occipital fasciculus. The curved arrow at the posterior end of the Sylvian fissure connects
superior temporal and inferior parietal areas, and has been termed the
posterior segment of either the arcuate fasciculus or the middle longitudinal
fasciculus, depending on the nomenclature. (b) Functional subdivisions and
connectivity of the language-related circuit. In the superior temporal gyrus,
areas 41 and 42 make up the auditory cortex, while Wernicke's area roughly
corresponds to posterior area 22. Broca's area, in a restricted sense, has been
defined as area 44-pars opercularis, and area 45-pars triangularis. The dorsal
language pathway has two components, one connecting Wernicke's area
mainly with area 44 and neighboring regions via the arcuate fasciculus
(black arrow), and the other connecting Wernicke's area with the inferior
parietal lobe, and then projecting to areas 44 and 45 via the superior longitudinal fasciculus (dark gray arrows). There are additional connections
between motor, premotor and somatosensory areas (light gray arrow). The
ventral pathway (segmented arrows) is a polysynaptic tract that connects the
anterior temporal gyrus (auditory component), and the middle and inferior
temporal gyri (visual component) with areas 45 and 47

Nonetheless, recent investigations have confirmed the existence of two parallel pathways connecting Wernicke and Broca's region (Fig. 2.3). One is the dorsal pathway, running through the arcuate fasciculus, whose interruption (or of the gray matter above it) leads to conduction aphasia. The second is the so-called ventral pathway, connecting the anterior temporal lobe and the inferior frontal gyrus along the extreme capsule, which has been proposed to participate in auditory recognition. The ventral pathway has been proposed as a better fit to Wernicke's original notion of a short connection to Broca's region beneath the insula (Saur et al. 2008; Weiller et al. 2011; Fridriksson et al. 2016). Again, Foville's Sylvian convolution fits these two pathways, the dorsal pathway/arcuate fasciculus running through the inferior parietal lobe, and the ventral pathway/extreme capsule running through the temporal lobe and below the insula to reach Broca's area. Furthermore, Reil's original depiction of the arcuate fasciculus as a curved tract running the length of the upper Sylvian convolution is also consistent with this notion. Possibly due to the neglect of the ventral pathway during most of the last century, the arcuate fasciculus came to be viewed only as the dorsal component linking Broca's and Wernicke's areas.

The Disconnection Syndrome

Since Wernicke's findings, an influential associationist tradition emerged in the late nineteenth and early twentieth centuries, in which disconnection syndromes were described in other brain areas beyond the language regions (Mesulam 2015). Wernicke's student Heinrich Lissauer described a patient with intact visual capacity but incapable of recognizing familiar objects by sight, a condition called visual agnosia that is due to interruption of the connectivity between visual areas and higher order association areas. Another student, Hugo Liepmann, described the apraxias resulting from disconnection of the motor centers from sensory regions and characterized by the incapacity to imitate meaningless movements or manipulating imaginary objects (Weiller 2011). Finally, Jules Déjérine coined the term pure alexia, meaning the acquired inability to read (while the capacity to write remains spared) due to a disconnection between visual areas and Wernicke's area. In 1881, Déjérine described a patient with a lesion in the fusiform gyrus (part of the inferior temporal lobe), who was unable to read but could write and otherwise had intact visual and language skills. Déjérine slightly departed from the pure associationist school by proposing a specific brain center dedicated to processing word images (Corsi et al. 1991). More recent research, notably by Stanislaas Dehaene, has identified a region called the visual word form area in the inferior temporal lobe, which is specifically involved in recognizing the shapes of words and letters, and projects to Wernicke's area where these visual percepts associate with auditory phonological representations (Cohen et al. 2002). The visual word form area does not activate with reading, and cannot do so, in illiterate people, and is the result of enculturation among the literate. Subsequent studies suggest the existence of a nearby visual number form area, and an area involved in graphemic motor control (called Exner's area), above Broca's region (Roux et al. 2009). As I mentioned in the Chapter 1, culture can make enormous changes in the structure and functional organization of our brains. Is language an example of enculturation, as the neural substrate is for reading?

The associationist school became firmly consolidated much later in 1965, with Norman Geschwind's monumental work *The disconnection syndromes in animals and man* (Geschwind 1965). Geschwind made an extensive account of acquired neurological symptoms that could be explained by the disconnection between different brain centers. He proposed a series of pathways connecting visual, auditory and somatosensory areas with each other, but also with motor and limbic areas whose specific damage yielded a particular neurological symptomatology. A key element in these networks was the inferior parietal lobe (the supramarginal and angular gyri, part of the Sylvian convolution), where auditory, visual, and somatosensory projections converged. Marco Catani and collaborators recently summarized these ideas in a diagram highlighting the inferior parietal lobe as a critical node for cortico-cortical connectivity, and appropriately called it "Geschwind's area" (Catani and ffytche 2005; Catani and Mesulam 2008b). Concerning the language circuits, Geschwind emphasized the case of conduction aphasia and the role of the arcuate fasciculus in conveying sensory information from Broca's to Wernicke's areas. Furthermore, he consolidated the now classical model of language areas that prevailed through the second half of last century, consisting of a posterior, perceptive Wernicke's region, connected via the arcuate fasciculus with Broca's anterior motor region.

In 1964, Geschwind published a little known article, called *The development of the brain and the evolution of language*, where he proposed that the capacity to establish direct cortico-cortical associations, especially between different sensory modalities (but also within a sensory modality), was particularly well developed in humans as opposed to other primates (Geschwind 1964). This allows us to name objects in the world and acquire symbolic representations. On the other hand, non-human primates are much slower in learning cross-modal associations, and require an intact limbic system to perform such associations. Humans, with their big brains, have freed themselves of the limbic connection by emphasizing direct cross-modal, cortico-cortical associations. This is not to say that in humans there are no limbic associations, but that much faster cortico-cortical associations can be readily made that allow us to rapidly associate words with objects. Again, an essential part of Geschwind's proposal was that the temporo-parietal junction serves as a node in which sensory information converges from the visual, tactile, and auditory modalities, and is connected to Wernicke's area in the superior temporal lobe. Later evidence that apes are able to learn a relatively extensive vocabulary using sign language has challenged this hypothesis. However, apes learn words through a long and painstaking training procedure, while children acquire their vocabulary rapidly and effortlessly.

In the twentieth century, human neuroanatomy made some discrete progress, particularly in the study of cytoarchitectonics and brain-behavior correlations, a field termed by Geschwind as "behavioral neurology" (Catani and Mesulam 2008a,b). Broca's area became circumscribed to two specific regions of the ventrolateral prefrontal cortex. One is the posterior part of Broca's area or pars opercularis, comprising Brodmann's area 44, more related to phonological and vocal articulatory processes, and the other is the anterior part or pars triangularis, which includes Brodmann's areas 45 and 47, and is related to lexical and semantic processing.

Nonetheless, there is a noticeable individual variability in the symptoms of classical Broca's aphasia. This condition now includes a wide spectrum of acquired speech dysfunctions, including more subtle speech articulation and fluency deficits, difficulties to find words, and some comprehension problems, particularly of complex grammatical sequences. Moreover, studies in the late twentieth century, notably by Nina Dronkers, Marco Catani and others, have found that Broca's aphasia can be produced by lesions in several regions surrounding areas 44 and 45, including neighboring cortical areas, the insula, the underlying white matter and the basal ganglia, which is in agreement with Pierre Marie's descriptions (see above) (Thiebaut de Schotten et al. 2015). Thus, instead of being a strictly localized brain region, Broca's area encompasses a wide network in the left ventrolateral prefrontal cortex. Moreover, damage restricted to areas 44 and 45 is now thought to produce only transient speech deficits, while long-lasting impairments may include lesions in white matter tracts that connect Broca's region with other areas, or in more extensive cortical regions. In this line, Alfredo Ardila proposes the term "Broca's complex" to account for Broca's aphasia symptomatology, which includes prefrontal areas 44, 45, 46, 47 and part of the ventral premotor cortex (area 6) (Ardila et al. 2016).

Dronkers and collaborators analyzed in detail the brains of Leborgne and Lelong, confirming Broca's original descriptions, but localizing Leborgne's lesion in the middle of the inferior frontal gyrus (Dronkers and Sanides 2007). The posterior part of this gyrus, where modern researchers have located Broca's region, is altered but is not the most damaged area. In Lelong's brain, there are signs of atrophy consistent with chronic dementia, but there is also evidence of a stroke located in the pars opercularis, sparing the pars triangularis. Further analyses using magnetic resonance imaging techniques show extensive damage in Leborgne's brain, restricted to the left hemisphere, including regions like the insula, superior temporal lobe and inferior parietal lobe, while in Lelong's brain resonance imaging confirms the lesion localized in the pars opercularis. This supports the idea that Broca's aphasia does not result from damage in a strictly localized brain region, but may require more extensive cortical, subcortical or white matter lesions. Nonetheless, anatomical studies have by necessity been restricted to a handful of areas, particularly areas 44 and 45, although sometimes including neighboring regions. Although this may only be part of a larger network for language production, science accumulates information step by step, from the particular to the general in order to keep the required simplicity for executing highly demanding technical procedures. Below, I will refer to some recent studies that use the more restricted definition of Broca's area, involving only areas 44 and 45 (and sometimes 47), a notion that, while criticized for reasons outlined above, has been extremely useful to trace the neural connectivity that makes up language and speech networks.

On the other hand, Wernicke's area remains ill defined, corresponding to a wide region including Brodmann's posterior area 22 and surrounding areas. This covers the posterior superior temporal gyrus and a triangular region within the lower bank of the Sylvian fissure called planum temporale. In front of the planum temporale are the gyri of Heschl, containing the primary and secondary auditory areas. Cytoarchitectonic studies in the 1960s by Friedrich Sanides, Deepak Pandya and their then student Albert Galaburda subdivided the auditory areas into three concentric rings, a "core" region containing primary and secondary auditory areas, which are successively surrounded by an intermediate auditory "belt" and an outer "parabelt". In the posterior parabelt, Galaburda and Pandya described a region called Tpt, which is thought to occupy a large part of the planum temporale, and has been ascribed (but not exclusively) to Wernicke's area (Galaburda and Sanides 1980, Galaburda and Pandya 1983). Notably, all the regions composing Broca and Wernicke's regions exist in monkeys and apes, indicating that they are highly conserved in evolution. How did these areas acquire a linguistic function? This is a major question I intend to address in this book, and will discuss in more detail in Chapter 7.

The Imaging Revolution

For most of the twentieth century, the study of the human brain was limited to postmortem, gross anatomical, and microscopic cytoarchitectonic studies. There were few possibilities of studying the brain in action (one exception being electroencephalography) or brain connectivity, as was being done with animals for most of that time. Anatomical and electrophysiological studies were yielding much information about animal brains, but to what extent these findings could be extrapolated to the human brain was in many cases a matter of question. At least since the 1980s, neuronal connections can be visualized in high detail in animals by injecting chemical tracers that are absorbed by the respective axons or neurons in one brain region, and then observing the distribution of the tracer in the rest of the brain in the postmortem tissue. Apart from some details, this technique continues to be used to trace connections in most animal brains. However, this cannot be done with humans, and until recently the only way to analyze connectivity was in postmortem specimens that had suffered brain stroke in life. When neurons die due to injury, their axonal projections undergo a degenerative process called Wallerian degeneration, which leaves traces in the neural tissue that can be observed after death. However, this method depends on the site and size of the lesion, and has very low resolution compared to animal tract-tracing procedures.

A different strategy emerged in the 1950s and 1960s, when neurosurgeons Wilder Penfield and Lamar Roberts made groundbreaking studies with patients undergoing brain surgery by electrically stimulating their brains and observing the behavioral reactions (Penfield and Roberts 1959). Since neurosurgery has to be done with the patient awake and using only local anesthesia, patients were conscious and able to respond to the stimulation procedure. Penfield and colleagues depicted the famous body homunculus in the sensory and motor cortices; and also identified areas whose stimulation elicited vocalizations, notably in the ventral precentral and supplementary motor regions of both hemispheres (areas 6 and 4, ventral). They further found that stimulating the ventrolateral prefrontal cortex (Broca's area), the motor and premotor cortices, and some regions around the Sylvian fissure, all in the left hemisphere, could lead to interference with or the arrest of speech.

But revolutionary discoveries were about to change the study of language for good. Since the 1960s, new brain imaging techniques were developed that made it possible for the first time to study local brain activity in living humans, even if they evidenced processes only indirectly associated with neuronal activity. The first of these techniques were SPECT (single photon emission computed tomography) and PET (positron emission tomography), which detect emissions from a radioactive tracer in the bloodstream, sensed by an array of detectors that anatomically localize the source of the emission in the brain. These techniques measure differences in blood flow, but also glucose consumption and even the binding of radioactive ligands to their receptors. An underlying assumption is that local differences in blood flow or glucose metabolism reflect changes in neuronal activity in the corresponding brain regions. However, the most influential neuroimaging technique has been magnetic resonance imaging (MRI), first developed by Paul Lauterbur, and optimized by Peter Mansfield (both received the Nobel Prize for their contribution), a totally non-invasive technique that measures the magnetic field orientation of water molecules in different tissues (Pearson 2003). MRI made it possible to generate high-resolution three-dimensional images of the brain for detailed quantitative analyses of brain morphology in living subjects. Moreover, two techniques derived from MRI have been the most relevant for the development of cognitive neuroscience and particularly for understanding the language neural networks. One is functional MRI (fMRI), which takes advantage of the magnetic properties of the oxygen-carrier protein hemoglobin, depending on whether or not it is oxygen-binding. Counterintuitively, brain regions show a larger oxygen supply when they are more, rather than less active, presumably because the overall increase in blood flow overcomes the higher oxygen consumption by active neurons. Compared to SPECT and PET, fMRI has higher neuroanatomical precision and, as noted, is totally non-invasive, as it does not require radioactive tracers, which also makes it more affordable. However, one drawback for language studies is that speech produces image distortions due to jaw movements, so subjects' responses are restricted to button pressing. As well, the machine is quite noisy, which complicates the delivery of auditory stimuli.

Another technical difficulty with imaging techniques is that the brain is never quiet, and blood flow is evident throughout the brain. One way to overcome this is a subtraction procedure, where the difference in activity between two related conditions is determined. In most instances, subjects have to perform two quite similar tasks, but differing only in one parameter. For example, imagine the N-back task, a procedure to assess short-term memory, where subjects are exposed to a semi-random string of numbers (avoiding the chance of repeated numbers), and at some point the sequence stops. Subjects are then asked to immediately recall the last number of the sequence. This is the 0-back condition, which requires attention from the subject, but on the other hand it puts little demand on short-term memory capacity. If the subject is then asked to recall the next-to-last number (1-back condition), the demand on memory is higher, and still more demanding if the subject has to recall the second-to-last number (2-back condition) (Gaspar et al. 2011). Thus, brain activation in the first 0-back task evidences networks involved primarily with attention, but that have less to do with memory, while activation patterns in the 1-back and 2-back tasks increasingly activate networks involved in memory and executive processes, but also activate attentional networks. If we subtract the activation pattern of the 0-back from that of the 1-back, we minimize activation due to attentional mechanisms and emphasize memory-related networks. By subtracting the 1-back and the 2-back conditions, we may obtain understanding of higher-level executive processes. The usual results are that a small group of areas are highlighted by the subtraction procedure.

However, the technique has its drawbacks, as it downplays connectivity and the participation of brain regions that may be highly relevant for the specific function but also participate in the control task. Furthermore, the specific areas that "light up" in a subtraction procedure may depend on the statistical method and criterion used to identify significant differences. Furthermore, results are usually (but not always) reported as grand averages of several trials with each subject, and then averaged among the subjects that compose the sample. Under these conditions, the observed activity locus is usually attributed to specific cytoarchitectonic areas. However, in practice, this is impossible to verify because of inter-individual differences in brain activity profiles and the neuroanatomy of cortical areas, where fissurization patterns are highly variable, and presumably so is the arrangement of cytoarchitectonic areas. The best we can get is an approximation of the cortical areas involved. Furthermore, Eklund et al. (2016) and collaborators recently performed a comprehensive study, finding an astonishing 70% of false-positives when analyzing imaging data with standard fMRI softwares, which calls into question the results of some 40,000 previous studies. There have been recent technical developments such as single-trial fMRI approaches, but these are still not widespread and have not yet produced important results. Most of the studies presented in this book rely on averaged samples of subjects.

Resting Brains

One alternative to rescue network thinking has come from a technique called functional connectivity, which is basically the statistical analysis of covariance in activity between different brain regions. That is, the activity level of a brain region is not constant but changes over time, either as a result of sensory stimulation, or by endogenous mechanisms. If we analyze different brain regions and find areas where activity changes more or less synchronically, we can say that these areas are functionally connected. This is not exactly the same as anatomical connectivity, as functional connectivity results from a statistical study of correlated variability between two areas. Thus, we can observe which area becomes preferentially activated in a given task, and then analyze the constellation of brain areas that are functionally connected to it to unveil the distributed brain network to which it belongs. One notable example of this was provided by the groundbreaking experiments by Marcus Raichle and his collaborators, who criticized the standard imaging protocols for always using a control task that requires an executive function, and then contrasting this with the experimental task. Raichle wondered what happens when the brain does not have to perform any task at all, as opposed to executing some sort of cognitive task. Thus, he asked participants to lie quietly on the fMRI machine with their eyes open while he recorded their brain activity. Then, he and colleagues compared the observed pattern with the average activations found for a series of cognitive tasks. His findings have become among the most relevant in the history of cognitive neuroscience, although not without controversy, as every respectable innovation should be (Raichle et al. 2001; Raichle 2015).

Raichle determined that in the resting condition, also called the default mode condition, there was a typical activity pattern in which some brain areas increase their activity. Notably, these are the dorsomedial prefrontal cortex and posterior cingulate cortex in the dorsal midline of the hemisphere (see Fig. 2.2), and a few other areas in the lateral aspect of the hemisphere. On the other hand, these same areas significantly decrease their activity when the brain engages in an executive task. In the latter condition, there is a different set of areas that increase their activity, including premotor areas that are involved in short-term memory processes, in eye movement control and others. When studying the functional connectivity in these networks, it was found that their activity was strongly oscillatory, with a notable within-network positive synchrony. That is, within the resting networks all areas activate and decrease their activities more or less at the same time; and conversely, within the executive network all areas also show a highly positive activity correlation. However, between networks there is strict anti-synchrony, that is, when the resting state network is active, the executive network goes down, and conversely, when the executive network engages, the resting state network disengages (Fox et al. 2005, 2007). As I said, this is an oscillatory process, in which we normally alternate in periods of one or more minutes from activating the executive networks and deactivating the resting network, and then activating the resting network and deactivating the executive network. Thus, we do not fully concentrate even when we are engaged in serious tasks, but from time to time disengage and make an update of our internal state and contextual situation, to again re-enter the task after a brief while. This fits quite well with our own personal experiences at work, when writing, as I am now, or in any other task. Thus, our cognitive or behavioral efficiency may relate better with the appropriate alternation between these two tasks than with keeping to the executive network at the expense of the resting network.

I used these long words to describe the resting state and default network because they are related to two mental processes that are highly relevant to language and to language origins: one is social behavior, as the default network has been associated with empathy and mentalization, the capacity to understand the other's mental states;

and the second is introspection and particularly daydreaming, which are related to the development of inner speech, a capacity that I will argue marked an inflection point in the evolution of speech and language. Importantly, the language network does not strictly belong to either the executive or the resting state networks, but rather is recruited by one or the other in different circumstances, say when daydreaming (activating the resting state network, as noted above), or for example when teaching a class or opening conference (activating the executive network). The speech circuits may actually contribute information stored in both networks and supply a way of transferring memories between them (See Chapter 4).

The Language Network Updated

The second derivation of MRI is tractographic diffusion tensor imaging (DTI), which measures the asymmetry of water diffusion in nerve fiber tracts. Inside a tract, water tends not to diffuse symmetrically in all directions, but diffuses in the same direction as the fibers. By measuring the direction of water flow in nerve tracts, it is possible to follow their trajectory in the living human brain and represent them in three dimensions. Using a combination of fMRI and DTI, we can find for example the areas that activate under a given experimental task, and then use these areas as "seeds" to trace their anatomical connections to the rest of the brain, thus visualizing the "hard" network to which each area belongs. Although DTI does not have the resolution to determine which fibers are afferents (incoming) or efferents (outgoing) to the respective area, practically all cortico-cortical fiber tracts are bidirectional, containing both kinds of axons. MRI and DTI do not yet have the same resolution as animal postmortem techniques, but they have provided invaluable information that was totally inaccessible some 50 years ago. As I said above, these findings have provided substantial evidence that the language circuit contains dorsal and ventral components that run in the dorsal and ventral aspects of the Sylvian convolution, respectively.

Early tractographic studies of the language regions, first by Marco Catani and later by several groups, including those led by James Rilling, Cornelius Weiller, Michael Petrides and Angela Friederici, confirmed the existence of an arcuate fasciculus connecting Wernicke's and Broca's regions, running deep to the inferior parietal lobe and the ventral somatosensory and motor cortices, which was larger on the left than on the right hemisphere (Catani et al. 2005b; Glasser and Rilling 2008, Saur et al. 2008, Frey et al. 2008, Friederici 2009, Brauer et al. 2013, Tremblay and Dick 2016; Fridriksson et al. 2016). In addition, Catani and Dominic ffytche noted an important connection from the inferior parietal lobe into Broca's region (Catani and ffytche 2005; Catani et al. 2005). The name of the tract containing these fibers differs among authors, and I will refer to it as being part of the superior longitudinal fasciculus. Furthermore, there is another tract that connects Wernicke's region with the inferior parietal lobe, therefore closing the circuit between the auditory cortex, the inferior parietal cortex and Broca's area. Again, this tract has received distinct names from different authors, and I will refer to it as the posterior middle longitudinal fasciculus (Petrides 2014; Catani and Bambini 2014). Adding to these projections that make up the dorsal stream, the above studies also described the so-called ventral pathway for language. This encompasses fibers along the superior temporal lobe, recruiting fibers from the anterior auditory regions, connecting them with the anterior temporal lobe, and reaching the anterior part of Broca's area and its vicinities (areas 47 and 45). The auditory and neighboring areas in the anterior temporal lobe play a role in semantic processing and identifying the speaker, as in some cases lesions in this region lead to anomia, that is, the inability to generate the names of categories of objects or perceptions like colors. The pathway connecting these areas includes two longitudinal tracts, the inferior longitudinal fasciculus, and the inferior fronto-occipital fasciculus. From now on, I will refer to it as the "ventral pathway" for speech or language (for a summary diagram, see Fig. 2.3).

Recently, Catani and Valentina Bambini summarized the language-related projections in the social communication and language evolution and development (SCALED) model, which separates the different tracts according to their distinct functions (Catani and Bambini

2014, Tremblay and Dick 2016). According to this model, (i) the arcuate fasciculus is involved in syntactic analysis; (ii) the inferior parietal projection to the posterior part of Broca's area participates in recognition and production of motor patterns. (iii) Wernicke's area and the inferior parietal lobe are connected via a tract (the posterior middle longitudinal fasciculus) involved in pragmatic aspects of speech. (iv) the ventral pathway, involving two longitudinal fascicles along the temporal lobe (middle and inferior longitudinal fascicles), and their connection to the anterior part of Broca's region via the uncinate fasciculus and the extreme capsule, is involved in lexical and semantic processing. I have to note that some 20 years ago, Ricardo García and I proposed a connectivity diagram for the language circuit containing essentially the same elements as this model (see Chapter 7) (Aboitiz and García 1997).

Based on these and other findings, Gregory Hickok and David Poeppel provided a functional-anatomical model of language processing, with an early stage of speech perception that takes place in the superior temporal lobe (auditory cortex, Wernicke's area) of both hemispheres, involving the analysis of auditory signals and early phonological processing (see Chapter 4) (Hickok and Poeppel 2004, 2007). From there, there is a pathway that runs along the temporal lobe (predominantly in the left hemisphere) and involves lexical representations, and a left-hemisphere dorsal pathway that controls articulatory processes. Following earlier authors like Ludwig Lichtheim and Antonio Damasio, Hickok and Poeppel proposed a diffuse "conceptual network" that interacts with these two pathways in an as yet unspecified manner. Interestingly, the right hemisphere auditory pathways participate in prosodic processing. Daniela Sammler, Pascal Belin and other coauthors made a thorough imaging study of the neural basis of prosody, evidencing that it takes dual routes in the ventral and dorsal auditory pathways of the right hemisphere, with a similar organization to that of left-hemisphere language networks (Sammler et al. 2015).

The separation of dorsal and ventral pathways prompted to a redefinition of the role of Broca's region in language processing. Angela Friederici and collaborators parcellated this region into three components, areas 45 (pars triangularis), area 44 (pars opercularis), and a region called the deep frontal operculum that borders the deep insular cortex (Friederici et al. 2006; Anwander et al. 2007). The dorsal pathway is associated with area 44 and participates in recursive syntactic processing, and verbal working memory. On the other hand, area 45 and its connections via the ventral pathway are linked to simple (non-recursive) grammatical forms, and semantic and lexical analyses. More recently, Friederici and collaborators have proposed a model for Broca's region in which area 45 receives auditory information from the ventral pathway and then areas 45 and 44 convert the phonological and lexical inputs into a vocal articulatory pattern that is conveyed to the premotor cortex to codify speech utterances (Skeide and Friederici 2016). Thus, Broca's area may not be directly involved in the production of speech, but rather coordinates the transformation from phonological representations into neuromuscular articulatory processes. This is consistent with the recent finding by Nina Dronkers and collaborators, who found that while Broca's area activates during word presentation in a vocal repetition task, at the time of the speech response there is activation of the ventral motor cortex, but not of Broca's region. Nonetheless, Broca's region activated when novel articulatory sequences had to be executed when presenting non-word stimuli, that is, phonetically correct but meaningless phonological sequences, like "dago", which requires conscious control of vocalization (Flinker et al. 2015).

Finally, Catani, Marsel Mesulam and other collaborators have discovered an additional tract, called the frontal aslant. This is a vertical fiber bundle that connects the supplementary and pre-supplementary motor areas in the superior frontal gyrus (dorsal prefrontal cortex) with the inferior frontal gyrus where Broca's area is located (Catani et al. 2013). Catani and his group found that the aslant tract was affected in a subgroup of patients with primary progressive aphasia (a neurodegenerative condition that results in progressive loss of speech), which is characterized by lack of fluency in speech or in its more serious condition, complete mutism. The aslant tract is also present in monkeys, and may be part of a secondary but ancestral vocalization system that includes the medial frontal cortex and its descending projections to the brainstem, which we will discuss in more detail in Chapter 10 (Ackermann et al. 2014).

Connecting It All

Perhaps surprisingly to some, the language areas are not different from other cortical areas in their intrinsic architecture. Angela Friederici, Wolf Singer and several others have emphasized that the synaptic organization of different cortical regions is essentially the same, based on a "canonical microcircuit" that repeats serially throughout the cortex (Friederici and Singer 2015). The idea of a modular organization of the cerebral cortex was introduced by Vernon Mountcastle in the 1950s, based on the vertical organization of neuronal clusters in the cerebral cortex, in arrays termed columns (Edelman and Mountcastle 1978; Mountcastle 1997). Mountcastle proposed that cortical columns have a conserved synaptic organization across the entire cortical mantle. There are minor differences between cortical areas arising from the relative development of distinct laminar components, for example, large pyramidal neurons in motor areas and abundant granular neurons in sensory areas. Mountcastle also asserted that each cortical region should be defined by the unique pattern of connectivity of each area with the rest of the brain, rather than by its cytoarchitectonic features. In this context, the specificity of functions of each given area depends more on the particular embedding of this area in a larger scale neural network rather than on its internal organization. Thus, localization emerges more as a consequence of the network configuration than as an intrinsic property of each brain region. Furthermore, recent evidence has revealed significant individual variability in the organization of these networks. Emily Finn and her collaborators have described an individual fingerprint in the connectome, which allows for distinguishing one subject from others. This indeed provides each of us with a specific signature, characterized by the organization of large-scale neural connections in our brains (Finn et al. 2015).

Network thinking has led to the connectome project, which is an ambitious computational endeavor that aims to account for all connections of the human brain. The connectome was independently proposed in 2005 by Olaf Sporns and Patric Hagmann, in analogy to the human genome project, and has been developed by the U.S. National Institute of Health as a major endeavor to describe the connectivity of the entire nervous system in humans and animals (Hagmann et al. 2008). Connectome models emphasize complex and distributed networks encompassing widespread brain areas, in which there are critical nodes where many connections converge and are therefore key regulators of the overall network. Stefan Fuertinger, Kristina Simonyan and collaborators proposed a speech-specific connectome model that includes the classical language networks, the dorsal and the ventral pathways described here, and other regions like the insula, anterior cingulate gyrus and other regions (Fuertinger et al. 2015). Notably, a critical node in this network is the posterior motor cortex, which can be considered a connector through which motor output is directed to brainstem centers. Pascale Tremblay and colleagues have proposed a complex network subserving language systems, emphasizing a descending cortical "motor stream" that includes Catani's frontal aslant tract, which anchors the distributed language network in a specific motor pathway (Dick et al. 2014). These findings are relevant for the origin of speech, as it has been commonly argued that the direct control of the descending cortical over laryngeal musculature was the key process that allowed the voluntary control of vocalizations and hence the appearance of speech as the main communicative modality.

These extended networks support the notion of a widespread region associated with Broca's aphasia. In this line, Evelina Fedorenko has subdivided the language-related networks into a functionally specialized "core" of coactive areas during speech and language processing (Broca and Wernicke's areas in the restricted sense), and a "periphery" that includes areas like the insular cortex, inferior parietal areas and other regions (Fedorenko 2014; Fedorenko and Thompson-Schill 2014; Chai et al. 2016). These areas contribute domain-general mechanisms like attention, short-term memory, motivation and motor control to linguistic processes, but may also provide cognitive control over other tasks. Furthermore, cortico-cortical connections are usually reciprocal, so that information can be transferred in both directions, from sensory-related to motor-related areas (bottom-up), and vice versa, from motor-related to sensory-related areas (top-down). A statistical methodology called dynamic causal modeling, developed in the 2000s by Karl Friston and collaborators, analyzes the effect that changes in activity in one region can have on activity in another connected region (Friston et al. 2003). Using this technique, Dirk-Bart den Ouden and collaborators determined a significant top-down effect of Broca's area and the adjacent premotor cortex into Wernicke's area, via the dorsal pathway, particularly for mechanisms of sentence processing (den Ouden et al. 2012). Other authors like Angela Friederici and Josef Rauschecker have also proposed a top-down regulation of Wernicke's area from Broca's area (Rauschecker 2012; Skeide and Friederici 2016). More specifically, the arcuate fasciculus and the adjacent tract stemming from the premotor cortex probably play an important role in modulating early stages of speech processing in function of current motor programs (see Chapter 7).

Thus, there is a much more intricate cortical network for language than was envisioned in the early models of Wernicke and Geschwind. This becomes even more complicated when we consider that these areas are not isolated from the rest of the brain and that they are highly interconnected with other neuronal systems. For example, the production of speech, writing or sign language requires the execution of complex motor patterns that are controlled by the cerebellum and the basal ganglia (Jeon et al. 2014; Ackermann et al. 2014; Leisman et al. 2014; Moberget and Ivry 2016; Krishnan et al. 2016). The basal ganglia are extensively connected with the cerebral cortex, and Broca's and Wernicke's areas, as well as the motor cortex controlling the vocal tract. People with lesions in these subcortical nuclei usually display speech deficits like dysarthria or apraxia (the incapacity to form and articulate speech sounds, although patients seem to know what they want to say). Furthermore, stuttering is also caused by basal ganglia dysfunction, and pharmacological blockage of dopamine (a neurotransmitter critical for basal ganglia function) can ameliorate these speech deficits. In addition, the basal ganglia are believed to participate in the execution of automatic speech patterns acquired over many years, like producing the past tense in regular verbs in English. In Parkinson's disease, a condition that primarily affects the basal ganglia, there is in fact difficulty in applying this rule to newly learned verbs. Another subcortical structure that is relevant for speech and language is the thalamus, a potato-shaped complex of nuclei at the base of the cerebral hemispheres that is highly and reciprocally connected to the cerebral cortex, to which some of its nuclei convey auditory, visual and somatosensory stimuli (Jeon et al. 2014; Klostermann et al. 2013; Bohsali et al. 2015). Lesions in the thalamus have been linked to aphasia, but the relationship with language or speech production is still difficult to understand and separate from cortical damage. A common effect of thalamic effects on language is dysnomia, which is thought to be due to insufficient arousal caused by damage to the thalamic reticular nucleus. The study of subcortical components in speech and language is only in its beginnings, and probably the coming years will witness exciting discoveries in this area. Finally, a recent study revealed that the hippocampus, a limbic structure of the temporal lobe involved in memory processing (see Chapter 6), participates in language processing by linking incoming words with stored semantic representations, possibly associated to the ventral language pathway (Piai et al. 2016).

Brain Waves

Another recent source of evidence on language processing has come from more direct measurements of neuronal activity, such as electro-encephalography (EEG, the analysis of electrical fields on the surface of the skull) and the much more recent magnetoencephalography (MEG), which measures the magnetic fields associated with electrical fields. Compared with imaging methods, whose time resolution analysis is on the order of minutes, EEG and MEG record electromagnetic activity every millisecond, which reveals the microdynamics of the brain in real time. However, they lack the anatomical resolution of imaging methods, as they are recorded directly from the skull, after tremendous distortions of the electromagnetic field as it crosses the braincase. The electrical activity of the brain surface was first analyzed in the 1870s by the American neurologist Richard Caton, and was subsequently measured by several other researchers (Caton 1875). However, it was the German psychiatrist Hans Berger who, in 1924, recorded the first human EEG on the skull surface (Berger 1929). Berger had studied mathematics before enrolling in medicine, and had an interest in the physics of the brain, but more than that, he was motivated by his belief in telepathy, and was trying to find physical evidence for this. His electrical recordings unveiled a complex oscillating electrical signal that was, however, much too weak to travel any significant distance away from the skull. He discovered the alpha rhythm of the EEG (an oscillatory activity of some 8–13 cycles per second), which is evident in occipital regions when subjects close their eyes, but is substituted by the faster beta rhythm (between 12 and 30 cycles per second) when subjects open their eyes. His findings revealed that the brain is actually an active network at all times, working as a highly complex oscillatory machine with electrical activity with cycles at many different frequencies at the same time. Brain oscillations come in different flavors, and the EEG signal is in fact a composite of many oscillatory activities that occur at frequencies from one tenth of a cycle per second or less, up to some 80 cycles per second or more. These frequencies can be separated, much the way white light can be broken down into its different frequencies or colors through a prism, by a mathematical method called Fourier analysis, or other more modern methods such as wavelet analysis. Thus, brain activity occurs at different timescales that, interestingly, fit spatial requirements so that high frequencies seem to be related to local processing, and are nested in wider networks operating at higher frequencies that serve as associative links between different regions.

Work in this century by György Buzsáki, Nikos Logothetis, Wolf Singer and many others have determined that neuronal oscillations are ubiquitous across species and brain regions, and have been found to be critical for brain activity, including cognitive processes (Buzsáki et al. 2013). Ongoing oscillatory activity is fundamental for controlling and synchronizing the "spiking" activity of neurons, that is, the generation of very strong but extremely brief all-or-none electrical signals called action potentials that make up the basis of neuronal signaling. In a seminal article, Eugenio Rodríguez, working with Francisco Varela and others, showed that high-frequency synchronization of neuronal oscillations across brain regions is associated with feature perception in human subjects (Rodríguez et al. 1999; Varela et al. 2001). Furthermore, my former student Conrado Bosman, working with Pascal Fries and me (in two separate papers) has recently proposed that the canonical cortical circuit discussed above is essentially an oscillatory device, highly conserved not only across cortical areas but also across many species (including birds, reptiles and perhaps some invertebrates) (Bosman and Aboitiz 2015, Lewis et al. 2015). This circuit serves basic computational processes inherent to a variety of sensory, motor and cognitive functions (see Chapter 9). As Angela Friederici and Wolf Singer have emphasized, the neuronal networks for language are no exception to this phenomenology (Friederici and Singer 2015). David Poeppel has advanced the hypothesis that brain rhythms are essential for language processing and that their nested organization partly reflects the hierarchical structure of language by packaging information at different temporal levels. Poeppel specifies three main levels of processing that fit distinct neuronal frequencies, namely phonemes are processed at very high frequencies (some 25–35 cycles per second or more, called the high beta or low gamma ranges), the syllabic rate occurs at around 4–7 cycles per second (the so-called theta frequency); and lexical and phrasal units are processed at slower frequencies, say 1–2 cycles per second (delta frequency). Additional studies have found that differences in the amplitude of gamma oscillations in auditory regions are also associated with differences in semantic contents, while the theta rhythm is related to short-term verbal memory, a capacity that is critical for language acquisition (Chapters 6 and 7) (Poeppel et al. 2012; Poeppel 2014; Giraud and Poeppel 2012; Ghitza et al. 2013; Chait et al. 2015, Hickok and Poeppel 2015). Noteworthy, a recent study mentioned above, indicating involvement of the hippocampus in language processing, revealed that modulation of theta oscillations in this region are associated with semantic expectations during speech perception (Piai et al. 2016).

Thus, speech and speech processing take place in an oscillatory domain where interrelated frequency ranges must be tightly coordinated for appropriate execution and perception. Provided that the speech rhythm is maintained, the nested organization of these activities is able to provide contextual cues (provided by low frequencies) to local processing (occurring at high frequencies). Under these conditions, it may be possible to solve perceptual ambiguities and facilitate comprehension. In the auditory cortex, ongoing oscillations in superficial layers, especially in the theta and gamma ranges, synchronize with the acoustically imposed rhythmic activity provided by the speech signal, which hits the middle layers of the cortex, and is projected to higher order cortical areas. On the motor side, speech itself is a highly rhythmic activity involving lip, tongue and vocal fold movements that also take place semi-periodically (just like many other motor activities). Furthermore, the tight coordination between the different organs involved in speech (lips, tongue, and vocal folds) requires fine coordination of the motor pacemakers located in the brainstem, which are controlled by brain oscillatory activity. In this same line, Nai Ding, Lucia Melloni, Poeppel and colleagues recently analyzed spectral activity at different timescales in subjects listening to fluent speech, observing that cortical activity accurately tracked the time course of words, phrases and sentences, while purely acoustic cues or the predictability of incoming words did not correlate with the recorded activity (Ding et al. 2016a). This suggests that grammatical constructions reflect a timescale hierarchy of neural processing, a point I will return to in Chapter 6. Some very recent studies have used intracranial recordings during surgery of epileptic patients. For example, the group led by Stanislaas Dehaene found that oscillatory activity in the left hemisphere increases as words are being read in a sentence (possibly reflecting working memory load), but this activity decreases in the moment the phrase is formed, which may relate to the syntactic function Merge (see Chapter 1) (Nelson et al. 2017).

Finally, another way of analyzing human brain electromagnetic activity has been the study of event-related potentials (ERPs), a technique developed in the 1930s by Pauline and Hallowell Davis (Davis et al. 1939). It consists of averaging EEG signals after many trials that are time-locked to the presentation of a stimulus in a sensory modality (visual, auditory or tactile). Since the recordings are time-locked, trial averaging eliminates all non-coherent variation in activity, unveiling a smooth signal that shows voltage or magnetic deflections at specific times after the presentation of a stimulus. These deflections are the ERPs, which are classified as early potentials (occurring around 100–200 milliseconds after the stimulus), which reflect activation of specific sensory cortices; and late potentials (300 milliseconds or later), reflecting multimodal cognitive operations. Although a relatively old technique, the study of ERPs has been revived in the last 30 years due to their usefulness in the study of attentional processes. As we will see in Chapter 5, there has been a steadily increasing number of ERP studies in language processing, partly triggered by the seminal reports of Marta Kutas and Steve Hillyard on semantic-related activity (Kutas and Hillyard 1980).

The time resolution of the ERP signal has allowed for establishing a sequence of events in speech processing that was elegantly summarized in a recent model proposed by Michael Skeide and Angela Friederici. According to them, speech information is first processed in the auditory cortex, and some 20–50 milliseconds after presentation, the phonological representation of words is recognized in the superior temporal sulcus. Then, two parallel streams run along the temporal lobe, one involved in morphosyntactic categorization (assigning syntactical categories to words) (40–90 milliseconds) and analysis of basic phrase structure (120–150 milliseconds in the anterior temporal lobe). The other stream is lexical-semantic processing in which, for example, words are distinguished from non-words (50–80 milliseconds), followed by lexical retrieval processes in which word meanings are fully recognized (110–170 milliseconds in the left anterior temporal lobe). These are bottom-up processes that are conveyed mainly by the ventral acoustic stream. Top-down mechanisms then ensue via a projection from the anterior temporal lobe to Broca's area. First (between 200 and 400 milliseconds), lexical information reaches areas 45 and 47 in the left hemisphere via the ventral pathway, where semantic analysis is performed. In addition (between 300 and 500 milliseconds), morphosyntactic input is conveyed to area 44, where higher-level syntax is processed. After this, both semantic and syntactic information are transmitted back from Broca's region to Wernicke's area, where syntactic and semantic information converge to generate a unified conceptual representation of the speech string. On the other hand, prosodic processing has a longer onset time, beginning at 200 milliseconds in the right auditory cortex, while activity related to prosodic information begins in the right ventrolateral prefrontal cortex at some 300 milliseconds post-stimulus (Skeide and Friederici 2016).

No doubt we have come a long way since Broca's time. Researchers have been able to identify a sophisticated network involved in speech processing, and accessory networks supplying basic cognitive processes to support the demands of linguistic behavior. Still, the evolutionary questions of how did these networks originate, and whether they emerged from some ancestral system present in the non-human primate brain remains unanswered. First, we need to explore other features of the human brain that are intimately related to our communicative capacity: the large size of our brain, hemispheric dominance and interhemispheric communication, and our memory system. After discussing these, I will begin to track the ancestry of our speech-related brain networks and behavior by looking for similar phenomena in non-human primates, other mammals and even non-mammals like birds.

References

Aboitiz F, García R (1997) The evolutionary origin of the language areas in the human brain. A neuroanatomical perspective. Brain Res Rev 25:381–396

Ackermann H, Hage SR, Ziegler W (2014) Brain mechanisms of acoustic communication in humans and nonhuman primates: an evolutionary perspective. Behav Brain Sci 37:529–546

Anwander A, Tittgemeyer M, von Cramon DY, Friederici AD, Knösche TR (2007) Connectivity-based parcellation of Broca's area. Cereb Cortex 17:816–825

Ardila A, Bernal B, Rosselli M (2016) How localized are language brain areas? A review of Brodmann areas involvement in oral language. Arch Clin Neuropsychol 31:112–122

Berger H (1929) Über das Elektroenkephalogramm des Menschen. Arch Psychiatr 87: 527–570

Bohsali AA, Triplett W, Sudhyadhom A, Gullett JM, McGregor K, FitzGerald DB, Mareci T, White K, Crosson B (2015) Broca's area – thalamic connectivity. Brain Lang 141:80–88

Bosman CA, Aboitiz F (2015) Functional constraints in the evolution of brain circuits. Front Neurosci 9:303

Brauer J, Anwander A, Perani D, Friederici AD (2013) Dorsal and ventral pathways in language development. Brain Lang 127:289–295

Broca P (1865) Sur le siège de la faculté du langage articulé. Bull Soc Anthrop Paris 6: 377–393

Broca P (2015) Comparative anatomy of the cerebral convolutions: the great limbic lobe and the limbic fissure in the mammalian series. J Comp Neurol 523:2501–2554

Brodmann K (1909) Vergleichende Lokalisationslehre der Grosshirnrinde. Johann Ambrosius Barth, Leipzig

Buzsáki G, Logothetis N, Singer W (2013) Scaling brain size, keeping timing: evolutionary preservation of brain rhythms. Neuron 80:751–764

Catani M, Bambini V (2014) A Model for Social Communication and Language Evolution and Development (SCALED). Curr Opin Neurobiol 28:165–171

Catani M, ffytche DH (2005) The rises and falls of disconnection syndromes. Brain 128:2224–2239

Catani M, Mesulam M (2008a) The arcuate fasciculus and the disconnection theme in language and aphasia: history and current state. Cortex 44:953–961

Catani M, Mesulam M (2008b) What is a disconnection syndrome? Cortex 44:911–913

Catani M, Jones DK, ffytche DH (2005) Perisylvian language networks of the human brain. Ann Neurol 57:8–16

Catani M, Mesulam MM, Jakobsen E, Malik F, Martersteck A, Wieneke C, Thompson CK, Thiebaut de Schotten M, Dell'Acqua F, Weintraub S, Rogalski E (2013) A novel frontal pathway underlies verbal fluency in primary progressive aphasia. Brain 136:2619–2628

Caton R (1875) Electrical currents of the brain. J Nerv Ment Dis 2:610

Chai LR, Mattar MG, Blank IA, Fedorenko E, Bassett DS (2016) Functional network dynamics of the language system. Cereb Cortex 26: 4148–4159

Chait M, Greenberg S, Arai T, Simon JZ, Poeppel D (2015) Multi-time resolution analysis of speech: evidence from psychophysics. Front Neurosci 9:214

Cohen L, Lehéricy S, Chochon F, Lemer C, Rivaud S, Dehaene S (2002) Language-specific tuning of visual cortex? Functional properties of the Visual Word Form Area. Brain 125:1054–1069

Corsi P, Jones EG, Shepherd GM (1991) The Enchanted Loom. Chapters in the History of Neuroscience. Oxford University Press, Oxford.

Davis H, Davis PA, Loomis AL, Harvey EN, Hobart G (1939) Electrical reactions of the human brain to auditory stimulation during sleep. J Neurophysiol 2:500–514

den Ouden DB, Saur D, Mader W, Schelter B, Lukic S, Wali E, Timmer J, Thompson CK (2012) Network modulation during complex syntactic processing. Neuroimage 59:815–823

Dick AS, Bernal B, Tremblay P (2014) The language connectome: new pathways, new concepts. Neuroscientist 20:453–467

Ding N, Melloni L, Zhang H, Tian X, Poeppel D (2016a) Cortical tracking of hierarchical linguistic structures in connected speech. Nat Neurosci 19:158–164

Ding SL, Royall JJ, Sunkin SM, Ng L, Facer BA, Lesnar P, Guillozet-Bongaarts A, McMurray B, Szafer A, Dolbeare TA, Stevens A, Tirrell L, Benner T, Caldejon S, Dalley RA, Dee N, Lau C, Nyhus J, Reding M, Riley ZL, Sandman D, Shen E, van der Kouwe A, Varjabedian A, Write M, Zollei L, Dang C, Knowles JA, Koch C, Phillips JW, Sestan N, Wohnoutka P, Zielke HR, Hohmann JG, Jones AR, Bernard A, Hawrylycz MJ, Hof PR, Fischl B, Lein ES (2016b) Comprehensive cellular-resolution atlas of the adult human brain. J Comp Neurol 525:407

Dronkers NF, Plaisant O, Iba-Zizen MT, Cabanis EA (2007) Paul Broca's historic cases: high resolution MR imaging of the brains of Leborgne and Lelong. Brain 130:1432–1441

Edelman GM, Mountcastle VB (1978) The Mindful Brain. Cortical organization and the group-selective theory of higher brain function. MIT press, Cambridge

Eklund A, Nichols TE, Knutsson H (2016) Cluster failure: Why fMRI inferences for spatial extent have inflated false-positive rates. Proc Natl Acad Sci U S A 113:7900–7905.

Fedorenko E (2014) The role of domain-general cognitive control in language comprehension. Front Psychol 5:335

Fedorenko E, Thompson-Schill SL (2014) Reworking the language network. Trends Cogn Sci 18:120–126

Finn ES, Shen X, Scheinost D, Rosenberg MD, Huang J, Chun MM, Papademetris X, Constable RT (2015) Functional connectome fingerprinting: identifying individuals using patterns of brain connectivity. Nat Neurosci 18:1664–1671.

Flinker A, Korzeniewska A, Shestyuk AY, Franaszczuk PJ, Dronkers NF, Knight RT, Crone NE (2015) Redefining the role of Broca's area in speech. Proc Natl Acad Sci U S A 112:2871–2875

Fodor J (1983) The Modularity of Mind. MIT Press, Cambridge

Fox MD, Snyder AZ, Vincent JL, Corbetta M, Van Essen DC, Raichle ME (2005) The human brain is intrinsically organized into dynamic, anticorrelated functional networks. Proc Natl Acad Sci U S A 102:9673–9678

Fox MD, Snyder AZ, Vincent JL, Raichle ME (2007) Intrinsic fluctuations within cortical systems account for intertrial variability in human behavior. Neuron 56:171–184

Frey S, Campbell JS, Pike GB, Petrides M (2008) Dissociating the human language pathways with high angular resolution diffusion fiber tractography. J Neurosci 28:11435–11444

Fridriksson J, Yourganov G, Bonilha L, Basilakos A, Den Ouden DB, Rorden C (2016) Revealing the dual streams of speech processing. Proc Natl Acad Sci U S A 113:15108–15113

Friederici AD (2009) Pathways to language: fiber tracts in the human brain. Trends Cogn Sci 13:175–181

Friederici AD, Singer W (2015) Grounding language processing on basic neurophysiological principles. Trends Cogn Sci 19:329–338.

Friederici AD, Bahlmann J, Heim S, Schubotz RI, Anwander A (2006) The brain differentiates human and non-human grammars: functional localization and structural connectivity. Proc Natl Acad Sci U S A 103:2458–2463

Friston KJ, Harrison L, Penny W (2003) Dynamic causal modelling. Neuroimage 19:1273–1302

Fuertinger S, Horwitz B, Simonyan K (2015) The functional connectome of speech control. PLoS Biol 13:e1002209

Galaburda AM, Pandya DN (1983) The intrinsic architectonic and connectional organization of the superior temporal region of the rhesus monkey. J Comp Neurol 221:169–184

Galaburda A, Sanides F (1980) Cytoarchitectonic organization of the human auditory cortex. J Comp Neurol 190:597–610

Gaspar PA, Bosman CA, Ruiz S, Zamorano F, Pérez C, Aboitiz F (2011) Parametric increases of working memory load unveil a decreased alpha oscillatory activity in schizophrenia. Schizophr Res 131:268–269

Glasser MF, Rilling JK (2008) DTI tractography of the human brain's language pathways. Cereb Cortex 18:2471–2482

Glasser MF, Coalson TS, Robinson EC, Hacker CD, Harwell J, Yacoub E, Ugurbil K, Andersson J, Beckmann CF, Jenkinson M, Smith SM, Van Essen DC (2016) A multi-modal parcellation of human cerebral cortex. Nature 536:171–178

Geschwind N (1964) The development of the brain and the evolution of language. Mon Ser Lang Ling 1:155–169

Geschwind N (1965) Disconnexion syndromes in animals and man. Brain 88:237–294; 585–644

Ghitza O, Giraud AL, Poeppel D (2013) Neuronal oscillations and speech perception: critical-band temporal envelopes are the essence. Front Hum Neurosci 6:340

Giraud AL, Poeppel D (2012) Cortical oscillations and speech processing: emerging computational principles and operations. Nat Neurosci 15:511–117.

Hagmann P, Cammoun L, Gigandet X, Meuli R, Honey CJ, Wedeen VJ, Sporns O (2008) Mapping the structural core of human cerebral cortex. PLoS Biol 6:e159

Hickok G, Poeppel D (2004) Dorsal and ventral streams: a framework for understanding aspects of the functional anatomy of language. Cognition 92:67–99.

Hickok G, Poeppel D (2007) The cortical organization of speech processing. Nat Rev Neurosci 8:393–402

Hickok G, Poeppel D (2015) Neural basis of speech perception. Handb Clin Neurol 129:149–160

Jeon HA, Anwander A, Friederici AD (2014) Functional network mirrored in the prefrontal cortex, caudate nucleus, and thalamus: high-resolution functional imaging and structural connectivity. J Neurosci 34:9202–9212

Klostermann F, Krugel LK, Ehlen F (2013) Functional roles of the thalamus for language capacities. Front Syst Neurosci 7:32

Krishnan S, Watkins KE, Bishop DV (2016) Neurobiological basis of language learning difficulties. Trends Cogn Sci 20:701–714

Kutas M, Hillyard SA (1980) Reading senseless sentences: brain potentials reflect semantic incongruity. Science 207:203–205

Leisman G, Braun-Benjamin O, Melillo R (2014) Cognitive-motor interactions of the basal ganglia in development. Front Syst Neurosci 8:16

Lewis CM, Bosman CA, Fries P (2015) Recording of brain activity across spatial scales. Curr Opin Neurobiol 32:68–77

Mesulam MM (2015) Fifty years of disconnexion syndromes and the Geschwind legacy. Brain 138:2791–2799

Moberget T, Ivry RB (2016) Cerebellar contributions to motor control and language comprehension: searching for common computational principles. Ann N Y Acad Sci 1369:154–171

Mountcastle VB (1997) The columnar organization of the neocortex. Brain 120:701–722

Nelson MJ, El Karoui I, Giber K, Yang X, Cohen L, Koopman H, Cash SS, Naccache L, Hale JT, Pallier C, Dehaene S (2017) Neurophysiological dynamics of phrase-structure building during sentence processing. Proc Natl Acad Sci U S A 114:E3669-E3678

Pearson H (2003) Magnetic pioneers met Nobel for putting medicine in the picture. Nature 425:547

Penfield W, Roberts L (1959) Speech and Brain Mechanisms. Princeton University Press, Princeton

Petrides M (2014) Neuroanatomy of Language Regions of the Human Brain. Academic Press, New York

Piai V, Anderson KL, Lin JJ, Dewar C, Parvizi J, Dronkers NF, Knight RT (2016) Direct brain recordings reveal hippocampal rhythm underpinnings of language processing. Proc Natl Acad Sci U S A 113:11366–11371

Poeppel D (2014) The neuroanatomic and neurophysiological infrastructure for speech and language. Curr Opin Neurobiol 28:142–149

Poeppel D, Emmorey K, Hickok G, Pylkkänen L (2012) Towards a new neurobiology of language. J Neurosci 32:14125–14131

Raichle ME (2015) The brain's default mode network. Annu Rev Neurosci 38:433–447.

Raichle ME, MacLeod AM, Snyder AZ, Powers WJ, Gusnard DA, Shulman GL (2001) A default mode of brain function. Proc Natl Acad Sci U S A 98:676–682

Rauschecker JP (2012) Ventral and dorsal streams in the evolution of speech and language. Front Evol Neurosci 4:7

Rodríguez E, George N, Lachaux JP, Martinerie J, Renault B, Varela FJ (1999) Perception's shadow: long-distance synchronization of human brain activity. Nature 397:430–433

Roux FE, Dufor O, Giussani C, Wamain Y, Draper L, Longcamp M, Démonet JF (2009) The graphemic/motor frontal area Exner's area revisited. Ann Neurol 66:537–545

Sammler D, Grosbras MH, Anwander A, Bestelmeyer PE, Belin P (2015) Dorsal and ventral pathways for prosody. Curr Biol 25:3079–3085

Saur D, Kreher BW, Schnell S, Kümmerer D, Kellmeyer P, Vry MS, Umarova R, Musso M, Glauche V, Abel S, Huber W, Rijntjes M, Hennig J, Weiller C (2008) Ventral and dorsal pathways for language. Proc Natl Acad Sci U S A 105:18035–18040

Schiller F (1992) Paul Broca. Explorer of the Brain. Oxford University Press, Oxford

Skeide MA, Friederici AD (2016) The ontogeny of the cortical language network. Nat Rev Neurosci 17:323–332

Steinberg DA (2009) Cerebral localization in the nineteenth century–the birth of a science and its modern consequences. J Hist Neurosci 18:254–261.

Steinberg DA (2014) The origin of scientific neurology and its consequences for modern and future neuroscience. Brain 137:294–300

Thiebaut de Schotten M, Dell'Acqua F, Ratiu P, Leslie A, Howells H, Cabanis E, Iba-Zizen MT, Plaisant O, Simmons A, Dronkers NF, Corkin S, Catani M (2015) From Phineas Gage and Monsieur Leborgne to H.M.: revisiting disconnection syndromes. Cereb Cortex 25:4812–4827

Tremblay P, Dick AS (2016) Broca and Wernicke are dead, or moving past the classic model of language neurobiology. Brain Lang 162:60–71

Varela F, Lachaux JP, Rodriguez E, Martinerie J (2001) The brainweb: phase synchronization and large-scale integration. Nat Rev Neurosci 2:229–239

Von Economo C, Koskinas GN (1925) Die Cytoarchitektonik der Hirnrinde des Erwachsenen Menschen. Springer Verlag, Wien

Weiller C, Bormann T, Saur D, Musso M, Rijntjes M (2011) How the ventral pathway got lost: and what its recovery might mean. Brain Lang 118:29–39

Wernicke K (1874) Der Aphasische Symptomencomplex. Eine Psychologische Studie auf Anatomischer Basis. M. Crohn and Weigert, Breslau

York GK 3rd, Steinberg DA (2011) Hughlings Jackson's neurological ideas. Brain 134:3106–3113

Zimmer C (2004) Soul Made Flesh. The Discovery of the Brain – and How it Changed the World. Free Press, New York

3

A Matter of Size

A feature early neurologists rapidly became aware of was that humans are endowed with unusually large brains compared to those of many other animals. This fact tempted many people to associate brain size with intelligence, not only across species but also among humans. Darwin claimed that the large size of the human brain, compared to that of the gorilla or orangutan, was closely related to the higher mental powers of humans, and noted that the effect of brain size was also found in insects, where social ants and bees had much larger cerebral ganglia than beetles (Darwin 1871). Darwin also asserted that one of the requisites to achieve language was to be endowed with higher mental capacity. As we will see throughout this book, it may have been the other way around, communication skills being a strong selective force for the increase in both brain size and cognitive capacity. In this chapter, I will review some aspects of the intense research agenda involved in determining the functional, developmental and evolutionary aspects of brain size differences. Not surprisingly, this continues to be a contentious topic as it is the most evident difference in brain anatomy between us and other primates.

© The Author(s) 2017
F. Aboitiz, *A Brain for Speech*,
DOI 10.1057/978-1-137-54060-7_3

Brain and Body

Animals like elephants and whales have brains much larger than ours. In fact, the brain is simply another organ of the body, subject to similar growth rules as other organs. Thus, larger animals tend to have larger brains than smaller animals, but are they smarter? Supporting the notion that brain size is a determinant of intelligence and learning capacity, in the early twentieth century Karl Lashley proposed the "principle of mass action", stating that the amount of damaged neural tissue is proportional to the amount of memory impairment produced, a concept that challenged the localizationist hypotheses at the time (Lashley 1929). Later on, Harry Jerison interpreted Lashley's concept in an evolutionary context and proposed the "principle of proper mass", which relates overall brain size to processing capacity across species (Jerison 1973). Jerison claimed that brain weight correlated best with the number of neurons in the brain, and that the amount of information processing per unit of volume was constant across species, implying that increased brain volume is directly associated with increased information capacity. Jerison statistically analyzed brain and body sizes of many species of vertebrates and found a consistent correlation between brain and body size among species, but little correlation in these variables within a species. In sexually dimorphic species (like humans), each sex was treated as a separate species. He graphically showed his results in standard allometric diagrams called log-log graphs in which both variables are displayed exponentially in each axis. With this method, exponential relations are displayed linearly and one can apply standard statistical methods to the data. If two variables (brain and body) have a linear relationship (a twofold increase in one implies a twofold increase in the other), the relationship is isometric and the slope of the graph is 1. If the slope is other than 1 in either direction, the relationship is allometric. In isometric growth, overall size increases result in scaled versions of the smaller versions, but in allometric growth, components (say body and brain) increase in size at different rates. Note that in an allometric relationship growth among different components still correlates, only some increase in size faster than others. A third possibility is that structures grow independently, that is, there is no correlated variability in size among distinct components of the body. The latter suggests little genetic correlation among the components, at least in relation to the determination of size. It is important to be clear about this, as some controversies have been caused by a lack of precision in describing comparative data.

In the case of body and brain, twofold increases in body size result in less than twofold increases in brain size, implying that smaller animals have larger brains for their body size than bigger animals. Jerison considered the strong body size dependency of brain size as the amount of neural tissue that was necessary for controlling bodily functions, and called it the "somatic factor", which was variable across vertebrate groups. Jerison's body-brain slope in mammals was about two-thirds, which fits the geometrical ratio between body size and body surface area. Therefore, he speculated that brain size scaled not with body weight but with the animals skin surface, as it needed to match the sensory receptors distributed in the skin. New analyses have revealed that the brain-body slope is not two thirds, but actually three-fourths, that is, if the body doubles in size, the brain increases 1.5 times in size (Martin 1981). According to this, a new interpretation for brain-body scaling is that brain size is determined by basal metabolic rate, which Max Kleiber showed to scale at three fourths with body size (Fig. 3.1) (Kleiber 1975). Since the brain is one of the most expensive organs in terms of energy needs (in humans it uses about 20% of total body energy), a lower metabolism in larger animals put limits to brain growth during gestation. However, no relationship was found between metabolic rate and brain size in a statistical analysis that eliminated body size (Pagel and Harvey 1988). In effect, metabolic rate and brain size only correlate because they both depend on body weight.

More detailed studies in the 1980s revealed that the variable that best fits the mammalian brain body slope is the period of prenatal body growth (Riska and Atchley 1985). During development, brain growth follows an exponential curve that can be subdivided into three distinct phases. There is an initial rapid growth phase in which the brain increases in size concomitant with body size and roughly corresponds to the period of prenatal growth. There is then a second

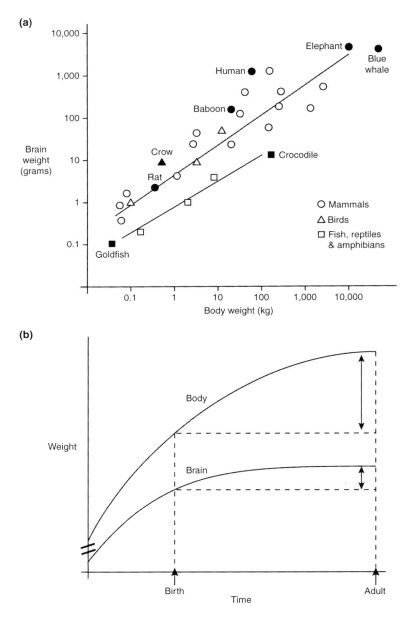

Fig. 3.1   Brain and body growth. (a) Brain weight depends on body weight across species. Birds and mammals tend to have larger brains for a given body

phase in which brain growth slows down with respect to body size and more or less fits the period around birth, and finally there is a postnatal period of slow brain growth in which the brain decouples from body growth, which maintains a high rate of growth. As species increase in body size, the period of postnatal body growth increases disproportionately to prenatal growth, which largely determines adult brain size. In evolution, this makes neonatal body size and adult brain size grow more slowly than adult body growth. This is important, as neurogenesis (the production of neurons during development) in mammals is largely restricted to the embryonic and fetal periods, with the notable exception of regions like the dentate gyrus, the olfactory bulbs and other brain regions where adult neurogenesis is, however, very limited. The brain keeps growing after birth by increasing neural ramifications (dendrites), increasing glial cells, myelination and glial cell production, but the neuronal population is largely determined by prenatal and early postnatal growth.

The length of the gestation period varies considerably among species, as altricial species like humans deliver their young prematurely and the period of rapid brain growth continues beyond birth. This makes the period of postnatal brain growth more important in determining adult brain size in these animals than it is in other species. Notwithstanding the variability of gestation period among mammals, brain development follows more or less the same schedule in all species. Barbara Finlay and colleagues (Workman et al. 2013, Finlay and Workman 2013)

Fig.3.1 (Continued)
size than other vertebrates, and primates and birds like crows have brains twice the size of those of other mammals or birds, respectively. Finally, although there is a statistical correlation between brain and body size, brain size grows more slowly than body size, so that larger animals tend to have smaller brains relative to their body size than smaller animals (humans are an exception). **(b)** The lifetime curve of body and brain growth of an average mammalian species. Most brain growth occurs prenatally, but the rest of the body keeps growing at a rapid rate long after birth. The postnatal period is increasingly important for the body growth of large-bodied species (double arrows) while postnatal brain growth is slower. Primates are unique in that their brains are larger at all ages, and grow more rapidly in the initial stages than the brains of other mammals of the same body size.

developed an extensive cross-species developmental timetable, showing that the ordering of many critical events like the initiation and end of neurogenesis, the appearance of important neural connections, and differentiation of cell types and nuclei all follow an extremely conserved sequence that scales logarithmically with post-conception time. Furthermore, the slope and the intercept of these curves increase steeply in species that end up with larger cerebral cortices, like humans. More recently, Andrew Halley showed that the rate of rapid brain growth in early development is somewhat conserved among mammals, although primates show a faster rate of growth, and even start their development with a larger fetal brain size relative to fetal body size than other species (Halley 2016). Notably, this is not due to more rapid brain growth, but to slower prenatal body growth in relation to other mammals.

The Anatomy of Intelligence

In the late nineteenth century, Francis Galton quantified the relationship between brain size and intelligence, by multiplying head length by width, and comparing this with the academic performance of about 1,000 Cambridge students (Galton 1907). He reported that the best students had a brain size around 4% larger than the rest. After that, speculation about differences in brain size among ethnic groups became widespread, Europeans supposedly having the largest brains and Africans the smallest. The idea that brain size correlates with intelligence was pervasive but still controversial during most of last century. In the early eighties, Stephen Jay Gould published his popular and highly influential book *The Mismeasure of Man*, where he strongly refuted the idea of racially based differences in brains and intelligence, showing categorically that there was no evidence for ethnic differences in intellectual ability (Gould 1981). He did recognize that there might be differences in brain size across human groups, but these were mostly related to differences in body height. Since then, sporadic reports suggesting racial differences in brain size or capacity have appeared, although these have produced more controversy than consensus. For example, Philippe

Rushton has been one of the main defenders of an association between brain size and intelligence, arguing for significant racial differences in both parameters, which has brought him under intense criticism, as would be expected (Rushton and Ankney 2009). In any case, should racial differences in IQ or brain size exist, these would be explained largely by cultural, socioeconomic or even alimentary differences rather than by genetic load.

Searching for differences in cognitive capacity among species, Jerison and others also showed that the brain-body relationship was not the same for all vertebrate groups. For any given body size, an average mammal has a larger brain than a reptile, and reptiles have larger brains than amphibians or fish (Jerison 1973). Birds have a brain-to-body ratio much like that of mammals. Furthermore, both are homeotherms, or warm-blooded, which points again to some relation between brain size and metabolism. Among mammals, primates have brains that are about twice as big as the brain of non-primate mammals of the same size. Transitional species like *Archaeopteryx* (the earliest bird) or *Triconodon* (an early mammal) have relative brain sizes intermediate between those of reptiles and birds or mammals, respectively. In addition, birds and mammals display more complex behaviors than small-brained, cold-blooded reptiles, and among mammals, primates are characterized by elaborate social lives. Thus, there seems to be at least some phylogenetic relationship between (absolute or relative) brain size and whatever we may call intelligence or cognitive abilities. Within each vertebrate group (birds, mammals or reptiles), a proportion of the brain-body data lies outside the best-fitting curve, yielding species with higher or lower than expected brain sizes for their given body size. The coefficient between the expected and actual body size has been defined as the encephalization quotient (EQ). An EQ greater than 1 indicates that a species has a larger brain than the average mammal with the same body size. This difference is interpreted as excess brain mass attributable to higher cognitive capacities (Jerison 1973). Humans are the most encephalized species of all, followed by dolphins and elephants. Whales have enormous brains, particularly the blue whale with a 7 kg brain, but their gigantic body size renders their EQ on the mammalian average. Among birds, crows and parrots have very large EQs.

Although it is a controversial measure, the encephalization quotient has shown a statistical relationship to certain behavioral capacities. For example, it varies with the predictability of food resources, such that extant carnivores tend to have higher EQs than herbivores and other animals that feed on abundant food (Aboitiz 1996). Among bats, echolocating insectivore species tend to have the lowest EQs, which increase in fruit-eating and nectarivorous bats, reaching a maximum in the hematophagous vampire (Pirlot and Pottier 1977). Among rodents, fossorial and folivorous species tend to have smaller EQs than terrestrial and granivorous species; and among primates, folivorous species usually have smaller brains for their body size than frugivorous species (Frahm et al. 1997). However, in many cases, it is not clear if these differences are due to the cognitive challenges involved in finding food, or to the quality of the food source, as abundant food is usually poor in nutrients. Social animals also tend to have larger EQs than non-social animals (Shultz and Dunbar 2010). Other studies have found that absolute brain mass, regardless of body weight, is indeed a relevant trait. Evan MacLean and collaborators compared performance in self-control tasks in about 36 species of mammals and found that absolute brain mass correlates better with behavior than brain mass corrected for body size (MacLean et al. 2014). Likewise, Jeffrey Stevens reported that absolute brain size was the best predictor of self-control, measured as the capacity to wait for the delivery of reward (Stevens 2014).

As noted, the quality of food has repeatedly been proposed as a limiting factor for brain growth, animals that feed on less nutritional food having smaller encephalization quotients. Humans stand out for their high encephalization quotient, and the evolutionary explanations range from selective pressure to compete in social environments to the increasing availability of energy rich nutrients provided by the invention of cooking over fire. A modern variant of the energy hypothesis of brain growth mentioned above was put forward as the "expensive tissue" hypothesis, which postulates a trade-off between the size of the brain and that of the digestive tract, both tissues requiring large amounts of energy. More specifically, Robert Foley and Leslie Aiello proposed that in human evolution, increasing brain size only became possible when humans acquired an energy rich carnivorous diet, allowing for a reduction of the gastrointestinal tract and the release of energy constraints to build a large brain (Foley and Lee 1991; Aiello and Wheeler 1995). In a similar line, Suzana Herculano-Houzel points out that apes, which spend much of the day eating large amounts of low calorie leaves, are limited in their energy intake by the duration of the active period of the sleep-wake cycle (Fonseca-Azevedo and Herculano-Houzel 2012; Herculano-Houzel 2015). Accordingly, cross-species increases in neuronal numbers are adaptively associated with decreasing sleep requirements. The shift by our recent ancestor to high-calorie meat liberated them from this limitation, contributing to the rapid increase in brain size. The anthropologist Richard Wrangham has further hypothesized that the advent of fire-based cooking, which made nutrients more accessible for digestion, was a critical event that permitted the increase in brain size and neuron numbers in early humans (Wrangham 2009). Likewise, among apes, humans exceed by far the other species in total energy expenditure, which is largely explained by an increase in basal metabolic rate (Pontzer et al. 2016). Still, the energy hypothesis remains controversial, and there are arguments for and against it. For example, Alianda Cornélio and collaborators made an extensive analysis of hominin brain volumes over time and found no relation between brain size increases and archeological evidence for the use of fire (Cornélio et al. 2016). Another energy variable that has been related to brain size is adipose tissue, which some authors have found to correlate negatively with brain size among mammals (Navarrete et al. 2011), although humans have been reported to have the highest percentage of body fat among apes (Pontzer et al. 2016).

Wrinkled Brains

Because brain size is largely determined by cortical surface, larger brains soon reach a point at which further cortical growth is limited by the volume of the cranium in which the brain is contained. Species with relatively small cortices tend to have smooth brains and are called lissencephalic, while species with larger cortices display convoluted, or gyrencephalic brains characterized by inward sulci and outward gyri that develop in the embryo as the brain increases in size. In larger brains, the cortex seen on the brain's surface is a very minor fraction of the total cortical area, as most of the cortex lies buried within highly intricate sulci. The anatomical pattern of sulci and gyri is specific for different mammalian orders, such that the brain of an elephant folds somewhat differently from that of a carnivore or a primate brain. Our brain folds follow a general primate pattern. This indicates a strong within-group genetic determinant of cortical folding mechanics, of which we still know little.

While gyrification does not necessarily reflect the development of neuronal networks in the brain, the developmental and mechanical factors involved in their generation have attracted the attention of many researchers, including myself. Explanations of gyrification have been proposed over the years, but we still have no real way of determining which of these, if any, is correct. The models fall into three main categories, one emphasizing the role of the deep ventricular surface of the brain, where neurons and the radial glia are produced, as proposed by Pasko Rakic, and Robert Hevner and Tao Sun (Rash and Rakic 2014; Sun and Hevner 2014). The radial glia is a critical cell type for brain development, whose cell body is located in the depth of the hemisphere and has a process that reaches the external surface of the brain (the pia mater), spanning the entire thickness of the developing hemisphere. We will come to other functions of this cell type below, but for now it is suffice to say that it is like a chord attached to the external (pia mater) and internal (ventricular epithelium) brain surfaces that produces mechanical tensions, for example, in the depth of sulci, as the cerebral cortex expands in development. Regions where radial glia are for some reason more elastic and can increase in length will grow and fold outwardly, while regions in which radial glia are "stiffer" will remain buried, close to the ventricular surface, forming the depth of sulci.

Other models emphasize a role of cortical expansion *per se*, implying the differential growth of the superficial layers of the cortex as opposed to the slower expansion of the deep layers, producing an intracortical mechanical pressure that leads to folding (Sun and Hevner 2014, Striedter et al. 2015). Another possibility is that cortical expansion generates mechanical pressure on the cranial cavity that leads to folding. Georg Striedter and collaborators recently proposed a mechanism by which newly arriving neurons to the developing cortex must intercalate in the horizontal plane between older neurons that arrived there earlier (Striedter et al. 2015). This produces a mechanical tension in the tangential direction, particularly in the superior cortical layers, that leads to the differential expansion of the cortex relative to deeper structures. According to Eric Lewitus, the onset of gyrification in a mammalian group depends on a critical neuron-number threshold, which is about 10^9 neurons (Lewitus et al. 2014). David Van Essen, and more recently Helen Barbas, proposed a different model, in which short-range cortico-cortical axonal connections exert mechanical tension between the connected areas such that as the cortex grows, these two areas tend to fold against each other, forming a gyrus. Long cortico-cortical connections, on the other hand, exert less tension and are allowed to grow underneath the depth of the sulci formed by adjacent gyri (van Essen 1997; Hilgetag and Barbas 2009).

Suzana Herculano-Houzel proposed a mixed model to account for connectivity and cortical expansion processes, and considers gyrification a strategy to optimize connectivity in a large brain, an idea that goes back to Georg Striedter (Striedter 2005). Herculano-Houzel found that the surface area of white matter increases less rapidly than the number of cortical neurons (Herculano-Houzel et al. 2010). In primates, whose cerebral cortex is particularly large, the scaling of white matter relative to neuron number is actually slower than that of other species like rodents, which means that primates have relatively less white matter. This implies a general decrease in connectivity in larger brains, presumably reflecting a strategy to minimize redundancy in connectivity. Furthermore, Herculano-Houzel claims that cortical folding in large brains contributes to solving the connectivity problem by minimizing the length of cortical connections with critical regions deeper in the brain. Moreover, Herculano-Houzel recently published a mathematical model for cortical folding in which the degree of folding depends on the product between surface of cortical area and the square root of average cortical thickness (Mota and Herculano-Houzel 2015). Notably, the model closely fits to what is found when folding paper sheets of different thicknesses: folding capacity is much higher with thinner than thicker sheets. In fact, human mutations in which the cortex is particularly thick have low folding indexes, and species with large brains but thin cortices like dolphins and whales have highly convoluted cortices, much more than that of humans. Georg Striedter contended that these models assume that the cerebral cortex folds once it has already grown (like a sheet of paper), but in fact the cortex folds as it develops and the model does not make any assumptions about the embryological mechanisms involved, apart from the general hypothesis of a tension-based mechanism from the underlying white matter (Striedter and Srinivasan 2015). Nonetheless, the model may well reflect the physical constraints involved in gyrification, to which the developmental mechanism must in last instance be subordinate.

Perhaps the most elegant physical model for cortical folding was recently published by Tuomas Tallinen, Jun Young Chung and collaborators, who developed a 3D printed gel model of a 22-week-old fetal human brain, coated with a layer of a different gel that absorbs liquid and progressively swells over time (Tallinen et al. 2014). Under these conditions, the surface gel expands tangentially and develops a complex pattern of gyri and sulci that strikingly resembles the normal fissural development in the human brain, closely reproducing the orientation of the major and secondary sulci. Note, however, that the 3D printed template already shows an incipient temporal lobe, an exposed insula and the superior operculum of the Sylvian fissure. Therefore, this model does not account for the initial formation of the most fundamental fissural components of the human brain, namely the Sylvian fissure and the insular lobe. Nevertheless, this and Herculano-Houzel's studies strongly imply that purely physical parameters are at the very least significant determinants of fissurization. However, this does not account for differences among individuals and species in cortical folding, or for hemispheric asymmetries. This variability may depend on the differential expansion of distinct cortical regions, or on other aforementioned factors like the mechanical influences of radial glia and subcortical white matter, which may be under genetic control.

Cell Counts

Following Harry Jerison's principle of proper mass, many of the above studies have assumed that in larger brains there will be more processing neurons, more connectivity among them and more information capacity. This is in line with the micro-modular organization of the neocortex that we discussed in the previous chapter, where the building block of the cerebral cortex is the cortical column. Thus, in larger brains there will be more columns, neurons, and processing capacity. As we will see now, this may be correct but only to some extent. Despite a general conservation of the basic module, the comparative evidence indicates that there are areal and species differences in some details of the canonical microcircuit, based on the variability of neuron number in each column, and the proportions of neuronal types.

After the classic study of Andrew Rockel and collaborators, who reported that the number of neurons underneath a unit of cortical area was constant throughout the cerebral cortex, the latter was considered by many as an extended sheet of tissue that increases mostly in surface and very little in depth (Rockel et al. 1980). However, some findings appeared not much later that partly challenged this notion. Some years after Rockel's study, Herbert Haug published an extensive account of neuronal densities across brain regions and species using a technique called stereology (Haug 1987). This is a standardized method to make a three-dimensional representation of a series of two-dimensional microscopic cross sections of neural tissue, yielding accurate information about the total number of neurons in a given volume. Haug found that neuronal density varies both across regions and across species. In addition, Haug reported that gray matter neuronal density was lower in species with larger brains than in species with smaller brains. Comparing most species, neuron numbers tend to increase with brain size, but at a lower rate than the increase in brain size. As a result, neuronal density tends to decrease with increased brain size, providing more space for neuronal connections for each neuron. This notion is consistent with many developmental studies that indicate that training induces lower neuronal density and higher dendritic growth in specific brain regions, which may be associated with increasing connectivity and processing capacity (Diamond et al. 1993, Diaz et al. 1994, Scheibel 1988).

In 2005, Suzana Herculano-Houzel presented a new methodology to count cells in brain tissue, called the isotropic fractionator, which has challenged some of the ideas discussed earlier in this chapter (Herculano-Houzel 2005, Herculano-Houzel et al. 2015c). The isotropic fractionator consists of dissociating cell nuclei in a given volume of tissue, suspending the nuclei in a chemical solution and then staining them for neuronal or non-neuronal markers with specific antibodies. This allows for discerning and accurately counting the number of neurons and glial cells. Herculano-Houzel and collaborators confirmed and extended Haug's earlier finding that in most mammals, there is an increase in neuron numbers with increasing brain size, but the rate of additional neurons is slower than the increase in brain size, resulting in lower neuronal density in larger brains (Herculano-Houzel et al. 2015a, b; Mota and Herculano-Houzel2014). Furthermore, she and colleagues have observed that the rate of neuronal increase in relation to brain size differs across mammalian orders, such that distant species with similar brain sizes can have very different neuron numbers. On the other hand, glial cells maintain a constant density across species and their number accurately reflects differences in brain size. Herculano-Houzel has therefore proposed that for comparative studies, an estimator of the total neurons per brain should be used, called the Neuronal Index. This measure, she argues, may be a better predictor of cognitive ability than the EQ or brain size.

According to Herculano-Houzel, primate brains are unique in their neuronal composition (Wong et al. 2013; Ventura-Antunes et al. 2013). This group is characterized by a very rapid rate of neuronal addition, in which an 11-fold larger brain contains 10 times more neurons (and about 12 times non-neuronal cells, mostly glial), which results in a nearly constant and very high neuronal density despite brain size increases. As a result, primate brains have many more neurons than non-primate brains of the same size, and humans are no exception to this. This may relate to the more rapid fetal brain growth relative to body size in primates than in other species as I mentioned above (Halley 2016). With their very large brain, humans have the highest absolute neuron number (regardless of body size), some 86 billion neurons (and an equal number of glial cells), of which about 16 billion are in the cerebral cortex (these numbers are at odds with the classical estimates of 100 billion total neurons and 1,000 billion glial cells). Contrary to claims of a disproportionate increase in cortical neurons in large-brained species, Herculano-Houzel argues that cortical neurons represent about 20% of the total neurons in the brain across many species, including humans (Herculano-Houzel et al. 2014). The elephant brain is three times as large as the human brain, but has only 5.6 billion neurons in the cerebral cortex. Likewise, dolphins and whales, despite having large brains, have characteristically fewer neurons in their cerebral cortex. Even the smaller-brained gorillas, with a brain size one-third that of humans, also have more brain neurons than elephants and false orcas! Importantly, Herculano-Houzel, working with Tecumseh Fitch and other researchers, showed that parrots and songbirds have on average twice the number of neurons as primates of the same size (Olkowicz et al. 2016). Furthermore, most of these neurons are located in the pallium, a region involved in higher cognitive processing, comparable in functions to the mammalian cerebral cortex (see Chapter 9).

How do we reconcile Herculano-Houzel's findings with the earlier literature on the EQ? The model of prenatal neuronal addition may hold some cues. If most neurons are added in the prenatal and early postnatal periods (depending on the species), neuronal number should be a better proxy for immature brain size than adult brain size. In fact, during early development most cell division results in neurogenesis, but in postnatal development cell division is produced mostly by glial cells, and neuronal density and size may vary significantly during postnatal life. Thus, the prenatal/early postnatal period of growth is the main determinant of neuron number. But why would primates and some birds achieve such high neuronal densities? Perhaps it has to do with the inherent physical costs of having a brain volume (and head) that becomes too large in relation to body size, plus computational difficulties due to longer nerve paths. If we had the same neuronal density as the average mammal, in order to keep the same number of neurons, our brains (and heads) would have to about twice the size they are now! The same constraints may hold for birds, especially as these animals have the additional constraint of minimizing head weight in order to be able to fly.

Nonetheless, Diarmuid Cahalane, Chistine Charvet, and Barbara Finlay have been particularly critical of the isotropic fractionator method, claiming that this technique has strong limitations in anatomical resolution (Cahalane et al. 2012). They compared different histological cell counting methods for the primary visual cortex and the entire cortex of rodents and primates and found significant outlier effects for the isotropic fractionator that resulted in differences of 50% or more from the counts obtained by other methods. Although determining the number and size of neuronal cells (as well as neuronal types) may be a much better way to estimate processing capacity than brain size or the EQ, we still need to do many more comparative and developmental studies and assess the different techniques against each other to get a consensual estimate of these critical variables.

How to Build a Big Brain

How are larger brains produced? We have seen that there is an increasing number of neurons and glia in larger brains, but we haven't yet addressed the mechanisms by which the brain increases in size, for which we will need to briefly review cellular processes involved in cortical development. In the 1970s, Pasko Rakic proposed the radial model of cortical development, in which neurons are produced in the deep surface of the brain and migrate outward to reach the cerebral cortex (Rakic 1978). In the early embryo, there are self-renewing progenitor cells, called radial glia because they have a long process that connects the internal or ventricular surface, with the external surface or pia mater of the brain. The cell bodies of radial glia are located deep in the ventricular zone, and undergo symmetric divisions (that is, each progenitor gives rise to two identical radial progenitors). Thus, their numbers grow exponentially as development proceeds. In later stages, these progenitors divide asymmetrically, where one daughter cell is an immature neuron that stays some time in the ventricular zone and then migrates toward the brain surface attached to the radial glia's process (Tamamaki et al. 2001; Noctor et al. 2002). Migration is arrested in the cortical plate by a stop signal, and the cell differentiates as a mature neuron. The stop signal is a molecule called reelin, which is secreted by a special kind of cell called the Cajal-Retzius cell. Once stopped, neurons arrange themselves into a laminar and columnar scaffolding (Rakic 2009; Geschwind and Rakic 2013). Neurons that migrate along the same glial cell are likely to derive from the same radial glia, and arrange themselves in columns in the cortical surface (Fig. 3.2) (Noctor et al. 2001; Kriegstein and Noctor 2004; Yu et al. 2009).

Although successful, Rakic's model has required important modifications. In the late 1990s, John Rubenstein and collaborators showed that while excitatory neurons use radial migration to reach the cortex, inhibitory neurons do not arise from the cortical ventricular zone, but are born in the ventral hemisphere, in the region where the basal ganglia develop (Fig. 3.3) (Anderson et al. 1997). Rubenstein and his group performed minute surgery on the brains of fetal mice, separating the basal ganglia primordium from the cortical primordium. Impressively, in these animals, no inhibitory neurons were observed in the developing cortex, although the number of excitatory neurons was normal. The embryonic basal ganglia were then recognized as the major site for production of inhibitory neurons in the cerebral hemisphere, while most excitatory neurons are generated in the cortical ventricular zone. Once born in the ventral hemisphere, inhibitory neurons migrate following a tangential route, that is, perpendicular to the orientation of radial glia and parallel to the brain surface, and end in the different cortical layers as the cortex develops.

Several developmental studies in the 2000s revealed that in late cortical development, a layer of cells called the subventricular zone (located just above the ventricular zone) contains highly active neural progenitors (Rakic 2009) called intermediate progenitors, which derive from radial glia but have not yet differentiated as neurons. Instead, they continue proliferating for two or three cell divisions, and then migrate outwardly to the developing cerebral cortex. Studies by Zoltán Molnár (Cheung et al. 2007, 2010), Christine Charvet, Arnold Kriegstein and others established that the subventricular zone is absent or barely discernible in reptiles and

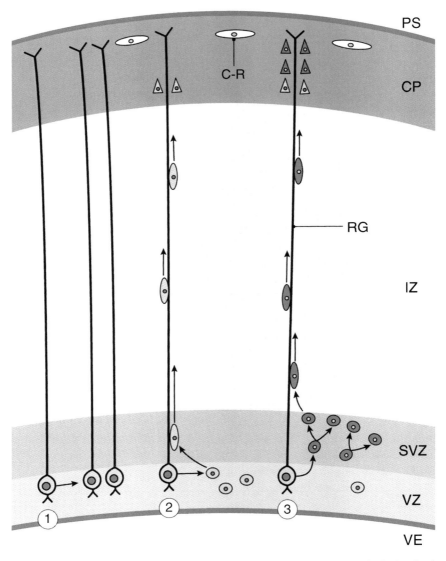

Fig. 3.2 Development of the cerebral cortex. In this region, radial glia (RG) extend a process that crosses the ventricular wall from the ventricular epithelium (VE) to the pial surface (PS). In early stages (1), radial glia divide symmetrically, their numbers increasing exponentially. In later development (2),

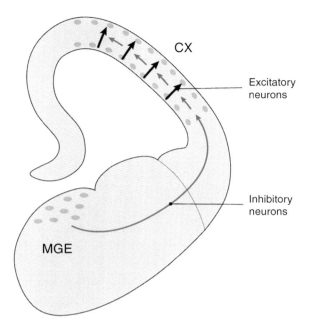

Fig. 3.3 Radial and tangential migration in brain development. A cross-section of the embryonic mammalian brain (one hemisphere), in which the cerebral cortex (CX) develops. Excitatory neurons migrate from the deep ventricular zone of the cortical primordium (black arrows). Inhibitory inter-neurons originate in a deep brain region, the medial ganglionic eminence (MGE), and arrive to the cortex by a process of tangential or horizontal migration (gray arrows)

Fig.3.2 (Continued)
these neurons divide asymmetrically, producing one radial glia and a daughter neuron (circles). These neurons migrate from the deep ventricular zone (VZ) (ovals) to the cortical plate (CP), attached to the glial process (RG) across the intermediate zone (IZ), to make up the deep cortical layers. In a third stage (3), radial glia produce daughter progenitors that proliferate in the subventricular zone (SVZ) and then migrate outwardly to form superficial cortical layers (but they also contribute to deep layers; not shown). Cajal-Retzius neurons (C-R) are located in the most superficial layer (called the marginal zone), and secrete the protein reelin, which controls the laminar arrangement of the cerebral cortex (see Chapter 9)

some marsupials, modest in rodents and highly developed in large-brained primates, including humans (birds have also developed a subventricular zone, likely independently of mammals but reflecting similar mechanisms of brain growth; see Chapter 9) (Charvet and Striedter 2011; Lui et al. 2011). Furthermore, a cell type called outer radial glia, which is present in the subventricular zone (as opposed to the canonical radial glia, located in the ventricular zone), is abundant in species with large brains, especially humans, producing further intermediate progenitors (Hansen 2010; Shitamukai et al. 2011; Florio and Huttner 2014).

The genetic cascade involved in this amplification process seems to be highly conserved across species, including birds. Pax6, a regulator gene originally found in the fruit fly and critical for eye development in most animals studied, from insects to vertebrates (see Chapter 10), is also a key promoter of radial glia self-renewal (Georgala et al. 2011). Increasing Pax6 activity results in more rapid production of neural progenitors, which at some point start invading the subventricular zone to keep dividing before migrating to the cortex. Thus, Pax6 is a key regulator of overall progenitor numbers, and together with downstream and related genes, has been proposed as an essential element of cortical expansion in mammalian brains. My students, particularly Juan Montiel and Francisco Zamorano (Aboitiz and Montiel 2007a, b; Aboitiz and Zamorano 2013) and I have further argued that amplification of a Pax6 cascade, or of related genes, was a key event in the origin of the mammalian cerebral cortex, as well as in the expansion of the avian brain, indicating a strongly conserved genetic cascade that underlies brain development and evolution, possibly in all vertebrates (see Chapter 9).

Pax6 is a key candidate for increasing neuronal numbers in mammalian and human brains, but there are also many other related genes that participate in this process, whose mutation could lead to smaller or larger brains (Georgala et al. 2011). One example is the genes involved in the regulation of neuronal death, such as Notch1 and CASP, which are also important in regulating neuronal cell numbers during development (Ables et al. 2011). Recently, Lei Wang and collaborators reported a role of a developmental regulatory gene called Hedgehog in the regulation of progenitor division and expansion of the cerebral cortex (Wang et al. 2016). Other evidence points to so-called microRNAs, small RNA pieces that do not code for a protein structure but regulate the activity of other genes. These tiny molecules can depress or enhance the activity of genes involved in progenitor division, finally affecting neuronal numbers (Somel and Khaitovich 2013).

Another source of evidence is genetic disorders that result in cortical malformations, particularly microcephaly, a condition well known now because of the Zika virus (Geschwind and Rakic 2013). Genes associated with this condition are MCPH and ASPM, both involved in the proliferation of neural progenitors (Pulvers et al. 2015). In contrast, macrocephaly is a condition in which there is an excessively large head, usually concomitant with a larger than normal brain. A larger brain can be the result of hydrocephalous or other conditions that affect the volume of the ventricular cavities, but can also be produced by megalencephaly (an abnormally large brain wall and cerebral cortex). Notably, over 20% of autism cases display macrocephaly to some degree. For example, over-activation of the gene AKT3 can result in megalencephaly, and its inhibition can result in microcephaly (Gai et al. 2015). Another interesting gene associated with macrocephaly is PTEN, which is also linked to autistic traits (Garcia-Junco-Clemente and Golshani 2014). Determining which of these and other genes have been involved in the evolution of our uniquely large brain is a matter of intense research today, with new and interesting candidates appearing every day. Still, there is a long way to go to provide a coherent picture of the genetics and evolution of human brain size.

The Brain Hangs Together

In 1995, Barbara Finlay and Richard Darlington published an influential paper showing that the evolution of brain size proceeds according to a highly conserved developmental schedule shared by most mammalian species (Finlay and Darlington 1995). They analyzed the sizes of major brain components in a huge sample of 131 species of primates, bats and insectivores, observing an extremely well-conserved correspondence between the volume of major brain components and the overall size of the brain. The only components that deviated from this relationship were limbic and olfactory-related components, which varied independently of brain size, and presumably in relation to ecological demands. Interestingly, the cerebral cortex scales disproportionately to other brain structures, so that species with larger brains tend to have relatively larger cerebral cortices. However, this explosive brain growth fits a clear allometric trend across species, which indicates that the cerebral cortex does not increase in size independently of other brain structures. In other words, all brain components (except olfactory/limbic) tend to grow together, although they do so at different rates. Considering this allometric growth, humans have the expected cortical size and proportions of a hypothetical primate of the same overall brain size. Finlay and Darlington concluded that there is only one way to increase the size of brain structures, which is by growing an overall larger brain. This conserved pattern has more recently been extended to all vertebrate groups, from sharks to mammals (Yopak et al. 2010). According to Finlay and Darlington, the independent development of brain components is not impossible, but very unlikely.

Subsequently, Finlay, Darlington, and collaborators expanded on their findings, presenting evidence for a conserved developmental schedule in mammalian brains, excepting limbic, and olfactory structures (Finlay et al. 1998; Workman et al. 2013). There is a neurogenetic gradient from back to front and from ventral to dorsal, such that anterior, late-generated brain components are disproportionately larger than posterior, early generated structures; and ventral (motor) structures tend to grow less than dorsal (sensory) structures. This meets Georg Striedter's dictum of "late equals large equals well-connected", meaning that late-developing structures tend to grow more and establish more interconnected networks (Striedter 2005), but adds the antero-posterior and dorso-ventral time gradients. According to Finlay and collaborators, this imposed gradient specifies a priori which structures will grow larger. Thus, it is not common to find species with a large brainstem component but very small cerebral hemispheres (with the exception of some rare species like mormyrid fish that have an hypertrophied cerebellum). In this line, the cerebral cortex is located exactly in the most expansive brain region, not because this is a functionally strategic region but because this is where it will grow faster. In other words, cognitive networks allocate in the most expanding regions, rather than cognitive functions specifying the brain regions that will expand. This line of thought is akin to Stephen Jay Gould and Richard Lewontin's notion that developmental mechanisms and constraints may be more important than the selective processes in shaping morphology in evolution (Gould and Lewontin 1979). In my opinion, this does not necessarily mean that development determines everything. The neurogenetic gradient is not a given, but responds to a basic functional constraint that has been the target of natural selection. The position of the brain subordinates to the oral end of the animal to regulate food intake. Likewise, sense organs are also localized near the oral end, making up the head. The postero-anterior neurogenetic gradient probably responds to this requirement, facilitating the formation of neural networks that regulate the most basic behaviors like orientation for food sources and other signals near the mouth and sense organs. In this sense, the disproportionate growth of anterior brain structures like the cerebral cortex may be the result of an ancient developmental mechanism that has been selected to favor the establishment of neural networks in the anterior end of the animal. Sensorimotor and cognitive networks, including those involved in language, are an extension of purposeful orientation behavior and develop atop this ancestral scaffolding. This perspective agrees with Robert Barton and colleagues' recent conclusion that allometric relations may ultimately result from functional rather than developmental constraints (Montgomery et al. 2016).

Specialist Brains

Finlay and Darlington acknowledge that the brain divisions they used are rather gross, and that there may be space for reallocation of functions within each division (Finlay and Darlington 1995). Furthermore, despite the observed correlations, Finlay and Darlington's data allow for two to threefold variation in the size of individual parts, which leaves space for independent variation of the different components. In this line, many authors have focused on the adaptation of specific brain systems to ecological conditions, considering their growth to be somewhat independent of that of other networks. A good example of this particulated strategy is food-storing birds, which have a larger hippocampus (a brain structure critical for the acquisition of memory, which we will discuss in Chapter 9) than that of non-foodstoring birds (Clayton 1998). This increase in size has been associated with postnatal addition of neurons, but there have been contesting reports. Likewise, in the brood parasitic cowbird, which lays its eggs on the nests other species, females have to remember the location of several nests of other species and wait until eggs are laid in one of these to deposit their own eggs there. Consequently, the hippocampus is larger in females than in males of this species (Sherry et al. 1993). However, part of this may be due to acquired increases in size, as in the famous study showing that London taxi drivers and bus drivers have larger hippocampi than control subjects (nowadays, with the help of satellite-directed navigators this character may be lost) (Maguire et al. 2006). In addition, migratory birds tend to have smaller encephalization quotients than all-year resident birds, presumably because they need more cognitive capacity to find food in the harsh winter. However, a recent report by Orsloya Vincze et al. 2015 and collaborators has shown that, despite having a smaller brain, migratory birds tend to have larger than expected relative sizes of the optic tectum in the brainstem, which is the main visual processing area in the bird brain. This character may be of benefit for visual orientation during migration.

Beginning in 1995, Robert Barton and collaborators published a series of extensive studies of visual and olfactory structures in primates, bats and insectivores and their evolutionary relationships (Barton et al. 1995; Harvey 2000; Barton 2004). After removing the effect of overall brain size, they found correlated changes in size among functionally related structures (visual with visual, and olfactory with olfactory structures), while correlations between visual and olfactory structures were negative in primates, nonsignificant in insectivores and positive in bats. In primates and insectivores, nocturnal habits are associated with larger olfactory systems and smaller visual systems, but there are also associations of visual structures with frugivory (color vision helps detect ripe fruit) in primates and insectivores, and between frugivory and olfaction, but only in bats.

Barton and Chris Venditti recently reported an important correlation between cerebellar and cerebral cortex growth (Barton 2012, Venditti 2014). Furthermore in apes and humans, the cerebellum increased in size more than would be expected based on cortical expansion. Barton proposed cerebellar growth was associated with extractive foraging, which consists of locating and processing food that is either underground (roots or ants, for example), or embedded in hard shells, which can require tool making, as has been shown in chimpanzees in the wild. This implies that cerebellar function has been an important achievement in ape and human evolution and may have been involved in social behavior, cognition and motor dexterity, possibly associated with making and throwing tools, and other behaviors relevant to early hominids. Supporting Barton and Venditti's claims, Herculano-Houzel also determined that the cerebral cortex does not grow alone, but as extra cells are added to this structure, there is a coordinated increase in neuronal numbers in the cerebellum (Herculano-Houzel 2010). Although the cerebellum only increases modestly in size with growing body size, the number of cerebellar neurons are added in tight correlation with increased body mass. Furthermore, the rate of addition of neurons is uneven; there being about 8 new cerebellar neurons and 2 cortical neurons for each neuron added to the rest of the brain. This results in a tremendous increase in neuronal density in the cerebellum of larger animals. Finally, a note on the developmental and evolutionary aspect of this correlation, while the correlation between the cerebral cortex and cerebellum probably results from the fact that both are late-generated structures (as argued by Finlay; see above), natural selection may have benefited lineages in which the neurogenetic schedules of these two structures synchronize.

The Cortical Mosaic

There is conserved developmental and architectural scaffolding in the regions of the cerebral cortex. Barbara Finlay and Ryutaro Uchiyama recently subdivided the cortex into an exteroceptive zone including visual, somatosensory and motor areas, and an interoceptive zone including temporal, insular and ventral frontal areas (oddly, auditory regions are labeled in the interoceptive zone) (Finlay and Uchiyama 2015). In this organization, sensory and motor areas are "seeds" shared by all mammals, while higher order and association areas appear and expand between them, concomitant with increasing brain size in mammalian evolution. A neurogenetic gradient is added to this in which neurogenesis continues in posterior cortical regions until later stages, and consequently neuron numbers and density are greater than in frontal regions where neurogenesis ends earlier (Charvet 2014; Cahalane et al. 2012). Cortical connections tend to arrange themselves in this same direction, preferentially aligning antero-posteriorly. According to Finlay, this conserved organization represents a compromise between network redundancy, providing robustness against perturbations, and evolvability by permitting genetic and environmental variability (Anderson and Finlay 2014). In this line, the group led by Henry Kennedy has made a thorough analysis of connectivity in the macaque and mouse, showing a conserved pattern of connectivity among cortical areas, where the density of interareal connections decreases exponentially with areal distance. Nonetheless, this decay is much more pronounced in the larger brain of the macaque than in the smaller mouse brain, indicating that there is a constraint for long-range connectivity as brains increase in size (Ercsey-Ravasz et al. 2013; Horvát et al. 2016). Even so, primates show a tendency to have more dense cortico-cortical connectivity than other mammals (Charvet et al. 2017).

In addition to this conserved scaffolding, there is evidence that cortical regions can vary in size in different directions among species. Using modern anatomical and electrophysiological mapping methods, Jon Kaas and others have exhaustively analyzed the areal composition of the cerebral cortex in different mammals, obtaining large species differences in the number and relative extent of these areas (Kaas 2011, 2013). Based on the presence of distinct cortical areas in all the studied mammal species, Kaas proposed that the ancestral mammal had only a few cortical regions, with four visual areas, four somatosensory areas, a gustatory and viscerosensitive (insular) area, and an auditory area. There was also a small frontal cortex with medial (cingulate cortex) and orbitofrontal components, and a small, multimodal parietal area. In the course of mammalian brain evolution, different areas have been added as the cerebral cortex has increased in size. A general process of areal separation and input segregation was first noted by Sven Ebbesson, who postulated the "parcellation theory" for brain development and evolution (Ebbesson 1980). Basically, Ebbesson argued that there are initially heterogeneous projections in both neural development and brain evolution that converge in specific brain regions. As the brain increases in size, there is a pervasive tendency of these projections to segregate into different areas that end up receiving more specific inputs, thus parcellating an ancestral multi-targeted convergence center, and favoring parallel processing. The idea sparked intense debate at the time, but eventually gained support, not as the exclusive mechanism for the evolution of brain projections, but as a common phenomenon. Parcellation is likely to occur especially as the convergence zone increases in size and allows for the spatial segregation of different inputs. This is in fact what happens in the cerebral cortex, because as the cortex grows in size disproportionately to the thalamic nuclei that relay information to it, the numbers of neurons receiving input from a specific source keep increasing, which favors the segregation of axons and the eventual separation of different brain areas.

Leah Krubitzer has proposed an updated version of Ebbesson's theory, in which small-scale mechanisms of afferent segregation also contribute to increasing input specificity and processing efficiency (Krubitzer 2009; Seelke 2012). The addition of new areas is considered a result of a process that includes increased size of a given area, subsequent within-area microscopic segregation of different inputs into distinct laminae or stripes, and eventually the separation of these areas in two regions. For example, the primary visual cortex is microscopically segregated into a laminar distribution of neurons according to responsiveness to specific kinds of visual stimuli, each of which then projects to distinct areas of the temporal and parietal lobes (see Chapter 7). This pattern of spatial amplification of microscopically segregated inputs may also take place during evolution, generating the observed diversification of cortical areas in the large brains of many species.

The main exception to the parcellation process is the well-known invasion of inputs to a region that up to then received few if any afferents from a given brain component. Examples of this are the connections between both cerebral hemispheres, and the corticospinal tract that sends axons from the cortex to the spinal cord, both tracts appearing only in mammals. Suzana Herculano-Houzel and collaborators have clarified that the disproportionate increase in descending axons from the cerebral cortex in primates, and especially in humans, is explained simply by the fact that the number of descending cortical projections invading the brainstem and spinal cord nuclei increases as the cortex grows in size (Herculano-Houzel et al. 2016). On the other hand, the number of cells in the brainstem and spinal cord nuclei does not increase as rapidly as does the cerebral cortex, and they are invaded by descending axons. To what extent is cortical control of human speech a consequence of this allometric scaling? I will discuss this question in Chapters 8 and 10.

The relative size of individual cortical areas can also change according to behavioral adaptations. For example, the somatosensory representation of the tactile vibrissae of rodents occupies a large extent of the cortex and is organized into a series of "barrels", each representing one whisker (Kaas 2011, 2013). Likewise, the star-nosed mole, a subterranean animal that has developed many tentacle-like protuberations in its nose to maximize tactile sensitivity, has a very enlarged representation of each of these tentacles in the cerebral cortex (Catania 1995). And the platypus, the only mammal known to have electrosensory capacities (located in its beak, which it uses to find prey in mud underwater), also has a hypertrophied beak representation in the somatosensory cortex (Krubitzer et al. 1995). Bats also have an enlarged auditory cortex, which I will describe in more detail in Chapter 10.

Evidence gathered in recent years shows that both plasticity-driven and genetically modulated mechanisms operate in concert to determine the differentiation of cortical regions. To show the effects of neural plasticity, Migranka Sur, Sarah Pallas, and collaborators have taken advantage of a common phenomenon in early brain development, namely transient exuberance of incoming cortical connections such that nuclei from one sensory modality (say visual) initially send axons to cortical areas destined to another modality (say auditory or somatosensory) (Sur et al. 1990). However, these connections soon retract during normal development. By surgically eliminating the natural auditory or somatosensory input to the presumptive auditory and somatosensory areas, researchers have found that the originally transient visual projections to the remaining areas stabilize, establishing functional synapses. Neurons in these areas become visually sensitive, having similar visual responses to those in the original visual cortex. Altogether, the evidence of transient exuberance of cortical projections and the subsequent retraction or segregation of these projections is in accord with Ebbesson's parcellation hypothesis, and also indicates a period of intense plasticity of projections that can be remodeled according to differential patterns of activity (recall the critical period of development, see Chapter 1). In normal circumstances, circuits processing different inputs (like visual or auditory) become largely separated and can perform their computations relatively independently of each other. However, if there is an imbalance in this process in early development caused by a lesion or deprivation, it is possible that circuits from a different modality take over. This occurs in people blind from birth, whose visual areas become auditory or somatosensory sensitive.

However, plasticity does not account for everything. There are also genetic mechanisms, perhaps not imposing a fixed mosaic pattern of cortical areas, but establishing continuous developmental gradients across the cortical surface, which serve as scaffolding for the differentiation of cortical areas. Three such gradients have been found at this point, the Pax6 gradient (the same gene involved in progenitor proliferation we saw above) distributed from lateral to medial cortex; a gradient including genes called Wnts and Emx2 among others, from posterior to anterior regions; and finally a gradient of a gene called FGF8 and related ones, from anterior to posterior. Dennis O'Leary and colleagues first observed that in mutant mice in which Pax6 is inactive, lateral structures (olfactory cortex, amygdala) and frontal areas, where Pax6 should be active, become strongly regressive (O'Leary and Sahara 2008; Bishop et al. 2002). Conversely, posterior (visual) areas where the Emx2 gene is normally active become regressive at the expense of amplification of frontal regions when this gene is mutated. Other experiments by Elizabeth Grove and collaborators showed that injecting the anterior signal FGF8 in the posterior cortex of the mouse produced a duplicate somatosensory area in the posterior cortex (Grove and Fukuchi-Shimogori 2003). Thus, differential modulations of these gradients may expand presumptive territories destined to different cortical areas, and furthermore, as the cortex increases in size, these gradients may also extend, providing more space for areal differentiation.

The current consensus about areal specification in the cerebral cortex is that gene patterning mechanisms play a role in establishing what is called a protomap or blueprint of the topographic arrangement of cortical areas, which is refined in later development by neuronal activity and plastic processes. Projecting this to evolution, both factors may play a role. Studies indicate that there may be more variability in the arrangement of sensory areas within each species than the variability seen among related species, indicating either that genetic variability is very high or that plastic mechanisms are relevant in establishing the final configuration of cortical areas. It is likely that both mechanisms were important in human evolution. Furthermore, considering that language must have arisen quite rapidly in evolutionary time, it is very likely that the advent of culture-induced plastic reorganizations of the brain, and at the same time, generated a selective pressure for mutations favoring these reorganizations.

Primates Are Different (Again)

Besides having a large brain, primates have privileged visual systems among mammals. While reptiles and birds have a rich color perception, in mammalian origins some of the genes involved in color vision were lost, presumably due to early adaptations to nocturnal life (see Chapter 9). As a consequence, most mammals have only two visual pigments, one detecting blue light and the other detecting a sort of green light. Another common adaptation to nocturnal life is frontal vision, which increases light and contrast sensitivity. Early primates are thought to have been both nocturnal and arboreal, a lifestyle that strongly selects for frontal vision (Aboitiz and Montiel 2015). When primates invaded the diurnal niches, they redeveloped color vision by duplicating the gene for the green pigment, and mutating one of these copies into a close-to-red light detecting pigment. Thus, primates are usually trichromats (have three color pigments) as opposed to most other mammals that are dichromats. In 2004, Robert Barton elegantly showed that the degree of optical convergence in primates is associated with the expansion of several visual brain components, which ends up increasing overall brain size (Barton 2004). This was shown by a tight correlation across species between optical convergence and the volume of thalamic visual nuclei, the visual cortex, and overall brain size, which were independent of increases in body size.

Another factor that has been invoked to explain the large brains of primates is social behavior. Robin Dunbar and his colleagues collected evidence for an increase in relative volume of the cerebral cortex (this time compared to total brain size) and social group size in different primates including humans (Schultz and Dunbar 2010). Likewise, Simon Reader and Kevin Laland made an exhaustive analysis of documented instances of behavioral innovation, social learning and tool use among primates (which tend to correlate among themselves) and found that these variables strongly correlate with both absolute and relative brain volumes (Reader and Laland 2002). However, a very recent study reports that a main determinant of brain size among primates is frugivorous diet rather than social complexity (DeCasien et al. 2017). The most likely possibility is that there are many factors influencing brain size, and determining the relative weight of each may depend on several variables.

One possibility to integrate these hypotheses is that with the development of a complex visual system and the regression of olfactory structures, the social life of primates underwent important modifications, increasingly based on visual and gestural cues rather than olfactory or pheromonal signals. There is a report that loss of olfactory receptor genes is concomitant with the development of trichromatric vision in primates (Gilad et al. 2004); and Rodrigo Suárez, Jorge Mpodozis and colleagues found that in sexually dimorphic species like primates, that rely more on visual signals for mating, there is a documented reduction of the pheromone-detecting system (Suárez et al. 2011). A visual, gesture-dominated communication system may have propelled the development of cognitive power, which benefited from increasing neuronal numbers and brain size. Gestural communication is also relevant for human speech and language, which would be in line with this possibility.

One of the brain regions that has received more attention in relation to human brain evolution is the frontal cortex, which is in front of the central sulcus that separates the parietal and frontal lobes. On the other hand, the prefrontal cortex covers most of the frontal cortex, but does not include the premotor and motor cortices, which are located just anterior to the central sulcus (Brodmann's areas 6 and 4). Interest in the prefrontal cortex originates from its involvement in characteristically human abilities like planning behavior, cognition and speech and language. Karl Brodmann was perhaps the first to claim that the frontal lobe represents a larger proportion of cortical surface in humans (28%) than in chimpanzees (17%) and macaques (11%), a concept that became deeply entrenched for most of the past century (Brodmann 1909). However, in the 1940s, Gerhardt von Bonin concluded that the human frontal lobe is the size that would correspond to a primate with that brain size, indicating that the main difference with apes is overall brain size rather than an expanded frontal cortex (von Bonin 1948). Debate about frontal lobe size has continued until now, as studies continue to present contradictory evidence. Many authors have reported different estimates of prefrontal size, including neuroimaging measures of white matter, gray matter, absolute and relative volumes, etc., producing more controversy than consensus (Passingham and Smaers 2014; Smaers et al. 2011; Smaers 2013; Sherwood and Smaers 2013; Barton and Venditti 2013a, 2013b; Smaers et al. 2017). Again, Herculano-Houzel and collaborators have attempted to resolve this issue by the isotropic fractionator method (Ribeiro et al. 2013; Gabi et al. 2016). They found that apart from overall differences in total neuron numbers, humans do not differ from other primates in the proportion of neurons in the prefrontal cortex (about 8% in all species). Furthermore, they claim that new neurons have been added uniformly across cortical areas, and that the main difference between humans and other primates lies in the larger total number of neurons. All in all, at this point it may be safe to say that if there are differences in the size or neuron numbers of the human prefrontal cortex with respect to other primates, they are small enough to strongly depend on the statistics and experimental methodologies used.

Increase Brain Power, Not Cell Numbers

Ursula Dicke and Gerhard Roth have pointed out the inconsistencies of studies attempting to correlate intelligence with general brain properties (Dicke and Roth 2016). They have proposed an estimator of information processing capacity that depends on the number of cortical neurons, neuronal packing density, interneuronal distance, and axon conduction velocity, to minimize delays because of increasing distances in large brains. Humans have the largest information capacity, followed by apes and monkeys. Despite their large brains, cetaceans and elephants score lower than primates in this estimate. On the other hand, some birds, like crows and parrots, have high neuronal densities that significantly increase their information processing capacity, which may explain their notable learning abilities.

Considering the apparent paradoxes and controversies concerning the relationship between brain size, body size and intelligence, in 1996 I proposed the hypothesis of dual processes of brain growth in evolution (Aboitiz 1996). Most researchers have assumed that as brains get larger or have more neurons, they are automatically better at processing information. But this assumption ignores all the intricate variability in connectivity and plasticity mechanisms that in the end may be more critical than the raw brain cell numbers. Consider, for example, echolocating bats, which, as discussed above, have quite small encephalization quotients. Nevertheless, their auditory cortex is particularly well developed (see Chapter 10). On the other hand, the statistical allometric relationship between body growth and brain growth is undeniable, so that the brain is developmentally coupled to the rest of the body, at least in early developmental stages. In a way, Jerison's "somatic factor" reflects this coupling, although not for the reasons he proposed. Therefore, there is one mechanism of brain growth, which I have called "passive growth" that results from simply following increases in body size. And the specific allometric relationship between body and brain (or number of neurons) depends on the particular developmental coupling between body and brain in each specific lineage, in prenatal and early postnatal stages. In this case, animals whose body size increases also grow a larger brain, but generally to perform the same functions they were doing before at smaller sizes.

There is another way by which brains can grow, which is by selective pressure on behavioral or functional capacities. In this case, it may be of benefit to produce more neurons, as there will be more possibilities of connectional rearrangements and network specialization (even if in some cases, as in echolocating bats, this can be done with fewer neurons). I call this process "active" brain growth, which is a strategy to facilitate the development of more efficient neural networks and increasing plasticity. Plastic rearrangements that increase processing capacity occur during the lifetime of individuals as a response to immediate environmental demands. Under these conditions, subjects having more neurons in their brains might be at some advantage over those with slightly fewer neurons. I highlighted a role of neural plasticity as a driver for human brain evolution in an early article, proposing that a minimum of genetic changes, mainly (but not exclusively) involved in increasing neural progenitor proliferation in the brain, might account for human brain evolution, while the rearrangement of connectivity would have been largely a byproduct of activity-dependent reorganization of the neural networks in these larger brains (Aboitiz 1988).

More neurons and larger brains may be of benefit for the development of learned social abilities, as Robin Dunbar has observed in primates (Shultz and Dunbar 2010; Gamble et al. 2014). It is conceivable that a sort of "arms race" (to use Richard Dawkins' term; Dawkins 1991) took place among our immediate ancestors, in which every increase in mental capacity resulted in higher fitness relative to the group. Or just to follow Leigh Van Valen's "Red Queen" hypothesis, individuals had to constantly adapt not only to gain fitness relative to others, but also to keep their social status in a rapidly changing social world (changes that were, in turn, produced by the advent of successive cultural innovations) (Liow et al. 2011). Thus, a virtuous circle may have been established in which pressure for increasing plasticity facilitated selection of large brains and more neurons, and in turn these large brains resulted in more intense social pressures and cultural innovations, again putting new selective demands to increase neuron numbers, and so on. Furthermore, increasing brain size may be a relatively simple genetic achievement that can be done in a short time in evolutionary terms.

Subsequently (but certainly not caused by my publication), many authors like Terrence Deacon and others also proposed plastic and epigenetic processes for the rapid evolution of the human brain (Deacon 1997). Very recently, Chet Sherwood and collaborators reported that the heritability of cortical anatomy is much higher in the chimpanzee than in the human, which firmly supports the concept of a plastic process in brain evolution (Gómez-Robles et al. 2015). They studied a series of human and chimp brains with known kin relationships, and determined variability in brain size and brain shape, measured from a geometric model of cortical anatomy. They then calculated an index of heritability, which is the proportion of variability that cannot be explained by genetics or kinship. Their finding is in line with a strong developmental plasticity of the human brain, which might simply be the result of increasing brain size (larger brains might have more developmental plasticity), an interesting possibility that requires further research.

Finally, I have to point out that things are not so clear-cut regarding the different modalities of evolutionary brain growth. First, in passive growth, brains still need to keep doing what they did before, but in larger networks and with more distance between neurons, which may produce unwanted delays in neuronal communication. As I said above, increasing neuronal density might be a factor contributing to minimizing brain expansion as neuron numbers increase. Furthermore, as mentioned in the previous chapter, oscillatory activity could be especially hampered in large brains. If the transmission delay of nerve impulses is too long, it may take a significant part of an oscillatory cycle, or be even longer than one cycle, which would interfere with the production of synchronized oscillations in large-scale networks, particularly at high frequencies where cycles are much shorter in time. Györgi Buzsáki, Nikos Logothetis and Wolf Singer recently highlighted that the "synaptic path length", or the number of synaptic relays between two connected regions, increases as the distance between these regions expands in larger brains (Buzsáki et al. 2013). Larger brains partly adapt to this situation by growing longer faster conducting axons that are larger in diameter, which serve as shortcuts for long connections (see Chapter 5). Thus, connectivity becomes more complex, with local connections, middle-range connections in different degrees, and long- and very long-range connections that act as shortcuts for different pathways. This pattern corresponds to what is called a "small world" organization, in which the balance among local, intermediate and long-range connections is optimized to maximize processing efficiency. Buzsáki and collaborators have also underlined the fact that the propagation of low frequency oscillations across the cerebral cortex is much faster in the large human brain than in the small brains of rats, pointing to a relative maintenance of transmission time intervals across the cortex in both species. We will come back to the issue of axonal conduction and brain size in Chapter 5, using the corpus callosum as a model tract for the evolution of brain connectivity.

Thus, there may be compensatory rearrangements during passive growth simply to maintain basic functional requirements. In addition, by increasing neuron number, passive growth provides space for further connectional rearrangements and opens a possibility for increasing behavioral capacity. In fact, in many cases, active growth may make use of general body size increases to increase the overall neuron number. This has happened in human evolution, where there has been a steady increase in body size accompanied with brain size increases, from 30 to 45 kg in Australopithecines and *Homo habilis* to 60 kg in *Homo erectus* and a larger average size in modern humans. However, body size has only doubled, while brain size has tripled from Australopithecines to modern humans, indicating that passive growth is not the only factor involved. Therefore, brain growth, coupled with body growth, may be one of the ways higher processing capacity has been achieved, but selection may also increase brain size (or neuron number) independent of body growth. Moreover, this could also explain why in some cases it is absolute neuron numbers, and in others the number of neurons relative to body size, that best accounts for behavioral capacities in different animal groups. Nonetheless, general brain size, plasticity and epigenetics could not have done it all. We have evolved a specific sensorimotor network, specialized to one hemisphere that enabled our ancestors to engage in complex vocal behavior. In the next chapter, I will refer to another attribute of the human brain, namely brain lateralization, which is an additional innovation that may have required distinct genetic mechanisms.

References

Ables JL, Breunig JJ, Eisch AJ, Rakic P (2011) Not(ch) just development: Notch signalling in the adult brain. Nat Rev Neurosci 12:269–283

Aboitiz F (1988) Epigenesis and the evolution of the human brain. Med Hypotheses 25:55–59.

References   121

Aboitiz F (1996) Does bigger mean better? Evolutionary determinants of brain size and structure. Brain Behav Evol 47: 225–245

Aboitiz F, Montiel J (2007a) Co-option of signaling mechanisms from neural induction to telencephalic patterning. Rev Neurosci 18:311–342

Aboitiz F, Montiel J (2007b) Origin and evolution of the vertebrate telencephalon, with special reference to the mammalian neocortex. Adv Anat Embryol Cell Biol 193:1–112

Aboitiz F, Montiel JF (2015) Olfaction, navigation, and the origin of isocortex. Front Neurosci 9:402

Aboitiz F, Zamorano F (2013) Neural progenitors, patterning and ecology in neocortical origins. Front Neuroanat 7:38

Aiello LC, Wheeler P (1995) The expensive-tissue hypothesis: the brain and the digestive system in human and primate evolution. Curr Anthropol 36:199–221

Anderson ML, Finlay BL (2014) Allocating structure to function: the strong links between neuroplasticity and natural selection. Front Hum Neurosci 7:918

Anderson SA, Eisenstat DD, Shi L, Rubenstein JL (1997) Interneuron migration from basal forebrain to neocortex: dependence on Dlx genes. Science 278:474–476.

Barton RA (2004) Binocularity and brain evolution in primates. Proc Natl Acad Sci U S A 101:10113–10115

Barton RA (2012) Embodied cognitive evolution and the cerebellum. Philos Trans R Soc Lond B Biol Sci 367:2097–2107

Barton RA, Harvey PH (2000) Mosaic evolution of brain structure in mammals. Nature 405:1055–1058

Barton RA, Venditti C (2013a) Human frontal lobes are not relatively large. Proc Natl Acad Sci U S A 110:9001–9006

Barton RA, Venditti C (2013b) Reply to Smaers: getting human frontal lobes in proportion. Proc Natl Acad Sci U S A 110: E3683–E3684

Barton RA, Venditti C (2014) Rapid evolution of the cerebellum in humans and other great apes. Curr Biol 24:2440–2444

Barton RA, Purvis A, Harvey PH (1995) Evolutionary radiation of visual and olfactory brain systems in primates, bats and insectivores. Philos Trans R Soc Lond B Biol Sci 348:381–392

Bishop KM, Rubenstein JL, O'Leary DD (2002) Distinct actions of Emx1, Emx2, and Pax6 in regulating the specification of areas in the developing neocortex. J Neurosci 22:7627–7638

Brodmann K (1909) Vergleichende Lokalisationslehre der Grosshirnrinde. Johann Ambrosius Barth, Leipzig

Buzsáki G, Logothetis N, Singer W (2013) Scaling brain size, keeping timing: evolutionary preservation of brain rhythms. Neuron 80:751–764

Cahalane DJ, Charvet CJ, Finlay BL (2012) Systematic, balancing gradients in neuron density and number across the primate isocortex. Front Neuroanat 6:28

Catania KC (1995) Magnified cortex in star-nosed moles. Nature 375:453–454

Charvet CJ (2014) Distinct developmental growth patterns account for the disproportionate expansion of the rostral and caudal isocortex in evolution. Front Hum Neurosci 8:190

Charvet CJ, Striedter GF (2011) Causes and consequences of expanded sub-ventricular zones. Eur J Neurosci 34:988–993

Charvet CJ, Hof PR, Raghanti MA, Van Der Kouwe AJ, Sherwood CC, Takahashi E (2017) Combining diffusion magnetic resonance tractography with stereology highlights increased cross-cortical integration in primates. J Comp Neurol 525:1075–1093

Cheung AF, Pollen AA, Tavare A, DeProto J, Molnár Z (2007) Comparative aspects of cortical neurogenesis in vertebrates. J Anat 211:164–176

Cheung AF, Kondo S, Abdel-Mannan O, Chodroff RA, Sirey TM, Bluy LE, Webber N, DeProto J, Karlen SJ, Krubitzer L, Stolp HB, Saunders NR, Molnár Z (2010) The subventricular zone is the developmental milestone of a 6-layered neocortex: comparisons in metatherian and eutherian mammals. Cereb Cortex 20:1071–1081

Clayton NS. (1998) Memory and the hippocampus in food-storing birds: a comparative approach. Neuropharmacology 37:441–452

Cornélio AM, de Bittencourt-Navarrete RE, de Bittencourt Brum R, Queiroz CM, Costa MR (2016) Human brain expansion during evolution is independent of fire control and cooking. Front Neurosci 10:167

Darwin C. (1871) The Descent of Man, and Selection in Relation to Sex. John Murray, London

Dawkins R (1991) The Blind Watchmaker. Penguin, New York

Deacon T (1997) The Symbolic Species. The Co-evolution of Language and the Brain. Norton Press, New York

DeCasien AR, Williams SA, Higham JP (2017) Pimate brain size is predicted by diet but not sociality. Nature Ecol Evol 1:1002

Diamond ME, Armstrong-James M, Ebner FF (1993) Experience-dependent plasticity in adult rat barrel cortex. Proc Natl Acad Sci U S A 90:2082–2086

Díaz E, Pinto-Hamuy T, Fernández V (1994) Interhemispheric structural asymmetry induced by a lateralized reaching task in the rat motor cortex. Eur J Neurosci 6:1235–1238

Dicke U, Roth G (2016) Neuronal factors determining high intelligence. Philos Trans R Soc Lond B Biol Sci 371:20150180

Ebbesson SO (1980) The parcellation theory and its relation to interspecific variability in brain organization, evolutionary and ontogenetic development, and neuronal plasticity. Cell Tissue Res 213:179–212

Ercsey-Ravasz M, Markov NT, Lamy C, Van Essen DC, Knoblauch K, Toroczkai Z, Kennedy H (2013) A predictive network model of cerebral cortical connectivity based on a distance rule. Neuron 80:184–197

Finlay BL, Darlington RB (1995) Linked regularities in the development and evolution of mammalian brains. Science 268:1578–1584

Finlay BL, Uchiyama R (2015) Developmental mechanisms channeling cortical evolution. Trends Neurosci 38:69–76

Finlay BL, Workman AD (2013) Human exceptionalism. Trends Cogn Sci 17:199–201

Finlay BL, Hersman MN, Darlington RB (1998) Patterns of vertebrate neurogenesis and the paths of vertebrate evolution. Brain Behav Evol 52:232–242

Florio M, Huttner WB (2014) Neural progenitors, neurogenesis and the evolution of the neocortex. Development 141:2182–2194

Foley RA, Lee PC (1991) Ecology and energetics of encephalization in hominid evolution. Philos Trans R Soc Lond B Biol Sci 334:223–231

Fonseca-Azevedo K, Herculano-Houzel S (2012) Metabolic constraint imposes tradeoff between body size and number of brain neurons in human evolution. Proc Natl Acad Sci U S A 109:18571–18576

Frahm HD, Rehkämper G, Nevo E (1997) Brain structure volumes in the mole rat, Spalax ehrenbergi (Spalacidae, Rodentia) in comparison to the rat and subterrestrial insectivores. J Hirnforsch 38:209–222

Gabi M, Neves K, Masseron C, Ribeiro PF, Ventura-Antunes L, Torres L, Mota B, Kaas JH, Herculano-Houzel S (2016) No relative expansion of the number of prefrontal neurons in primate and human evolution. Proc Natl Acad Sci U S A 113:9617–9622

Gai D, Haan E, Scholar M, Nicholl J, Yu S (2015) Phenotypes of AKT3 deletion: a case report and literature review. Am J Med Genet A 167:174–179

Galton F (1907) Inquiries into Human Faculty and Its Development. JM Dent & Sons, London

Gamble C, Gowlett J, Dunbar R (2014) Thinking Big: How the Evolution of Social Life Shaped the Human Mind. Thames and Hudson, New York

Garcia-Junco-Clemente P, Golshani P (2014) PTEN: A master regulator of neuronal structure, function, and plasticity. Commun Integr Biol 7:e28358

Georgala PA. Carr CB, Price DJ (2011) The role of Pax6 in forebrain development. Dev Neurobiol 71:690–709

Geschwind DH, Rakic P (2013) Cortical evolution: judge the brain by its cover. Neuron 80:633–647

Gilad Y, Przeworski M, Lancet D (2004) Loss of olfactory receptor genes coincides with the acquisition of full trichromatic vision in primates. PLoS Biol 2:E5

Gómez-Robles A, Hopkins WD, Schapiro SJ, Sherwood CC (2015) Relaxed genetic control of cortical organization in human brains compared with chimpanzees. Proc Natl Acad Sci U S A 112:14799–14804

Gould SJ (1981) The Mismeasure of Man. WW Norton, New York

Gould SJ, Lewontin RC (1979) The spandrels of San Marco and the panglossian paradigm: a critique of the adaptationist programme. Proc Roy Soc Lond B 205:581–598

Grove EA, Fukuchi-Shimogori T (2003) Generating the cerebral cortical area map. Annu Rev Neurosci 26:355–380

Halley AC (2016) Prenatal brain-body allometry in mammals. Brain Behav Evol 88:14–24

Hansen DV, Lui JH, Parker PR, Kriegstein AR (2010) Neurogenic radial glia in the outer subventricular zone of human neocortex. Nature 464:554–561

Haug H (1987) Brain sizes, surfaces, and neuronal sizes of the cortex cerebri: a stereological investigation of man and his variability and a comparison with some mammals (primates, whales, marsupials, insectivores, and one elephant). Am J Anat 180:126–142

Herculano-Houzel S (2010) Coordinated scaling of cortical and cerebellar numbers of neurons. Front Neuroanat 4:12

Herculano-Houzel S (2015) Decreasing sleep requirement with increasing numbers of neurons as a driver for bigger brains and bodies in mammalian evolution. Proc Biol Sci 282:20151853

Herculano-Houzel S, Lent R (2005) Isotropic fractionator: a simple, rapid method for the quantification of total cell and neuron numbers in the brain. J Neurosci 25:2518–2521

Herculano-Houzel S, Mota B, Wong P, Kaas JH (2010) Connectivity-driven white matter scaling and folding in primate cerebral cortex. Proc Natl Acad Sci U S A 107:19008–19013

Herculano-Houzel S, Manger PR, Kaas JH (2014) Brain scaling in mammalian evolution as a consequence of concerted and mosaic changes in numbers of neurons and average neuronal cell size. Front Neuroanat 8:77

Herculano-Houzel S, Catania K, Manger PR, Kaas JH (2015a) Mammalian brains are made of these: a dataset of the numbers and densities of neuronal and nonneuronal cells in the brain of glires, primates, scandentia, eulipotyphlans, afrotherians and artiodactyls, and their relationship with body mass. Brain Behav Evol 86:145–163

Herculano-Houzel S, Messeder DJ, Fonseca-Azevedo K, Pantoja NA (2015b) When larger brains do not have more neurons: increased numbers of cells are compensated by decreased average cell size across mouse individuals. Front Neuroanat 9:64

Herculano-Houzel S, von Bartheld CS, Miller DJ, Kaas JH (2015c) How to count cells: the advantages and disadvantages of the isotropic fractionator compared with stereology. Cell Tissue Res 360:29–42

Herculano-Houzel S, Kaas JH, de Oliveira-Souza R (2016) Corticalization of motor control in humans is a consequence of brain scaling in primate evolution. J Comp Neurol 524:448–455

Hilgetag CC, Barbas H (2009) Sculpting the brain. Sci Amer 2:66–71

Horvát S, Gămănuţ R, Ercsey-Ravasz M, Magrou L, Gămănuţ B, Van Essen DC, Burkhalter A, Knoblauch K, Toroczkai Z, Kennedy H (2016) Spatial embedding and wiring cost constrain the functional layout of the cortical network of rodents and primates. PLoS Biol 14:e1002512

Jerison HJ (1973) Evolution of the Brain and Intelligence. Academic Press, New York

Kaas JH (2011) Reconstructing the areal organization of the neocortex of the first mammals. Brain Behav Evol 78:7–21

Kaas JH (2013) The evolution of brains from early mammals to humans. Wiley Interdiscip Rev Cogn Sci 4:33–45

Kleiber M (1975) Metabolic turnover rate: a physiological meaning of the metabolic rate per unit body weight. J Theor Biol 53:199–204

Kriegstein AR, Noctor SC (2004) Patterns of neuronal migration in the embryonic cortex. Trends Neurosci 27:392–399

Krubitzer L (2009) In search of a unifying theory of complex brain evolution. Ann N Y Acad Sci 1156:44–67

Krubitzer LA, Seelke AM (2012) Cortical evolution in mammals: the bane and beauty of phenotypic variability. Proc Natl Acad Sci U S A 109 (Suppl 1):10647–10654

Krubitzer L, Manger P, Pettigrew J, Calford M (1995) Organization of somatosensory cortex in monotremes: in search of the prototypical plan. J Comp
Neurol 351:261–306

Lashley KS (1929) Brain Mechanisms and Intelligence. University Of Chicago
Press, Chicago

Lewitus E, Kelava I, Kalinka AT, Tomancak P, Huttner WB (2014) An
adaptive threshold in mammalian neocortical evolution. PloS Biology 12:
e1002000

Liow LH, Van Valen L, Stenseth NC (2011) Red Queen: from populations to
taxa and communities. Trends Ecol Evol 26:349–358

Lui JH, Hansen DV, Kriegstein AR (2011) Development and evolution of the
human neocortex. Cell 146:18–36

MacLean EL, Hare B, Nunn CL, Addessi E, Amici F, Anderson RC, Aureli F,
Baker JM, Bania AE, Barnard AM, Boogert NJ, Brannon EM, Bray EE,
Bray J, Brent LJ, Burkart JM, Call J, Cantlon JF, Cheke LG, Clayton NS,
Delgado MM, DiVincenti LJ, Fujita K, Herrmann E, Hiramatsu C, Jacobs
LF, Jordan KE, Laude JR, Leimgruber KL, Messer EJ, Moura AC, Ostojić
L, Picard A, Platt ML, Plotnik JM, Range F, Reader SM, Reddy RB, Sandel
AA, Santos LR, Schumann K, Seed AM, Sewall KB, Shaw RC, Slocombe
KE, Su Y, Takimoto A, Tan J, Tao R, van Schaik CP, Virányi Z, Visalberghi
E, Wade JC, Watanabe A, Widness J, Young JK, Zentall TR, Zhao Y (2014)
The evolution of self-control. Proc Natl Acad Sci U S A 111:E2140–E2148

Maguire EA, Woollett K, Spiers HJ (2006) London taxi drivers and bus
drivers: a structural MRI and neuropsychological analysis. Hippocampus
16:1091–1101

Martin RD (1981) Relative brain size and basal metabolic rate in terrestrial
vertebrates. Nature 293:57–60

Montgomery SH, Mundy NI, Barton RA (2016) Brain evolution and development: adaptation, allometry and constraint. Proc Roy Soc B
283:20160433.

Mota B, Herculano-Houzel S (2014) All brains are made of this: a fundamental
building block of brain matter with matching neuronal and glial masses.
Front Neuroanat 8:127

Mota B, Herculano-Houzel S (2015) Cortical folding scales universally with
surface area and thickness, not number of neurons. Science 349:74–77

Navarrete A, van Schaik CP, Isler K (2011) Energetics and the evolution of
human brain size. Nature 480:91–93

Noctor SC, Flint AC, Weissman TA, Dammerman RS, Kriegstein AR (2001) Neurons derived from radial glial cells establish radial units in neocortex. Nature 409:714–720

Noctor SC, Flint AC, Weissman TA, Wong WS, Clinton BK, Kriegstein AR (2002) Dividing precursor cells of the embryonic cortical ventricular zone have morphological and molecular characteristics of radial glia. J Neurosci 22:3161–3173

O'Leary DD, Sahara S (2008) Genetic regulation of arealization of the neocortex. Curr Opin Neurobiol 18:90–100

Olkowicz S, Kocourek M, Lučan RK, Porteš M, Fitch WT, Herculano-Houzel S, Němec P (2016) Birds have primate-like numbers of neurons in the forebrain. Proc Natl Acad Sci U S A 113:7255–7260

Pagel MD, Harvey PH (1988) How mammals produce large-brained offspring. Evolution 42:948–957

Passingham RE, Smaers JB (2014) Is the prefrontal cortex especially enlarged in the human brain allometric relations and remapping factors. Brain Behav Evol 84:156–166

Pirlot P, Pottier J (1977) Encephalization and quantitative brain composition in bats in relation to their life-habits. Rev Can Biol 36:321–336

Pontzer H, Brown MH, Raichlen DA, Dunsworth H, Hare B, Walker K, Luke A, Dugas LR, Durazo-Arvizu R, Schoeller D, Plange-Rhule J, Bovet P, Forrester TE, Lambert EV, Thompson ME, Shumaker RW, Ross SR (2016) Metabolic acceleration and the evolution of human brain size and life history. Nature 533:390–392

Pulvers JN, Journiac N, Arai Y, Nardelli J (2015) MCPH1: a window into brain development and evolution. Front Cell Neurosci 9:92

Rakic P (1978) Neuronal migration and contact guidance in the primate telencephalon. Postgrad Med J 54 (Suppl 1):25–40

Rakic P (2009) Evolution of the neocortex: a perspective from developmental biology. Nat Rev Neurosci 10:724–735

Rash BG, Rakic P (2014) Genetic resolutions of brain convolutions. Science 343:744–745

Reader SM, Laland KN (2002) Social intelligence, innovation, and enhanced brain size in primates. Proc Natl Acad Sci U S A 99:4436–4441

Ribeiro PF, Ventura-Antunes L, Gabi M, Mota B, Grinberg LT, Farfel JM, Ferretti-Rebustini RE, Leite RE, Filho WJ, Herculano-Houzel S (2013) The human cerebral cortex is neither one nor many: neuronal distribution reveals two quantitatively different zones in the gray matter, three in the white matter, and explains local variations in cortical folding. Front Neuroanat 7:28

Riska B, Atchley WR (1985) Genetics of growth predict patterns of brain-size evolution. Science 229:668–671

Rockel AJ, Hiorns RW, Powell TP (1980) The basic uniformity in structure of the neocortex. Brain 103:221–244

Rushton JP, Ankney CD (2009) Whole brain size and general mental ability: a review. Int J Neurosci 119:691–731

Scheibel AB (1988) Dendritic correlates of human cortical function. Arch Ital Biol 126:347–357

Sherry DF, Forbes MR, Khurgel M, Ivy GO (1993) Females have a larger hippocampus than males in the brood-parasitic brown-headed cowbird. Proc Natl Acad Sci U S A 90:7839–7843

Sherwood CC, Smaers JB (2013) What's the fuss over human frontal lobe evolution? Trends Cogn Sci 17:432–433

Shitamukai A, Konno D, Matsuzaki F (2011) Oblique radial glial divisions in the developing mouse neocortex induce self-renewing progenitors outside the germinal zone that resemble primate outer subventricular zone progenitors. J Neurosci 31:3683–3695

Shultz S, Dunbar R (2010) Encephalization is not a universal macroevolutionary phenomenon in mammals but is associated with sociality. Proc Natl Acad Sci U S A 107:21582–21586

Smaers JB (2013) How humans stand out in frontal lobe scaling. Proc Natl Acad Sci U S A 110:E3682

Smaers JB, Steele J, Case CR, Cowper A, Amunts K, Zilles K (2011) Primate prefrontal cortex evolution: human brains are the extreme of a lateralized ape trend. Brain Behav Evol 77:67–78

Smaers JB, Gómez-Robles A, Parks AN, Sherwood CC (2017) Exceptional Evolutionary Expansion of Prefrontal Cortex in Great Apes and Humans. Curr Biol 27:714–720

Somel M, Liu X, Khaitovich P (2013) Human brain evolution: transcripts, metabolites and their regulators. Nat Rev Neurosci 14:112–127

Stevens JR (2014) Evolutionary pressures on primate intertemporal choice. Proc Biol Sci 281:1786

Striedter GF (2005) Principles of Brain Evolution. Sinauer Associates, Sunderland

Striedter GF, Srinivasan S (2015) Knowing when to fold them. Science 349:31–32

Striedter GF, Srinivasan S, Monuki ES (2015) Cortical folding: when, where, how, and why? Annu Rev Neurosci 38:291–307

Suárez R, Fernández-Aburto P, Manger PR, Mpodozis J (2011) Deterioration of the Gαo vomeronasal pathway in sexually dimorphic mammals. PLoS One 6(10):e26436

Sun T, Hevner RF (2014) Growth and folding of the mammalian cerebral cortex: from molecules to malformations. Nat Rev Neurosci 15:217–232

Sur M, Pallas SL, Roe AW (1990) Cross-modal plasticity in cortical development: differentiation and specification of sensory neocortex. Trends Neurosci 13:227–233

Tallinen T, Chung JY, Biggins JS, Mahadevan L (2014) Gyrification from constrained cortical expansion. Proc Natl Acad Sci U S A 111:12667–12672

Tamamaki N, Nakamura K, Okamoto K, Kaneko T (2001) Radial glia is a progenitor of neocortical neurons in the developing cerebral cortex. Neurosci Res 41:51–60

Van Essen DC (1997) A tension-based theory of morphogenesis and compact wiring in the central nervous system. Nature 385:313–318

Ventura-Antunes L, Mota B, Herculano-Houzel S. (2013) Different scaling of white matter volume, cortical connectivity, and gyrification across rodent and primate brains. Front Neuroanat 7:3

Vincze O, Vágási CI, Pap PL, Osváth G, Møller AP (2015) Brain regions associated with visual cues are important for bird migration. Biol Lett 11 pii: 20150678

Von Bonin G (1948) The frontal lobe of primates; cytoarchitectural studies. Res Publ Assoc Res Nerv Ment Dis 27:67–83

Wang L, Hou S, Han YG (2016) Hedgehog signaling promotes basal progenitor expansion and the growth and folding of the neocortex. Nat Neurosci 19:888–896

Wong P, Peebles JK, Asplund CL, Collins CE, Herculano-Houzel S, Kaas JH (2013) Faster scaling of auditory neurons in cortical areas relative to subcortical structures in primate brains. Brain Behav Evol 81:209–218

Workman AD, Charvet CJ, Clancy B, Darlington RB, Finlay BL (2013) Modeling transformations of neurodevelopmental sequences across mammalian species. J Neurosci 33:7368–7383

Wrangham R (2009) Catching Fire: How Cooking Made Us Human. Profile Books, London

Yopak KE, Lisney TJ, Darlington RB, Collin SP, Montgomery JC, Finlay BL (2010) A conserved pattern of brain scaling from sharks to primates. Proc Natl Acad Sci U S A 107:12946–12951

Yu YC, Bultje RS, Wang X, Shi SH (2009) Specific synapses develop preferentially among sister excitatory neurons in the neocortex. Nature 458:501–504

4

Broken Symmetry

As I mentioned in Chapter 2, Marc Dax was the first to document left-hemisphere specialization in speech, something that in the beginning was not evident for either Broca or Wernicke (Schiller 1992). By the early twentieth century, the notion that the faculty of speech was localized in the left hemisphere was already accepted among neurologists, but hemispheric specialization was still not a significant issue. In the 1960s, Norman Geschwind's work on disconnection syndromes contributed to establishing the notion of brain lateralization, with the left hemisphere dominant for language and hand control (Geschwind 1965). However, it was with the Nobel Prize winning study by Roger Sperry and his student Michael Gazzaniga on what they termed split-brain patients that the concept became widely known among the scientific community and the public. Together with the neurosurgeon Joseph Bogen, Sperry, and Gazzaniga were interested in patients undergoing a new neurosurgical technique called callosotomy, which consists of sectioning the corpus callosum, a massive tract of fibers that connects the left and right hemispheres of the brain (of which I will talk extensively in the next chapter). This procedure has been performed since the 1940s on patients with intractable epilepsy to avoid the development of a

© The Author(s) 2017
F. Aboitiz, *A Brain for Speech*,
DOI 10.1057/978-1-137-54060-7_4

mirror focus in the other hemisphere, which contributes to propagating seizures. The surgery was very successful in medical terms, providing a series of "split-brain" patients in which the two cerebral hemispheres were largely disconnected. One of the most striking observations was that such patients were able to live reasonably normal lives. However, some of them experienced hand discoordination, in which the left hand (controlled by the right hemisphere) seemed to act on its own and did not follow the patient's will, or at least according to the patients' verbal reports (which depends on the left hemisphere). This was an important indication that the right hemispheres of these patients were blind to language processes.

Two Minds

Sperry became widely respected in the 1950s for his groundbreaking work on the regeneration of the optic nerve in amphibians (neural regeneration is common in these animals, unlike in higher vertebrates) (Sperry 1947). He showed that changing the eye's orientation by rotating it did not result in modifying its central connections when these were reestablished. Sperry took advantage of the fact that the geometry of the eye inverts the image projected on the retina like an optical photographic camera, so that the lower retina normally faces the superior visual field and the upper retina faces the inferior visual field. After sectioning the optic nerve, he rotated the frog's eye by 180 degrees, so that the normally lower retina was now in an upper position facing the lower visual field and vice versa. After allowing the sectioned nerve to regenerate, Sperry studied the frog's visual behavior by presenting food (a fly) in the frog's upper or lower visual field. When the fly was positioned in the lower visual field, the frog lunged upwardly to catch it, while if it was presented in the upper visual field; the frog lunged downwardly, as it would have done before the eye rotation. The world had turned upside down to the frog, but it was unable to adjust to this change. Of course, sectioning the optic nerve and allowing it to regenerate without rotating the eye did not produce this effect. These findings implied that axons located in the superior (or inferior) retina were labeled to establish connections with central regions representing the upper (or lower) visual field, regardless of the eye's orientation. This conclusion supported the chemical label theory of how axons find their synaptic targets; as opposed to the resonance theory that claimed axons connect with their postsynaptic partners based on similarities in electrical activity patterns.

Sperry and collaborators continued studying the visual system, this time using cats to section a structure called the optic chiasm, where fibers of the optic nerve cross to the opposite hemisphere (Miner et al. 1956; Myers and Sperry 1958; Schrier and Sperry 1959). In frontal viewing species like cats and humans, each eye projects visual fibers to both cerebral hemispheres, so sectioning the optic chiasm made visual stimuli from each eye send fibers to the same hemispheric side, and not the other hemisphere. That is, the left eye was only connected to the left hemisphere, and the right eye to the right hemisphere (Fig. 4.1). Sperry then taught the cats a visual task with one eye blinkered, so that only one of their hemispheres (the one receiving input from the unblinkered eye) could learn the task. Cats learned the task well with the unblinkered eye. Experimenters then blinkered the eye with which the cat had learned the task, and unblinkered the other one (the untrained eye). Notably, cats also did well in the task because information that originally reached the hemisphere that had learned the task could be transferred to the other hemisphere through the corpus callosum. In a second step, Sperry and team performed two operations, one sectioning the optic chiasm, and the other sectioning the corpus callosum to interrupt interhemispheric communication. The cats did well in the task with the eye originally exposed to the task, but were unable to do it with the untrained eye. This suggested that the hemisphere that had learned the task was unable to transfer the knowledge to the hemisphere connected to the blinkered eye.

In a third step, Sperry, together with Michael Gazzaniga, studied the human split brain (Gazzaniga et al. 1962, 1965,; Gazzaniga and Sperry 1967). With the help of Joe Bogen, they recruited several split-brain patients to analyze their behavior under restricted conditions. Because sectioning the human optic chiasm was not an option, Sperry and Gazzaniga took advantage of the arrangement of retinal projections to the brain in binocular, or

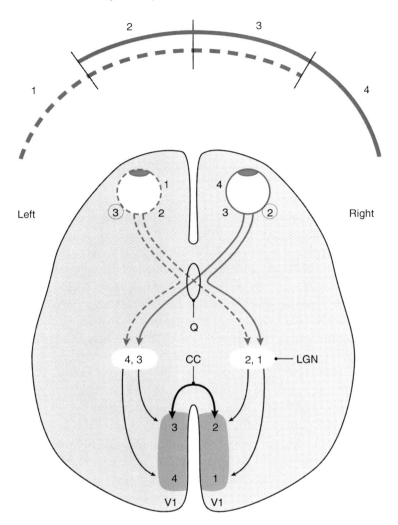

Fig. 4.1 The visual pathway to the cerebral cortex. The visual field (curved lines 1–4) is subdivided into the left (1, 2) and the right (3, 4) visual hemifields. The left eye (segmented lines) sees the left hemifield (ipsilateral, 1, 2), and only the medial right hemifield (contralateral, 3). Conversely, the right eye sees the right hemifield (ipsilateral, 4, 3), and only the medial left hemifield (contralateral, 2). In the optic chiasm (Q), fibers from the ipsilateral visual field representation from each eye cross to the other hemisphere, while fibers from the contralateral representation from each eye remain in the same hemisphere.

frontal viewing species like humans and cats. In animals with binocular vision, each eye can see on both sides of the head (called left and right visual fields, respectively). However, connectivity is arranged so that in both the left and right eyes, the part of the retina that sees the left visual field is projected to the right hemisphere. Conversely, objects on the right visual field are projected by both eyes to the left cerebral hemisphere (Fig. 4.2). The short story is that when you are looking frontally, whatever is to your right is seen by the left hemisphere and everything to your left is seen with the right hemisphere. Gazzaniga and Sperry put their patients in front of a screen divided in two (left and right), and instructed them to fix their sight on a central point. They then presented stimulus on only half of the visual field (left or right), so that the stimulus would be projected only to the contralateral hemisphere (right or left, respectively). Gazzaniga and Sperry found that the left hemisphere of split-brain patients (receiving stimuli from only the right visual field) was perfectly able to perform all reading tasks, while the reading capacity of the right hemisphere (facing the left visual field) was much more limited, being restricted to simple words for most patients. Furthermore, subjects might not be able to verbally recall stimuli presented to the right hemisphere, but using the left hand, the subject was able to point to the observed object, so, for example, if the subject was presented with a word like "pencil" in the right hemisphere, he/she could recognize the object with his left hand even if it was out of sight (this showed a limited reading ability of the right hemisphere), but when asked what he/she had done, the subject could not report this verbally since language is located in the left hemisphere.

Later in the seventies, another of Sperry's students Eran Zaidel designed an ingenious contact lens (the Z-lens) that presented stimuli to only one eye, in which half of the stimulus was seen by the left hemisphere and the other half by the right hemisphere (Zaidel 1975). At the time this was a great innovation as the previous design required constantly checking to ensure that subjects had not moved their eyes

Fig.4.1 (Continued)
The result is that in the visual cortex (V1), the left visual field is represented in the right hemisphere, and the right visual field is represented in the left hemisphere. Both hemifields are connected in the visual cortex by fibers of the corpus callosum (CC). LGN, lateral geniculate nucleus

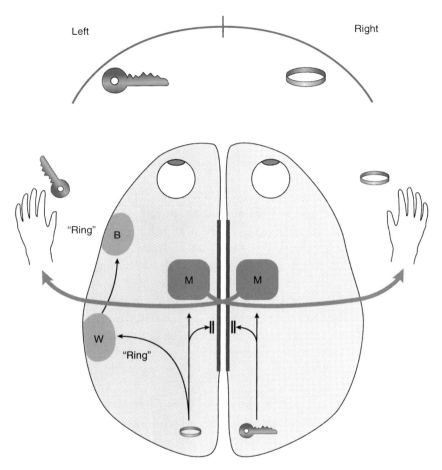

Fig. 4.2 The split brain. If the corpus callosum is sectioned at the midline, sensory information (in this case, visual) reaching only one hemisphere is disconnected from the other hemisphere. If two different stimuli are presented to the two halves of the visual field (say, a key on the left side and a ring on the right side), each hemisphere will have access to only one stimulus. If the subject is asked to grasp the presented object, he/she will take the key with the left hand, and the ring with the right hand, because the descending motor pathway from the motor cortex (M) is crossed. Note that the motor pathway to the hand crosses to the contralateral side in the brainstem, and not through the corpus callosum. On the other hand, if the subject is asked to say what he/she saw, he/she will say "Ring" as the language regions (W and B) are located in the left hemisphere in most people

from the center of the screen (if they did, they allowed both hemispheres access to the stimulus). In subsequent studies, Zaidel demonstrated that the right hemisphere of split-brain patients has a language representation of its own, and is able to perform some basic syntactic operations (Zaidel 1976, 1983; Zaidel and Peters 1981). Furthermore, not all people have left-hemisphere language dominance, as about 10% of people have right-sided language representation. To complicate things further, there may be significant variability in the degree of language or speech lateralization, and in the specific linguistic functions that are lateralized. This issue will be dealt with below in this chapter, specifically when I discuss speech perception and production.

Nonetheless, the left hemisphere was found to be deficient in simple tasks involving spatial orientation, visual searches, drawing a cube, or imagining the rotation of three-dimensional objects; tasks that the right hemisphere had no problem doing (Sperry 1961, Springer and Deutsch 1981; Hellige 1993). Other studies of patients with right hemisphere damage reported specific deficits in attentional capacity. In particular, patients usually show left-sided neglect, which is a specific denial of the events that take place on the left side, be they external to the subject or even parts of his/her own body (the left arm, for example), despite there being no problem in sensory capacity on this side. Right hemisphere patients can also have deficits in the capacity to recall dates, times or places, in organizing discourse, and facial recognition. In addition, some language-related functions like music (in musically uneducated persons) and prosody are better processed in the right hemisphere (see Chapter 2). Thus, while in most people the left hemisphere is dominant for speech, the right hemisphere performs better in visual orientation and other tasks like speech prosody. Furthermore, split-brain subjects display conflicts in bimanual tasks, as in what is called the alien hand syndrome, where the two hands behave in opposite ways, for example, one hand choosing one piece of clothing from a closet and the other choosing another; or one turning on a light and the other turning it off. In extreme cases, one hand has even become aggressive against the patient. This condition is not only caused by callosal sectioning, but can also occur after localized lesions of the frontal or parietal lobes. Thus, the corpus callosum was found to be necessary for the integration and resolution of conflicting experiences between the two hemispheres. Nonetheless, the observation that otherwise split-brain subjects showed no major behavioral dysfunctions implied that whatever its function, an intact corpus callosum was not critical for daily behavior.

Another lateralized behavior is emotion, which Charles Darwin described as lopsided, noting that defiant facial expressions were markedly asymmetrical (Darwin 1872). John Hughlings Jackson later noted that patients with lesions in the right hemisphere were impaired in producing and perceiving emotions (York and Steinberg 2011). Likewise, facial expressions display evident lateralization. The inferior aspect of the face, where most emotional expression takes place, is contralaterally innervated by the motor muscles of the brainstem. Consequently, emotional expressions tend to appear more rapidly and more intensely on the left side of our faces (controlled by the right hemisphere) (Springer 1981, Hellige 1993). Finally, the right hemisphere has usually been associated with creativity and art, a speculation that as yet has no scientific basis. Dahlia Zaidel, another of Sperry's students (who met and married Eran Zaidel while working in Sperry's lab), recently criticized this unwarranted assumption, claiming that this was originally a popular notion that filtered into science and has misled research on neuroaesthetics in recent years (Zaidel 2013).

Roger Sperry was awarded the Nobel Prize in 1981. Eran Zaidel once told me that he witnessed how Sperry had worked his way to earn this recognition. It is very likely that such awards are as much the result of scientific as political work. And this may not have been without consequences. The award generated a deep rift with Michael Gazzaniga, who may have felt that he should have shared the prize, as he designed and performed the initial split-brain experiments (Corballis 2015a). After that, Sperry and Gazzaniga "split" in Michael Corballis' words. As a graduate student of Eran Zaidel, who remained close to Sperry, I could feel the tension between the two groups, which for a long time did not have any interaction whatsoever. While Sperry turned to more philosophical issues concerning the phenomenology of consciousness (Sperry 1980, 1984, 1998), Gazzaniga focused on the hypothesis that the left hemisphere works as an "interpreter" that provides a coherent account of fragmented perceptions and memories, thus contributing to the unity of mind (Gazzaniga 1998, 2000, 2015a, b). On the other hand, Zaidel remained perhaps the most experimentally oriented, and developed a laboratory dedicated to studying different kinds of functional asymmetries in the brain, and especially information transfer across the hemispheres.

The impact of Gazzaniga and Sperry's work on both science and the public was tremendous. The notion that we have two brains, one specialized for logic and language and the other for visual orienting and creativity soon became widespread among the public and was non-critically and superficially applied to many aspects of daily behavior. There would be "right-brained" and "left-brained" people, with different capacities, goals, etc. Moreover, men were proposed to have more right-hemisphere skills and women more left-hemisphere skills. For laypersons, this has been perhaps the most influential and at the same time the most misunderstood discovery in the history of neuroscience. A more accepted interpretation among scholars is that the left hemisphere is specialized in time-related matters and sequential processing, while the right hemisphere is devoted to holistic, gestaltic processing (Corballis 2014, 2015b). Although this may generally be true, and we will see evidence of different patterns of connectivity between the left and the right hemispheres, it is important to emphasize that many of the differences between hemispheres are more a matter of degree than of kind.

Lateralization Is Complex

One limitation of the studies by Sperry, Gazzaniga, Zaidel and others was that the experimental designs were based on visual stimulation, while speech is audio-vocal. The problem is that one cannot simply separate the auditory inputs to the left hemisphere from those to the right, as both ears project to both hemispheres. This is just like the visual system, you might say, but with the complication that auditory stimuli from either side of the head are not segregated from stimuli from the other side, as happens with the left and right visual fields. Each hemisphere receives auditory input from both ears, and also from both sides of the head, although with a small difference in timing; as sounds produced on one side of the head reach the ear of that side sooner than the ear on the other side. The delay between the two ears is used by the brain to calculate the source of a sound. This computation is made at low hierarchical levels in the brainstem, but there are indications that this also takes place in the auditory cortex.

There have been two main ways to experimentally circumvent the acoustical problem. One is the Wada test, which consists of injecting the sedative sodium amytal (a relative of "truth serum") into one hemisphere via the carotid artery, which temporarily inhibits the respective hemisphere while the other hemisphere remains awake (Strauss and Wada 1983). This procedure is still used with epilepsy patients to determine the hemispheric localization of language before surgery. Another, less invasive method is the dichotic listening test, which consists of simultaneously presenting two different but similar syllables like /ba/ and /pa/, one in the left ear and the other in the right ear. In conditions of dichotic input, individuals whose left hemisphere is dominant for language will better detect the syllable presented to the right ear (Bryden 1962). This is believed to occur due to a process called ipsilateral suppression, where the input from the left ear is inhibited when a competing stimulus appears from the other ear. Studies using the Wada and dichotic listening tests supported the early lesion studies of language lateralization, and Sperry and Gazzaniga's' main findings of a strong left hemisphere specialization for speech and language in most people.

However, David Poeppel, whom we met in Chapter 2, presented evidence that in some cases speech perception is a bilateral rather than left dominant process (Poeppel 2003, 2014; Chait et al. 2015, Silbert et al. 2014; Hickok and Poeppel 2007). First, he found that the condition that most affects speech perception is pure word deafness (which is not the same as Wernicke's original concept of word deafness; see Chapter 2) or auditory verbal agnosia, which predominantly affects the perception of consonants, and is only produced by bilateral lesions in the auditory areas. In other words, both the left and the right auditory cortices need to be impaired for this condition to occur. Pure word deafness patients have no auditory problems except for their incapacity to understand spoken words (they describe what they hear as being like a foreign language). Furthermore, Poeppel reported strong, bilateral, electromagnetic activity in both hemispheres when presenting speech-like stimuli. Intrigued by these findings, Gregory Hickok reexamined the classical example of Wernicke's aphasia (produced by lesions in the left hemisphere), where patients are said to have a deficit in speech perception, and concluded that instead of a speech recognition problem, the perceptual impairment emerges from a difficulty at higher sentence processing levels (Hickok 2014). But how do we deal with the established evidence of a left-hemisphere dominance for syllable perception, as seen in dichotic listening studies? Hickok and Poeppel argue that speech perception is a complex phenomenon, occurring at different levels of linguistic structure, and includes discrimination of phonemes and words and recognition of phrases and sentences (Hickok and Poeppel 2007). While some stroke patients have difficulty in distinguishing similar syllables like /ba/ and /da/, their capacity to distinguish the words /bad/ and /dad/ remains. Conversely, other patients are able to discriminate isolated syllables but have trouble with words. This points to dissociation between syllable and word perception. Thus, the capacity to distinguish pairs of isolated syllables that sound similar, as in dichotic listening studies, is not the same as word perception. These authors also claimed that dichotic listening requires cognitive as well as perceptual skills. Most syllable discrimination tasks put a load on phonological working memory, as they require conscious awareness of speech sounds; something we automatically do while reading, but not when hearing speech. During normal listening, we do not listen to phonemes but rather to words and their meanings. Thus, analyzing the phonological structure of speech signal puts a load on phonological working memory, which depends on the dorsal language pathway, which is left hemisphere dominant (see Chapters 2 and 6). This may explain the leftward bias in dichotic listening studies, but it remains to be experimentally demonstrated. Notably, Gregory Cogan and collaborators recorded electrical activity from the cortical surface with epilepsy patients while they were performing a word repetition task in which subjects had to either hear a word and then say it two seconds later, or to silently mouth words they had just heard (Cogan et al. 2014). Somatomotor activity (i.e. activity in both the auditory and the production phases) occurs bilaterally in language-related areas, suggesting that the sensorimotor component of the dorsal stream is also bilateral. This intriguing finding may imply that articulatory processes in the dorsal pathway are also bilateral, which would leave hemispheric dominance only to complex syntactic processing (see Chapter 2). More studies are needed in this line.

Although early stages of speech perception take place bilaterally, Poeppel claims there is a division of functions between the two hemispheres, with low-frequency theta sampling (syllabic level) dominated by the right auditory cortex while high-frequency gamma sampling (phonemic processing) is driven by the left hemisphere. Regarding the above discussion on the lateralization of dichotic listening, it is possible that this task requires high frequency processing of sounds, which is left hemisphere dominant. This might be a simpler explanation than invoking working memory requirements for the task. Robert Zatorre, Pascal Belin and others (Zatorre et al. 2002; Belin and Zatorre 2000) have advanced similar interpretations, emphasizing that auditory perception is constrained by a tradeoff between fine time-discrimination and the analysis of frequency composition. This is a general constraint of signal processing mechanisms in which a sufficient window of time must be compressed to extract information about the frequency composition (depending on the wavelengths to be analyzed), within which information is lost about specific events. In auditory physiology, this is called "acoustic uncertainty". It has been hypothesized that language processing has optimized this dilemma by specializing the right hemisphere in frequency analysis, and the left hemisphere in high-resolution temporal analysis. In turn, word discrimination may depend on a combination of both time and spectral analyses of speech stimulus (besides semantic processing), making it a bilateral process. On the other hand, Robert Shannon and collaborators argue that the relevant signals from speech emerge mostly from an envelope component that captures the bulk of the variability of air pressure (Shannon 2005). Conversely, the fine temporal structure of speech is less relevant. In fact, cochlear implants rely on envelope information to transmit speech signals. This contrasts with the acoustically relevant cues from music, which according to Shannon derive from its fine temporal structure. It has not yet been fully established how the two hemispheres interact in speech perception. This will probably be resolved by further experiments.

Hemispheric dominance might be evident with motor functions. However, studies using transcranial magnetic stimulation (TMS) have shown that the process is more complicated than expected. TMS is a non-invasive technique used with awake subjects that provides brief, highly localized magnetic pulses on the surface of the skull. This produces a transient alteration of neural activity in the site to which it is applied, and can reveal the role of specific brain areas in distinct tasks by suppressing their normal processing capacity. Yasuo Terao, Ichiro Kanazawa, and collaborators applied TMS in the motor area controlling oral speech movements of subjects undergoing a task in which they had to respond vocally after presentation of a visual cue (Terao et al. 2001). Recall that Broca's region is not motor or premotor cortex, it is prefrontal cortex and upstream from premotor and motor areas controlling speech muscles. TMS produced a delay in the vocal response, when applied to either the left or the right motor areas. However, there were hemispheric differences in the specific timing in which stimulation was more effective. If TMS was applied at a relatively long interval before vocalization (50–100 msec), left hemisphere interruption produced a slightly longer delay than when it was applied to the right hemisphere. However, if it was applied just before the onset of vocalization (0–50 msec), the effect was much longer when TMS was produced in the right hemisphere than in the left hemisphere. Thus, there seems to be an alternation between the two hemispheres when the motor command is downstream from the motor cortex. All this evidence indicates that rather than one hemisphere being totally dominant over the other for speech; they interact closely and play different roles in speech perception and execution. Perhaps the neural substrates for lateralization are to be found at higher levels in the processing hierarchy.

Connectivity Within or Between?

Jonathan Peelle, a scholar who has been working on speech perception, has proposed another model in which more basic aspects of hearing and speech perception, like the perception of pure tones or more complex signals, is strongly bilateral. Word perception is in an intermediate position, with weak left hemisphere specialization in lexical and semantic memory processes, while processing larger structures like phrases or sentences primarily depends on the left hemisphere (Peelle 2012). In this model, speech lateralization depends on the differential organization of large-scale networks in each hemisphere, which may be consistent with differences in early processing between the two hemispheres. In fact, there is brain-imaging support for asymmetries in large-scale networks in the cerebral hemispheres. Using resting-state fMRI, Hesheng Liu and collaborators studied the functional connectivity of different large-scale cortical networks (Wang et al. 2014). These included the default mode or resting state network, the executive frontoparietal network, and attentional networks that partly overlap with the frontoparietal system. While the frontoparietal network is strongly coupled with attentional networks in the right hemisphere, it links with the default-mode network and the language network in the left hemisphere. This is relevant to our interests, as it indicates that language networks in the left hemisphere are linked to both the executive and resting state networks, both of which display antisynchronic activity. This points to a double standard of the language networks, participating in internal state dynamics via mechanisms of inner speech, while at the same time being engaged in executive processes when using external language (see also Chapter 2). Furthermore, Liu and colleagues found that the higher level networks mentioned above display a preference for establishing within-hemisphere, rather than between-hemisphere connectivity, which contrasts with the sensorimotor networks that display strong interhemispheric coherence. Thus, there might be a trade-off between inter-hemispheric and intra-hemispheric connectivity, promoting brain lateralization when there is an increase in within-hemisphere associations relative to between-hemisphere couplings. This will be an important topic in the next chapter, when I talk about the role of the corpus callosum in the origin of brain lateralization. Finally, Liu's work also showed a lateralized pattern in the cerebellum, mirroring the one observed in association cortices.

Finally, hemispheric lateralization has been observed in other brain regions like the hippocampus, a structure that participates in forming new memories (see Chapter 6). Epilepsy patients undergoing resection of a large part of the hippocampus in one hemisphere develop verbal memory impairments in the case of left hemisphere surgery, while in right hemisphere resections patients show deficits in memory of faces and abstract figures. In addition, there is functional evidence of preferential activation of the right hippocampus in spatial memory and the left in verbal memory (Springer 1981).

From Function to Form

An important issue regarding the early studies of brain lateralization was that although the functional evidence for hemispheric differences was very strong, there was no accompanying structural evidence of asymmetries in the human brain. In 1968, Norman Geschwind and Walter Levitsky contributed a now classical postmortem study showing notable hemispheric difference in an auditory region of the Sylvian fissure called planum temporale (see Chapter 2) (Geschwind and Levitsky 1968). This structure was reported to be larger in the left hemisphere than in the right in about two thirds of the population. Subsequently, Albert Galaburda, working with Geschwind and other collaborators, reported that the asymmetry of the planum temporale could be observed in the lateral surface of the hemisphere as a longer Sylvian fissure on the left side, an asymmetry that is already evident in the fetus (Galaburda et al. 1978a). Furthermore, based on skull morphology, they claimed that Neanderthals also had Sylvian asymmetries. In the same year, Galaburda, Geschwind and the expert on cytoarchitectonics, Friedrich Sanides, found asymmetry in the size of the cortical area Tpt, a posterior auditory area that occupies a large part of the planum temporale (Galaburda et al. 1978b).

I did my Ph.D. thesis in Eran Zaidel's lab, working on the interaction between brain asymmetry and callosal connectivity in humans. Therefore, I spent quite some time looking at the lateral surfaces of brains to measure the length and depth of the Sylvian fissure in postmortem specimens. There were no computer-based morphometric algorithms to automatize area or curved length measures, and I had to do all this using simple but ingenious methods, which nevertheless were time-consuming. Surprisingly, I found that the Sylvian fissure does not always run straight in the lateral surface of the hemisphere, but has an inflection point in the posterior aspect, from which it either curves upwardly to the parietal lobe, or remains horizontal (Fig. 4.3). The straight pattern is prevalent in the left hemisphere, while the upward deviation appears more often in the right

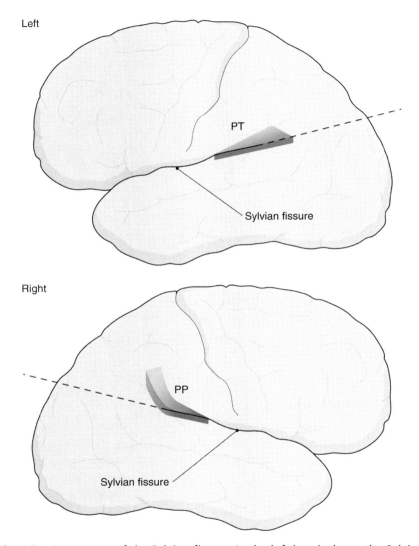

Left

Right

Fig. 4.3 Asymmetry of the Sylvian fissure. In the left hemisphere, the Sylvian fissure runs horizontally, while in the right hemisphere it usually turns upward. The planum temporale (PT) is located in the Sylvian fissure, and depicted here as a triangle. The posterior region of the planum temporale is called planum parietale (PP) when it runs into the parietal lobe. When the brain is sectioned in the plane of the Sylvian fissure, the region corresponding to the planum temporale appears smaller in the right hemisphere.

(Aboitiz et al. 1992; Ide et al. 1996). In the same line, the groups led by Sandra Witelson and by Lutz Jäncke and Heinz Steinmetz made similar observations and referred to the region in the upward deflection as the planum parietale (Jäncke et al. 1994; Witelson and Kigar 1992). It is possible that in many cases Geschwind and Levitsky sectioned the upward deviation when exposing the planum temporale in the Sylvian fissure. As the upward branch is more common in the right side, they may have sectioned it more often in the right than in the left hemisphere, yielding an apparent difference in size. In fact, when measuring the total length of the Sylvian fissure, considering both the horizontal and the upward branches, the asymmetry is minimized. Geschwind and Levitsky did observe significant asymmetry, but it was not so much in the depth or length of the Sylvian fissure as in its orientation.

However, the relationship between planum temporale asymmetry and functional lateralization has been elusive. For example, Jäncke and Steinmetz were unable to detect any correlation between different versions of the dichotic listening task and planum asymmetry (Jäncke and Steinmetz 1993). However, together with Gottfried Schlaug, the same authors noted strong asymmetry (larger in the left) of the planum temporale in musicians with perfect pitch, which is the capacity to recognize musical notes without a reference note, an ability Mozart shared with other musicians (Schlaug et al. 1995). Asymmetry in these subjects was greater when compared to asymmetries in other musicians and non-musicians. Other reports indicated abnormal asymmetry in dyslexia, autism, schizophrenia and other conditions, but again these findings have often been inconsistent.

Anatomical asymmetries have been found in other brain regions as well. My former student Andrés Ide observed fissurization is more pronounced on the left than on the right of Broca's region (Ide et al. 1999). Ide also described asymmetry in the sulcal pattern of the inferior parietal lobe and the cingulate cortex in the medial frontal lobe, with folding again being more marked in the left hemisphere. Shortly before our paper, Anne Foundas, Katryn Amunts, and collaborators reported leftward asymmetry in the volume of the pars triangularis (anterior Broca's area), as seen in MRI images (Keller et al. 2009). Furthermore, these authors described asymmetries in size (larger on the left) in areas

44 and 45, but there are also reports contrary to these findings. More recently, François Leroy, Ghislaine Dehaene-Lambertz and collaborators recently described robust asymmetry (larger on the right) in the depth of the superior temporal sulcus (below the Sylvian fissure) of humans but not apes, which is present before birth (Leroy et al. 2015). Another type of consistent brain asymmetry is the so-called petalias, corresponding to torsion of the hemispheres in which anteriorly, the right frontal lobe protrudes to the left of the midline, and posteriorly, the left occipital lobe protrudes to the right of the midline. Petalias are found in fossil hominids and great apes, although in modern humans they tend to be more significant (Galaburda et al. 1978a).

As I said above, although there is evidence of gross anatomical asymmetries in the human brain, many are not convinced that there is relationship to functional laterality. There are still many conflicting reports and the relationship with functional asymmetry has not found consistently. Perhaps measures of white matter tracts will be more reliable and correlate better with functional measures. Using neuroimaging tractographic techniques, Geoffrey Parker and his group were the first to document that the arcuate fasciculus and related fibers have more extensive connections in the left than in the right hemisphere, while the ventral language pathway showed a symmetric pattern (see Chapter 2) (Parker et al. 2005). This was confirmed by several authors like Angela Friederici and her team, who even showed the asymmetry of the arcuate fasciculus to be present in newborns, as opposed to the tracts making up the ventral language pathway, which are equivalent in the two hemispheres from birth (Perani et al. 2011). An important recent study by Marco Catani and colleagues used DTI to analyze the projections to Broca's area from the superior temporal lobe via the arcuate fasciculus, and from the inferior parietal lobe via the superior longitudinal fasciculus, in a large sample of subjects of different ages including monozygotic and dizygotic twins (see Chapter 2) (Budisavljevic et al. 2015). They found strong lateralization of both projections, which is established before adolescence and remains stable from then on. Notably, the projection from the superior temporal lobe (arcuate fasciculus) is more robust on the left hemisphere, while that from the inferior parietal lobe (superior longitudinal fasciculus) is more developed in the right hemisphere. These pathways were reported to be concordant among twins, although Michael Corballis and collaborators described a significant degree of variability in the arcuate fasciculus of monozygotic twins (Häberling et al. 2013). I must mention the apparent correspondence between the leftward asymmetries of the arcuate fasciculus and the planum temporale on the one hand, and between the rightward asymmetries of the ventral superior longitudinal fasciculus and the planum parietale on the other hand. Whether these tractographic and gross anatomy asymmetry measures in fact correlate is a matter for future studies.

Asymmetries in language regions have also been sought at the cellular level. In 1985 Arne Scheibel (my Ph.D. thesis co-advisor) showed that neurons in the left and right pars opercularis of Broca's area, and in the adjacent facial area of the premotor and motor cortices, displayed more dendritic branching on the left than the right side in subjects that had been right-handed in life (Scheibel et al. 1985). The asymmetry pattern was less consistent in left-handers. Likewise, my student Ricardo García studied a specific type of pyramidal neuron that contains an enzyme called acetylcholinesterase, and observed larger neuronal sizes in Broca's area than in its right hemisphere equivalent (García et al. 2004). These neurons are sensitive to the neurotransmitter acetylcholine, a neuromodulator that regulates cortical excitability and participates in memory mechanisms. In the auditory regions, Bob Jacobs (then a student of Scheibel's) made an exhaustive analysis of the dendritic structure of Wernicke's area, in which they found some sex differences, and reported only a slight left-hemisphere advantage in dendritic length that was however not always consistent at the individual level (Jacobs and Scheibel 1993; Jacobs et al. 1993). What did have a substantial effect on dendritic length was educational level, which speaks of an important effect of plasticity and literacy on the late dendritic development of the language regions. In the auditory regions, Ralf Galuske, Wolf Singer and others detected hemispheric differences in the cellular organization of Wernicke's area, cortical columns were about 20% further apart in the left hemisphere than in the right (Galuske et al. 2000). Not long after this Daniel Buxhoeveden and his group reported that the columns of the planum temporale were larger, with more interneuronal space and more neurons in humans than in monkeys (Buxhoeveden et al. 2001).

Furthermore, they only observed hemispheric asymmetry in column structure in humans, while non-human primates exhibited no asymmetry. Summarizing most studies suggest that asymmetries in the language regions and associated areas occur at different scales, from the cellular to the network to gross anatomy. However, the challenge remains to associate these traits at different anatomical levels, and correlate them with functional lateralization.

Monkeying with Brain Dominance

Another of Sperry's students, Charles Hamilton was probably the first to investigate functional cerebral lateralization in monkeys. In 1977, he published a study of split-brain monkeys, in which he found hemispheric equivalence for a variety of tasks (Hamilton 1977). Hamilton concluded that there was as yet little support for hemispheric specialization in non-human mammals, but it was worth pursuing the question a little more before abandoning it. In a subsequent study he and collaborators described a positive correlation between handedness in monkeys and the hemisphere that was faster in learning visual discrimination tasks (Hamilton and Vermeire 1982). From then on, he consistently observed hemispheric differences in facial discrimination (better in the right hemisphere) and spatial orientation (particularly to discriminate the angle of tilted lines, in which the left hemisphere was better). Hamilton concluded that monkeys are good models for studying the neurobiology of brain lateralization (Hamilton 1983; Hamilton and Vermeire 1988). Other studies used acoustic orienting tasks, notably Michael Petersen and his group. These authors presented stimuli randomly to the left or the right ear of monkeys, and compared discrimination capacity between the two sides (Petersen et al. 1978). They recorded calls from the Japanese macaque repertory and presented the stimuli to Japanese macaques and other macaque species that have distinct calls. They found a clear right ear preference only in Japanese macaques. Other monkey species learned the task equally well, but had no ear advantage, indicating that the laterality effect was restricted to species-specific calls. However, an imaging analysis by Ricardo Gil-da-Costa and collaborators observed that species-specific calls elicit strong bilateral activation of the homologs of Broca and Wernicke's areas in macaques (see Chapter 7) (Gil-da-Costa et al. 2006). There may be a difference between behavioral lateralization and lateralization as seen in brain imaging, and the two measures may not always correspond. Other studies have reported left hemisphere advantage for same-species calls in domestic dogs, the house mouse and other species. Notably, a very recent imaging study found lateralization for human speech perception in dogs, with left-hemisphere dominance for perception of words, and right hemisphere dominance for intonation patterns (Andics et al. 2016).

Anatomical asymmetries in regions comparable to human language areas were soon reported in non-human primates. Patrick Gannon and collaborators reported that the planum temporale was larger on the left side in 17 of 18 chimpanzees (a proportion higher than in humans!), and found a human-like rightward asymmetry of the planum parietale (Gannon et al. 1998, 2005). These findings were confirmed by William Hopkins, James Rilling and others, who noted that a planum temporale was present only in great apes and not in monkeys, and that it was asymmetric in all species of apes (Hopkins et al. 1998). Furthermore, Hopkins and colleagues also reported a correlation between the hand preference for clapping and planum asymmetries (chimps usually clap with one hand over the other, and the dominant hand is considered to be the one above, which keeps the rhythm) (Meguerditchian et al. 2012). Broca's area was not left behind. Claudio Cantalupo and Hopkins used MRI reconstructions of the inferior frontal lobe to report significant asymmetry in the homologue of the posterior Broca's area of chimps (the pars opercularis), but this has been contested on the basis that the individual variability is too great (Cantalupo and Hopkins 2001; Sherwood et al. 2003). Considering these and other findings, Hopkins and colleagues have concluded that asymmetries in gross brain anatomy are present in non-human apes, but are less pronounced than in humans (Hopkins 2013; Meguerditchian et al. 2013). Importantly, human-like size asymmetry in the chimp arcuate fasciculus was also reported, which to my knowledge is the only measure yet made of this structure in non-human primates (Rilling et al. 2008). More recently, Dietrich Stout, Todd Preuss and collaborators reported asymmetry in the superior longitudinal fasciculus of the chimpanzee, which I will discuss below in the context of tool making (Hecht et al. 2015a).

Lateralization of facial expressions is also found in non-human primates, particularly associated with vocalization behavior. In chimpanzees, voluntary communicative vocalizations are accompanied by more movements of the right side of the face (mainly left hemisphere), while more automatic, emotional signals appear more intensely on the left side of the face. Likewise, communicative gestures and sounds made with the lips and mouth show a right face bias (left hemisphere), whereas innate vocalizations display left facial dominance. In addition, emotional perception has also been reported to be asymmetric. Jacques Vauclair and colleagues have extensively documented lateralization for emotional gestures in baboons, and have shown a right hemisphere advantage for emotional perception (Vauclair et al. 2013). Thus, although studies of brain dominance in non-human primates have not always reached consensus, they do suggest a weaker degree of lateralization and asymmetry than in humans, sometimes in the same direction as humans. This brings us to the question of whether these asymmetries provided the scaffolding for the origin of language lateralization in the human species.

Throwing with the Right

Since Broca's time, the association of handedness with speech dominance in the left hemisphere of most people has been a subject of interest. About 90% of people are right-handed, but this depends on the criterion used for assessing handedness. In humans, handedness for object-use usually appears before 1 year of age and becomes fully established by 3 years of age. On the other hand, left-handers are not considered mirror images of right-handers, but rather represent a less lateralized group than most right-handers (Springer 1981, Hellige 1993). Thus, the hemispheric coincidence for handedness and speech, and the use of tools associated with handedness in early humans, have led many to speculate that language circuits evolved from a left-hemisphere already specialized for skilled actions like throwing and making tools.

One of the most enthusiastic proponents of this association is William Calvin, who wrote a highly popular book in 1983 in which he attributed the ability to throw objects with one hand to the development of handedness and other lateralized skills, including language and writing (Calvin 1983). Calvin speculated that human babies were carried with their mothers' left arm and hip because they could better feel the heart-beat, leaving the right arm free to collect food, point to indicate directions, and throw objects. He further argued that most females carried their babies on the left side, while fathers, who like mothers, are also predominantly right-handers, have no side preference for carrying (personally, I am right handed and have carried my own babies preferentially with the left arm!). According to Calvin, this implies that right-handed bias originated as an adaptation by women for carrying their infants. Partly in support of Calvins's hypothesis, a study of the group led by William Hopkins observed that in the chimpanzee there is a relationship between the ability to throw objects, communicative ability and the white-to-gray ratio in Broca's area homolog (Hopkins et al. 2012). However, as I will argue below, the relationship between handedness and speech in humans is not as clear-cut as one would expect.

Another advocate of the handedness theory of language origins is Michael Corballis, who has hypothesized a specific role of handedness, and particularly manual gestures in the origin of speech (Corballis 1991). His proposal is largely based on the correlation between hand dominance and hemispheric dominance for speech across people, in which right-hand dominance in the left hemisphere was probably the initial factor leading to right hemisphere dominance for visuospatial processing as a secondary event. However, the association between right-handedness and left-sided language lateralization is not as strong as expected. According to some studies by Corballis' group (Badzakova-Trajkov et al. 2010), about 97% of right-handers, but also 70% of left-handers, show left hemisphere dominance for language. Furthermore, other lateralized capacities like spatial attention (in which the right hemisphere tends to be dominant) do not correlate with either language or handedness lateralization, which suggests that lateralization in different skills may be relatively independent. Additional studies by Corballis' group reported that handedness and language lateralization in the left hemisphere correlates with right-hemisphere specialization for perceiving facial emotions

(Badzakova-Trajkov et al. 2015). According to them, left-hemisphere dominance for both facial and manual communicative gestures may have driven the displacement of facial emotion processing to the right hemisphere.

Dorothy Bishop, working with Magriet Groen and other collaborators, investigated the possible correlation between three tests for handedness, and a language lateralization measure based on ultrasound assessment of blood flow through the left and right middle cerebral arteries while subjects verbally recalled a speechless video (Groen et al. 2013). They found limited correlation between handedness and language lateralization, in which handedness predicted no more than 16% of the total variance in language lateralization. Moreover, they strongly recommended against using handedness as a proxy for language or speech lateralization as there is considerable independence between the two variables. Furthermore, Bishop recently reviewed the literature on the relationship between language disorders and brain lateralization and concluded that contrary to current notions, weak cerebral lateralization is unlikely to be genetically associated with language impairments (Bishop 2013). Alternatively, she argues that lateralization is not a stable heritable character, and that alterations of normal asymmetric development are more likely the consequence than the cause of language impairments. In my opinion, the relationship between handedness and speech lateralization remains obscure. On the one hand, the two traits are strongly asymmetric in the population, and both are in the same direction, which intuitively suggests that they may be related. However, looking more closely this relationship tends to vanish. A possible explanation is that there is an underlying trait biasing handedness and speech laterality in the same direction, even if the two variables have no direct relationship between them.

There are many reports on hand preferences in non-human animals. Asymmetry in paw preference is common among individuals of a species, but in different directions in distinct subjects, so that at the population level there is no left or right bias. However, kangaroos and wallabies are strongly left-handed, a characteristic associated with bipedalism among marsupials that may have to do with the evolution of human handedness (Giljov et al. 2015). Additionally, some species of parrots have strong foot-grasping lateralization, sometimes to the right side, and more often to the left. Some days ago while writing this book, I saw a group of seven wild Argentinian parrots (a pest in my country, Chile) eating dandelions, all of them handling the flowers with their left foot, and standing on the fence with their right. This might have been just chance, but in any event it was a curious observation. Unfortunately, handedness is not so clear in non-human primates. Peter MacNeilage reported that most primates display a left-hand preference to reach for objects, which he speculated was related to coordinated preference for object manipulation with the right hand, which may have served as scaffolding for tool use in early humans (MacNeilage 2013). As I mentioned, some studies of apes, including those of Hopkins' group and of the team led by Jacques Vauclair, have described hand preferences for reaching, clapping, handling, tool use and manual gestures. Despite the attractiveness of these reports, other studies have not confirmed a consistent species-level hand preference among non-human primates. Reviewing this literature, Tecumseh Fitch and Stephanie Braccini reasonably concluded that if there is a handedness population effect among monkeys or apes, it is relatively small, depending on the specific task observed and on the difficulty of the task (Fitch and Braccini 2013). This points to a specifically human amplification of handedness, perhaps related to full bipedalism and the acquisition of tool-making capacities.

Man the Toolmaker

A more reliable association of handedness is toolmaking, which requires a great deal of bimanual coordination. In the mid-twentieth century, Kenneth Oakley published an influential book called *Man the Tool Maker*, in which he eloquently argued that toolmaking was the main factor that propelled human and human brain evolution (Oakley 1949). Early human-made tools required a painstaking procedure to be produced, and our early ancestors must have spent large amounts of time making them. Dietrich Stout has studied the cognitive processes involved in making stone tools and has shown that this is an extremely laborious and difficult task (Stout and Chaminade 2012, 2016). Collaborating with Tierry Chaminade and other colleagues, Stout has shown that learning to make such tools involves different processes in time (Hecht et al. 2015b). In one study, Stout's students were PET scanned after a toolmaking session, and in another study students were scanned by fMRI while passively viewing movies of toolmaking apprentices. In both studies, they found that at early stages of learning, students show increased activity in visual areas, but as they become more skillful, they started activating bilateral regions of the inferior parietal lobes and ventral premotor areas. Stout and colleagues also compared brain activation while learning either the more primitive Oldowan technique or the more elaborate Acheulean technique. They found that the latter was associated with increased activation in the right inferior frontal gyrus (roughly equivalent to Broca's region in the right hemisphere), and bilaterally in other brain regions, which to them implies increasing demands of cognitive control for making the more sophisticated tools. Furthermore, Stout and Erin Hecht performed a tractographic study of the superior longitudinal fasciculus that connects the parietal and frontal lobes, areas that showed increased activation with toolmaking (Hecht et al. 2015a). Notably, they found that this tract is larger in humans than in apes, particularly its ventral aspect, which is also larger on the right side in humans. This finding agrees with the study of Sanja Budisavljevic, Marco Catani and others, mentioned above, and may provide a useful functional explanation for this asymmetry (Budisavljevic et al. 2015). Nonetheless, the possibility I mentioned before is also a plausible explanation, namely that the rightward asymmetry of the superior longitudinal fasciculus relates to the asymmetry of the planum parietale, and the leftward asymmetry of the arcuate sulcus relates to the asymmetry of the planum temporale.

There is a benefit to left and right hand specialization in toolmaking, so that in bimanual tasks there is a division of labor and conflict is minimized. In toolmaking, one hand holds the object while the other (usually the right) makes repetitive and rhythmic movements to shape the future tool. Natalie Uomini and others have characterized this as complementary role differentiation, in which one hand (usually the left) performs low-frequency movements, changing the position and orientation of the tool, while the other hand (usually the right) performs more accurate high frequency movements (Uomini 2009; Uomini and Meyer 2013). According to this view, hemispheric dominance arose due to the separation of two neural processing strategies that compete with each other, one involved in complex sequencing behaviors like skilled hand movements, and the other relating to coarse motor programs. Similarly, Stout and Chaminade argue that tool manufacturing is a hierarchically organized behavior, resembling the nested and recursive structure of human syntax (Stout and Chaminade 2012). Finally, Thomas Morgan and colleagues found that students learned to make stone tool faster if they were verbally instructed, which points to a co-evolution between toolmaking and speech (see Chapter 8) (Morgan et al. 2015). However, there are some dissenting opinions. Mark Moore and Yinika Preston forced an experienced human toolmaker to focus on each step of flake making instead of thinking of the final result while the subject was producing an Oldowan-type hand axe (Moore and Perston, 2016). The resulting tool was a reasonable instrument, without having benefited from a predetermined goal. The authors argue that the geometrical constraints of stone fracture may yield results of apparently complex thought. Even if the authors are right, this toolmaking strategy requires a good deal of bimanual coordination and functional specialization, so that is possible that in early stages of toolmaking behavior, our ancestors did not manufacture tools according to an elaborate plan but just found that breaking stones would leave them with useful sharp edges. In later stages, planning behavior may have been needed to make more sophisticated tools, as in the Mousterian industry. Again, we may never know exactly how our ancestors planned toolmaking, but most likely they had to rely on bimanual coordination and hand specialization to perform such tasks.

Hand-based toolmaking is not uniquely human, however. Archaeological evidence from chimpanzee sites some 1–4 thousand years ago, and more recently, from pre-Columbian sites attributed to Brazilian capuchin monkeys, indicate that non-human primates have been using stones to break hard shelled food for some time (Haslam et al. 2016). South American capuchin monkeys usually use stones to crack open nuts or digging. More recently, they have been observed breaking stones into sharp-edged flakes similar to early hominid tools, although they apparently do not use them for any purpose (Proffitt et al. 2016). Modern day chimpanzees capture termites by cleaning a stick and poking it into a hole in a termite nest and then removing the stick and licking off the termites adhering to it. In this and other toolmaking or tool-using behaviors, some groups have been found to be right dominant, and others left dominant (Humle and Matsuzawa 2009). Furthermore, individuals with stronger handedness scores are more efficient in this behavior (McGrew and Marchant, 1999). Thus, there is a tendency for the development of hand preference in individuals, but it does not reach a population level in which the large majority of subjects consistently prefer one hand to the other, as in humans. Analyzing the shape of prehistoric tools, Uomini has concluded that our direct ancestors like *Homo habilis* and Neanderthals were predominantly right-handed, which fits the toolmaking hypothesis of right-handedness (Uomini 2009). What would be the advantage of having a majority of right-handers (or left handers)? It might be related to tool use; all left-handers know what it is to live in a right-handed world, where most things are made to be used with the right hand. Nonetheless, there might be some advantages in being different from the majority, which would make left handers more fit for some tasks. For example, left-handed fighters, especially boxers, are known to be more difficult to deal with by the majority of right-handers. This might help explain the maintenance of left-handers in our species, as long as they are a minority.

In summary, handedness may relate to different kinds of tasks, the left hand involved in low-level but skilled sequential processes, while the right hand provides broader contextual and support elements. These two properties have also been associated with brain lateralization, the left hemisphere emphasizing sequential processing while the right hemisphere is more involved with gestaltic and visuospatial processing. It may be that a weak initial hemispheric bias independently shaped the asymmetries of sensorimotor systems involved in speech, and in toolmaking. This suggests an ancient but relatively weak developmental tendency for hemispheric specialization, from which different functions like toolmaking and speech benefitted independently. This is not to say that toolmaking and speech did not interact in human evolution. The point is that the developmental mechanisms may not be directly related to each other.

Whence Asymmetry?

As I said, language and handedness may not be the only or the most common instance of lateralization or asymmetry in animals. There are other ancient lateralized functions in the brain that may have contributed to frame asymmetric networks in which functions like language and handedness found ground for hemispheric specialization (Springer 1981; Hellige 1993). Furthermore, cerebral asymmetries have been described in several non-primate species (even in fish and invertebrates), and in systems far from hand control or communication. For instance, we all have a preferred foot to kick with, and a preferred eye to look with (which some studies have related to handedness, particularly throwing capacity). Likewise, eye preferences are common in birds. Chicks develop a visual asymmetry based on the enhanced exposure to light of the eye that faces the eggshell while the other eye faces the body as the chick folds its neck inside the egg. The eye more exposed to light (usually the left) is better at detecting movement and shapes, while the eye less exposed to light is better at discriminating details like food grains. This asymmetry is also modulated by maternal hormone levels at egg laying, and during development induces cognitive asymmetries at central levels. Similar eye asymmetries have been reported in fish (Güntürkün and Ocklenburg 2017). Perceptual lateralization as seen in the chicken eye might lead to selective disadvantages, as relevant stimuli can appear on any side and one would think that the animal might be better off having equal perceptual abilities on both sides. However, studies indicate that both in birds and fish, more asymmetric individuals are more efficient in foraging for food in presence of predators (Güntürkün and Ocklenburg 2017). More spectacular and related to human speech, songbirds have developed a lateralized circuit for singing that relates to peripheral asymmetry in the innervation and musculature of the syrinx (analogous to our vocal tract), which is the subject of Chapter 9.

Functional interpretations of the evolution of lateralization and asymmetry abound, although no one has as yet provided a coherent perspective of this phenomenon. It may well be that asymmetries serve different kinds of functions, and cannot be pooled together in one overarching evolutionary explanation. Others have argued that in vertebrates, brain asymmetries for cognitive functions or behaviors serve a specialization rule, like the time versus frequency processing conflict mentioned above; or that there are some functions that are better performed in a well-packed network, and distributing this network in two hemispheres would hamper processing efficiency. In this line, complex motor functions performed by midline structures in speech (the tongue and larynx) and birdsong (the syrinx) might benefit from being specialized in only one hemisphere to favor neuronal coordination. Another possibility is that brain dominance is the consequence of another adaptive process like increased brain size, which would favor hemispheric independence, again for the benefit of processing efficiency. Giorgio Vallortigara and Leslie Rogers have argued that species-level lateralization results from social selection mechanisms that promote behavioral coordination among individuals, in which there might be interference by certain socially relevant cognitive functions (like sequence and pattern discrimination), which is solved by hemispheric specialization (Vallortigara et al. 1999). Possibly like human speech, left-right dominance in other species builds on a preexisting hemispheric bias that has arisen for reasons unrelated to the function that is currently being selected. Subsequently, the new function may benefit from being lateralized in one hemisphere.

However, the biological development of asymmetries may in the end show more cross-species commonalities than its selective causes. The field of comparative genetics has advanced impressively in recent years, evidencing highly conserved genetic regulatory mechanisms for the development of widely different traits. Therefore, although cerebral lateralization may respond to different functional requirements across species, there may be restricted genetic and developmental mechanisms underlying these different instances. The development of brain asymmetries was for a long time a little examined topic, and very few hypotheses appeared about the embryonic or genetic mechanisms underlying it. Below, I will review some of the studies to unveil the developmental and genetic processes underlying brain asymmetry in humans and in other species.

In the 1980s Norman Geschwind, Peter Behan and Albert Galaburda provided one of the earliest interpretations of the developmental origins of human brain lateralization. In his clinical practice, Geschwind noticed a curious association between left-handedness, developmental learning disorders, immune-related conditions and migraines. Geschwind and Behan published a first article reporting these findings, and then Geschwind started working with Galaburda in an extensive three-part review, emphasizing the intrauterine environment as a main determinant of anatomical asymmetries (Geschwind and Behan 1982;

Geschwind and Galaburda 1985). Abnormal sex hormone levels disrupted normal asymmetric development and produced immune-related pathologies as a side effect. Geschwind passed away in 1984 and did not live to see this article published in 1985. Subsequent studies in humans and other species have reported sex differences in lateralization, and relations between hormone levels and brain lateralization and anatomical asymmetry, but at this point the topic remains controversial.

Is there a genetic determinant of human brain dominance? As far as we have reviewed here, the evidence for this proposal is not strong. Likewise, studies of gene expression levels have not revealed significant differences between cerebral hemispheres. There have been a few large-scale studies of gene polymorphism (i.e. high-frequency alleles of a gene in a population that are sometimes associated with phenotypic differences). For example, Philippe Pinel, Stanislaas Dehaene, and others reported that alleles of the speech-associated gene FOXP2 and of related genes are more common in individuals showing altered patterns of brain lateralization as seen in functional imaging studies (Pinel et al. 2012). Timothy Crow, a psychiatrist well known for his groundbreaking classificatory work on schizophrenia (Crow 2008), has advanced a more theoretical proposal. Crow has argued for some time that this pathology is found only in humans (which is very likely), and appeared as an unwanted consequence of acquiring language. In his words, schizophrenia is the price we have to pay for having language. His proposal is that there was a single genetic mutation occurring in the sex chromosomes some 6 million years ago, in the last common ancestor of humans and chimps, which affected some cell-surface adhesion molecules. A subsequent mutation producing a right-shift factor that propelled language and increased risk of schizophrenia appeared about 150–200 thousand years ago. While some association has been reported between abnormal brain lateralization and schizophrenia (Royer et al. 2015), the identification and specific functions of Crow's putative genes has been more confusing than elucidating.

It is possible that more insights into asymmetric development will come not directly from language-related regions, but from much simpler but no less important brain structures. One such system is the epithalamus, a small region in the roof of the diencephalon (its name means "over the thalamus") that connects with several lower brain centers that regulate basic behaviors, including reproduction, feeding, water intake and basic components of emotional behavior including stress response. The epithalamus contains mainly two components, the pineal gland or parietal eye, and the parapineal organ, two eye-shaped structures located in the midline. In some vertebrates, these organs are exposed to the surface and serve a photoreceptive function that regulates, via the hormone melatonin, the sleep/wake cycle according to ambient light. In other vertebrates like mammals, these structures remain buried inside the braincase, indirectly receiving photic input via retinal projections. The pineal and parapineal organs are supported by a small stalk that contains the habenular nucleus, which connects them to other brain structures. The habenula and associated nuclei have been the subject of many recent studies about their role in the control of behavior and neuropsychiatric conditions (Hikosaka 2010). Notably, in many species the parapineal organ is located on the left side of the midline, and sends its projections only to the left habenula, which is consequently highly asymmetric in size, neuronal composition and internal structure. The asymmetry of the habenular nuclei has been reported in species from mammals to fish, particularly in the zebrafish, a common aquarium fish that is also amenable to genetic and developmental research. Consequently, this little fish has been used as an animal model to study the mechanisms underlying cerebral asymmetries in vertebrates (Concha and Wilson 2001). Furthermore, in zebrafish and in other fish, habenular asymmetries have been found to relate to behavioral lateralization, fear responses, anxiety and other characters like asymmetries in eye development in flounders. More interestingly, studies by Miguel Concha and Stephen Wilson established that the direction of habenular asymmetry in the zebrafish is initially random (left or right) in development, but the expression of a gene called *Nodal*, and the signaling cascade associated with it, is critical in directing this asymmetry to the left side (Concha et al. 2009). Other factors, including environmental stimuli and hormonal levels, can also modulate the robustness of this asymmetry. Thus, the action of *Nodal* produces a consistent shift in the direction of lateralization, making it a population-level phenomenon that otherwise would be obscured by the random distribution of left- or right-sided asymmetries. Moreover, *Nodal* controls asymmetric body development in very primitive animals that lack a pineal or parapineal organ, indicating that its function is more general than just determining epithalamic asymmetry. In humans, *Nodal* and other genes participate in generating asymmetry of critical structures like the heart and lungs, but evidence for its involvement in brain lateralization or asymmetry is still lacking (Hirokawa et al. 2006). In fact, humans with situs inversus, where asymmetric organs are placed in a mirror image pattern with respect to normals, display normal handedness and language lateralization (Güntürkün and Ocklenburg 2017). In this line, a pioneering study led by Caleb Webber and Silvia Paracchini used the technique of meta-analysis to unveil common genetic determinants of handedness (Brandler et al. 2013). Meta-analysis is a systematic, statistical analysis of data reported in large numbers of publications to find common ground that may be obscured by inherent errors in each of the studies. In their study, Webber and Paracchini reported an intriguing association between a variant or polymorphism in a gene called PCSK6, known to regulate *Nodal* activity, and relative hand skill in dyslexics but not in the general population. Other genes are LRRTM1, whose methylation patterns have been linked to handedness, and genes associated with glutamatergic neurotransmission (Güntürkün and Ocklenburg 2017).

A word of caution is needed here. I am not even close to saying that there is only one gene involved in asymmetric development; we have seen that several laterality measures do not show significant correlations between them, which may be produced by environmental effects, or by different genetic systems involved in them. The development of asymmetries may be highly flexible, being modulated by many epigenetic and genetic variables. Nonetheless, some genes may participate in many instances of asymmetric development, in different organs and species. Thus, studying the development of asymmetries in other systems may yield clues to the mechanisms underlying language lateralization. However, as I mentioned above, genetic research on lateralization or asymmetry is still in its infancy.

Lateralization of brain function and asymmetry began as a brilliant finding that promised to explain many of our conflicting behaviors and provide ground for philosophical and pseudo-philosophical interpretations. However, as research went into the details, the picture was found to be much more complex than expected, and it was difficult to make broad generalizations from the obtained results. Much of the evidence was controversial if not confusing, and a unified model of functional lateralization is still lacking. However, there are some facts more or less established. The left hemisphere supports more language-related functions than the right hemisphere, particularly those associated with the dorsal stream of language processing (sequencing, articulation and time analysis). The ventral stream apparently has a strong bilateral component. Likewise, there is rightward lateralization of some functions like visuospatial processing, emotional responses and prosody, but these functions are actually bilateral, the right hemisphere being only better at them than the right hemisphere in most people. The relationship between structural asymmetry and functional lateralization is still not clear, and there is not yet a good explanatory hypothesis for these relationships. A promising candidate to unveil such associations is the study of white matter connectivity, which to date has provided more consistent results than gross anatomy measures. Finally, as I said, our understanding of the development and genetics of brain asymmetry is weak to say the least. In the rest of this book, we will have to keep in mind that at least some components of the dorsal language pathway are better developed in the left hemisphere, and that this may provide benefit for some fast processing functions like sequencing and time analysis. However, as I once heard Alfonso Caramazza say, it may not matter which hemisphere does any specific function, what is really important is to know how it is processed.

References

Aboitiz F, Scheibel AB, Zaidel E (1992) Morphometry of the Sylvian fissure and the corpus callosum, with emphasis on sex differences. Brain 115:1521–1541

Andics A, Gábor A, Gácsi M, Faragó T, Szabó D, Miklósi Á (2016) Neural mechanisms for lexical processing in dogs. Science 353:1030–1032

Badzakova-Trajkov G, Häberling IS, Roberts RP, Corballis MC (2010) Cerebral asymmetries: complementary and independent processes. PLoS One 5:e9682

Badzakova-Trajkov G, Corballis MC, Häberling IS (2015) Complementarity or independence of hemispheric specializations? A brief review. Neuropsychologia 93:386–393

Belin P, Zatorre RJ (2000) "What", "where" and "how" in auditory cortex. Nat Neurosci 3:965–966

Bishop DV (2013) Cerebral asymmetry and language development: cause, correlate, or consequence? Science 340:1230531

Brandler WM, Morris AP, Evans DM, Scerri TS, Kemp JP, Timpson NJ, St Pourcain B, Smith GD, Ring SM, Stein J, Monaco AP, Talcott JB, Fisher SE, Webber C, Paracchini S (2013) Common variants in left/right asymmetry genes and pathways are associated with relative hand skill. PLoS Genet 9:e1003751

Bryden MP (1962) Order of report in dichotic listening. Can J Psychol 16:291–299

Budisavljevic S, Dell'Acqua F, Rijsdijk FV, Kane F, Picchioni M, McGuire P, Toulopoulou T, Georgiades A, Kalidindi S, Kravariti E, Murray RM, Murphy DG, Craig MC, Catani M (2015) Age-related differences and heritability of the Perisylvian language networks. J Neurosci 35:12625–12634

Buxhoeveden DP, Switala AE, Litaker M, Roy E, Casanova MF (2001) Lateralization of minicolumns in human planum temporale is absent in nonhuman primate cortex. Brain Behav Evol 57:349–358

Calvin WH (1983) The Throwing Madonna: Essays on the Brain. McGraw-Hill, New York

Cantalupo C, Hopkins WD (2001) Asymmetric Broca's area in great apes. Nature 414:505

Chait M, Greenberg S, Arai T, Simon JZ, Poeppel D (2015) Multi-time resolution analysis of speech: evidence from psychophysics. Front Neurosci 9:214

Cogan GB, Thesen T, Carlson C, Doyle W, Devinsky O, Pesaran B (2014) Sensory-motor transformations for speech occur bilaterally. Nature 507:94–98

Concha ML, Wilson SW (2001) Asymmetry in the epithalamus of vertebrates. J Anat 199:63–84

Concha ML, Signore IA, Colombo A (2009) Mechanisms of directional asymmetry in the zebrafish epithalamus. Semin Cell Dev Biol 20:498–509

Corballis MC (1991) The Lopsided Ape. Evolution of the Generative Mind. Oxford University Press, Oxford

Corballis MC (2014) Left brain, right brain: facts and fantasies. PLoS Biol 12: e1001767

Corballis MC (2015a) A life of splits. Brain 138:3128–3130

Corballis MC (2015b) What's left in language? Beyond the classical model. Ann N Y Acad Sci 1359:14–29

Crow TJ (2008) The "big bang" theory of the origin of psychosis and the faculty of language. Schizophr Res 102:31–52

Darwin C (1872) The Expression of Emotions in Man and Animals. John Murray, London

Fitch WT, Braccini SN (2013) Primate laterality and the biology and evolution of human handedness: a review and synthesis. Ann N Y Acad Sci 1288:70–85

Galaburda AM, LeMay M, Kemper TL, Geschwind N (1978a) Right-left asymmetrics in the brain. Science 199:852–856

Galaburda AM, Sanides F, Geschwind N (1978b) Human brain. Cytoarchitectonic left-right asymmetries in the temporal speech region. Arch Neurol 35:812–817

Galuske RA, Schlote W, Bratzke H, Singer W (2000) Interhemispheric asymmetries of the modular structure in human temporal cortex. Science 289:1946–1949

Gannon PJ, Holloway RL, Broadfield DC, Braun AR (1998) Asymmetry of chimpanzee planum temporale: humanlike pattern of Wernicke's brain language area homolog. Science 279:220–222

Gannon PJ, Kheck NM, Braun AR, Holloway RL (2005) Planum parietale of chimpanzees and orangutans: a comparative resonance of human-like planum temporale asymmetry. Anat Rec A Discov Mol Cell Evol Biol 287:1128–1141

García RR, Montiel JF, Villalón AU, Gatica MA, Aboitiz F (2004) AChE-rich magnopyramidal neurons have a left-right size asymmetry in Broca's area. Brain Res 1026:313–316

Gazzaniga MS (1998) Brain and conscious experience. Adv Neurol 77:181–192; discussion 192–193

Gazzaniga MS (2000) Cerebral specialization and interhemispheric communication: does the corpus callosum enable the human condition? Brain 123:1293–1326

Gazzaniga MS (2015a) The split-brain: rooting consciousness in biology. Proc Natl Acad Sci U S A 111:18093–18094

Gazzaniga MS (2015b) Tales from Both Sides of the Brain. Harper Collins, New York.

Gazzaniga MS, Sperry RW (1967) Language after section of the cerebral commissures. Brain 90:131–148

Gazzaniga MS, Bogen JE, Sperry RW (1962) Some functional effects of sectioning the cerebral commissures in man. Proc Natl Acad Sci U S A 48:1765–1769

Gazzaniga MS, Bogen JE, Sperry RW (1965) Observations on visual perception
after disconnexion of the cerebral hemispheres in man. Brain 88:221–236

Geschwind N (1965) Disconnexion syndromes in animals and man. Brain
88:237–294; 585–644

Geschwind N, Behan P (1982) Left-handedness: association with immune
disease, migraine, and developmental learning disorder. Proc Natl Acad
Sci U S A 79:5097–5100

Geschwind N, Galaburda AM (1985) Cerebral lateralization. Biological
mechanisms, associations, and pathology: I, II and III. A hypothesis and a
program for research. Arch Neurol 42: 428–459; 521–552; 634–654

Geschwind N, Levitsky W (1968) Human brain: left-right asymmetries in
temporal speech region. Science 161:186–187

Gil-da-Costa R, Martin A, Lopes MA, Muñoz M, Fritz JB, Braun AR (2006)
Species-specific calls activate homologs of Broca's and Wernicke's areas in
the macaque. Nat Neurosci 9:1064–1070

Giljov A, Karenina K, Ingram J, Malashichev Y (2015) Parallel Emergence of
True Handedness in the Evolution of Marsupials and Placentals. Curr Biol
25:1878–1884

Groen MA, Whitehouse AJ, Badcock NA, Bishop DV (2013) Associations
between handedness and cerebral lateralisation for language: a comparison
of three measures in children. PLoS One 8:e64876

Güntürkün O, Ocklenburg S (2017) Ontogenesis of Lateralization. Neuron
94:249–263

Häberling IS, Badzakova-Trajkov G, Corballis MC (2013) Asymmetries of the
arcuate fasciculus in monozygotic twins: genetic and nongenetic influences.
PLoS One 8:e52315

Hamilton CR (1977) An assessment of hemispheric specialization in monkeys.
nAnn N Y Acad Sci 299:222–232

Hamilton CR (1983) Lateralization for orientation in split-brain monkeys.
Behav Brain Res 10:399–403

Hamilton CR, Vermeire BA (1982) Hemispheric differences in split-brain
monkeys learning sequential comparisons. Neuropsychologia 20:691–698

Hamilton CR, Vermeire BA (1988) Complementary hemispheric specialization in monkeys. Science 242:1691–1694

Haslam M, Luncz LV, Staff RA, Bradshaw F, Ottoni EB, Falótico T (2016)
Pre-Columbian monkey tools. Curr Biol 26:R521–R522

Hecht EE, Gutman DA, Bradley BA, Preuss TM, Stout D (2015a) Virtual dissection and comparative connectivity of the superior longitudinal fasciculus in chimpanzees and humans. Neuroimage 108:124–137

Hecht EE, Gutman DA, Khreisheh N, Taylor SV, Kilner J, Faisal AA, Bradley BA, Chaminade T, Stout D (2015b) Acquisition of Paleolithic toolmaking abilities involves structural remodeling to inferior frontoparietal regions. Brain Struct Funct 220:2315–2331

Hellige JB (1993) Hemispheric Asymmetry. What's Right and What's Left. Harvard University Press, Cambridge

Hickok G (2014) The Myth of Mirror Neurons: The Real Neuroscience of Communication And Cognition. Norton Press, New York

Hickok G, Poeppel D (2007) The cortical organization of speech processing. Nat Rev Neurosci 8:393–402

Hikosaka O (2010) The habenula: from stress evasion to value-based decision-making. Nat Rev Neurosci 11:503–513

Hirokawa N, Tanaka Y, Okada Y, Takeda S (2006) Nodal flow and the generation of left-right asymmetry. Cell 125:33–45

Hopkins WD (2013) Neuroanatomical asymmetries and handedness in chimpanzees (Pan troglodytes): a case for continuity in the evolution of hemispheric specialization. Ann N Y Acad Sci 1288:17–35

Hopkins WD, Marino L, Rilling JK, MacGregor LA (1998) Planum temporale asymmetries in great apes as revealed by magnetic resonance imaging (MRI). Neuroreport 9:2913–2918

Hopkins WD, Russell JL, Schaeffer JA (2012) The neural and cognitive correlates of aimed throwing in chimpanzees: a magnetic resonance image and behavioural study on a unique form of social tool use. Philos Trans R Soc Lond B Biol Sci 367:37–47

Humle T, Matsuzawa T (2009) Laterality in hand use across four tool-use behaviors among the wild chimpanzees of Bossou, Guinea, West Africa. Am J Primatol 71:40–48

Ide A, Rodríguez E, Zaidel E, Aboitiz F (1996) Bifurcation patterns in the human sylvian fissure: hemispheric and sex differences. Cereb Cortex 6:717–725

Ide A, Dolezal C, Fernández M, Labbé E, Mandujano R, Montes S, Segura P, Verschae G, Yarmuch P, Aboitiz F (1999) Hemispheric differences in variability of fissural patterns in parasylvian and cingulate regions of human brains. J Comp Neurol 410:235–242

Jacobs B, Scheibel AB (1993) A quantitative dendritic analysis of Wernicke's area in humans. I. Lifespan changes. J Comp Neurol 327:83–96

Jacobs B, Schall M, Scheibel AB (1993) A quantitative dendritic analysis of Wernicke's area in humans. II. Gender, hemispheric, and environmental factors. J Comp Neurol 327:97–111

Jäncke L, Steinmetz H (1993) Auditory lateralization and planum temporale asymmetry. Neuroreport 5:169–172

Jäncke L, Schlaug G, Huang Y, Steinmetz H (1994) Asymmetry of the planum parietale. Neuroreport 5:1161–1163

Keller SS, Crow T, Foundas A, Amunts K, Roberts N (2009) Broca's area: nomenclature, anatomy, typology and asymmetry. Brain Lang 109:29–48

Leroy F, Cai Q, Bogart SL, Dubois J, Coulon O, Monzalvo K, Fischer C, Glasel H, Van der Haegen L, Bénézit A, Lin CP, Kennedy DN, Ihara AS, Hertz-Pannier L, Moutard ML, Poupon C, Brysbaert M, Roberts N, Hopkins WD, Mangin JF, Dehaene-Lambertz G (2015) New human-specific brain landmark: the depth asymmetry of superior temporal sulcus. Proc Natl Acad Sci U S A 112:1208–1213

MacNeilage PF (2013) Vertebrate whole-body-action asymmetries and the evolution of right handedness: a comparison between humans and marine mammals. Dev Psychobiol 55:577–587

McGrew WC, Marchant LF (1999) Laterality of hand use pays off in foraging success for wild chimpanzees. Primates 40:509–513

Meguerditchian A, Gardner MJ, Schapiro SJ, Hopkins WD (2012) The sound of one-hand clapping: handedness and perisylvian neural correlates of a communicative gesture in chimpanzees. Proc Biol Sci 279:1959–1966

Meguerditchian A, Vauclair J, Hopkins WD (2013) On the origins of human handedness and language: a comparative review of hand preferences for bimanual coordinated actions and gestural communication in nonhuman primates. Dev Psychobiol 55:637–650

Miner N, Sperry RW, Stamm JS (1956) Relearning tests for interocular transfer following division of optic chiasma and corpus callosum in cats. J Comp Physiol Psychol 49:529–533

Moore MW, Perston Y (2016) Experimental insights into the cognitive significance of early stone tools. PLoS One 11:e0158803

Morgan TJ, Uomini NT, Rendell LE, Chouinard-Thuly L, Street SE, Lewis HM, Cross CP, Evans C, Kearney R, de la Torre I, Whiten A, Laland KN

(2015) Experimental evidence for the co-evolution of hominin tool-making teaching and language. Nat Commun 6:6029

Myers ER, Sperry RW (1958) Interhemispheric communication through the corpus callosum: mnemonic carry-over between the hemispheres. AMA Arch Neurol Psychiatr 80:298–303

Oakley K (1949) Man the Tool-Maker. Bulletin of the British Museum of Natural History, London

Parker GJ, Luzzi S, Alexander DC, Wheeler-Kingshott CA, Ciccarelli O, Lambon Ralph MA (2005) Lateralization of ventral and dorsal auditory-language pathways in the human brain. Neuroimage 24:656–666

Peelle JE (2012) The hemispheric lateralization of speech processing depends on what "speech" is: a hierarchical perspective. Front Hum Neurosci 6:309

Perani D, Saccuman MC, Scifo P, Anwander A, Spada D, Baldoli C, Poloniato A, Lohmann G, Friederici AD (2011) Neural language networks at birth. Proc Natl Acad Sci U S A 108:16056–16061

Petersen MR, Beecher MD, Zoloth SR, Moody DB, Stebbins WC (1978) Neural lateralization of species-specific vocalizations by Japanese macaques (Macaca fuscata). Science 202:324–327

Pinel P, Fauchereau F, Moreno A, Barbot A, Lathrop M, Zelenika D, Le Bihan D, Poline JB, Bourgeron T, Dehaene S (2012) Genetic variants of FOXP2 and KIAA0319/TTRAP/THEM2 locus are associated with altered brain activation in distinct language-related regions. J Neurosci 32:817–825

Poeppel D (2003) The analysis of speech in different temporal integration windows: cerebral lateralization as "asymmetric sampling in time". Speech Comm 41: 245–255

Poeppel D (2014) The neuroanatomic and neurophysiological infrastructure for speech and language. Curr Opin Neurobiol 28:142–149

Proffitt T, Luncz LV, Falótico T, Ottoni EB, de la Torre I, Haslam M (2016) Wild monkeys flake stone tools. Nature 539:85–88

Rilling JK, Glasser MF, Preuss TM, Ma X, Zhao T, Hu X, Behrens TE (2008) The evolution of the arcuate fasciculus revealed with comparative DTI. Nat Neurosci 11:426–428

Royer C, Delcroix N, Leroux E, Alary M, Razafimandimby A, Brazo P, Delamillieure P, Dollfus S (2015) Functional and structural brain asymmetries in patients with schizophrenia and bipolar disorders. Schizophr Res 161:210–214

Scheibel AB, Paul LA, Fried I, Forsythe AB, Tomiyasu U, Wechsler A, Kao A, Slotnick J (1985) Dendritic organization of the anterior speech area. Exp Neurol 87:109–117

Schiller, F (1992) Paul Broca. Explorer of the Brain. Oxford University Press, Oxford

Schlaug G, Jäncke L, Huang Y, Steinmetz H (1995) In vivo evidence of structural brain asymmetry in musicians. Science 267:699–701

Schrier AM, Sperry RW (1959) Visuomotor integration in split-brain cats. Science 129:1275–1276

Shannon RV (2005) Speech and music have different requirements for spectral resolution. Int Rev Neurobiol 70:121–134

Sherwood CC, Broadfield DC, Holloway RL, Gannon PJ, Hof PR (2003) Variability of Broca's area homologue in African great apes: implications for language evolution. Anat Rec A Discov Mol Cell Evol Biol 271:276–285

Silbert LJ, Honey CJ, Simony E, Poeppel D, Hasson U (2014) Coupled neural systems underlie the production and comprehension of naturalistic narrative speech. Proc Natl Acad Sci U S A 111: E4687–E4696

Sperry RW (1947) Nature of functional recovery following regeneration of the oculomotor nerve in amphibians. Anat Rec 97:293–316

Sperry RW (1961) Cerebral Organization and Behavior: The split brain behaves in many respects like two separate brains, providing new research possibilities. Science 133:1749–1757

Sperry RW (1980) Mind-brain interaction: mentalism, yes; dualism, no. Neuroscience 5:195–206

Sperry R (1984) Consciousness, personal identity and the divided brain. Neuropsychologia 22:661–673

Sperry RW (1998) A powerful paradigm made stronger. Neuropsychologia 36:1063–1068

Springer SP, Deutsch G (1981) Left Brain, Right Brain. WH Freeman & Company, New York

Stout D (2016) Tales of a stone age neuroscientist. Sci Amer 4:20–27

Stout D, Chaminade T (2012) Stone tools, language and the brain in human evolution. Philos Trans R Soc Lond B Biol Sci 367:75–87

Strauss E, Wada J (1983) Lateral preferences and cerebral speech dominance. Cortex 19:165–177

Terao Y, Ugawa Y, Enomoto H, Furubayashi T, Shiio Y, Machii K, Hanajima R, Nishikawa M, Iwata NK, Saito Y, Kanazawa I (2001) Hemispheric lateralization in the cortical motor preparation for human vocalization. J Neurosci 21:1600–1609

Uomini NT (2009) The prehistory of handedness: archaeological data and comparative ethology. J Hum Evol 57:411–419

Uomini NT, Meyer GF (2013) Shared brain lateralization patterns in language and Acheulean stone tool production: a functional transcranial Doppler ultrasound study. PLoS One 8:e72693

Vallortigara G, Rogers LJ, Bisazza A (1999) Possible evolutionary origins of cognitive brain lateralization. Brain Res Brain Res Rev 30:164–175

Vauclair J, Fagard J, Blois-Heulin C (2013) Lateralization, praxis, and communicative gestures: developmental and comparative perspectives. Dev Psychobiol 55:575–576

Wang D, Buckner RL, Liu H (2014) Functional specialization in the human brain estimated by intrinsic hemispheric interaction. J Neurosci 34:12341–12352

Witelson SF, Kigar DL (1992) Sylvian fissure morphology and asymmetry in men and women: bilateral differences in relation to handedness in men. J Comp Neurol 323:326–340

York GK 3rd, Steinberg DA (2011) Hughlings Jackson's neurological ideas. Brain 134:3106–3113

Zaidel E (1975) Technique for presenting lateralized visual input with prolonged exposure. *Vis Res* 15:283–289

Zaidel E (1976) Auditory vocabulary of the right hemisphere following brain bisection or hemidecortication. Cortex 12:191–211

Zaidel E (1983) A response to Gazzaniga. Language in the right hemisphere, convergent perspectives. Am Psychol 38:542–546

Zaidel DW (2013) Split-brain, the right hemisphere, and art: fact and fiction. Prog Brain Res 204:3–17

Zaidel E, Peters AM (1981) Phonological encoding and ideographic reading by the disconnected right hemisphere: two case studies. Brain Lang 14:205–234

Zatorre RJ, Belin P, Penhune VB (2002) Structure and function of auditory cortex: music and speech. Trends Cogn Sci 6:37–46

5

Bridging Hemispheres

The experiments of Sperry, Gazzaniga, and collaborators with calloso-tomized patients shed profound light on the lateralization of human brain functions, but did not provide much additional insight into the functions normally subserved by the corpus callosum. Work on split brains in humans and animals had made it clear that the corpus callosum was essential for transferring information across the hemispheres when it was available to only one hemisphere. Although this process is relevant to our lateralized brain, it is not necessarily so in the brains of animals that show a much lower degree of functional laterality.

The functions of the corpus callosum have in fact been an enigma for many researchers over time. In the 1600s, Thomas Willis, of whom I spoke in Chapter 2, suggested that the callosum receives sensory input after it has been amplified by the lentiform body (i.e. the basal ganglia), much as a lens does, and projects this information to the gray matter of the cerebral cortex (Zimmer 2004). According to Willis, the corpus callosum was associated with imagination by connecting the different regions of the cerebral cortex. More modern interpretations have pointed to a role of the corpus callosum in coordinating sensory and motor information across the hemispheres, and some have argued that

© The Author(s) 2017
F. Aboitiz, *A Brain for Speech*,
DOI 10.1057/978-1-137-54060-7_5

its emergence propelled further growth of the cerebral cortex by allowing more extensive and integrated neural networks to operate synchronically. However, there is an apparent contradiction between the evolutionary conservation of such a massive tract, and the relatively mild symptomatic effects produced by surgical callosotomy on human patients and animals, which can only be characterized in controlled laboratory conditions. In this chapter, I will attempt to explain the origin and functions of this massive tract, the largest of the human brain, and its relationship to brain lateralization and hand control, features that are relevant for speech and language origins.

Holding the Hemispheres Together

My Ph.D. thesis, with Eran Zaidel and Arne Scheibel as co-advisors, was initially aimed at understanding the relationship between callosal anatomy and anatomical brain asymmetry in postmortem brains. Earlier works, notably by Sandra Witelson, had reported sex and handedness differences in callosal size, with females and left-handers having larger callosums than right-handed males (Witelson 1985). This suggests that there is an inverse relationship between interhemispheric connectivity and brain lateralization. My interest was to make a direct anatomical-to-anatomical comparison, assessing the extent of morphological asymmetries, and to directly estimate fiber counts in the callosum instead of using cross-sections of the callosal area as had been done in previous studies.

Human postmortem and monkey tract-tracing studies suggested that different callosal regions bridge different cortical areas, such that the callosum contains a back-to-front topographic map of the cortical regions that project through it. Therefore, one could look for specific callosal sectors in relation to circumscribed anatomical asymmetries, like those of the planum temporale and the Sylvian fissure. Following Witelson, we cross-sectioned the callosum at the midline between the hemispheres, and parcellated it into a series of segments from back to front, each presumably connecting different cortical areas (Aboitiz et al. 1992a). Since there are no clear anatomical landmarks to parcel this tract, the standard procedure was to subdivide it geometrically into thirds according to its straight length (see Fig. 5.1). The anterior third is called the genu, and the mid-third the callosal body. The posterior third is subdivided into the posterior fifth, called the splenium, and the region between the posterior third and the posterior fifth is called the isthmus. The isthmus is usually the most slender callosal region, and there is postmortem evidence that fibers from the planum temporale and adjacent areas cross at this level to the other hemisphere. In my thesis, I found no relationship between the callosal cross-section area and callosal fiber density, supporting the notion that larger callosal sizes imply more fibers crossing through, although with substantial interindividual variance. In addition, I found partial support for my original hypothesis that asymmetries in the planum temporale are associated with a smaller isthmus area and fiber number, but only in males. However, the callosal region we were targeting for planum asymmetries may have been the wrong one, as recent studies by Giorgio Innocenti and collaborators

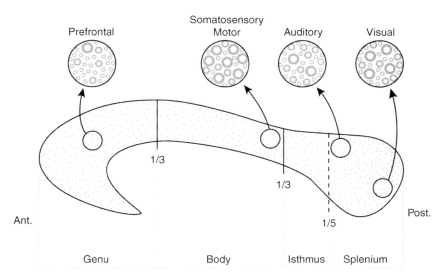

Fig. 5.1 A midsagittal section of the corpus callosum. This structure is geometrically subdivided into thirds, and in the posterior fifth. Insets show a schematic of the distribution of fiber diameters in callosal regions connecting different cortical areas

indicate that callosal fibers connecting the left and right planum tem-
porales are located in the midportion of the callosal splenium (posterior
fifth), rather than in the isthmus as we speculated (Caminiti et al. 2013;
Innocenti et al. 2014). The relationship between callosal anatomy and
brain lateralization is still unclear as there have been many discrepant
reports, largely related to the different procedures used to determine
callosal connectivity, anatomical asymmetries and functional lateralization (Dorion et al. 2000; Josse et al. 2008; Luders et al. 2010). Perhaps
due to the lack of confirmatory findings, the subject has lost much of its
initial impetus.

Nonetheless, there have been findings that support an association
between callosal connectivity and interhemispheric coordination. A
revealing study in this line was recently provided by Marcus Raichle's
laboratory, the discoverer of the default-mode brain network (see
Chapter 2). Using fMRI, Raichle and collaborators analyzed slow spontaneous fluctuations (more than 10 seconds per cycle) in cortical activity
across the hemispheres in a child that had undergone a complete
callosotomy (Johnston et al. 2008). After surgery, they found that
while intrahemispheric correlations remained similar to condition before
surgery, interhemispheric correlations were practically lost post-surgery,
generating independent activity patterns in each hemisphere. In the
previous chapter, I mentioned the fMRI study by Hesheng Liu and
collaborators, in which interhemispheric correlations were higher in
sensorimotor than in higher-order cortical areas, indicating that callosal
connectivity is stronger for low-level processing regions; and that activity
in higher-level ipsilateral networks is organized asymmetrically (Wang
et al. 2014). In a more recent large-scale fMRI study, Kelly Shen and
collaborators evaluated the strength of functional connectivity between
homotopic regions across hemispheres, and compared these values with
heterotopic functional connectivity in different resting state conditions
(Shen et al. 2015). Heterotopic connectivity could be contralateral, that
is, connecting different cortical regions in separate hemispheres, or
ipsilateral, that is, connecting different cortical regions within a single
hemisphere. Notably, they observed that functional connectivity
between homotopic points in both hemispheres remained robust and
stable across conditions, while contralateral, or ipsilateral heterotopic

connectivity was less stable, depending on the resting condition. Furthermore, functional connectivity between homotopic regions depended on the specific connections through the corpus callosum, being stronger in sensory than association areas. This indicates that the integration of information is stronger between homotopic regions than between ipsilateral or contralateral heterotopic regions. Overall, this evidence points to callosal participation in the maintenance of interhemispheric integration. Nonetheless, in order to get more precise insight into the functions of this structure, we need to go into some anatomical detail about the microscopic structure of the callosum and its evolutionary and developmental underpinnings, which I will do in the rest of this chapter.

Mammals Are More Connected

Although it is the largest cerebral tract, the corpus callosum is not an ancient structure. It is present only in placental mammals (i.e. rats, cats, cows, monkeys, humans and many others), but is absent in marsupials (like opossums and kangaroos) and monotremes (echidnas and platypodes). However, marsupials and monotremes have abundant interhemispheric fibers, mainly running across the anterior commissure, a tract located in the deep forebrain, which is disproportionately large in these animals. A much smaller tract that also contributes to interhemispheric communication is the hippocampal commissure, which connects the two hippocampi in the dorsal hemisphere. In placental mammals, the corpus callosum probably served as a shortcut for interhemispheric fibers, as the pathway via the anterior commissure used by marsupials is quite long and tortuous. An alternative attempt to minimize interhemispheric axonal length is what is termed the fasciculus aberrans in large-brained marsupials like kangaroos, which somewhat shortens the distance traveled from the cerebral cortex to the anterior commissure (Aboitiz and Montiel 2003). In non-mammals (birds, reptiles and amphibians) there is a modest pallial commissure, homologous to the hippocampal commissure of mammals, and an anterior commissure connecting limbic regions like the amygdala. However, there are no reciprocal connections between the most expanding regions of the cerebral hemispheres, which are comparable to the cerebral cortex of mammals (Aboitiz and Montiel 2003). In addition, mammals are unique in the conspicuous laminar arrangement of the cerebral cortex, while the cerebral hemispheres of non-mammals have an overall globular shape, with no evident lamination (I will come back to this below, and in Chapter 9).

The corpus callosum originated in evolution through a major developmental innovation. Some 30 years ago, Michael Katz and collaborators originally proposed that a "glial sling" bridging the two embryonic hemispheres appeared in early placental mammals, allowing axons to cross the midline (Katz et al. 1983). Subsequently, Linda Richards and her team described in more detail the generation of this interhemispheric bridge, which includes several glial specializations, and demonstrated that it serves as a substrate for growth of cortical axons across the midline between hemispheres (Lindwall et al. 2007; Suárez et al. 2014). As brains get larger, as in humans, the glial bridge becomes increasingly complex, with different cellular components involved.

As in other instances mentioned in this book, the genetic basis for the generation of commissural connections seems to be significantly conserved in evolution. There is a detailed molecular mechanism that allows axons to grow across the midline and invade the other side of the brain, which has been found at all levels in the nervous system of vertebrates, insects and worms. This is based on the interplay between three key proteins, called *Robo, Slit* and *Comm. Slit* is located in the midline and repels *Robo*, which is expressed in axons that are impeded from crossing to the other side. However, developing commissural axons stop expressing *Robo* at some point and join another midline molecule, *Comm*, which facilitates their growth across the midline (Dickson and Gilestro 2006). Notably, once axons have reached the other side, they start expressing *Robo* again at their tip, which makes them unable to cross back again. Richards and colleagues have found that different forms of *Slit* are indeed expressed in cells of the callosal glial wedge, and *Robo* is present in growing cortical axons. Likewise, mutant mice with inactivated *Slit* or *Robo* genes display severe malformations in the developing corpus callosum, as well as in many other fiber tracts. In addition to its axonal repellent function, *Slit* is required for the formation of the glial bridge that serves as a substrate for callosal axon growth (Richards 2002; Edwards et al. 2014; Unni et al. 2012). Thus, it appears that a major genetic rearrangement took place in placental mammals, involving the regulation of *Slit, Robo* and other genes, and the formation of a glial pathway that permitted the growth of callosal fibers across the midline. More recently, Richards and her team have reported a role of another protein, Netrin, in callosal axon guidance and regulating *Slit* expression during the formation of the corpus callosum (Fothergill et al. 2014).

There are rare genetic conditions in which the corpus callosum is not present in humans or selected rodent breeds (Edwards et al. 2014). In these cases, a robust longitudinal nerve tract called Probst's bundle develops on both sides of the brain, which may consist of prospective callosal fibers that turn back on the same hemisphere, or may simply reflect the compaction of a preexisting fiber tract (the cingulum bundle) that normally becomes disaggregated as callosal fibers cross through it to reach the midline (Stefanko 1980). Some genetic conditions, such as X-chromosome-linked lissencephaly (a type of cerebral malformation), Aicardi syndrome (also linked to the X chromosome), and ciliopathies, in which cellular cilia (tiny and movable "hairs" in the cells) are defective, have been associated with callosal agenesis. Callosal agenesis is also related to relatively severe cognitive impairments, including visual, motor and cognitive deficits and autistic behavior. Thirty percent of subjects with callosal agenesis have autistic symptomatology, and many individuals with autism spectrum disorder have congenital reduction of the callosal area. However, it is not known to what extent this correlation is due to the absence of the callosum *per se,* or to a more pervasive effect of the genetic disorder, affecting other neural and bodily systems. Many individuals with callosal agenesis have adequate intelligence levels and live relatively normal lives (if there is such a thing as a normal life).

Thus, interhemispheric connections are a new evolutionary acquisition, possibly associated with the origin of the mammalian cerebral cortex. However, its original functions are still somewhat of a mystery. As I have said, the interpretation of a role of the callosum in the integration of the cerebral hemispheres makes sense. However, this does not explain what its function was originally, when it was still a small tract (unless it appeared all at once, which I consider unlikely). It also leaves open the question of how birds have developed such sophisticated behavioral and cognitive skills without the help of interhemispheric connectivity. In order to understand this, we will need to delve into some anatomic and functional details that, although somewhat intricate, can be enlightening in these points.

160 Million Fibers

The corpus callosum is by far the largest fiber tract in the brain, which in humans contains some 160 million nerve fibers crossing the midline. This is a number I know quite well as it was perhaps the main result of my Ph.D. dissertation (Aboitiz et al. 1992b). I was not the first, however, to study this famous tract. At about the same time, Anthony LaMantia, working in his thesis with Pasko Rakic, was making an electron microscopy analysis of the fine callosal structure in the monkey brain (LaMantia and Rakic 1990a). Electron microscopy is a highly detailed technique that cannot be reliably used with humans because it requires pre-mortem preparation of tissue that cannot be performed on humans. But despite its elegance, LaMantia's work was with monkeys, not humans. However, in 1954, the anatomist Joseph Tomasch published a light-microscopy description of the fiber composition of four human callosums, a report that had gone largely unnoticed (Tomasch 1954). I decided to increase the sampling to 40 subjects, 20 males and 20 females. When I started my thesis I had no idea how painstaking a job this was going to be. At the time there were no adequate automatic counting procedures and I had to count fibers of different cross-section diameters for quite a long time. When I closed my eyes at night all I could see were the tiny circles and dots depicting the cross-sectioned myelinated and non-myelinated fibers under the intense light coming through the microscope lens. In a way, I felt reassured reading Ramón y Cajal's autobiography at the time, as he mentioned that when he went to sleep after a day of histological observations all the neuronal shapes he had seen in the day would come back to mind to produce a synthesis of the most important and relevant features among the effervescent diversity of neuronal types (Ramón y Cajal 2006).

One of the first relevant observations among this tedious work was that callosal fiber sizes are quite variable (Fig. 5.1). There are many small unmyelinated or slightly myelinated fibers, smaller than a micrometer in diameter. In addition, there are progressively smaller proportions of myelinated, medium-diameter (1 to 3 micrometers) and large-diameter fibers (larger than 3 micrometers) (myelin is a sheath that covers some axons to increase the propagation speed of nerve signals). Furthermore, different fiber types, particularly the large-diameter fibers, are not homogeneously distributed along the callosum. I first realized this when observing the posterior corpus callosum of a subject that showed a striking concentration of very large diameter fibers in the posterior-most region, where fibers connecting primary and secondary visual areas travel. This was a hint that fiber composition was indeed variable from subject to subject. However, looking at all the data in all callosal regions and across all subjects, a conserved pattern appeared, with two peaks of concentration of large diameter fibers. The first and largest is in the posterior part of the callosal body (the posterior middle third), and the second largest is located in the posterior most callosum (the back of the splenium). These are regions that connect primary and secondary somatosensory and motor areas (the posterior body), and visual areas (the posterior splenium). On the other hand, the callosal genu (the anterior third), which connects frontal and prefrontal areas, is characterized by high densities of small unmyelinated fibers. It was very stimulating to see that the findings by Tomasch with his small human sample, and by LaMantia with macaques were highly consistent with my own. These findings were not just an anatomical curiosity, as fiber diameter, together with myelin wrapping, determines the conduction velocity of nerve impulses. Therefore, they were of high functional relevance, meaning that these are fibers connecting primary or secondary sensory and motor areas that transmit their nerve impulses much faster than the average callosal fiber, while in higher order or association areas (particularly in the frontal region), callosal connectivity is generally slower. Subsequent MRI studies, again including Giorgio Innocenti's group, have assessed callosal fiber microstructure by fractional anisotropy, the basis for tractographic analyses that I mentioned in Chapter 2 (Caminiti et al. 2013). As I said, water diffusion is highly constrained by the orientation of axons and myelin sheaths, and is more constrained when the tract is highly packed and myelinated. Thus, a higher anisotropy value in a tract implies more myelination and increased packing. This technique is still in its beginnings, but in the future, it may provide a non-invasive assessment of callosal fiber variability across subjects.

The Zipper Hypothesis

Why would fibers connecting early stage sensory and motor areas be so fast-conducting? To get some insight into this question, we must first go into some details about the development of callosal connectivity in sensory and higher-order association areas. Innocenti, Caminiti and colleagues first showed in the cat that there is an initial excess of callosal fibers crossing the callosum, which decreases substantially soon after birth, with only about a quarter of the callosal fibers at birth being retained beyond the postnatal period (Innocenti et al. 1977; Innocenti 1981; Koppel and Innocenti 1983; Berbel and Innocenti 1988). These findings concurred with those of LaMantia and Rakic with monkeys (LaMantia and Rakic 1990b). Considering that I calculated 160 million callosal fibers in humans, this means that in the human newborn there could be as many as 640 million callosal fibers, with 480 million retracting shortly after birth. This retraction process can also be observed in gross morphology, as the cross-sectional area of the callosum transiently diminishes after birth, only to begin growing again due to increased fiber thickness, myelination and decreased fiber density. The number of callosal fibers stabilizes in later development and for most of adulthood, except with disease and advanced aging. Furthermore, this initial exuberance indicates that there is a strong intrinsic tendency of many fibers to cross the callosum, many more than are actually supported in adult life. Note that this process of terminal retraction is not exclusive for callosal connectivity, but has been found to be a major feature of the development of ipsilateral cortico-cortical connections as well, and may be related to the existence of critical periods for sensor-imotor development, including language (see Chapter 10).

The studies by Innocenti's group showed that concomitant with major fiber loss, there is a drastic rearrangement of callosal projections around birth, when initially callosal fibers evenly innervate all cortical regions (Innocenti et al. 1977; Innocenti 1981, 1986; Innocenti Bressoud 2003; Koppel and Innocenti 1983; Berbel and Innocenti 1988; Aggoun-Zouaoui and Innocenti 1994). From then on, callosal development differs between fibers connecting primary and secondary sensorimotor areas on the one hand, and higher order cortical areas on the other. Only in primary and secondary sensory (visual, somatosensory and auditory) and motor areas, is there a topographic map of the sensory or motor surface. This is the "homunculus" in sensory and motor cortices, and the representation of the visual field in visual areas. You will recall that these maps only correspond to the opposite part of the sensory surface. In auditory areas, the situation is slightly different, as there is a "tonotopic" representation, corresponding to different auditory tones that are segregated in the cochlea of the inner ear. Moving to higher order cortical areas, the sensory or motor topography becomes diffuse, as these regions are involved in more abstract processing mechanisms. Notably, the process of callosal terminal retraction is much more pronounced in the primary and secondary areas than in higher order areas of the cortex. In the former, callosal projections become restricted to a strip located in the borders between adjacent sensory (or motor) areas, while fibers connecting higher order areas are evenly eliminated across the surface (Fig. 5.2). Still, many more fibers may remain connecting higher order areas than sensorimotor regions. The projecting callosal strip that remains in sensory and motor cortices is the representation of the sensory or motor midline of the adjacent areas, so that the only sensorimotor regions connected through the callosum are those corresponding to the medial part of the body and the sensory field, like the visual midline, or the midline of the body surface. Since each hemisphere only receives input from the contralateral side, callosal fibers in these regions serve to connect the two hemi-representations in the midline, forming a continuous sensory and motor field across the hemispheres. In the regions of sensory or motor areas that are far from the midline, representing say the periphery of the visual field,

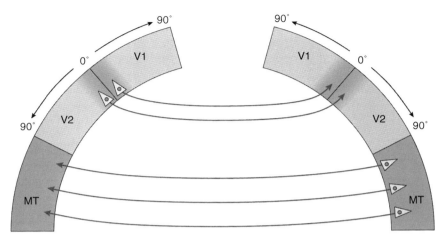

Fig. 5.2 The anatomical arrangement of adult callosal connections. Although in the newborn, neurons project to the corpus callosum throughout the sensory areas (in this case, V1 and V2), these projections undergo severe retraction after birth and only those that connect regions related to the sensory midline remain (0°), while those that represent peripheral regions of the visual field (→90°) are lost. In higher-order areas, there is also profound retraction, but evenly distributed across the respective areas (in this case, area MT). The remaining neurons in adults continue projecting to and from all parts of the respective areas, as well as projecting to additional areas. For simplicity, connections between primary and secondary sensory areas are depicted only from left to right, and in area MT, these are shown from right to left. In fact, all these projections are bidirectional.

there are very few callosal fibers, if any. Likewise, callosal fibers connecting the hand region of motor or somatosensory cortex are negligible, as in these areas most callosal fibers connect midline body regions. Therefore, tasks that are learned with one hand need to be transferred to the other hemisphere via the higher-order areas that are intensively connected via the callosum, and not by primary/secondary areas. Audition is in a way an exception to this rule, as the surface of the cochlea does not map space locations of sounds but rather different tones, with high tones at one extreme and low tones at the other. Callosal projections in auditory areas of the cortex cover different tonalities, but are still restricted to the edges of auditory regions.

The uneven distribution of fiber sizes in the callosum now makes some sense. In the first steps of visual or somatosensory processing, the events that occur around the midline are usually the most relevant, and must be rapidly processed in order for there to be continuous perception across the two hemispheres. Ramón y Canal first proposed the midline rule, asserting that callosal and other commissural connections establish the continuity of the two halves of the sensory map across the hemispheres (Ramón y Cajal 1898). Further studies, including those by the Nobel Prize winners David Hubel and Torsten Wiesel, supported the notion that callosal fibers extend the visual network across hemispheres (Hubel 1988). More specifically, Jean-Christophe Houzel and others have proposed that callosal fibers participate in the process of adaptation to and prediction of a moving object, that passes in front of an observer from one visual field to the other by crossing the vertical midline (Houzel et al. 2002). A beautiful experiment in this line was recently made by Kerstin Schmidt and collaborators, who lightly anesthetized the right visual cortex of a cat by lowering its temperature, and recorded neurons in the left hemisphere while presenting moving stimuli in the contralateral visual field (i.e. right) (Peiker et al. 2013). They found that these neurons activated more strongly when stimuli entered the midline, predictably to cross to the opposite visual field, as opposed to activation with movement toward the periphery of the visual field. Thus, visual neurons may anticipate the movement of objects across the midline, perhaps in addition to other functions involved in fusing the two visual images. This may require very rapid communication across the callosum, and a similar situation may hold for motor and somatosensory areas (both regions displaying the highest concentration of large diameter fibers through the callosum).

Moving Maps to the Cortex

The fine anatomy of callosal fibers and its variability among species give some hints about the original function of interhemispheric connections, and may explain why other large-brained animals like birds never developed this arrangement. We know that embryonic specialization in early placental mammals permitted fiber growth across the midline, and that the callosum was advantageous because it provided a shortcut to the other side of the brain. Nonetheless, we still have no clues about what processing benefits they provided when they first appeared given there must have been selective pressure favoring their development.

To clarify this point, let me remind the reader that the mammalian cerebral cortex is quite different in shape from that of other vertebrates. It is organized as a bidimensional sheet or lamina consisting of several layers, as opposed to the brain of birds, which develops as a well-packed three-dimensional neuronal network. The bidimensional arrangement of the sensory cerebral cortex of mammals is particularly suited for the development of topographically arranged maps of the sensory surfaces, like the somatosensory homunculus or the representation of the visual field (see above). Conversely, in reptiles, birds and other vertebrates, spatial information about the environment is not processed in the cerebral hemispheres, but in a laminar brainstem structure called the optic tectum (see Fig. 5.3). In these animals, the cerebral hemispheres behave like higher-order cortical areas, with no clear topographic sensory or motor organization (Aboitiz and Montiel 2003). These differences are reflected in the relatively small size of the mammalian superior colliculus, the structure homologous to the bird's tectum, an example supporting Robert Barton's hypothesis of evolutionary independence of different neural processing systems (see Chapter 3).

Thus, in mammals there has been a shift in the early sites of spatial processing from the brainstem to the cerebral cortex. As I discussed above, spatial processing poses the problem of midline fusion as each side of the brain receives input from only half of the sensory surface. Non-mammals have solved this problem by developing a tectal commissure that connects the two halves of the sensory field in the midbrain. But as spatial maps moved to the cerebral hemispheres of mammals, the problem of midline fusion became an issue, and interhemispheric connections came as a solution. In the beginning, as in monotremes and marsupials, the only available path for these fibers was through the anterior commissure, which was still a long way but was perhaps better than nothing. The corpus callosum came as an improvement that permitted a shorter travelling distance. One could even stretch this hypothesis and say that without interhemispheric connectivity mammals

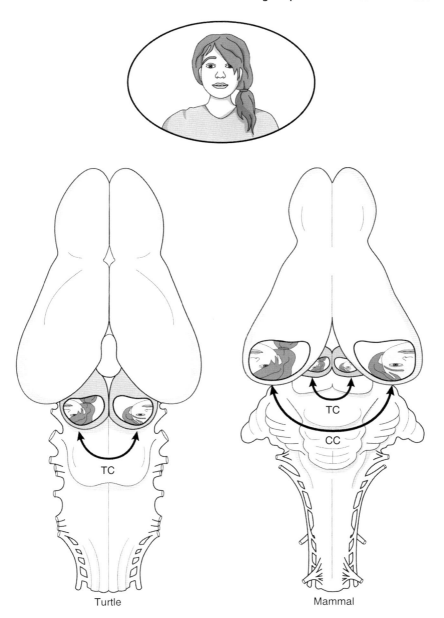

Fig. 5.3   The topographic representation of visual inputs in a reptile and a mammal. In reptiles, the visual map is established in the optic tectum (gray),

would never have generated or at least expanded the cerebral cortex as we know it, not because of developmental but rather functional limitations.

Despite the attractiveness of the hypothesis of midline fusion, the great majority of callosal fibers connects areas other than the sensory or motor regions and is directed mainly to higher-order and association areas involved in higher cognitive processes. It is likely that when this pathway became available, first via the anterior commissure and then through the corpus callosum, not only sensory and motor but also many other fibers were able to traverse to the other hemisphere. As a side effect of the initial benefit of midline fusion, fibers from other cortical regions also made their way across the hemispheres, contributing to other aspects of interhemispheric integration. This may have had the benefit of generating more interconnected networks, but it still remains to be proven that this design is any better than that of other animals without interhemispheric connections, such as birds.

Robin Mihrshahi proposed that besides perceptual midline fusion, interhemispheric integration of motor areas played a key role in the evolution of the callosum (Mihrshahi 2006). In fact, some behavioral functions may have strongly benefited from the development of cross-hemispheric communication, such as bimanual coordination, a mammal-specific behavioral pattern that relies on interhemispheric axons connecting higher-order cortical areas. Bimanual coordination is observed in most mammals, excepting those that have undergone anatomical specializations for walking, swimming or digging; and is pretty much absent in other vertebrates. Moreover, bimanual coordination depends on hand dexterity, which is supported by the cortico-spinal tract, another invention of the mammalian brain. Thus, bimanual coordination is a result of the interplay between these two tracts, the callosum and the cortico-spinal tract, and is extremely useful for beha-

Fig.5.3 (Continued)
and there is a tectal commissure (TC) that fuses both halves of visual representation. In mammals, in addition to the optic tectum (in mammals this structure is called superior colliculus), the visual map is also generated in the visual cortex, where the corpus callosum serves to fuse the two representations at the midline.

viors like nest building and especially food manipulation, features that may have been very important in early mammalian evolution. Bimanual coordination and hand dexterity are especially important in primates, and foreshadowed the capacity for toolmaking and communication in our immediate ancestors. William Hopkins and colleagues observed chimpanzees fishing for termites with sticks, as they do in the wild. They assessed the degree of hand preference and performance in this task, and took tractographic measures of the fiber integrity of the corpus callosum of all individuals (Phillips et al. 2013). They found increasing connectivity through the corpus callosum in individuals with stronger hand preference and performance, regardless of direction (left- or right-handers), which supports the concept of an increasing sensorimotor (but not necessarily higher-level) communication between hemispheres in association with hand specialization. The authors also measured the regional size of the corpus callosum and found no differences in relation to handedness, which emphasizes the use of tractographic instead of area analysis to study callosal connectivity.

There is ample evidence that the corpus callosum in humans is required for everyday bimanual coordination tasks, like typing or eating with a knife and fork, and of course toolmaking in our ancestors. Most of us learn these tasks easily and they become daily routines, but acallosal patients have difficulty with them, especially when these tasks are new and subjects have to learn them. You will recall the alien hand syndrome I mentioned in the previous chapter. While patients who underwent callosal surgery tend to do badly in bimanual coordination tasks, subjects with callosal agenesis (who are born without a corpus callosum) do much better in such tasks, showing some compensatory capacity during development. Gazzaniga and collaborators recently studied a patient undergoing callosotomy in successive stages, where the anterior corpus callosum was sectioned in an initial operation, and the posterior part was resected in a second procedure (Eliassen et al. 2000). With each hand, the patient had to simultaneously draw either mirror image or non-mirror image figures following a model presented to her. Mirror image drawings require tight bimanual coordination, for which an intact corpus callosum may be needed. The patient was evaluated before and after the first operation and after the second. Before surgery, the non-mirror images were drawn poorly, but mirror images were drawn reasonably well. Sectioning the anterior callosum in the first operation had little effect on either the mirror image or non-mirror image drawings. Nonetheless, after sectioning the posterior callosum in the second operation, mirror image drawing deteriorated, while non-mirror drawings improved, presumably because there was less interference between the two hands. The authors concluded that bimanual spatial coordination in visuomotor tasks is significantly impaired by the absence of the corpus callosum, and considering the critical role of the posterior callosum in this task bimanual integration is likely conveyed by the parietal cortex.

Helene Sisti and collaborators used a bimanual task in which healthy subjects had to move a cursor on a computer screen using two dials, with different levels of difficulty during a learning period (Sisti et al. 2012). The researchers studied the callosal regions of the subjects tractographically and found a positive correlation between fractional anisotropy and behavioral performance, but only in regions connecting prefrontal areas. This was found only after a period of training, as the correlation was not significant during early training sessions. In motor regions, the group led by Ulf Ziemann assessed callosal fractional anisotropy and a functional measure of interhemispheric connectivity using TMS with normal subjects and neurologic patients that performed a bimanual finger-tapping task (Wahl et al. 2015). They found that both structural and functional parameters correlated with task performance. Thus, the callosal region, through which bimanual coordination is executed, may depend on the specific task being assessed. As I said above, callosal fibers from primary and secondary motor areas are unlikely to participate in this task as these fibers are concentrated in the body midline rather than in the hand or arm representation.

Transferring Sounds

The above holds well for visual, somatosensory and motor transfer, but not so much for audition. We have seen that the auditory cortex is different from the somatosensory or visual areas, as it has no spatial representation of the auditory scene. Likewise, it appears that auditory callosal fibers do not fit the pattern of visual and somatosensory fibers, as they tend to be located in the anterior part of the splenium, which has an association area-like fiber composition. This may make sense because in audition, much side-to-side information transfer already takes place at very early neural processing levels in the brainstem. In the visual pathway of mammals, brainstem side-to-side connectivity is very limited, and is mainly performed via the tectal or collicular commissure. Thus, cortico-cortical interhemispheric transfer may not need to be as rapid for audition as it does for vision and touch. This has been shown by a series of studies that measure interhemispheric transfer in the visual and the auditory modalities that are based on a simple neuropsychological procedure called the simple reaction time task.

In the 1800s, Franciscus Donders designed the reaction time task to measure the time required to perform a given computation (Newell 1989). In this task, subjects had to respond automatically to a visual or auditory stimulus by pressing a button. The time taken to press this button is the result of the sum of perceptual, motor and cognitive processes. By manipulating the cognitive task and keeping the perceptual and motor components constant Donders estimated the time the brain takes to perform a specific cognitive process. Thus, he compared the response time for automatic tasks and tasks that required a perceptual choice, and found that the latter involved more time. A variant of this task was used by John Stroop in the 1920s, in which subjects were shown the names of colors (red, blue, green) written in different colored ink, so that, for example, the word "red" was written in the same color or a different color (Stroop 1935; MacLeod 1992). Subjects had to respond to the color of the ink and not to the word. For example, if the word "red" was written in blue, the correct answer was "blue". Subjects took longer to respond when the word was different from the color of the ink. Around the same time, psychologist Albert T. Poffenberger designed an experimental paradigm to measure the time needed for interhemispheric transfer of sensory information, consisting of pressing a button with one hand (left or right) as fast as possible after the appearance of a lateralized stimulus in one visual field (left or right) (Poffenberger 1912). When the stimulus was presented in the same visual field as the responding hand (left visual field and left hand, or right visual field and right hand), the response times were shorter than when the stimulus was presented to the visual field opposite to the responding hand (left visual field and right hand, or right visual field and left hand). The difference was about 5 milliseconds, depending on the specific task. When the visual field and responding hand were on the same side, the stimulus reached the contralateral hemisphere, which also commands the contralateral hand (see previous Chapter). However, if visual field presentation and responding hand were crossed, the stimulus had to be transferred to the opposite hemisphere to perform the manual response. This time difference is considered an estimate of sensory interhemispheric transfer through the corpus callosum.

However, Marco Iacoboni and Eran Zaidel showed that visual inter-hemispheric transfer is quite different from auditory transfer. They analyzed the crossed-uncrossed reaction time difference for auditory and visual stimuli with a patient that had undergone a complete callosotomy (Iacoboni and Zaidel 1999; Zaidel and Iacoboni 2003). They found that the auditory crossed-uncrossed difference was rather small and highly variable (less than 5 milliseconds), while the visual crossed-uncrossed difference was much greater (between 25 and 45 milliseconds), indicating that the auditory crossed-uncrossed difference is not a reliable estimate of callosal interhemispheric transfer. Rebecca Woelfle and Jessica Grahn also found in normal humans that interhemispheric transfer took less time when auditory rather than visual cues were used (Woelfle and Grahn 2013). The subjects, who were trained musicians and non-musicians, performed a simple reaction task of pressing in button in response to a visual or auditory stimulus. The crossed-uncrossed difference was less for auditory than for visual stimuli, and was slightly greater in musicians than non-musicians. As I have mentioned, the smaller crossed-uncrossed difference for auditory stimuli may be explained by the fact that acoustic information can cross the midline already in the brainstem, while in the visual system this occurs mostly at cortical levels; or, in the case of normal subjects, because visual callosal connections require longer axons than auditory connections due to the anatomy of the neural pathways (see below). A recent and intriguing finding in this line by Giorgio Innocenti and collaborators is a callosal projection to the corpus striatum in monkeys and humans (Innocenti et al. 2016) that is carried by thin fibers, with an estimated interhemispheric transfer time of about 2 and 4 milliseconds in monkeys and humans, respectively, which fits with the results of standard neuropsychological studies of interhemispheric transfer. Furthermore, callosal corticostriatal axons originate mainly from sensory, motor and premotor cortices (with an important exception in humans, which I will discuss below), suggesting that simple sensorimotor interhemispheric transfer is mediated by crossed cortico striatal projections through the corpus callosum.

Time is of the Essence

Different species have different brain sizes and consequently interhemispheric distance varies accordingly, such that in large-brained species like us, callosal fibers are much longer than in mice. Furthermore, interhemispheric delay may be especially detrimental when information has to cross back and forth between the hemispheres, as happens with more complex processing. In this line, James Ringo, Robert Doty, Steve Demeter and Patrice Simard conjectured in 1994 that more time is required to transmit information across the hemispheres in species with larger brains as they have on average a longer interhemispheric distance (Ringo et al. 1994). This imposes an additional delay that they argued is detrimental for fine time-critical neural computations in which multiple passes across the callosum would make processing prohibitively slow. A simple solution is to keep high-resolution processing, or reciprocal neural loops involved in higher processing, restricted to a single hemisphere, leading to hemispheric specialization. A not yet confirmed prediction from their hypothesis was that all large-brained species like elephants and cetaceans would also show a high degree of hemispheric specialization (interestingly, elephants and cetaceans are also good vocal learners; see Chapter 10).

Partly motivated by the above conjecture, my student Ricardo Olivares made a comparative analysis of fiber composition in the posterior corpus callosum of several domestic species of different brain sizes (mouse, rabbit, cat, cow and horse) (Olivares et al. 2001). Ricardo noticed that in each species, fiber sizes are distributed in an asymmetric bell-like curve in which one side of the bell (the left, closer to zero) is very short and the other (the right), containing higher values, has a very long tail. The peak of the curve includes the large majority of fibers and reflects the most common diameter, or modal value. This shape is similar to probability functions like Poisson's or ex-Gaussian distribution. What is more striking is that the modal value changes little across species regardless of brain size. Following Ringo and his colleagues, this implies that interhemispheric transfer is in fact delayed in larger brained species, as most callosal fibers do not significantly increase conduction velocity concomitant with the physical separation of the two hemispheres. On the other hand, the few largest-diameter fibers (the long tail at the right of the bell) noticeably increased in diameter and consequently in conduction velocity in larger brains. This strongly suggests that some kinds of information can be rapidly transferred even in big brains. As we saw earlier, many (but not all) of these large fibers correspond to sensory and motor regions and may participate in midline fusion. Nonetheless, provided that nerve fiber conduction velocity increases linearly with fiber diameter, and scales directly with increasing interhemispheric distance, we calculated the expected increases in fiber caliber required for interhemispheric delay to remain constant, regardless of brain size. We found that the increased size of the largest fibers is not sufficient to maintain a constant interhemispheric delay as brains get bigger, so that there is a toll on interhemispheric transmission.

Furthermore, we searched the literature for information about interhemispheric transfer velocity and transmission times of visual fibers in different animals, and found that species with laterally-directed eyes like rabbits have very long transfer times as opposed to cats, with frontally-directed eyes and shorter interhemispheric transfer times. The laterally placed eyes of rabbits cover a visual field of almost 360 degrees around their heads to maximize detection of predators, while carnivores like cats and dogs depend strongly on frontal vision, and visual midline fusion may be important for them to catch prey. Likewise, Olivares showed that cats and dogs have a higher proportion of large or very large splenial fibers than would be expected in ungulates, rabbits or rodents of the same brain size, all of the latter having laterally placed eyes to different degrees (Olivares et al. 2001). In addition to these findings, we found a significant difference in the relative size of the posterior callosum in relation to total callosal area in frontal-looking species like carnivores and humans, compared to laterally-looking species (mostly herbivores), suggesting that these species devote a higher proportion of visual fibers to the callosum, or have larger visual fibers (Olivares et al. 2000).

After our report, two laboratory groups published similar findings, but with different samples of species. The first was led by Samuel Wang, and included Patrick Hof as one of their collaborators. Wang's group has for some time been interested in describing scaling regularities among different cellular brain components and brain size. Shortly after our publication, these authors published preliminary findings with a small sample of species similar to ours (adding a primate, the macaque), and confirmed an increase in the diameter of the large fibers in species with larger brains (Harrison et al. 2002). They later confirmed these findings in a broader sample of species from shrews to whales, and measured fibers in the posterior and anterior portions of the callosal body (Wang et al. 2008). In line with our conclusions, they showed that while modal fiber diameter remained relatively constant across species, maximal fiber diameters and the degree of myelination of these fibers rose steeply with increasing brain size. Nonetheless, the associated increase in conduction velocity was not sufficient to maintain a constant interhemispheric transmission time, which ranged from one to two milliseconds in the smallest species to about 5 milliseconds in whales (in humans, this value was calculated to be about 4 milliseconds). Wang explains these findings in terms of a functional tradeoff between the need to increase conduction velocity in larger brains on the one hand, and the energy cost and the anatomical difficulty of packing larger axonal volumes on the other, which is a reasonable hypothesis that has to be tested.

The second finding was made by Giorgio Innocenti, Roberto Caminiti, Patrick Hof and others, who analyzed the diameter and anatomic position of callosal fibers originating from specific cortical regions in different primate species (Caminiti et al. 2009). In a series of important articles, they confirmed the previous findings of anterior to posterior distribution of callosal fibers according to cortical topography, and the distribution of fiber diameters described before. The shortest interhemispheric delays were found in areas connecting motor and sensory regions, consistent with previous findings. Moreover, comparing the sizes of axons from motor regions in the macaque, chimpanzee and human, they reported conservatism in modal fiber diameter, and progressively greater maximal axon diameters in relation to increased brain size. Again, the largest axons were not sufficiently fast to render a constant interhemispheric delay. Moreover, differences in maximal axon diameter were not evident from chimp to human. Notably, although frontal regions have very thin callosal fibers, their interhemispheric delays are rather short, because the distance traveled by axons is shorter than in more posterior regions. On the other hand, fibers connecting visual regions have to travel a long distance to the midline, and consequently the interhemispheric delay is relatively high despite there being a high proportion of coarse diameter fibers connecting these areas. Another important point made by Innocenti's group was that there is greater intrinsic variability of fiber sizes and transmission times in species with larger brains. Here, humans ranked higher than chimps. Greater intrinsic variability was observed across callosal regions, but also among fibers connecting specific brain regions. They concluded that there tends to be a wider range of conduction velocities in species with larger brains, which implies that there is a wider time frame for segregating neuronal circuits, particularly considering oscillatory activity. More recently, Kimberley Phillips, Chet Sherwood, Patrick Hof and others described the fiber composition of the corpus callosum in 14 primate species, including humans, again confirming the same essential findings (Phillips et al. 2015).

Finally on this point, Innocenti, Caminiti and Hof extended their previous findings to language-related regions, finding cross-species conservatism in the size of callosal fibers originating from the planum temporale in humans and chimpanzees (Innocenti et al. 2010). In addition, William Hopkins, Chet Sherwood and colleagues found that planum temporale asymmetries in the chimpanzee were associated with a smaller proportion of large diameter fibers in the posterior corpus callosum (Hopkins et al. 2012), which in a way is reminiscent of my early results described at the beginning of this chapter (Aboitiz et al.

1992b). Although in principle this is an interesting finding, in my opinion this data needs to be consistently replicated before it can be considered a fact.

Travelling Waves

As I said in Chapter 2, oscillatory activity is a hallmark of brain function, speech and language being no exceptions to this. As David Poeppel and colleagues have evidenced, speech processing takes place in a nested symphony of neuronal oscillations in a wide but continuous frequency range, from high frequency gamma activity involved in phoneme perception to low-frequency delta oscillations related to large-scale language processing like complex grammar and semantic associations (Chait et al. 2015). We also saw in Chapter 4 that speech perception and production may involve complex bilateral interactions, therefore the question of how these oscillations are coordinated across the hemispheres is crucial. To achieve cross-hemispheric coordination information must be rapidly transmitted across the hemispheres, very likely conveyed by high oscillatory frequency codes. Motor and somatosensory cortices contain the largest axons in the corpus callosum, and are concentrated in the representation of the sensorimotor midline, which includes the organs of speech: the tongue, larynx and lips. However, we know little about interhemispheric transmission during vocalizations. The study of inter-hemispheric synchronization during normal and pathological speech production may prove a valuable field of study that could be of clinical relevance when considering neural plasticity mechanisms and compensatory effects in speech-impaired individuals.

In Chapter 3, I mentioned an article by György Buzsáki, Nikos Logothetis and Wolf Singer that highlighted the conservation of oscillatory brain activity across a wide variety of mammals from bats and mice to humans, from very high frequencies at 100 or more cycles per second that take place in the hippocampus, to very slow frequencies of about 10 seconds per cycle (Buzsáki et al. 2013). Just to remind the reader classical human electroencephalographic waves are found in most mammals and other vertebrates, including gamma, alpha, beta and theta waves, and have been associated with similar functions in all species. High-frequency oscillations like gamma (at 40 cycles per second or more) are considered to reflect local processing and cognitive contents, and are distinguished from low-frequency oscillations (theta or slower waves) that underlie the workings of large-scale networks that integrate different local processes and contextual elements. The rainbow of oscillatory brain frequencies is thus a highly preserved character across species regardless of brain size, and probably reflects aspects of neuronal network dynamics that are essential for local-global integration and self-organization. A critical requirement for oscillatory dynamics is that stimuli or signals are delivered at appropriate times in the respective neuronal groups, which must be achieved by several physiological processes including synaptic activity, dendritic integration, inhibitory processes and, especially important for our concerns, close regulation of axonal conduction velocity in the different circuits. Thus, in the same line as Ringo and colleagues, Buzsáki, Logothetis and Singer claim that with increasing brain size, time constraints become especially important for oscillatory activity, which is partly compensated for by increasing conduction velocity in a small group of axons. Our work and Innocenti's on the corpus callosum have shown that the range of axonal conduction velocities amplifies as brains grow larger, which may have important consequences for the dynamics of local-global processing in larger brains.

Interhemispheric distance is no more than 1 cm in the mouse brain, but can reach 10–14 cm or more in the human brain, depending on the regions being connected. Conduction velocity of the most abundant, relatively small fibers (about 0.8 microns in diameter) is calculated to be 5–8 meters per second, producing an interhemispheric delay of about 2 milliseconds in the mouse, and 15 and 25 milliseconds in the human. Low oscillatory frequencies like theta have periods of 100–250 milliseconds per cycle, so a delay of 2 milliseconds (mouse) or 20 milliseconds (human) makes up a small proportion of the oscillatory cycle in both species. In other words, these delays may do no harm to low-frequency coordinated activity across the hemispheres. Even in humans, the transmission delay takes about a tenth of the entire cycle, a variability that is within the expected range. On the other hand, at higher frequencies like gamma (40 cycles per second), with cycles lasting only 25 milliseconds, the situation becomes more complicated for the human brain. While in the mouse, 2 milliseconds of delay may not affect high-frequency interhemispheric synchrony, the resulting delay in humans is impossibly long to maintain accurate synchrony if callosal connections are made via the average fibers. Larger callosal fibers, say more than 3 microns in diameter, transmit impulses at about 40 meters per second, while the largest 0.1% of fibers, with axons 10 micrometers in diameter or more, can transmit at 120 meters per second. This yields interhemispheric delays of about 3 milliseconds for fibers 3 micrometers in diameter, and close to 1 millisecond for the largest fibers, which may fit within a 10% tolerance in the variability of gamma oscillatory gamma cycles. These large fibers could allow high-frequency interhemispheric synchrony in the human and other big brains (Aboitiz et al. 2003).

But is there any high frequency synchrony between hemispheres after all? In the visual system, there are fast-conducting callosal fibers, but the longer interhemispheric distance results in increased transmission delay. With single cell recording techniques, Andreas Engel, Wolf Singer and collaborators were the first to observe interhemispheric synchrony in pairs of neurons of the primary visual area of the cat. Synchrony became disrupted after sectioning the corpus callosum (Engel et al. 1991). Later, Engel, Ina Peiker and colleagues moved to humans, using magnetoencephalography, a technique that records magnetic field variations in the skull surface (as opposed to recording electric fields in the EEG) (Peiker et al. 2015). They assessed visual integration deficits in autistic subjects performing an object discrimination task with partially occluded figures. While controls showed increased gamma coherence (a measure indicative of synchronic activity) in visual temporal areas during tasks that require information from both hemispheres, autistic subjects failed to show this increase in such tasks. But high frequency interhemispheric communication may be more complex than a straightforward fit in the phase of the fast cycles. Rafael Malach and his group used electrodes located directly on the cortical surface of five individuals suffering pharmacologically intractable epilepsy, while monitoring brain activity during surgery (Nir et al. 2008). They observed strong, spontaneous slow-frequency cross-hemispheric fluctuations in the activity of high-frequency oscillations, particularly gamma (above 40 cycles per second). That is, the intensity of rapid oscillations fluctuate slowly, and these fluctuations are synchronized in both cerebral hemispheres, a finding that is reminiscent of the low-frequency interhemispheric synchrony reported with fMRI by Marcus Raichle and collaborators (see above in this chapter).

On the other hand, callosal fibers connecting auditory regions usually do not reach diameters as large as those of visual or somatosensory or motor fibers, and consequently there is likely a smaller fiber contingent able to support high frequency interhemispheric synchrony. However, interhemispheric distance is shorter for auditory than for visual fibers, which works in their favor. Saskia Steinmann, Christoph Mulert, Angela Friederici, and other authors conducted a high-density EEG study with healthy subjects participating in a dichotic listening task (Steinmann et al. 2014). Besides analyzing the synchrony, the authors employed a source estimation algorithm that, in combination with tridimensional MRI brain reconstructions, allowed for reconstructing the deep location of surface activity recorded on the scalp with EEG. Notably, the authors found a specific increase in gamma synchrony between the right and left auditory cortices, when subjects consciously perceived the syllable presented to the non-dominant ear (the left ear, projecting principally to the right hemisphere). This is taken as evidence for high-frequency interhemispheric transfer of auditory linguistic information. Considering the close interhemispheric coupling that takes place with speech perception and production, it is likely that cross-hemispheric, high-frequency synchronic ensembles are relevant for speech perception and production, and perhaps for bimanual motor tasks, a process that must depend on a small contingent of fast-conducting fibers.

Integrating Speech, Emotion and Meaning

Callosal fibers may also play a role at higher levels of speech and language processing in the temporal coordination of different speech processes, especially the exchange of information between right-dominant and left-dominant streams. A widely used strategy to study language and semantic processing is the N400 event-related potential, a negative voltage deflection occurring about 400 milliseconds after sti-mulus presentation (see Chapter 2). N400 and other similar potentials have been associated with cognitive incongruencies in which two or more stimuli are contradictory to each other. In the early eighties, Marta Kutas discovered the N400 in a semantic congruence/incongru-ence task where she presented phrases word-by-word on a screen that had expected endings like "The coffee was too hot to . . . ". In this sentence, the last word is expected to be "drink" (Kutas and Hillyard 1980). Kutas presented different ending words, the expected one ("drink"), and unexpected ones (say, "eat", or even more unexpected, "walk"). Comparing the event-related EEG curves for the expected and unexpected ending words, there was an evident negative deflection occurring at some 400 milliseconds for the incongruous words, which was more pronounced the more incongruous the word was with the content of the sentence. This was termed the semantic incongruency effect, and was marked by N400 potential. Angela Friederici took advantage of this technique to study interhemispheric processing in partially callosotomized patients. Since syntax is represented mainly on the left hemisphere, and prosody is right-hemisphere dominant, the corpus callosum might be important to integrate the two processing streams. Instead of semantic incongruency, Friederici's group presented inconguencies between the prosodic contour of a phrase and its syntactic structure (Sammler et al. 2010). Notably, while normal subjects devel-oped a good N400 effect after prosodic-semantic incongruencies, patients with lesions in the posterior third of the corpus callosum failed to show this effect. However, patients did show a normal semantic N400 effect, indicating that the deficit was specific for tasks being processed in different hemispheres. In a subsequent study, Friederici's team also showed that patients with anterior callosal lesions displayed a normal prosodic-syntactic N400 incongruency effect, supporting the participa-tion of parieto-temporal interhemispheric connections in the integration between intonation and phrase structure. This evidence is in line with studies showing that patients with callosal agenesis perform poorly in tasks requiring affective or nonliteral sentence understanding, like meta-phors or proverbs (Paul et al. 2003; Rehmel et al. 2016). Analyzing the callosal projection to the corpus striatum that I mentioned above,

Innocenti found that only in humans does this projection originate in temporoparietal areas that fit Geschwind's area in the language network of the left hemisphere (Innocenti et al. 2016). Furthermore, this projection crosses through the callosal isthmus, and is proposed by Innocenti's group to participate in syntactic-prosodic integration.

There have been findings supporting interhemispheric interplay in semantic processing. In an early study, Eran Zaidel and collaborators presented subjects with words belonging to different semantic categories (say, content words vs. action words) either in the left or the right visual fields, or presented the same word simultaneously in both visual fields (Mohr et al. 1994). Bilateral presentation improved recognition, but this did not occur when pseudo words (phonetically correct, but meaningless sequences of letters) were used as stimuli. This indicates that cross-hemispheric interactions are in fact relevant for processing semantic information. Warren Brown and his team also showed that subjects with agenesis of the corpus callosum display poorer narrative contents compared to IQ-matched controls, and have specific difficulties in semantic and pragmatic interpretations of the discourse (Turk et al. 2010).

Large-scale processes involved in semantic and higher syntactic analysis might relate to lower frequency neuronal oscillations that are more likely associated with contextual information. In this line, my student Enzo Brunetti conducted a variant of a lexical decision task in which words belonging to different semantic categories (animals, man-made objects, abstract nouns) and pseudo words were binaurally presented to subjects that had to say whether or not the word they heard corresponded to one of the pre-defined semantic categories, say animals (Brunetti et al. 2013). Enzo observed overall phase synchronization increments at low frequencies that were specific for the semantic category that was being used at the moment, whichever it was as there were no differences among semantic categories. However, the average topography of the synchronic networks was specific for each category, despite there being significant individual variability. Enzo also showed early increases in gamma synchrony associated with semantic relevance for the task. Source analysis of this data suggests that the synchronic networks at work are bilateral, at least for low-frequency oscillations. This finding underscores the role of callosal communication in higher aspects of speech and language processing. Overall, these findings are consistent with the recent report by Alexander Huth and collaborators, who identified a widespread semantic representation across the cerebral cortex, whose anatomical organization seems to be conserved across subjects (Huth et al. 2016).

All in all, the corpus callosum provides a massive pathway for cross-hemispheric integration, and despite time constraints, synchronic oscillatory activity can be performed in our large brains at relatively high frequencies, although through a limited contingent of large and very large diameter fibers. Its role in midline control, providing continuity across the sensorimotor representations, may represent one of the most basic and earliest functions of interhemispheric fibers, while processes like bimanual coordination and some aspects of speech perception and production (the corpus callosum may participate, but is not essential for speech processes), may have appeared as late acquisitions. Another question that remains is whether having such abundant interhemispheric connectivity provides any processing advantage to the mammalian brain over that of birds, some of which have shown cognitive capacities as elaborate as those of many mammals, or even more so. Comparative research in the organization of large-scale networks in mammals and birds is needed to provide insight into this issue.

References

Aboitiz F, Montiel J (2003) One hundred million years of interhemispheric communication: the history of the corpus callosum. Braz J Med Biol Res 36:409–420

Aboitiz F, López J, Montiel J (2003) Long distance communication in the human brain: timing constraints for inter-hemispheric synchrony and the origin of brain lateralization. Biol Res 36:89–99

Aboitiz F, Scheibel AB, Zaidel E (1992a) Morphometry of the Sylvian fissure and the corpus callosum, with emphasis on sex differences. Brain 115:1521–1541

Aboitiz F, Scheibel AB, Fisher RS, Zaidel E (1992b) Fiber composition of the human corpus callosum. Brain Res 598:143–153

Aggoun-Zouaoui D, Innocenti GM (1994) Juvenile visual callosal axons in kittens display origin- and fate-related morphology and distribution of arbors. Eur J Neurosci 6:1846–1863

Berbel P, Innocenti GM (1988) The development of the corpus callosum in cats: a light- and electron-microscopic study. J Comp Neurol 276:132–156

Brunetti E, Maldonado PE, Aboitiz F (2013) Phase synchronization of delta and theta oscillations increase during the detection of relevant lexical information. Front Psychol 4:308

Buzsáki G, Logothetis N, Singer W (2013) Scaling brain size, keeping timing: evolutionary preservation of brain rhythms. Neuron 80:751–764

Caminiti R, Ghaziri H, Galuske R, Hof PR, Innocenti GM (2009) Evolution amplified processing with temporally dispersed slow neuronal connectivity in primates. Proc Natl Acad Sci U S A 106:19551–19556

Caminiti R, Carducci F, Piervincenzi C, Battaglia-Mayer A, Confalone G, Visco-Comandini F, Pantano P, Innocenti GM (2013) Diameter, length, speed, and conduction delay of callosal axons in macaque monkeys and humans: comparing data from histology and magnetic resonance imaging diffusion tractography. J Neurosci 33:14501–1411

Chait M, Greenberg S, Arai T, Simon JZ, Poeppel D (2015) Multi-time resolution analysis of speech: evidence from psychophysics. Front Neurosci 9:214

Dickson BJ, Gilestro GF (2006) Regulation of commissural axon pathfinding by slit and its Robo receptors. Annu Rev Cell Dev Biol 22:651–675

Dorion AA, Chantôme M, Hasboun D, Zouaoui A, Marsault C, Capron C, Duyme M (2000) Hemispheric asymmetry and corpus callosum morphometry: a magnetic resonance imaging study. Neurosci Res 36:9–13

Edwards TJ, Sherr EH, Barkovich AJ, Richards LJ (2014) Clinical, genetic and imaging findings identify new causes for corpus callosum development syndromes. Brain 137:1579–1613

Eliassen JC, Baynes K, Gazzaniga MS (2000) Anterior and posterior callosal contributions to simultaneous bimanual movements of the hands and fingers. Brain 123:2501–2511

Engel AK, König P, Kreiter AK, Singer W (1991) Interhemispheric synchronization of oscillatory neuronal responses in cat visual cortex. Science 252:1177–1179

Fothergill T, Donahoo AL, Douglass A, Zalucki O, Yuan J, Shu T, Goodhill GJ, Richards LJ (2014) Netrin-DCC signaling regulates corpus callosum formation through attraction of pioneering axons and by modulating Slit2-mediated repulsion. Cereb Cortex 24:1138–1151

Harrison KH, Hof PR, Wang SS (2002) Scaling laws in the mammalian neocortex: does form provide clues to function. J Neurocytol 31:289–298

Hopkins WD, Pilger JF, Storz R, Ambrose A, Hof PR, Sherwood CC (2012) Planum temporale asymmetries correlate with corpus callosum axon fiber density in chimpanzees (Pan troglodytes). Behav Brain Res 234:248–254

Houzel JC, Carvalho ML, Lent R (2002) Interhemispheric connections between primary visual areas: beyond the midline rule. Braz J Med Biol Res 35:1441–1453

Hubel DH (1988) Eye, Brain and Vision. Scientific American Library, New York

Huth AG, de Heer WA, Griffiths TL, Theunissen FE, Gallant JL (2016) Natural speech reveals the semantic maps that tile human cerebral cortex. Nature 532:453–458

Iacoboni M, Zaidel E (1999) The crossed-uncrossed difference in simple reaction times to lateralized auditory stimuli is not a measure of interhemispheric transmission time: evidence from the split brain. Exp Brain Res 128:421–424

Innocenti GM (1981) Growth and reshaping of axons in the establishment of visual callosal connections. Science 212:824–827

Innocenti GM (1986) General organization of callosal connections in the cerebral cortex. In: Jones EG, Peters A (eds) Cerebral Cortex. Volume 5. Sensory Motor Areas and Aspects of Cortical Connectivity. Plenum Press, New York, p 291–354

Innocenti GM, Bressoud R (2003) Callosal axons and their development. In: Zaidel E, Iacoboni M (eds) The Parallel Brain. Cognitive Neuroscience of the Corpus Callosum. MIT Press, Cambridge, p 11–26

Innocenti GM, Fiore L, Caminiti R (1977) Exuberant projection into the corpus callosum from the visual cortex of newborn cats. Neurosci Lett 4:237–242

Innocenti GM, Caminiti R, Hof PR (2010) Fiber composition in the planum temporale sector of the corpus callosum in chimpanzee and human. Brain Struct Funct 215:123–128

Innocenti GM, Vercelli A, Caminiti R (2014) The diameter of cortical axons depends both on the area of origin and target. Cereb Cortex 24:2178–2188

Innocenti GM, Dyrby TB, Andersen KW, Rouiller EM, Caminiti R (2016) The crossed projection to the striatum in two species of Monkey and in

Humans: behavioral and evolutionary significance. Cereb Cortex pii: bhw161 [EPub ahead of Print]

Johnston JM, Vaishnavi SN, Smyth MD, Zhang D, He BJ, Zempel JM, Shimony JS, Snyder AZ, Raichle ME (2008) Loss of resting interhemispheric functional connectivity after complete section of the corpus callosum. J Neurosci 28:6453–6458

Josse G, Seghier ML, Kherif F, Price CJ (2008) Explaining function with anatomy: language lateralization and corpus callosum size. J Neurosci 28:14132–14139

Katz MJ, Lasek RJ, Silver J (1983) Ontophyletics of the nervous system: development of the corpus callosum and evolution of axon tracts. Proc Natl Acad Sci U S A 80:5936–5940

Koppel H, Innocenti GM (1983) Is there a genuine exuberancy of callosal projections in development? A quantitative electron microscopic study in the cat. Neurosci Lett 41:33–40

Kutas M, Hillyard SA (1980) Reading senseless sentences: brain potentials reflect semantic incongruity. Science 207:203–205

LaMantia AS, Rakic P (1990a) Cytological and quantitative characteristics of four cerebral commissures in the rhesus monkey. J Comp Neurol 291:520–537

LaMantia AS, Rakic P (1990b) Axon overproduction and elimination in the corpus callosum of the developing rhesus monkey. J Neurosci 10:2156–2175

Lindwall C, Fothergill T, Richards LJ (2007) Commissure formation in the mammalian forebrain. Curr Opin Neurobiol 17:3–14

Luders E, Cherbuin N, Thompson PM, Gutman B, Anstey KJ, Sachdev P, Toga AW (2010) When more is less: associations between corpus callosum size and handedness lateralization. Neuroimage 52:43–49

Macleod CM (1992) The Stroop task: the "gold standard" of attentional measures. J Exp Psychol: General 121:12–14

Mihrshahi R (2006) The corpus callosum as an evolutionary innovation. J Exp Zool B Mol Dev Evol 306:8–17

Mohr B, Pulvermüller F, Zaidel E (1994) Lexical decision after left, right and bilateral presentation of function words, content words and nonwords: evidence for interhemispheric interaction. Neuropsychologia 32:105–124

Newell FW (1989) Franciscus Cornelis Donders (1818–1889). Am J Ophthalm 107:691–693

Nir Y, Mukamel R, Dinstein I, Privman E, Harel M, Fisch L, Gelbard-Sagiv H, Kipervasser S, Andelman F, Neufeld MY, Kramer U, Arieli A, Fried I, Malach R (2008) Interhemispheric correlations of slow spontaneous neuronal fluctuations revealed in human sensory cortex. Nat Neurosci 11:1100–1108

Olivares R, Michalland S, Aboitiz F (2000) Cross-species and intraspecies morphometric analysis of the corpus callosum. Brain Behav Evol 55:37–43

Olivares R, Montiel J, Aboitiz F (2001) Species differences and similarities in the fine structure of the mammalian corpus callosum. Brain Behav Evol 57:98–105

Paul LK, Van Lancker-Sidtis D, Schieffer B, Dietrich R, Brown WS (2003) Communicative deficits in agenesis of the corpus callosum: nonliteral language and affective prosody. Brain Lang 85:313–324

Peiker C, Wunderle T, Eriksson D, Schmidt A, Schmidt KE (2013) An updated midline rule: visual callosal connections anticipate shape and motion in ongoing activity across the hemispheres. J Neurosci 33:18036–18046

Peiker I, David N, Schneider TR, Nolte G, Schöttle D, Engel AK (2015) Perceptual integration deficits in autism spectrum disorders are associated with reduced interhemispheric gamma-band coherence. J Neurosci 35:16352–16361

Phillips KA, Schaeffer JA, Hopkins WD (2013) Corpus callosal microstructure influences intermanual transfer in chimpanzees. Front Syst Neurosci 7:125

Phillips KA, Stimpson CD, Smaers JB, Raghanti MA, Jacobs B, Popratiloff A, Hof PR, Sherwood CC. (2015) The corpus callosum in primates: processing speed of axons and the evolution of hemispheric asymmetry. Proc Biol Sci 282:20151535. Erratum in: Proc Biol Sci. 2016, 283:1826. Proc Biol Sci. 2015, 282:1819

Poffenberger AT (1912) Reaction time to retinal stimulation with special reference to the time lost in conduction through nerve centers. Arch Psychol 23:1–73

Ramón y Cajal S (1898) Estructura del quiasma óptico y teoria general de los entrecruzamientos nerviosos. Rev Trim Micrograf 3:2–18

Ramón y Cajal S (2006) Recuerdos de mi Vida. Crítica Editorial, Barcelona

Rehmel JL, Brown WS, Paul LK (2016) Proverb comprehension in individuals with agenesis of the corpus callosum. Brain Lang 160:21–29

Richards LJ (2002) Surrounded by Slit–how forebrain commissural axons can be led astray. Neuron 33:153–155

Ringo JL, Doty RW, Demeter S, Simard PY (1994) Time is of the essence: a conjecture that hemispheric specialization arises from interhemispheric conduction delay. Cereb Cortex 4:331–343

Sammler D, Kotz SA, Eckstein K, Ott DV, Friederici AD (2010) Prosody meets syntax: the role of the corpus callosum. Brain 133:2643–2655

Shen K, Mišić B, Cipollini BN, Bezgin G, Buschkuehl M, Hutchison RM, Jaeggi SM, Kross E, Peltier SJ, Everling S, Jonides J, McIntosh AR, Berman MG (2015) Stable long-range interhemispheric coordination is supported by direct anatomical projections. Proc Natl Acad Sci U S A 112:6473–6478

Sisti HM, Geurts M, Gooijers J, Heitger MH, Caeyenberghs K, Beets IA, Serbruyns L, Leemans A, Swinnen SP (2012) Microstructural organization of corpus callosum projections to prefrontal cortex predicts bimanual motor learning. Learn Mem 19:351–357

Stefanko SZ (1980) Fasciculus callosus longitudinalis (bundle of Probst) and its relation to the corpus callosum. Patol Pol 31:263–272

Steinmann S, Leicht G, Ertl M, Andreou C, Polomac N, Westerhausen R, Friederici AD, Mulert C (2014) Conscious auditory perception related to long-range synchrony of gamma oscillations. Neuroimage 100:435–443

Stroop JR (1935) Studies of interference in serial verbal reactions. J Exp Psychol 18:643–662

Suárez R, Gobius I, Richards LJ (2014) Evolution and development of interhemispheric connections in the vertebrate forebrain. Front Hum Neurosci 8:497

Tomasch J (1954) Size, distribution, and number of fibres in the human corpus callosum. Anat Rec 119:119–135

Turk AA, Brown WS, Symington M, Paul LK (2010) Social narratives in agenesis of the corpus callosum: linguistic analysis of the Thematic Apperception Test. Neuropsychologia 48:43–50

Unni DK, Piper M, Moldrich RX, Gobius I, Liu S, Fothergill T, Donahoo AL, Baisden JM, Cooper HM, Richards LJ (2012) Multiple Slits regulate the development of midline glial populations and the corpus callosum. Dev Biol 365:36–49

Wahl M, Lauterbach-Soon B, Hattingen E, Hübers A, Ziemann U (2015) Callosal anatomical and effective connectivity between primary motor cortices predicts visually cued bimanual temporal coordination performance. Brain Struct Funct 221:3427–3443

Wang SS, Shultz JR, Burish MJ, Harrison KH, Hof PR, Towns LC, Wagers MW, Wyatt KD (2008) Functional trade-offs in white matter axonal scaling. J Neurosci 28:4047–4056

Wang D, Buckner RL, Liu H (2014) Functional specialization in the human brain estimated by intrinsic hemispheric interaction. J Neurosci 34:12341–12352

Witelson SF (1985) The brain connection: the corpus callosum is larger in left-handers. Science 229:665–668

Woelfle R, Grahn JA (2013) Auditory and visual interhemispheric communication in musicians and non-musicians. PLoS One 8:e84446

Zaidel E, Iacoboni M (2003) Introduction: Poffenberger's simple reaction time paradigm for measuring interhemispheric transfer time. In: Zaidel E, Iacoboni M (eds) The Parallel Brain. Cognitive Neuroscience of the Corpus Callosum. MIT Press, Cambridge, p 1–7

Zimmer C (2004) Soul Made Flesh. The Discovery of the Brain – and How it Changed the World. Free Press, New York

6

A Loop for Speech

Our minds are made of memories. Our past, our present and even our imagined future are memory representations of recent or past events, transformed in different ways by the neural networks that shape our behavior. Everything we do is strongly shaped by the many kinds of memory we have, from recognizing someone familiar, organizing a dinner, driving a car, our consciousness and the image of ourselves, not to mention the memory we need for proper education and the autobiographical memory that gives us a sense of identity. Furthermore, memory is not a single, unitary process but rather is composed of many different mechanisms involved in generating representations of past events in different sensory modalities. Early researchers in the field of memory recognized that there were at least two forms of memory, one permanent with infinite (or better, unknown) capacity, which remains stable over time, and the other of recent events, which lasts a few seconds and represents a gateway to form enduring memories. Recent memory is vivid, and makes our experiences combine in what seems a continuous stream of events forming the essence of our minds. Eloquently, the Nobel laureate Gerald Edelman titled one of his books on consciousness "*The Remembered Present*" (Edelman 1989).

© The Author(s) 2017
F. Aboitiz, *A Brain for Speech*,
DOI 10.1057/978-1-137-54060-7_6

Memento

Perhaps the first person to recognize the difference between short- and long-term memory was William James at the end of the nineteenth century, who referred to primary memory, which represented "the trailing edge of the conscious present" (James 1890). On the other hand, past memories corresponded to secondary memory, possibly under the assumption that short-term memory is a first stage required to establish long-term memories. In the 1940s Donald Hebb introduced the concept of short-term memory, which was dependent on electrical brain activity, as opposed to long-term memory, which was produced by neurochemical changes (Hebb 1949). Hebb proposed a basic principle for the generation of memories (now called Hebb's rule), based on the maintenance of synapses that successfully exert changes in activity in the next neuron, while synapses that fail to produce a postsynaptic effect are doomed to be eliminated. Hebb's principle has had a tremendous impact on neuro and cognitive science, as it provides a simple mechanism to explain short-term memory, long-term learning and neural plasticity, including the critical periods of neuronal development discussed in the Chapter 1. In the last century, evidence had accumulated that memories decay rapidly if there is no opportunity to rehearse them behaviorally or mentally. The studies by George Miller in the 1950s provided a deeper understanding of the nature of short-term memory, by showing that it has a limited capacity, allowing the storage of no more than about seven separate items in experimental subjects (Miller 1956). One of the earliest tests to assess short-term memory was the digit span test, which requires serial recall of random sequences of digits. As might be expected, the shorter sequence, the more accurate the performance.

What would life be without being able to develop new memories? Guy Pearce provided an eloquent interpretation of this condition in Christopher Nolan's movie "Memento", where the main character has lost his capacity to acquire new knowledge, as his short-term memory vanishes as soon as he changes his focus of attention. This results in a total loss of the sense of continuity and consequent disorientation that deeply affects the subject's daily life. But such profound impairment is not just fiction. In the early 1950s, a patient called Henry Molaison, also known as HM, underwent profound brain surgery at the age of 16 to treat intractable temporal lobe epilepsy. The surgical procedure eliminated most of his medial temporal lobes bilaterally, including the hippocampus and adjacent structures. Fortunately, this massive surgery alleviated his condition, but on the other hand he was left with severe anterograde amnesia, that is, the incapacity to transfer new information from short-term to long-term memory. Brenda Milner, who had been studying the role of the primate medial temporal lobe in memory, was impressed with this case and made a thorough neuropsychological study of HM (Scoville and Milner 1957). Notably, HM had a preserved short-term memory (evidenced in a normal performance in the digit span test) and procedural memory (the capacity to learn and remember motor programs like riding a bicycle), but was not able to use newly acquired information over the long term. He also had some retrograde amnesia, that is, he could not remember events that happened some 2 years before the surgery, suggesting that these memories were still in the process of being consolidated as enduring long-term memories. By the end of his life in 2008, he was capable of incorporating some new memories and modifying preexisting ones, which indicates a degree of plasticity in the networks controlling his behavior (Banks et al. 2014).

Since the findings by Milner and others, there have been many studies of short-term memory (Baddeley 2007). The earliest formal models of short-term memory, developed in the 1960s, considered in general three stages in memory processing, the first being a sensory memory that could be visual (iconic memory) or auditory (echoic memory). After this, there was a short-term or working memory storage box, which transiently held information, but was also related to direct behavioral control. Finally, there was long-term store of enduring memories. Long-term memories could go back to the short-term store to participate in behavioral responses. It was assumed that the short-term memory store was one and the same for all kinds of memory, and there was no proposal for a specific mechanism involved in transferring memories from the short- to the long-term store. The main determinant of the probability of transfer to the long-term store was assumed to be the length of time remaining in the short-term box. However, several studies showed that the behavioral or cognitive context in which recent memories were acquired is more important for transfer to long-term memory than time. For example, simple classification of items results in poor long-term acquisition, while items that have to be verbalized are more likely to be retained, and highly meaningful items or ones with emotional content are even more strongly maintained. In addition, assuming that there is only one short-term memory box suggests that short-term memory patients are deficient in all kinds of short-term memory tasks. However, many such patients live relatively normal lives, like running a shop or driving taxi. This means that some types of short-term memory are indeed spared, even though such patients perform poorly on tests like the digit span. Cases like HM are in a way extreme, while most short-term memory patients are not as impaired as he was. The exact process by which short-term memory rapidly decays with time has been a matter of much discussion and is not yet settled. Two main hypotheses have been presented, one is that memory traces spontaneously decay over time, and the other suggests that this decay is based primarily on interference from other sources of activity. In the latter view, inhibitory mechanisms actively repress interfering processes, and control the maintenance of memory traces. Additionally, behavioral rehearsal mechanisms such as vocalizing the remembered items could be an important factor that counteracts the effects of interference or spontaneous decay.

A special case of memory encapsulation was offered by patients with verbal short-term memory deficits. Several papers were published, notably by Elizabeth Warrington and Tim Shallice, describing brain lesion patients with deficits in short-term memory for words and numbers, while visual short-term memory was intact (Warrington and Shallice 1969). Noteworthy, in such patients the lesions were usually located in the left temporoparietal region and not the medial temporal lobe. Furthermore, despite their memory impairment, these subjects were perfectly able to sustain simple routine conversations, and spoke normally, that is, they were not speech impaired. Note that this symptom is very different from aphasia, as in addition to short-term memory deficits; in the latter there is a serious speech condition. Warrington and Shallice interpreted these symptoms as selective disruption of verbal short-term memory (particularly auditory), and spoke of a temporal buffer that maintains perceived speech for a couple of seconds, but was clearly not necessary for everyday speech. At about the same time, Alan Baddeley and Graham Hitch were working with a model for verbal short-term memory based on motor output, that is, constant vocal articulation of the remembered items to sustain the memory trace. However, the findings of verbal short-term memory patients without speech problems called for a revision of this interpretation. Thus, Baddeley and collaborators decided to include an additional component to their articulatory model of verbal short-term memory, a phonological storage buffer that transiently maintains auditory representation while reverberation of the articulatory loop refreshes the memory trace. As we will see below, this component has turned out to be one of the most controversial in Baddeley's model. In this context, in the 1970s Baddeley and Hitch introduced and popularized the model of working memory, as a limited capacity system that maintains information in the short-term, while one performs cognitively demanding tasks such as reasoning, comprehension or learning (Baddeley and Hitch 1974).

Perhaps no one can better tell the genesis of the concept of working memory better than Baddeley. In his influential book *Working memory, Thought and Action*, he provides a very clear account of these developments, which I will succinctly review here (Baddeley 2007). Although Baddeley confessed to having been reluctant to write this book for a long time, many of us are grateful to him for having done so. Moreover, I felt particular empathy with him when he acknowledged his wife at the beginning of the book for her support and encouragement to a husband that wandered about talking to himself instead of doing household chores. Initially, Baddeley and collaborators had shown double dissociation between short- and long-term memory impairments; that is, patients could have deficits in the former and not the latter, or conversely perform normally in short-term memory tests and show long-term memory impairments. An experimental paradigm, called the recency effect well illustrated the difference between the two kinds of memory (Baddeley 1968; Baddeley and Hitch 1993). This phenomenon is seen when subjects have to repeat in whatever order a list of words they have been shown. If recall is immediately after seeing the list, the last items on the list are better recalled than the first ones. However, if there is a short interval between the list and the recall time, this effect tends to vanish, and items presented earlier can be recalled just as well as the later ones. Long-term memory amnesic patients show a strong recency effect as their short-term memory is good, but tend to fail when recalling the early items. On the other hand, short-term memory patients perform the other way around, doing well with the earlier items and badly with later ones.

Subsequently, Baddeley and Hitch asked normal subjects to continuously rehearse a random sequence of digits while performing a verbal reasoning task like responding true or false to sentences like "A follows B → BA" (true), or "B is not preceded by A → AB" (false), and other combinations (Baddeley and Hitch 1974). Verbally repeating only one digit during the task (say one, one, one, etc.) impeded overt vocal reasoning, while randomly repeating a rising number of digits involved a load on working memory that progressively demanded processing capacity. Notably, as the number of digits to be rehearsed increased from 0 to 8, the time required to respond increased significantly but modestly, from 2.2 seconds to only 2.9 seconds. Moreover, subjects made only about 4% errors in the task regardless of the digit load, that is, this had no effect on the rate of successful trials. Baddeley and Hitch concluded that the observed effect was far less than was predicted from the single unit short-term memory model, and decided to move on to a different, multicomponent model of working memory.

Baddeley's Memories

George Miller and others like Richard Shiffrin used the term "working memory" to refer to a kind of short-term memory used for problem solving. However, Baddeley and Hitch formalized this concept into a model of memory processing involving different components and processing stages. Baddeley and Hitch conceived of working memory as a limited capacity system that maintains information in the short-term while one performs cognitively demanding tasks like reasoning, comprehension or learning. In effect, working memory involves storage and manipulation of elements in the context of a behavioral task, while the more general term short-term memory refers to a passive, short-term imprinting of events that eventually are extinguished or transformed into long-term memories (Baddeley 2007, 2012).

Baddeley and Hitch's multicomponent model of working memory consists of two modality-specific and limited-capacity storage systems, one for visuospatial behavior, called the visuospatial sketchpad, and the other for auditory-vocal behavior, called the phonological loop (Fig. 6.1) (Baddeley and Hitch 1974). While the former is involved in tasks related to spatial orientation and visual search, the latter keeps vocal and acoustic information online and is involved in inner speech. Maintenance of visuospatial sensory information in these stores partly depends on motor rehearsal involving head, eye, and possibly hand movements, or attentional displacements. Phonological rehearsal involves overt or covert speech (also called inner speech). These sensorimotor components are in turn supervised by a multimodal attentional

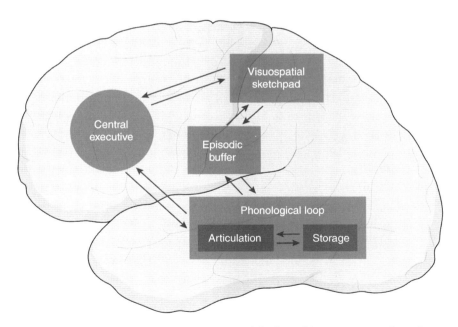

Fig. 6.1 Baddeley's multicomponent model of working memory. There is no precise statement in the model about the anatomical location of the components

control system, the central executive, which manipulates the items in the sensory loops according to cognitive or behavioral demands. The visuospatial sketchpad was initially assessed with a visual orienting task in which there were two alternative ways to recall a path through the university campus, one using rote verbal rehearsal and the other based on visual imagery, recalling relevant points and then mentally connecting them. Subjects performed better in the latter (Baddeley 2007). In a second step, subjects had to complete a visuomotor tracking task parallel to doing the test. With this additional requirement, the advantage observed in the visual imagery task disappeared and performance fell to the level in rote verbal recall. Thus, visuomotor performance impaired visuospatial tracking as it interfered with the rehearsal component of visuospatial working memory.

Baddeley and Hitch assumed that the phonological loop, which is of the utmost relevance for this book, consists of a phonological store and an articulatory rehearsal mechanism. The authors tapped the phonological store with the phonological similarity effect, which is based on the tendency to confuse similar sounding letters like /d/and /t/. Baddeley found that visually presented strings of phonetically similar monosyllabic words were more difficult to recall in the short-term than strings of dissimilar words (Baddeley 1966). This effect was more pronounced than when comparing semantically similar vs. semantically dissimilar word strings. Conversely, in long-term memory tests, semantic similarity impairs recall more than does phonological similarity. This finding underscores the role of phonological processing (as opposed to semantic processing) in short-term memory, even with visually presented stimuli. Basically, visual stimuli have to be first translated into an auditory memory trace that is subvocalized before it is recognized. Another strategy to disrupt phonological storage capacity was to use the irrelevant speech effect, which basically consists of presenting irrelevant sounds while subjects memorize a string of words or letters (Salamé and Baddeley 1982, 1990). These stimuli need not be speech, as they can also be irregular sounds that compete with the phonological trace in auditory short-term memory. According to Baddeley, complex auditory information obliges access to the phonological store, there being no filter to separate relevant from irrelevant input (Baddeley 2000a).

The articulatory component of the phonological loop can be reflected in a phenomenon called the word length effect, in which the recall of recently presented word strings declines with longer words (after controlling for the different exposure times to long versus short word strings with equal numbers of words) (Baddeley et al. 1975). The short-term auditory memory trace tends to fade rapidly unless it is reactivated by a motor process. Therefore, immediate recall is limited by the decay of the auditory trace and the articulatory speed capacity of the subject. Longer words take more time to be articulated and therefore decay more rapidly than shorter words. However, there is still discussion regarding the exact process involved in the word length effect, whether it owes to the longer rehearsal time per se or to the greater phonological complexity of longer words. Finally, articulatory suppression is an experimental manipulation, consisting of covertly repeating an irrelevant sound during the task while word strings are presented acoustically (Murray 1968). This inhibits motor rehearsal and strongly impairs performance, but suppresses the word length effect. However, the phonological similarity effect is spared, which depends on the phonological store. The effect of articulatory suppression is best observed with visual presentation of verbal stimuli, in which the visual image has to be translated into a phonetic representation. In this condition, articulatory suppression eliminates both the word length and the phonological similarity effects. The latter is eliminated because the translation of the seen stimulus into a sound cannot be readily executed. Thus, neither the auditory trace nor the articulatory speed has any effect on memory maintenance, generating poor performance at all levels. Later in this chapter, I will discuss imaging studies that purport to localize the phonological store and the articulatory system, and criticisms of these findings.

The executive component of working memory was more difficult to tackle, and its conceptualization was derived from Donald Norman and Tim Shallice's schema of attentional control developed in the 1980s (Norman and Shallice 1983). The authors distinguished two attentional mechanisms at work during daily behavior. The first is an automatic habit-based system that one uses to drive home from work, and the second, of more relevance to Baddeley's model, is a supervisory attentional system that involves contextual awareness and permits circumventing the habit system when it is no longer appropriate or when one is in a novel setting. These two components may be also separated anatomically, the automatic system putting more emphasis on basal ganglia or striatal networks, while the supervisory attentional system is biased to parietal-prefrontal cortical networks. However, Baddeley realized that an additional component was necessary that feeds long-term memory input into the working memory network to address more complex forms of working memory like recalling the elements of a discourse. This was investigated by more complicated studies on working memory span, in which subjects were presented a list of sentences and had to remember the last word of each. This measure is a good predictor of many cognitive capacities, and requires the use of long-term skills in addition to the simple mental manipulation assumed for the initial working memory model. Baddeley conceived the episodic buffer as an interface between the phonological loop, the visuospatial sketchpad and the central executive, which binds incoming information in integrated episodes that can be maintained in the mid-term (Baddeley 2000b). This is different from episodic memory, which is a long-term memory of experiences acquired in a single shot, in that the episodic buffer is transient in nature and related to the specific task. Nonetheless, episodic memory is strongly dependent on the hippocampus, and there is much recent evidence indicating hippocampal involvement in working memory tasks (Baddeley et al. 2011).

Images of Memory

Baddeley's working memory model inspired studies using imaging methods to establish the neuroanatomical regions involved in the different components of this model. Initially many studies concentrated on the phonological loop, which is more amenable to experimental analyses than the visuospatial sketchpad or the central executive. The first of these studies by Eraldo Paulesu, Chris Frith and Richard Frackowiak (Paulesu et al. 1993) used PET to compare brain activation patterns in subjects doing two different tasks, one consisting of short-term memorization of visual letters that supposedly engages both the phonological store and the subvocal articulatory system. This was contrasted to a similar task using Korean characters, a language that none of the subjects knew. Subtracting the activities in the two conditions highlighted the areas specifically involved in the phonological loop, including both the rehearsal and storage systems, as Korean letters were perceived only as visual stimuli. After this, Frith and Frackowiak applied an additional task requiring rhyming judgments. This was assumed to involve only the subvocal rehearsal mechanism and not the phonological store, as articulatory suppression specifically impairs rhyming judgment capacity. Furthermore, Giuseppe Vallar and Baddeley had shown that in patients with verbal storage deficits there was no deficit in rhyming judgments, indicating that the phonological store is not required for this task (Vallar et al. 1991). By subtracting the activity seen in the letter memorization task from that of the rhyming task, they expected to evidence the locus of activation of the phonological store system only, as it was supposed to be inactive (or less active) during the rhyming task, while the rehearsal system was active in both conditions. The main findings were activation of the left inferior parietal lobe (anterior part, Brodmann's area 40) associated with the phonological store, and activation in posterior Broca's area (pars opercularis, Brodmann's area 44), associated with subvocal rehearsal. These findings provoked a lot of excitement because patients with damage to the inferior parietal area and with deficits in phonological working memory had been reported earlier, although many of the lesions in these patients also involved temporal areas (Baddeley 2007; Vallar et al. 1991; Warrington and Shallice 1969).

Some years later, Bradley Buchsbaum and Mark D'Esposito criticized the report by Paulesu and collaborators, citing evidence that the rhyming task indeed activates the phonological storage system, even if it is not necessary for the task (Buchsbaum and D'Esposito 2008). Therefore, the difference observed in activation does not accurately reflect a phonological store system. It can reasonably be counter-argued that there may be a difference in metabolic activity when a structure is necessary for a task from when the structure participates in the task but is not required for it, and this is reflected in the observed difference between the two tasks. In other words, even if the phonological store is activated during the rhyming task, it may be less active than in the visual letter memorization task because it may not be critical for rhyming judgment. Nonetheless, this possibility needs to be tested experimentally. Buchsbaum and D'Esposito also made more serious objections to these findings, which I will describe in a few more paragraphs.

In the same year as Paulesu's report, John Jonides and collaborators published a PET study assessing brain activation in a visuospatial working memory task that consisted of showing a subject an array of three dots on a screen and after three seconds the subject was presented with a spot that matched or did not match the location of the previous dots. This was contrasted with a similar task that required minimal memory, that is, there was no delay between probe and target (Jonides et al. 1998). In the memory condition, Jonides and team found increased activation in area 40 of the right hemisphere (the same as in Paulesu's study but in the other hemisphere), in left frontal regions and in visual areas. Jonides' group subsequently developed a series of studies aimed at distinguishing the activation patterns of verbal versus spatial working memory processes and confirmed the association between phonological storage tasks with activation of the left inferior parietal lobe, although the precise inferoparietal area activated seemed to depend on the specific task used. Their findings were also consistent with a link between verbal rehearsal tasks and activation of Broca's region. The participation of right inferior parietal and frontal areas in the visuospatial network was also consistently observed. Using more complex designs, such as the N-back task (see Chapter 2), Jonides and collaborators found that verbal material activated the same regions in the left hemisphere as in the previous verbal tasks, but with prefrontal activation that increased with memory load, reflecting the recruitment of executive processes. There were other areas that evidenced activation, like the right cerebellum, and in highly demanding tasks there was also a mild activation of equivalent areas of the right hemisphere. This experiment is open to criticism as the N-back task heavily involves executive processes, and it has been claimed that it does not put increasing demands on phonological storage given that the number of digits in the store is probably constant regardless of the load. However, this assumption has not been verified experimentally. There were other studies that failed to detect left inferior parietal-Broca activation in verbal working memory tasks, but these tasks used semantically meaningful stimuli that confuse the processes being analyzed.

Jonides and collaborators also analyzed the rehearsal mechanisms involved in visuospatial working memory, focusing on attentional direction during the memorization interval (Smith and Jonides 1997). They did not address eye movements, perhaps a more natural effector system for attentional displacement, as these were at the time difficult to monitor and subjects were asked to fix their sight on the center of the screen. Instead, the authors employed a classical design by Michael Posner, who pioneered cognitive studies of attentional mechanisms (Posner and Petersen 1990). Basically, Posner's experiments showed that response to a visual stimulus is more rapid if it coincides with the region where attention is allocated, even if the eyes are not fixed on that position. In the working memory experiment of Jonides' group subjects had to memorize a spatial location, and concurrently a stimulus appeared either within the region kept in memory or outside it, that had to be discriminated. Discrimination evoked a stronger response when the stimulus fell into the patch the subject had to keep in mind, indicating that attention was located in this place. Finally, the central executive proved to be very elusive for imaging studies, as it has been very difficult to design a task that isolates executive processes. Attempts to do so have been inconclusive or contradictory until now. There is general consensus that the central executive probably relies heavily on prefrontal cortex activity, but agreement stops there. In parallel to these studies, several electrophysiological experiments were taking place by other researchers using visual working memory tasks with monkeys, which I will discuss more extensively in the next chapter. These studies revealed two parallel circuits, one via the parietal lobe that processes object location, and the other via the temporal lobe that processes object identity.

Boxes or Networks?

In their critique of imaging studies of working memory, Buchsbaum and D'Esposito referred to a meta-analysis of the data from the group of Julie Fiez (Fiez et al. 1995). The authors emphasized the variability of the activated locus in the inferior parietal lobe, which ranged from area 40 (supramarginal gyrus) to the more posterior area 39 (angular gyrus), and dorsally up to the intraparietal sulcus bordering the superior parietal lobe. The precise locus of activity was highly dependent on the precise task. For example, activation of intraparietal areas was more evident when using visual-demanding protocols. Furthermore, and perhaps more importantly, Fiez's group noted that if Baddeley's notion of obligatory access to the phonological loop was correct, inferior parietal activation should be observed when subjects listen passively to speech, which had not been reported. Furthermore, studies with monkeys had shown sustained patterns of activation of individual neurons during the delay period of a visual working memory task (see the next chapter). This is the period between presenting a stimulus and response, where sensory information must be kept active as the animal waits for the next response. These neurons were interpreted as memory-related cells. Thus, if a storage system is present, it should be active especially during the delay period, which is when information has to be maintained online. However, previous reports had averaged brain activity throughout the memory task, so it was not possible to determine which areas showed this specific maintained activity. Consequently, Buchsbaum, D'Esposito, Gregory Hickok and others searched for regions of the brain that become active during both the passive presentation of speech sounds and in the memory delay period. In one study, Hickok, Buchsbaum and Colin Humphries used an auditory verbal working memory task with multisyllabic pseudowords (Hickok et al. 2003). They observed only two brain regions that showed persistent activity during both the presentation of the stimulus and the delay period: the posterior superior temporal sulcus, where phonemes are integrated into word forms (see Chapter 2), and a small region in the posterior depth of the Sylvian fissure at the intersection of the temporal and parietal lobes, which they appropriately called Spt (for Sylvian, parietal and temporal). Further studies indicated that these areas also show sustained activation with nonsense speech and musical stimuli. In addition, these areas are active with both visual verbal and auditory verbal stimuli, but the superior temporal sulcus has some preference for auditory stimuli. Activity in these areas decays over time, which is consistent with a fading memory trace. It was also noted that these areas are by no means speech-specific and therefore are not exclusively phonological. These findings are consistent with aforementioned reports, indicating that many of the verbal working memory-impaired patients also had temporal lobe lesions in addition to damage to the inferior parietal (Baddeley 2007; Vallar et al. 1991; Warrington and Shallice 1969).

Area Spt and the superior temporal sulcus are embedded in the auditory processing circuits and are difficult to separate from early stages of sound analysis. Damage to these areas leads to severe speech deficits, unlike the purely short-term memory condition described by Shallice and Vallar. Considering this, Buchsbaum and D'Esposito argued that the phonological store is a psychological construct, without a neuroanatomical correlate in the brain (Buchsbaum and D'Esposito 2008). They further claimed that the rarity of the pure verbal short-term memory condition, with only 15 reported cases, suggests that these patients are indeed special cases, in which, for example, the right hemisphere may have assumed many language functions, albeit relying on a less robust network that evidences deficits like pure short-term memory. Buchsbaum and collaborators designed a dual-modality continuous recognition task, in which sequences of words were presented simultaneously in the auditory and visual modalities (Buchsbaum et al. 2011a). Subjects had to ignore the auditory stimuli, and discriminate whether each visually presented word had been visually presented before, or if it was a new word. Nonetheless, some of the visually presented words had been presented previously, not in the visual but in the acoustic modality. These visual stimuli were supposedly "new", as the acoustic stimuli had to be ignored. While overall subjects performed well in the task, fMRI-assessed bilateral activation of the inferior parietal lobe decreased with longer distances between the visually repeated words (increasing difficulty). Conversely, areas in the superior parietal and frontal lobes showed higher levels of activity with longer delays between words, which is consistent with their involvement in the difficulty of the task. Furthermore, this study confirmed dissociation between inferior parietal deactivation and activity in area Spt. More recently, D'Esposito and collaborators have criticized the notion that persistent activity in the prefrontal cortex actually represents memory storage, rejecting any claim of a localized storage buffer in the brain (D'Esposito and Postle 2015). As they argue, the only sites that store high-fidelity memory information are the sensory cortices, which is consistent with many recent findings indicating sensory activity during working memory tasks.

What function does area Spt serve? This region is considered an auditory-motor interface that binds acoustic representations with articulatory patterns in Broca's area, possibly via the arcuate fasciculus. Therefore, it represents a core component of the language network. Conduction aphasia, the symptoms of which include naming deficits, impaired verbal repetition and importantly, deficient verbal working memory, was initially believed to be caused by the disconnection between Broca's and Wernicke's areas via the arcuate fasciculus, but more recent studies have shown a significant involvement of gray matter in many patients (See Chapter 2). In an MRI study of 15 patients with conduction aphasia, Hickok, Nina Dronkers and colleagues found that the region of maximal lesion overlap fits the location of area Spt, which according to them explains most of the symptomatology of this condition (Buchsbaum et al. 2011b). This area may be connected to Broca's region, or to the vocal premotor cortex via the arcuate fasciculus or some adjacent tract (Saur et al. 2008). Complementary to this, Angela Friederici and her team assessed sentence processing and verbal working memory performance in a patient with a lesion involving the white matter underlying the left superior temporal gyrus, but sparing gray matter (Meyer et al. 2014). MRI examination revealed the absence of the arcuate fasciculus and the superior longitudinal fasciculus, the latter connecting parietal and frontal areas. Concomitantly, the patient performed poorly in verbal working memory tests, and in memory of sentences involving complex word order and long words, while performing better in tasks requiring long word storage. Another study by Friederici's group with normal subjects revealed that in normal speech, manipulation of phrase ordering (as in subject-first vs. object-first German sentences) primarily involved activation of Broca's area, while storage functions (phrases intervening between object and verb) were more associated with activation of the left temporoparietal junction and tractographic integrity of the arcuate fasciculus/superior longitudinal fasciculus (Meyer et al. 2012). Together, these findings imply that the connectivity of area Spt to

Broca's region via the arcuate fasciculus and other tracts is a critical component of verbal working memory. Likewise, Hickok's group confirmed a role of Broca's region and motor articulatory mechanisms in verbal working memory (Hickok et al. 2014). They assessed short-term verbal memory (assessed with a digit span task), and speech articulation deficits (apraxia of speech) with a series of stroke patients in the very early stages, before the onset of compensatory reorganizations of the damaged neuronal networks. Articulatory deficits were related to damage in posterior Broca's area, motor areas, insula and somatosensory areas, while verbal working memory was related mainly to posterior Broca's and motor areas. This indicates a close overlap in sensorimotor systems involved in speech production and verbal working memory.

So much for the search for a localized phonological store, especially in the inferior parietal lobe. Although the debate has not yet been settled, we will see in the next chapter that animal studies have shown that there no need for a specific storage system in the neural networks underlying visuospatial working memory. More generally, the notion that neuropsychological capacities are encapsulated in modular systems does not fit neuroscientific evidence. Nonetheless, besides the evidence shown here, there have been many other reports that have consistently found involvement of the inferior parietal lobe in verbal working memory tasks. It may be that these areas are recruited because verbal working memory demands attentional capacity, partly controlled by the inferior parietal lobe (as argued by Buchsbaum and D'Esposito), or that the inferior parietal lobe plays some role in rehearsal mechanisms, or that it contributes to the goal-directed component of working memory. For example, Baldo and Nina Dronkers tested patients with either inferior parietal or inferior frontal cortex damage in phonological storage tasks (including auditory rhyming, repetition and digit span), and in articulatory tasks (an n-back task and a visual rhyming task) (Baldo and Dronkers 2006). While inferior frontal patients were specifically impaired in rehearsal tasks, inferior parietal patients showed a deficit circumscribed to storage tasks. Using fMRI, Oliver Gruber and collaborators have done studies using the articulatory suppression condition to eliminate verbal strategies when performing working memory tasks like memory of letter names, colors or shapes, and found largely overlapping parieto-frontal networks associated with these different modalities (Gruber 2001; Gruber and von Cramon 2001). Furthermore, Gruber showed that during verbal working memory tasks performed under articulatory suppression, activation increased in the posterior inferior parietal lobe (instead of area 44) and anterior prefrontal areas. More recently, Gruber studied two selected patients, one with a bilateral lesion in the frontal pole and the other with a lesion restricted to Broca's area (Trost and Gruber 2012). The former had normal articulatory rehearsal capacity (measured in a subvocalization letter memory task) but impaired non-articulatory phonological working memory (that is, the same task under articulatory suppression), while the Broca's area patient showed intact non-articulatory verbal memory but was highly deficient in articulatory rehearsal tasks. This suggests that phonological storage mechanisms partly depend on networks other than the classical language networks, encompassing parieto-prefrontal systems.

Einat Lienbenthal and collaborators used dichotically presented syllables and chirps in an auditory recognition task with a combined ERP and fMRI protocol (Liebenthal et al. 2013). They found early syllable-specific activations in the auditory areas in the inferior parietal lobe and the ventral motor cortex. Moreover, concurrent left hemisphere activation in the inferior parietal and motor areas preceded the activation of left auditory areas, suggesting an anticipatory role. Dorothy Saur, Cornellius Weiller and collaborators found that the inferior parietal lobe contributed to both the ventral and dorsal language pathways (Kellmeyer et al. 2013). This team investigated the structural connectivity of areas involved in manipulations of segmental (shifting vowels) and suprasegmental (shifting stress placement) elements of pseudo words. The authors reported that connections between the left inferior parietal lobe and pars opercularis in Broca's area (area 44) participated in suprasegmental manipulations (dorsal pathway), while connections between the inferior parietal lobe and pars triangularis in Broca's region (area 45) participated in segmental manipulations (ventral pathway). These findings underscore the supporting role of parietal-frontal networks in phonological processing, even if they are not related to the phonological storage module. In another study of interest, Anne Sophie

Champod and Michael Petrides used an event-related fMRI design to assess the role of the inferior parietal cortex (particularly the intraparietal sulcus) in manipulating verbal information (Champod and Petrides 2010). They presented subjects with lists or abstract disyllabic words that had to be remembered in precise order. Subjects were then required to reorder the list (manipulation task) or to note the occurrence or non-occurrence of certain words from the remembered list when a new list was presented (monitoring task). A control task was simply to recall the words presented in each trial. While they observed increased activity in the prefrontal cortex during both manipulation and monitoring of progressively longer words, increased activity in the posterior parietal sulcus was related to manipulation but not monitoring information. Very recently, Cathy Price and collaborators assessed the participation of the supramarginal gyrus in a variety of phonological tasks, and identified specific subregions involved in articulatory sequencing, auditory short-term memory and lexical processing, which again supports the role of the inferior parietal lobe in the phonological loop (Oberhuber et al. 2016). Other components that have been involved in working memory circuits are the basal ganglia and the cerebellum. Both structures connect intensely with large regions of the cerebral cortex. Christopher Chatham, Michael Frank and David Badre proposed that the corpus striatum participates in input and output stimulus selection during working memory, mediated by contextual information provided by the frontal cortex (Chatham et al. 2014). Jutta Peterburs, Dominic Cheng and John Desmond have recently evidenced involvement of the cerebellum in controlling human eye movement in visual working memory tasks, which are dependent on memory load and independent of eye movements involved in stimulus analysis (Peterburs et al. 2015). While these designs have used mostly visuospatial tasks, it is possible that these systems play similar roles in verbal working memory.

Considering the above, parietal-prefrontal and subcortical networks may contribute to verbal working memory through indirect mechanisms, although they may not contain the memory elements that are kept online. Instead, these networks exert top-down influence over sensory regions in terms of the desired outcome or the motor programs that are to be selected. This view emphasizes a distributed system, encompassing sensory and higher order areas that support working memory tasks. In this way, activity in sensory regions is modulated, and possibly stabilized against interference by backward inputs from inferior parietal and frontal regions involved in motor programming and goal directed planning. In addition to these supporting components, increasing evidence indicates significant hippocampal involvement in the digit span and other working memory tasks (Baddeley 2000b). As with Baddeley's episodic buffer, working memory depends on the vivid representation of sensory input, which is provided by episodic memory, possibly via theta oscillations that propagate from the hippocampus to the cerebral cortex. A core circuit for verbal working memory therefore contains the arcuate fasciculus, connecting the auditory area Spt with the posterior of Broca's area, but includes surrounding components as subsidiary elements, as Evelina Fedorenko and collaborators have correctly emphasized (Chapter 2) (Fedorenko 2014).

In general, Baddeley's multicomponent model for working memory has been very influential, but it needs to be updated and revisited in the context of new neuroscientific evidence. The model of boxes involved in specific cognitive processes like articulation and storage is too simplistic for neuroscientific work, and will probably be replaced by a network-level model in which overlapping and distributed systems participate in different processes. Nonetheless, we owe Baddeley for introducing the concept of working memory as a kind of explicit short-term memory to be used in the near future, and especially to this book's purpose, for the concept of the phonological loop as a sensorimotor device that allows verbal acquisition, and may be unique to our species.

Tracking Sentences

Baddeley wondered what function verbal working memory serves, especially with subjects with low verbal working memory capacity that do reasonably well in normal life and are able to employ and understand forms of speech used in daily life. One possibility is that phonological memory is needed to understand complex forms of speech that cannot be processed automatically. Baddeley and Giuseppe Vallar worked with PV, a patient who was perfectly able to speak normally, with appropriate vocabulary and syntax, and normal speed and prosody (which rules out any speech processing deficit) (Vallar et al. 1991; Baddeley 2007). However, she was unable to understand relatively long and intricate sentences, especially passive ones, which required her to keep track of the initial elements to understand their meaning at the end. Linguists refer to these relations between distant elements in a phrase as long distance dependencies, while these are in fact time dependencies as whether in speech or reading, the relation between distant components is mediated by time and necessarily invoke some kind of memory. During reading, one can come back to the original words above on the page to help in understanding, while in speech one has to rely exclusively on memory, or else say, "Could you say that again?"

Thus, one possibility is that the loop serves to integrate complex sentences and track elements in memory phrases that are needed to understand the phrase as it is unfolding. This resembles the N-back task described in Chapter 2. However, this is not a simple retention memory task, as it requires manipulation of the items as they enter and exit the attention window, keeping their order in sequence. Thus, it also involves executive processes that may be at work during natural speech processing. Furthermore, there are additional elements in complex sentences that go beyond a mere string of concatenated elements. Steve Pinker argued that this is a critical element for language, requiring a special kind of memory that allows for keeping the first elements of sentences active as new words arrive (Pinker 1994). Some years ago, Eleanor Saffran went beyond the phonological dimension of working memory, putting forward a model that includes several parallel but interacting working memory systems involved in phonological, syntactic and semantic processing (Saffran and Marin 1975). Likewise, David Caplan has argued the existence of separate working memory systems for semantic and for syntactical processing (Caplan and Waters 1999). These ideas agree with Joaquín Fuster's notion that memory is a property of cognitive circuits, rather than a separate system in the brain (see Chapter 7). Circuits involved in different linguistic processes like syntax, semantics and phonology, may have their own memory capacities, even if they show significant overlap. In a similar line, Aniruddh Patel analyzed two existing models for syntactic and harmonic processing of music, the Dependency Locality Theory (DLT) and the Tonal Pitch Space Theory, respectively (Patel 2003). In both theories, distances between items (words or chords) have to be computed and stored while the sequence is still being perceived. In his words, "in DLT, integration can be understood as activating the representation of an incoming word while also reactivating a prior dependent word whose activation has decayed in proportion to the distance between words. In TPS, integration can be understood as activating an incoming chord while maintaining activation of another chord which provides the context for the incoming chord's interpretation" (Patel 2003, p. 678). Although Patel does not mention a memory system involved in this process, this is quite similar to the online management of information during working memory tasks.

Therefore, phonological, syntactical and semantic circuits may use different but overlapping short-term memory processes that contribute to creating a contextual framework in which linguistic elements are organized into a coherent whole. In this sense, an algorithm may be necessary to translate a sequential phonological working memory code into a visuospatial working memory code provided by lexical and semantic contents. Some of my students and I have argued that this algorithm is contained in the hierarchical organization of phrases that transforms the sequential auditory code into a visuospatial code. In this sense, syntax works as an interface between phonology on one side, and the lexicon and semantics describing actions or events, on the other (Aboitiz et al. 2006a, b). Furthermore, this interface may be represented by the nested time scale organization of oscillatory activity during speech processing, as the group of David Poeppel has recently found (Chait et al. 2015; Ding et al. 2016; see Chapter 2). In this, our brains are probably unique, as no other species is known to make translations of this kind in the context of short-term memory.

In Broca's aphasia there seems to be a specific difficulty in keeping the memory traces that connect phrase components in special verb tenses like passives, in which the canonical order of a sentence is reversed (for example, "The boy kissed the girl" → "The girl was kissed by the boy"). Something similar happens with some interrogative sentences, as in "Where did you go?" This operation is called "syntactic movement", and it is believed to be a consequence of the recursive property of language, in which components can be inserted within others, or moved from place to place, as if they were Leggo blocks. In order to recompose the canonical structure of the sentence, phrasal constituents keep connected with traces that bind them to their canonical place. As I said above, such traces have to be mnemonic in nature, as the brain processes sentence structure over a time interval. Yosef Grodzinsky, who first noted that Broca's aphasics have difficulty with syntactic movement, proposed the "trace deletion hypothesis", claiming that in Broca's aphasia, traces of syntactic movement are specifically erased (Grodzinsky 2000). As expected, the longer and more complex the dependencies, the more trouble patients have to understand them. Grodzinsky did not mention any memory deficit in these patients, and specifically referred to the elimination of formal syntactic operations. However, as I told Josef at one time, no matter what formal elements are missing, the main problem is the neurocognitive process by which the brain keeps these traces. Grodzinsky has responded that a direct connection between formal syntactic elements and working memory has yet to be demonstrated, which is correct but for now seems to be a reasonable neurobiological and cognitive explanation for these findings. However, I am not saying that working memory explains syntactic movement or long distance dependencies in complex grammars. Clearly, there is a lot more to these processes than short-term memory, like hierarchical organization and appropriate labeling and ordering of the phrasal components. But these syntactic operations are probably limited by short-term memory capacity, which, if impaired, results in a restriction of the syntactical operations that can be performed.

Broca's area has been considered critical for complex syntactic processing, as evidenced by studies showing activity changes associated with grammatically correct sentences compared with ungrammatical sentences. Notably, this area is also active during harmonic musical processing and mathematical calculations (both involving a sort of grammar). Disengaging the syntactic and mnemonic processes in these instances can be very difficult, as has been discussed by several authors (Fiebach et al. 2005). Michiru Makuuchi, working in Angela Friederici's laboratory, made an fMRI study in which they compared German sentences with two manipulated variables: hierarchical organization, tapping grammatical processing; and long distance dependencies that put a preferential load on working memory (Makuuchi et al. 2009). For example, phrases like "*Maria, die Hans, der gut aussah, liebte, Johann geküsst hatte*" ("Maria, who loved Hans who was good looking, had kissed Johann") vs. "*Maria, die weinte, Johann geküsst hatte und zwar gestern abend*" ("Maria, who cried, had kissed Johann and that was yesterday night"). Both phrases are highly hierarchical but the former has more long distance dependencies than the latter, as shown by the distance between the main subject "*Maria*" and the verb "*hatte*" in each of them (8 words in the former, 4 in the latter). On the other hand, phrases like "*Achim den grossen Mann gestern am späten Abend gesehen hatte*" ("Achim saw the tall man yesterday late at night") and "*Achim den grossen Mann gesehen hatte und zwar am abend*" ("Achim saw the tall man at night and that was late") are simple in hierarchical organization but again the former sentence has a longer distance dependency than the latter (8 words as opposed to 4 between "*Achim*" and "*hatte*"). Makuuchi found that hemodynamic activity in the left pars opercularis correlated more with structural complexity, while a slightly more ventral region (the left inferior frontal sulcus) was more sensitive to long distance dependencies. However, there was a very strong overlap between the activated regions for each variable, as well as a significant functional connectivity between these areas. Thus, they were able to partially segregate these two functions, but in my opinion the most important finding is the strong interconnectivity observed between the involved regions, which increased with higher syntactic complexity. This argues in favor of a tight relationship between syntactical processing and working memory load. As judged by the images presented, the activated areas in this study do not exactly fit the restricted notion of Broca's area, which involves only the inferior frontal gyrus (located just ventrally to the sites of activation). This underscores the point I made in Chapter 2, that

Broca's region may be functionally more extended than the pars triangularis and pars opercularis of the inferior frontal gyrus. Furthermore, the subtracting design of fMRI experiments emphasizes differences in activity but tends to eliminate areas that may be very necessary but coactive under different conditions (see also Chapter 2).

The Loop is for Learning

Interesting as the evidence and theories above may be, Baddeley correctly argued that it is difficult to think that the main benefit of the phonological loop is that we can understand complex and unusual sentences. My students and I have also argued that the development of complex syntax may have benefited from the acquisition of a sufficiently robust phonological loop, but clearly this does not explain its initial development (Aboitiz and García 1997; Aboitiz et al. 2006a, b). More than complex language processing in adults, the ease for learning a language may represent a more critical process for human development, and must have been a critical selective factor in early humans. Baddeley then focused on language acquisition, first with adults learning a second language, and later with children learning their mother tongue.

Baddeley asked the aforementioned patient PV to associate Russian words (a language that PV did not master) with their Italian translations (her native language), as opposed to learning associations between semantically and structurally distinct Italian words (Baddeley 2007; Vallar et al. 1991). PV was especially impaired in learning Russian-to-Italian associations, while Italian-to Italian pairs were recalled perfectly well. Control subjects did well in both tasks. The same findings were obtained when a graduate student with poor phonological working memory was assessed. Vallar described a patient with Down syndrome that had an outstanding verbal working memory capacity and had mastered three languages despite having a low IQ, (Vallar and Papagno 1993). Other studies successfully used articulatory suppression to interfere with learning foreign words, while the same procedure had no effect on associations between native words (Baddeley 2007).

Baddeley and colleagues then moved on to children with specific language impairment. This is a partly hereditary condition characterized by delayed language development in otherwise normal children that do not suffer hearing loss, vocal deficits or other developmental delays. Baddeley and colleagues observed that these children had a notable impairment when it came to repeating spoken non-words of different lengths (something reminiscent of conduction aphasia, although not the same, where the deficit consists of repeating spoken phrases or words). Baddeley and colleagues tested 8-year-old patients that performed at the level of normal 4-year-old children (Baddeley and Hitch 1993; Baddeley et al. 1998; Baddeley 2007; Gathercole et al. 1994). The non-word repetition test proved more reliable than other measures of phonological working memory, as it relies on novel phonological combinations that have not been overlearned as real words and numbers have. It has also been found that tests of non-word recognition, instead of repetition can be useful in assessing phonological storage capacity, especially with subjects with speech production problems. Returning to our point, the next step was to test non-word repetition capacity in normal children and find whether it could predict aspects of speech and language development. As expected, with children of a given age, verbal IQ significantly correlated with non-verbal IQ. However, non-word repetition was a better predictor than non-verbal IQ of verbal IQ performance. Furthermore, Baddeley and colleagues did a follow-up study that initially assessed vocabulary levels, and performance with two kinds of non-words, one type similar to English words, like "prindle", and the other dissimilar to English words like "stikicult". A year later the same children were evaluated for vocabulary richness again. Acquisition of new words during the year strongly correlated with earlier performance in the less English-like non-words but did not correlate with performance in the more English-like non-words. The point here is that children with more capacity to keep and repeat novel utterances are able to learn new words more rapidly.

But as many say, correlation does not mean causation. To get stronger evidence that better phonological working memory was indeed causing the difference in vocabulary acquisition, Baddeley and his group made what is called a cross-lagged correlation study, in which 4-year old children were tested on non-word repetition and on vocabulary (as had been done before), and after 1 year were tested again on both non-word repetition and vocabulary (Baddeley et al. 1998; Baddeley 2007). The point of this design was to determine which variable better explains the changes in the other. They found that non-word repetition at 4 more strongly correlated with vocabulary at 5 than vocabulary at 4 with non-word repetition at 5. This rules out the possibility that vocabulary itself is the main factor increasing phonological working memory. In fact, there is a positive effect of increasing vocabulary on working memory capacity, but it is much weaker than the effect that working memory capacity has on vocabulary acquisition. Finally, Baddeley and colleagues looked for evidence of the influence of working memory on grammatical development in children. They found indirect support for this, such as a study of two highly intelligent bilingual siblings, one with deficits in phonological memory accompanied with slow vocabulary and syntactic development, while the other was good at both (Baddeley 2007). Other studies have found correlations between phonological working memory capacity and the mean length of utterances, and grammar learning in a second language. Further studies of working memory and syntax development, as well as on working memory and other aspects of language and speech are strongly needed.

To end, the analysis related to errors in the digit span task has provided further insight into the mechanisms of verbal working memory. It has been known for some time that if a sequence of numbers increases beyond storing capacity, all the items are still remembered but are recalled in the wrong order, typically transposing two adjacent digits. Likewise, in studies using consonant-vowel-consonant (CVC) non-words like /wux/- /caz/, a common error is to transpose the consonants and retain the vowel order intact, for example, recalling /cux/- /waz/ after presentation of the above non-words. Furthermore, lists of CVC non-words similar in vowel sounds (/dah/, /fah/, /gah/) are more difficult to recall than non-words differing in their vowels (/di/, /dah/, /doh/). Baddeley and colleagues found that closed item sets (that is, using the same words in different trials), resulted in complete word transposition deficits, while with an open set (that is, new words in each trial), words themselves were often misreported, with a predominant shift of consonant order (for example /hat/- /pen/to /pat/- /hen/) (Baddeley 2007). These experiments make an important point, which is that order information tends to be carried by vowels instead of consonants, while consonants can be seen as the "junctures" between vowels (see Chapter 10).

Amplified Working Memory

There are about 37,000 articles in the scientific search page PubMed on working memory, the majority of which involve human subjects. In fact, the concept of working memory was conceived as a human trait, and initially there was little interest in its evolutionary development. Peter Carruthers recently published an interesting review of the comparative issues raised by working memory research (Carruthers 2013). Many objections have been raised to the idea that other animals display working memory capacities, including the incapacity to maintain sensory information for a relatively long period (2 seconds or so), the incapacity to resist interference, the inability to generate top-down control of memory traces, and the absence of rehearsal mechanisms that refresh working memory. Traditionally, it has been argued that if animals have any working memory capacity, it is very limited (no more than two objects) and they are unable to manipulate items in memory. Furthermore, animals only use working memory in contingent behavioral situations and not during mind-wandering and inner speech, as human commonly use it. And finally, only in humans does working memory operate in a communicative context. Although there has been little research directly comparing memory capacities in humans and non-human animals, there is evidence at least in higher vertebrates and especially monkeys and some birds, which challenges many of these assumptions. Studies have shown higher than expected memory spans and capacities in non-human species, as well as evidence of the capacity to resist interference in certain tasks (even in mice), and crows have been described as performing "mental travels", which is the capacity to recall one's past or future, a function dependent on episodic memory that is activated in working memory (see Chapter 9). Basically, tests involved in assessing this capacity rely on the animal's being able to forecast a complex future event, or to accurately recall the three W's of an event: what, when and where did something happen. Crows perform admirably well in these tasks, which implies that they can create vivid images of past or future events. Likewise, chimpanzees have shown the ability to rehearse actions mentally and plan strategies for cognitively complex behaviors. For example, Carruthers refers to a case of a captive chimp in an open-plan zoo that amused itself by collecting stones that he would later throw at the human visitors. Zookeepers then started removing his stone stashes, to which the chimp responded by concealing his projectiles and using new materials to throw. In this context, a very recent article by Hjalmar Kuhl Ammie Kalan and collaborators reported widespread stone accumulating behavior in wild chimpanzees (Kuhl et al. 2016). Notably, some chimps have the habit of throwing stones at certain trees, or tossing them inside tree holes, which result in piles of stones inside or around apparently targeted trees. Moreover, several species have shown the ability to mentally manipulate volumes, being able to recognize among other alternatives a three-dimensional object after it has been rotated to hide its initial appearance. The notion that animals engage little in daydreaming (or mind-wandering) and are more limited in the ways they use working memory capacities seem to be better sustained at the moment, as there is an apparent relationship between speech and mind-wandering in humans. Cerebral patterns of resting state activity similar to humans have been reported in chimpanzees, macaques and rodents (Rilling 2014), but whether these involve any mental imagery is still a big question. In my opinion, these patterns do not necessarily involve working memory capacity, as the phonological loop, using inner speech, may be an important element in maintaining the stability of mental contents. As I have said before, the language circuit may have a double role, connecting with executive networks for problem solving but also engaging with the default network at rest, providing continuity to our daydreams.

Working memory is directly related to mechanisms of cognitive control, which is a key element for appropriate social behavior. Executive function, which depends on working memory, is critical to revisit judgments that may be produced automatically but can be repressed or controlled by top-down mechanisms. In this line, Baddeley refers to Donald Norman and Tim Shallice's supervisory attentional system as a key element inhibiting automatic behavioral patterns in order for individuals to behave appropriately in social contexts. This system may have undergone strong selective pressure in human evolution (Norman and Shallice 1983). Nelson Cowan and others have argued that working memory has been expanding in response to increasing social and technological demands, but it is not clear whether this alleged increase is due to genetic selection or to learning or brain plasticity mechanisms, including epigenetic factors (Cowan 2005, 2009). Another proposal by Michael Vendetti and Silvia Bunge attributes relational thinking capacity, that is, the ability to represent relations between several items, to the lateral frontoparietal networks (Vendetti and Bunge 2014). In human development increased connectivity among these areas is associated with better relational thinking. Other authors, including Richard Passingham, have highlighted the role of dorsal prefrontal-parietal networks in foraging behavior in different species, by integrating information about metrics, distances, proportions and order (Genovesio et al. 2014). In the next chapter, I will mention additional functions of the parieto-frontal pathway that very likely played a significant role in the origin of speech and vocal communication. Finally in this line, working memory is intimately linked to attention, and increasing working memory capacity is dependent on a concomitant enhancement of attentional systems. In human evolution, both functions must have interacted closely, and the case of language origins and the generation of the phonological loop may not be exceptions to this. We still need to disentangle better the participation of attentional mechanisms in verbal working memory, to envision their role in the evolutionary origin of speech. In my opinion this is a highly promising direction for future research.

Perhaps no one has more explicitly pursued the amplification of working memory in human evolution than Fred Coolidge and Thomas Wynn, who proposed that an expansion of working memory capacity was a key event in late human evolution, separating modern humans from Neanderthals (Coolidge and Wynn 2007). It is supposed that working memory expansion was associated with expansion of the inferior parietal lobe and globularization of the brain, facilitating planning behavior and the development of progressively sophisticated technologies and social organization. Coolidge and Wynn put special emphasis on abilities like communicating in the subjunctive mode, referring to events that are not real and may never occur, and the capacity to understand metaphors or jokes, which has been associated with inferior parietal lobe activation. As I said in Chapter 3, the associations between gross brain anatomy or cranial features and cognitive abilities still require empirical support, and are highly reminiscent of Franz Galls's phrenology doctrine. The archaeological evidence of less sophisticated technology may however give us clues about early human behavior, and indicates that the technological revolution only took place in modern humans, which implies that a profound change in cognitive development was occurring at that time. I will come back to these issues at the end of the book (Chapter 11), while in the next chapter I will focus on a more restricted aspect of working memory, which is the phonological loop, and of evidence suggesting its possible evolutionary history. This, however, will bring us far back from the Neanderthal-modern human split, and we will have to look for evidence in non-human primates to get a glimpse of its neural underpinnings.

References

Aboitiz F, García R (1997) The evolutionary origin of the language areas in the human brain. A neuroanatomical perspective. Brain Res Rev 25:381–396

Aboitiz F, García RR, Bosman C, Brunetti E (2006a) Cortical memory mechanisms and language origins. Brain Lang 98:40–56

Aboitiz F, García R, Brunetti E, Bosman C (2006b) The origin of Broca's area from an ancestral working memory network. In: Grodzinsky Y, Amunts K (eds) Broca's Region. Oxford University Press, Oxford, p 3–16

Baddeley AD (1966) The influence of acoustic and semantic similarity on long term memory for word sequences. Quart J Exp Psychol 18:302–309

Baddeley AD (1968) Prior recall of newly learned items and the recency effect in free recall. Can J Psychol 22:157–163

Baddeley AD (2000a) The phonological loop and the irrelevant speech effect: some comments on Neath. Psychon Bull Rev 7:544–549

Baddeley A (2000b) The episodic buffer: a new component of working memory? Trends Cogn Sci 4:417–423

Baddeley A (2007) Working Memory, Thought and Action. Oxford University Press, Oxford

Baddeley A (2012) Working memory: theories, models, and controversies. Annu Rev Psychol 63:1–29

Baddeley AD, Hitch GJ (1974) Working memory. In: Bower GA (ed) Recent Advances in Learning and Motivation (vol. 8). Academic Press, New York, p 47–89

Baddeley AD, Hitch G (1993) The recency effect: implicit learning with explicit retrieval? Mem Cognit 21:146–155

Baddeley AD, Thomson N, Buchanan M (1975) Word length and the structure of short-term memory. J Verb Learn Verb Behav 14:575–589

Baddeley A, Gathercole S, Papagno C (1998) The phonological loop as a language learning device. Psychol Rev 105:158–173

Baddeley A, Jarrold C, Vargha-Khadem F (2011) Working memory and the hippocampus. J Cogn Neurosci. 23:3855–3861

Baldo JV, Dronkers NF (2006) The role of inferior parietal and inferior frontal cortex in working memory. Neuropsychology 20:529–538

Banks SJ, Feindel W, Milner B, Jones-Gotman M (2014) Cognitive function fifty-six years after surgical treatment of temporal lobe epilepsy: a case study. Epilepsy Behav Case Rep 2:31–36

Buchsbaum BR, D'Esposito M (2008) The search for the phonological store: from loop to convolution. J Cogn Neurosci 20:762–778

Buchsbaum BR, Ye D, D'Esposito M (2011a) Recency Effects in the Inferior Parietal Lobe during Verbal Recognition Memory. Front Hum Neurosci 5:59

Buchsbaum BR, Baldo J, Okada K, Berman KF, Dronkers N, D'Esposito M, Hickok G (2011b) Conduction aphasia, sensory-motor integration, and phonological short-term memory – an aggregate analysis of lesion and fMRI data. Brain Lan 119:119–128

Caplan D, Waters GS (1999) Verbal working memory and sentence comprehension. Behav Brain Sci 22:77–94; discussion 95–126

Carruthers P (2013) Evolution of working memory. Proc Natl Acad Sci U S A 110 (Suppl 2):10371–10378

Chait M, Greenberg S, Arai T, Simon JZ, Poeppel D (2015) Multi-time resolution analysis of speech: evidence from psychophysics. Front Neurosci 9:214

Champod AS, Petrides M (2010) Dissociation within the frontoparietal network in verbal working memory: a parametric functional magnetic resonance imaging study. J Neurosci 30:3849–3856

Chatham CH, Frank MJ, Badre D (2014) Corticostriatal output gating during selection from working memory. Neuron 81:930–942

Coolidge FL, Wynn T (2007) The working memory account of Neandertal cognition–how phonological storage capacity may be related to recursion and the pragmatics of modern speech. J Hum Evol 52:707–710

Cowan N (2005) Working Memory Capacity. Psychology Press, Hove

Cowan N (2009) Working memory from the trailing edge of consciousness. Neuron 62:13–15

D'Esposito M, Postle BR (2015) The cognitive neuroscience of working memory. Annu Rev Psychol 66:115–142

Ding N, Melloni L, Zhang H, Tian X, Poeppel D (2016) Cortical tracking of hierarchical linguistic structures in connected speech. Nat Neurosci 19:158–164

Edelman GM (1989) The Remembered Present: A Biological Theory of Consciousness. Basic Books, New York

Fedorenko E (2014) The role of domain-general cognitive control in language comprehension. Front Psychol 5:335

Fiebach CJ, Schlesewsky M, Lohmann G, von Cramon DY, Friederici AD (2005) Revisiting the role of Broca's area in sentence processing: syntactic integration versus syntactic working memory. Hum Brain Mapp 24:79–91

Fiez JA, Raichle ME, Miezin FM, Petersen SE, Tallal P, Katz WF (1995) PET studies of auditory and phonological processing: effects of stimulus characteristics and task demands. J Cogn Neurosci 7:357–375

Gathercole SE, Willis CS, Baddeley AD, Emslie H (1994) The Children's Test of Nonword Repetition: a test of phonological working memory. Memory 2:103–127

Genovesio A, Wise SP, Passingham RE (2014) Prefrontal-parietal function: from foraging to foresight. Trends Cogn Sci 18:72–81

Grodzinsky Y (2000) The neurology of syntax: language use without Broca's area. Behav Brain Sci 23:1–21; discussion 21–71

Gruber O (2001) Effects of domain-specific interference on brain activation associated with verbal working memory task performance. Cereb Cortex 11:1047–1055

Gruber O, von Cramon DY (2001) Domain-specific distribution of working memory processes along human prefrontal and parietal cortices: a functional magnetic resonance imaging study. Neurosci Lett 297:29–32

Hebb DO (1949) Organisation of Behaviour. Wiley Press, New York

Hickok G, Buchsbaum B, Humphries C, Muftuler T (2003) Auditory-motor interaction revealed by fMRI: speech, music, and working memory in area Spt. J Cogn Neurosci 15:673–682

Hickok G, Rogalsky C, Chen R, Herskovits EH, Townsley S, Hillis AE (2014) Partially overlapping sensorimotor networks underlie speech praxis and verbal short-term memory: evidence from apraxia of speech following acute stroke. Front Hum Neurosci 8:649

James W (1890) The Principles of Psychology. Henry Holt Press, New York

Jonides J, Schumacher EH, Smith EE, Koeppe RA, Awh E, Reuter-Lorenz PA, Marshuetz C, Willis CR (1998) The role of parietal cortex in verbal working memory. J Neurosci 18:5026–5034

Kellmeyer P, Ziegler W, Peschke C, Juliane E, Schnell S, Baumgaertner A, Weiller C, Saur D (2013) Fronto-parietal dorsal and ventral pathways in the context of different linguistic manipulations. Brain Lang 127:241–250

Kühl HS, Kalan AK, Arandjelovic M, Aubert F, D'Auvergne L, Goedmakers A, Jones S, Kehoe L, Regnaut S, Tickle A, Ton E, van Schijndel J, Abwe EE, Angedakin S, Agbor A, Ayimisin EA, Bailey E, Bessone M, Bonnet M, Brazolla G, Buh VE, Chancellor R, Cipoletta C, Cohen H, Corogenes K, Coupland C, Curran B, Deschner T, Dierks K, Dieguez P, Dilambaka E, Diotoh O, Dowd D, Dunn A, Eshuis H, Fernandez R, Ginath Y, Hart J, Hedwig D, Ter Heegde M, Hicks TC, Imong I, Jeffery KJ, Junker J, Kadam P, Kambi M, Kienast I, Kujirakwinja D, Langergraber K, Lapeyre V, Lapuente J, Lee K, Leinert V, Meier A, Maretti G, Marrocoli S, Mbi TJ, Mihindou V, Moebius Y, Morgan D, Morgan B, Mulindahabi F, Murai M, Niyigabae P, Normand E, Ntare N, Ormsby LJ, Piel A, Pruetz J, Rundus A, Sanz C, Sommer V, Stewart F, Tagg N, Vanleeuwe H, Vergnes V, Willie J, Wittig RM, Zuberbuehler K, Boesch C (2016) Chimpanzee accumulative stone throwing. Sci Rep 6:22219

Liebenthal E, Sabri M, Beardsley SA, Mangalathu-Arumana J, Desai A (2013) Neural dynamics of phonological processing in the dorsal auditory stream. J Neurosci 33:15414–15424

Makuuchi M, Bahlmann J, Anwander A, Friederici AD (2009) Segregating the core computational faculty of human language from working memory. Proc Natl Acad Sci U S A 106:8362–8367

Meyer L, Obleser J, Anwander A, Friederici AD (2012) Linking ordering in Broca's area to storage in left temporo-parietal regions: the case of sentence processing. Neuroimage 62:1987–1998

Meyer L, Cunitz K, Obleser J, Friederici AD (2014) Sentence processing and verbal working memory in a white-matter-disconnection patient. Neuropsychologia 61:190–196

Miller GA (1956) The magical number seven, plus or minus two: some limits on our capacity for processing information. Psychol Rev 63:81–97

Murray DJ (1968) Articulation and acoustic confusability in short-term memory. J Exp Psychol 78: 679–684

Norman DA, Shallice T (1983) Attention to action –willed and automatic control of behaviour. Bull Psychon Soc 21:354–354

Oberhuber M, Hope TM, Seghier ML, Parker Jones O, Prejawa S, Green DW, Price CJ (2016) Four functionally distinct regions in the left supramarginal gyrus support word processing. Cereb Cortex 26: 4212–4226

Patel AD (2003) Language, music, syntax and the brain. Nat Neurosci 6:674–681

Paulesu E, Frith CD, Frackowiak RS (1993) The neural correlates of the verbal component of working memory. Nature 362:342–345

Peterburs J, Cheng DT, Desmond JE (2015) The association between eye movements and cerebellar activation in a verbal working memory task. Cereb Cortex 26:3802–3813

Pinker S (1994) The Language Instinct. Penguin Books, London

Posner MI, Petersen SE (1990) The attention system of the human brain. Annu Rev Neurosci 13:25–42

Rilling JK (2014) Comparative primate neuroimaging: insights into human brain evolution. Trends Cogn Sci 18:46–55

Saffran EM, Marin OS (1975) Immediate memory for word lists and sentences in a patient with deficient auditory short-term memory. Brain Lang 2:420–443.

Salamé P., Baddeley AD. (1982) Disruption of short term memory by unattended speech. Implications for the structure of working memory. J Verb Learn Verb Behav 21:150–164

Salamé P, Baddeley AD (1990) The effects of irrelevant speech on immediate free recall. Bull Psychon Soc 28:540–542

Saur D, Kreher BW, Schnell S, Kümmerer D, Kellmeyer P, Vry MS, Umarova R, Musso M, Glauche V, Abel S, Huber W, Rijntjes M, Hennig J, Weiller C (2008) Ventral and dorsal pathways for language. Proc Natl Acad Sci U S A 105:18035–18040

Scoville WB, Milner B (1957) Loss of recent memory after bilateral hippocampal lesions. J Neurol Neurosurg Psychiatr 20:11–21

Smith EE, Jonides J (1997) Working memory: a view from neuroimaging. Cogn Psychol 33:5–42

Trost S, Gruber O (2012) Evidence for a double dissociation of articulatory rehearsal and non-articulatory maintenance of phonological information in human verbal working memory. Neuropsychobiology 65:133–140

Vallar G, Papagno C (1993) Preserved vocabulary acquisition in Down's syndrome: the role of phonological short-term memory. Cortex 29:467–483

Vallar G, Papagno C, Baddeley AD.¡ (1991) Long-term recency effects and phonological short-term memory. A neuropsychological case study. Cortex 27:323–326

Vendetti MS, Bunge SA (2014) Evolutionary and developmental changes in the lateral frontoparietal network: a little goes a long way for higher-level cognition. Neuron 84:906–917

Warrington EK, Shallice T (1969) The selective impairment of auditory verbal short-term memory. Brain 92:885–896

Part II

Before Speech

7

Monkey Brain, Human Brain

Around the time Baddeley and Hitch proposed their tripartite model of working memory, some researchers were beginning what would later become an explosion of articles on the functions of the monkey prefrontal cortex. These advances were largely based on single-neuron electrical recording with microelectrodes (also known as single-unit recording). This marked the beginning of a period devoted to mapping the electrical activity of individual neurons in different parts of the central nervous system. Single-unit recording was a revolutionary technique that allowed for the first time to record the electrical responses of neurons, elicited by sensory stimuli and associated with behavioral patterns. The first studies, with notable exceptions, focused on vision and provided a fundamental conceptual framework for the development of cognitive neuroscience. Some key notions that emerged from this research were then applied to other sensory systems, particularly auditory and language processing. Consequently, it is important to give an overview of these early findings in order to provide the neurobiological bases on which the study of language has been built.

© The Author(s) 2017   **249**
F. Aboitiz, *A Brain for Speech*,
DOI 10.1057/978-1-137-54060-7_7

The Visual Paradigm

In the late 1950s, titanic researchers consolidated the single-unit recording technique in neuroscience. This was science at its best, starting with the studies by John Eccles on motor neurons of the spinal cord, for which he was honored with the Nobel Prize in 1963 (Eccles 1967). Another crucial advance was made by Steven Kuffler and Horace Barlow, who recorded electrical activity from retinal cells in response to light stimuli (Spillman 2014). After them, the team led by Jerome Lettvin, in which Humberto Maturana was a key author, made a substantial discovery analyzing the visual responses of single neurons in the frog retina and optic tectum, a midbrain structure that is the main visual processing component of lower vertebrates. Lettvin and collaborators had been motivated by Roger Sperry's earlier studies on the development of the frog visual system, in which he sectioned the optic nerve, detaching the eye, and then allowing the visual fibers to regenerate their severed projections into the optic nerve (see Chapter 4). Maturana, Lettwin and coworkers began studying the visual responses of frog retinal cells, following Kuffler's method of directly illuminating the eye and recording neuronal electrical activity. In an earlier study, Maturana and coworkers sectioned the frog optic nerve as Sperry had done before and physiologically confirmed Sperry's behavioral findings that regenerated fibers grew into their original positions even after having rotated the eye (Maturana et al. 1959). But the group's most important finding came soon after this. As Maturana told the story, one day he was alone in the lab with a frog with an implanted electrode while his co-workers were at lunch when he made perhaps one of the most serendipitous discoveries in the history of neuroscience. He accidentally moved his hand in front of the frog's eye and observed a strong electrical response from the retinal neuron that was being recorded. Maturana's finding was that not only light, but also a moving shadow could provoke a visual response. The team began searching for specific kinds of stimuli that could trigger visual responses in the retina, and observed that the frog eye has only four separate visual operations: detection of sharp boundaries, detection of convex borders ("bug perceivers", presumably involved in catching prey), moving edge detection (as with Maturana's hand), and light dimming detection (Maturana et al. 1960). These cell types had different electrophysiological properties and their axons differed in terms of myelination. Furthermore, they projected to distinct layers in the optic tectum, where the presence of these same response types was confirmed. Lettvin, Maturana and collaborators published an influential paper titled *What the frog's eye tells the frog's brain*, in which they argued for the existence of "feature detectors" that extract behaviorally relevant cues according to basic perceptual configurations (Lettvin et al. 1968; Spillman 2014). With that the search began for operations that detect stimulus regularities to construct the visual world. This perspective had strong impact on the field of computer science, with efforts to construct image-processing devices. Maturana and Lettvin were nominated for the Nobel Prize for their findings, but the prize went in the end to the aforementioned David Hubel and Torsten Wiesel, who went more deeply into these findings in the monkey, and extended their studies on neuronal development in cats. Subsequently, Maturana took up epistemological issues regarding the nature of reality in terms of the operation of the nervous system. He refuted the paradigm he had contributed to constructing, and concluded that it makes no sense to speak of detecting features or information processing in the nervous system, as it is a dynamic system and its internal operations are much more relevant than its external interactions. This notion came together with an overarching conceptualization of the organization of living forms, defined by Maturana as "autopoietic", that is, self-producing machines. Although influential in the social sciences, Maturana's views have had limited acceptance in biology and neuroscience.

At about the same time as Maturana and Lettvin, Hubel and Wiesel began a series of studies to analyze neuronal response to specific configurations of stimuli (Hubel and Wiesel 1977; Hubel 1988). They characterized neurons according to their response selectivity when different kinds of stimuli were presented. For example, neurons in the retina or the lateral geniculate nucleus of the thalamus (the main relay nucleus to the cerebral cortex) respond to very simple stimuli, such as spots of light. In the mid-layers of the primary visual area (also called V1), neurons are more responsive to a light bar in a specific angular orientation (they called these "simple cells"), while in more superficial cortical layers, "complex cells" are more sensitive to attributes like the direction of movement (say left or right), and respond to a wider range of stimuli than do simple cells. Even more cryptic than these are the "hypercomplex cells", usually located in secondary visual areas and very difficult to describe in terms of their stimulus-response properties. The simplest hypothesis for these findings is that several aligned spot-detecting thalamic cells converge to form a simple cell, which would explain the preference for linear stimuli in a specific orientation. Subsequently, several simple cells converge to form a complex cell in the superficial layers of the visual cortex, and several of these converge to form hypercomplex cells in other areas. Extending this idea implies that recognition of complex patterns, such as faces, depends on the progressive convergence of many simple attributes of the visual stimuli that are sequentially integrated to construct a specific perceptual scene, which is perceived by one or more neurons located somewhere in the brain. This notion led to Jerry Lettvin's ironic concept of the "grandmother cell", a neuron that specifically recognizes one's own grandmother. Among the main objections to this interpretation was that this architecture is not compatible with the system's plasticity, and that too many of these grandmother-like cells would be needed to account for all the things we are able to perceive, let alone the complex percepts we learn in our lives. Alternative models were proposed based on lateral interactions between neighboring cells and the establishment of distributed large-scale networks involving different areas, but to date none of these hypotheses has been unequivocally supported by the evidence. Perhaps the most likely situation is that there is a bit of both, that is, a hierarchical processing network that is strongly modulated by preexisting activity in neighboring and distant regions. Some years ago, Rodrigo Quian Quiroga and collaborators reported a subset of hippocampal neurons in human subjects, selectively firing in response to specific images of known faces (like Jennifer Aniston, Halle Berry or Luke Skywalker), places, objects or animals (Quiroga et al. 2005). From then on, the "grandmother cell" rejuvenated into the "Jennifer Aniston neuron", with much more glamor. However, there is not just one neuron in the brain preferring Jennifer Aniston, but rather about a million (about one in every thousand hippocampal neurons). Furthermore, some of these neurons also fire in response to related faces, such as co-stars in the same series. The result is that there are overlapping neuronal networks involved in the responses to specific semantic stimuli, rather than a single hierarchically positioned neuron involved in complex recognition. Furthermore, Quiroga doubts that these cells are specifically involved in individual recognition. Rather he postulates that these neuronal ensembles participate in generating associative networks with preexisting memories that permit consolidating memory and recall of contextual information about a perception (Quiroga et al. 2008; Quiroga 2012).

Subsequent studies depicted a mixed organization of the visual system, where together with hierarchical organization, parallel streams are involved in processing different attributes of the visual scene. The work on the visual system was fundamental for recognizing the dorsal and ventral pathways for speech and language, and I will succinctly review it here (Zeki 1993). The visual pathway begins in the retina, the ganglion neurons of which send axons to the lateral geniculate nucleus of the thalamus, which then projects to the primary visual cortex or V1. There are two main kinds of ganglion neurons in the retina. The first are parvocellular neurons, selective for chromatic or color stimuli and visual details (the "P" pathway); and the other are magnocellular neurons, selective for movement and gross shapes (the "M" pathway). The two neuronal types project to different layers in the lateral geniculate nucleus (P and M layers, respectively), and neurons in these layers project to different subdivisions of the mid-layers in the primary visual cortex, such that the laminar segregation acquired in the thalamus is maintained in the visual cortex (Fig. 7.1). Information from visual detail from the P-receiving sublayer projects to superficial layers of V1; and the chromatic-responding neurons cluster in these layers in small cellular aggregates called "blobs" (Hubel 1988; Zeki 1993).

There are a series of stripes in the secondary visual area (V2) that cover all layers and run the length of the area in a sort of zebra stripe pattern. The stripes can be distinguished by the activity of a mitochondrial enzyme, cytochrome oxidase. There are three types of stripes, thick, thin and what are termed inter-stripes. From the P pathway, the color-processing blobs of V1 project to the thin stripes of V2, and the

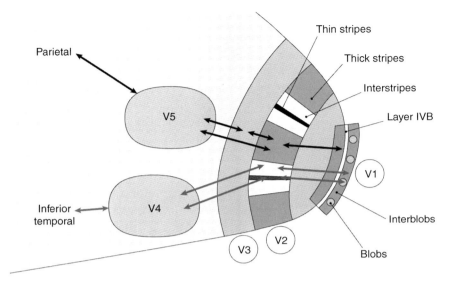

Fig. 7.1 Connections between visual areas. In gray arrows, the ventral pathway, processing object information and details. In black arrows, the dorsal pathway, processing spatial and movement information. Area V1 is separated in its laminar components, while area V2 is composed of tangential "stripes". Different laminar and stripe elements convey distinct kinds of visual information

superficial layers of V1 connect with the inter-stripe band. Neurons from the M-receiving sublayer of V1 project directly into the thick stripes of V2. Thus, the laminar segregation of inputs in V2 is transformed into micro-areal segregation, where different stripes convey different attributes of the visual stimulus. At higher levels of the visual processing network, V2 micro-areal segregation becomes large scale areal separation into two main processing pathways (Hubel 1988; Zeki 1993).

Area V2 projects to third-order visual areas called V3, V4 and V5, which receive different types of inputs from the former. For example, area V4, located in the inferior temporal lobe, receives color (thin stripes) and detailed visual (inter-stripes) information from V2. V4 is essential for the subjective perception of color. Lesions in this area produce a condition called achromatopsia in which patients become partly color-blind in the visual field contralateral to the site of the lesion. Notably, color perception is not exactly the same as the ability to discriminate wavelengths. The studies by Semir Zeki and others have provided substantial evidence that the perception of color is a subjective phenomenon, and depends on contextual variables (Zeki 1993). To understand this, we first have to realize that objects do not have color by themselves, as the light they reflect depends on the light by which they are illuminated. Thus, a red object could be made to reflect more green than red light, if illuminated with intense green light and faint red light. The brain compensates for this effect in a phenomenon called color constancy, where despite different lighting conditions, the object remains the same color, within some limits of course. What the brain actually does is to calculate how much red light and how much green light the object is emitting compared to ambient light. Thus, regardless of how much red and green light the object reflects at any instant, it will reflect more red and less green light compared to its immediate surroundings if the ambient is illuminated with the same light, and surrounding objects have a balanced chromatic composition. Thus, the object is labeled as "red" because it reflects more red light than its surroundings, and is not "green", even if it reflects more green than red light. This object-surroundings computation occurs in visual area V4, as chromatic cells in the retina and V1 are strictly responsive to light wavelength. That is, the hypothetical red object illuminated with mostly green light would be labeled in V1 as "green". There are ways to fool the system by altering the chromatic properties of the surroundings, which produces what is called color shadows, in which one sees colors that are not present (Zeki 1993). A good example of this is a dress that recently circulated in the Internet that appeared blue or white depending on the observer and contextual conditions. I have taken this small detour because I will make a similar argument in Chapter 10, but in the area of speech perception.

Area V4 connects extensively with many areas in the inferior temporal lobe, containing neurons selective to distinct objects such as faces (recall Quiroga's Jennifer Aniston neurons), hands and inanimate objects or places. Bilateral lesions of the inferior temporal lobe produce visual agnosia, which is the incapacity to recognize objects, of which the most dramatic is prosopagnosia, referred to as the inability to recognize the faces of familiar persons. This condition is usually caused by severe brain injury, although there are examples of developmental prosopagnosia in absence of evident neurological lesions. Some celebrities like Brad Pitt have claimed to be prosopagnosic, possibly a good excuse for ignoring many of the people that approach them. It would in any event be interesting to find out what happened with his Jennifer Aniston neurons. Visual areas from the inferior temporal lobe are highly connected to the anterior tip of the temporal lobe (the temporal pole), which serves as an interface between these sensory areas and limbic regions involved in emotional processing and memory. On the other hand, the dorsal visual pathway runs in the parietal lobe, in which area V3 receives projections from the M pathway (thick bands of V2 and the M-receiving sublayers of V1), and projects to V5 (also called MT). These areas are selective for gross shapes and movement, and lesions in V5 sometimes lead to a rare condition called akinetopsia, in which subjects are unable to perceive movement. They have difficulty crossing streets, as they cannot tell the velocity of vehicles or filling a teacup because they cannot tell how full it is. These patients report not being able to sense continuous movement but instead visualize a series of static photographs that keep changing. V5 and other areas from the inferior and posterior parietal lobe connect with higher order parietal areas that in turn project into frontal areas for motor action (Zeki 1993).

Thus, two main streams were recognized in visual processing, a ventral one running via the inferior temporal lobe, associated with object recognition (the P pathway), and the other running dorsally to the parietal lobe (the M pathway), associated with spatial information and movement or space-time processing. These two pathways are usually dubbed as the "what" (or "who") and the "where" pathways, respectively, although more recent interpretations prefer to nickname the dorsal stream as the "how" pathway, as it links visuospatial processing with motor commands in the frontal cortex via the parietal lobe. The ventral pathway is involved in recognition, emotional and semantic processing, while the dorsal pathway codes for context-dependent behavioral patterns. However, this is not to say that these two streams are totally independent; there are well known connections between the two that may serve to maintain an integrated perception of say, a bouncing colorful beach ball. The general problem of perceptual integration has intrigued neuroscientists for some time, and has been referred to as the binding problem. Synchronic oscillatory activity was proposed by Wolf Singer, Francisco Varela and others as the main mechanism by which distributed areas of the brain involved in different processing domains might integrate their activities contributing to a unified perceptual image (Singer 1999; Varela et al. 2001). In this context, Jason Yeatman and collaborators recently used tractographic imagery to analyze the human vertical occipital fasciculus, which connects the dorsolateral and ventrolateral visual cortices (see Chapter 2) (Yeatman et al. 2014). This tract was originally described by Wernicke in non-human primates, and may serve as a main channel to integrate the ventral and dorsal visual pathways.

Mapping Memory

In the 1970s, electrophysiologists began studying the activity of neurons in higher-level cortical areas of the monkey to understand the mechanisms underlying higher cognitive processes like memory and attention. These studies were largely inspired by the groundbreaking work in the 1930s of Carlyle Jacobsen, who pioneered a controversial operation, the lobotomy (Jacobsen 1938). Jacobsen showed that monkeys with bilateral prefrontal lesions (more precisely, in the dorsolateral prefrontal cortex) had no problem solving complex puzzles if the required information was available on sight, but the moment there was an interruption of even a few seconds the monkeys could no longer continue the task. This mirrored the observations by earlier neurologists like John Hughlings Jackson of human patients with prefrontal lesions, and reflected a significant deficit in short-term memory, which many researchers later likened to Baddeley's visuospatial working memory (York and Steinberg 2011). Jacobsen even advanced the concept that short-term memory must be maintained by some sort of sustained activity in the absence of stimuli, or by recall of past events. Other researchers like Karl Pribram and Mortimer Mishkin also made important contributions to understanding the role of the prefrontal cortex in behavior, with studies indicating distractibility, inflexibility and perseverative behavior following lesions in this region (Pribram and Mishkin 1956; Mishkin and Pribram 1955, 1956).

Two scientists were key in providing insights into the neurobiological underpinnings of working memory. One was Joaquín Fuster, who trained monkeys in the delayed match-to-sample task (Fuster and Alexander 1971; Fuster 1995, 2003), which consists of briefly presenting stimuli on a screen (the sample), followed by a short delay of a few seconds in which stimuli are erased, after which a second set of stimuli is presented. The animal then has to select stimuli from the second set that fit properties from the first sample. For example, the sample could be a colored dot, and the monkey has to remember the color during the delay and match it to the same color in the new set of stimuli. In 1971, Fuster and Garrett Alexander, in one paper and Kisou Kubota and Hiroaki Niki in another described sustained firing of prefrontal and thalamic neurons during the performance of a delayed response task (Fuster and Alexander 1971; Kubota and Niki 1971). The two papers reported a variety of neuronal responses during the task, some of which activated with the presentation of the sample, others activated just before the response, and still others activated precisely during the delay when no stimulus was present. These cells were selective for the sample and were not considered to reflect a general attentional state. Rather, their activity was interpreted as encoding or "keeping in mind" the information that was required for a near-future task. In the previous chapter, I mentioned Mark D'Esposito's critique of this assumption (D'Esposito and Postle 2015). In subsequent studies, Fuster, and others observed a variety of "memory cells", some firing more intensely at the beginning of the delay and then decaying, others with the reverse pattern of firing more at the end, and others still that showed a truly sustained pattern of activity during the delay (Fuster 1995, 2003). Nonetheless, Fuster is reluctant to use the term "working memory" and uses the term "active memory", making reference to a more general process in which information not only from the environment but also stored in long-term memory is activated by sustained firing. Fuster envisions active memory as a broad associative network formed by interactions between different brain systems that are maintained as a memory fragment in the context of a behavioral outcome in the short term. In this way, Fuster gets closer to the non-localizationist tradition that views the brain as resulting from the operation of large-scale and pervasive networks that encode multi-modal information. Moreover, he views the brain as a hierarchically orga-nized system with distributed executive processes in the frontal lobe, connecting with perceptual memories in the posterior brain (parietal, tem-poral and occipital lobes). Lower-level representations from sensory and motor networks are nested in these large-scale networks in an organization that reflects the different levels at which memory operates, from contextual to sensorimotor. One of his well-known dictums is that there is no system in the brain for memory, but rather there is the memory of different systems. He views memory as a property of the distinct sensorimotor networks involved in behavior, rather than as a separate cognitive system involved in the storage of different kinds of information. Finally, Fuster claims that from birth, mem-ories are formed by associative interactions that depend on experience, and build over phylogenetically established frameworks that connect sensory and motor domains, a point that I will discuss further in the next chapter.

The other main contributor to the neurobiology of working memory was Patricia Goldman (later, Patricia Goldman-Rakic), who followed Jacobsen's studies and attempted to define the region of the frontal cortex that is critically involved in short-term spatial memory (Goldman and Rosvold 1970). She found that animals with lesions in the dorsolateral prefrontal cortex, located dorsally to the ventrolateral prefrontal cortex where Broca's region is located, had short-term spatial memory impairments. However, the animals were able to do spatial tasks that did not require memory. Goldman then worked with the renowned neuroanatomist Walle Nauta in visualiz-ing the connectivity of these areas with tract tracing methods and found columnar organization of inputs in the dorsolateral prefrontal cortex, reminiscent of what David Hubel and Torsten Wiesel had described earlier in the visual system (Goldman and Nauta 1977). Together with Carmen Cavada and other researchers, Goldman-Rakic found that the principal sulcus of the prefrontal lobe, involved in spatial working memory, is closely connected to the parietal association cortex, particularly in the intraparietal sulcus and neigh-boring areas (more technically, areas 7a and 7lip) (Cavada and Goldman-Rakic 1989a, b). Moreover, these two regions are intensely connected to other frontal, temporal and parietal areas involved in different aspects of perception and behavior, as well as with many subcortical nuclei (Fig. 7.2).

After becoming acquainted with Fuster's and Kubota's works, Goldman-Rakic started working with Shintaro Funahashi using a delayed match-to-sample task in which the animal did not have to push buttons as in previous experiments, but was only required to move its eyes to a location (Funahashi et al. 1989, 1991). Eye movements were precisely monitored by an eye-tracking device, an apparatus that is now commonplace in cognitive neuroscience laboratories. Goldman-Rakic used spatially located samples as cues, instead of object properties like color or shape, and identified spatial-specific delay cells that fire continuously with the location of an object that is maintained in memory, and suppress firing when other locations are remembered. Notably, small lesions in the cell's

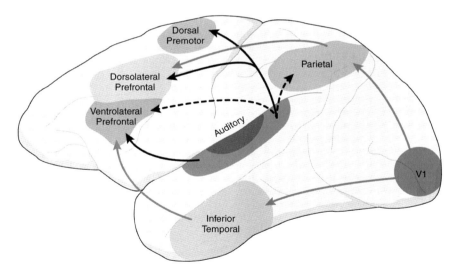

Fig. 7.2 Dorsal and ventral pathways for vision and audition. The diagram depicts the arrangement of the visual- prefrontal (gray arrows) and auditory-prefrontal (black arrows) projections in the macaque, each depicting ventral and dorsal components. Segmented arrows indicate projections that are less developed in the monkey than in humans

surroundings produced impairment in the memory but not in the perception of the precise location. This finding apparently challenges Michael D'Esposito notion that memory is strictly represented in sensory areas (Chapter 6) (D'Esposito and Postle 2015), but these higher order areas may work by stabilizing neural activity in sensory regions by top-down mechanisms that contribute to maintaining the memory trace. In additional experiments, Goldman-Rakic and her collaborators separated prefrontal neurons selective for locations in more dorsal regions of the prefrontal cortex from neurons encoding stimulus features such as color, shape and even faces in more ventral prefrontal positions. Together with Amy Arnsten, Goldman-Rakic identified the neuronal types involved in sustained firing, located mainly in cortical layer 3 and displaying extensive axonal arborization to neighboring neurons with similar perceptual properties (Arnsten et al. 1994). These connections engage in relatively extended circuits that maintain activity during the delay period due to recurrent excitation. Recurrent excitation during working memory tasks is modulated by inhibitory interneurons, and more notably by the neurotransmitter dopamine. Dopamine has a bell-shaped dose-response relationship in which an intermediate doses provides optimal results while doses that are too low or too high result in functional impairment associated with distractibility or anxiety, respectively. Goldman-Rakic then focused on the study of prefrontal function in schizophrenia, providing important insights before her unexpected death in 2003 (Arnsten 2013).

Goldman-Rakic and Fuster agreed that these neurons are the cellular basis of mental representations, but Goldman-Rakic's interpretations were more on the localizationist side than Fuster's. Following the scaffolding provided by research on the visual system, Goldman-Rakic distinguished two separate circuits involved in visual working memory (Fig. 7.2) (Goldman-Rakic 1990, 1995; Goldman-Rakic et al. 1999). The first is a dorsal stream selective for spatial cues that involves the primary visual area, posterior parietal cortices, and dorsal regions of the dorsal prefrontal cortex. The second circuit is a ventral stream that conveys object and facial information, involving the primary visual area, the inferior temporal lobe and more ventral regions of the lateral prefrontal cortex. Note that these two circuits together fit Louis Foville's longitudinal subdivision of the brain described in Chapter 2, while Foville's Sylvian convolution corresponds to the dorsal and ventral auditory pathways to be described below. Anatomically, connectivity between superior parietal areas and dorsal prefrontal areas that subserve visuospatial working memory is provided by the superior longitudinal fasciculus, the massive tract of fibers that connects the parietal and frontal lobes. On the other hand, the inferior longitudinal fasciculus, running along the temporal lobe, contributes to the object and face-related ventral stream. There are several tracts from the anterior temporal lobe that may connect the ventral stream with the ventro-lateral prefrontal cortex, like the capsula externa, the capsula extrema and the uncinate fasciculus. Goldman's Rakic's depiction of a dorsal visuospatial pathway, and a ventral object/face pathway for working memory made a strong impact on the neuroscientific community, and contributed significantly to the exponential increase in publications involving working memory and the prefrontal cortex.

These experiments intrigued John Jonides and collaborators, who developed a design to distinguish object and spatial working memory in humans (Jonides et al. 1993). Subjects had to retain either the spatial location or the shape of three objects for three seconds. While the spatial task induced strong right hemisphere activation (occipital, parietal and prefrontal areas), the object task activated left hemisphere regions, particularly inferotemporal and parietal areas. This confirmed the dissociation between a dorsal spatial-related network, and an object-related ventral network, also revealing differences in hemispheric specialization. Further studies showed that lateralization for object working memory depends on the nature of the stimulus, with the left hemisphere dominant with abstract shapes and the right dominant for faces. These were seminal studies for understanding the neural substrates of visual working memory. However, little information was available in the seventies and eighties about the neuroscience of auditory working memory, which could be a lot more interesting for people working on language.

The Search for Homology

As a biology undergraduate in the seventies, and then a graduate student in neuroscience in the eighties, I was deeply intrigued by the Geschwind/ Wernicke neuronal model of language, which at the time was depicted as a circumscribed circuit with no counterpart in non-human primates. The evolutionary origin of this circuit was a complete mystery that practically no one at that point had tried to solve. My undergraduate mentors Humberto Maturana and Francisco Varela were reluctant to recognize the existence of localized systems in the brain and adhered to the concept of dynamic large-scale networks in which the anatomical delineation of neural systems was less relevant than their functional dynamics. However, when I moved to the United States in the late 1980s, first to the lab of Al Galaburda, and then to the labs of Eran Zaidel and Arne Scheibel, the perspective was more localizationist, and the notion of a brain subdivided into distinct modules specialized for different functions was well accepted. As I said earlier in this book, the systemic or holistic paradigm provides a wealth of theoretical perspectives, but the localizationist approach has nourished us with substantial empirical evidence and has allowed us to chart the first maps of brain function. The combination of the two views of the brain may actually represent the optimal approximation of brain function, working with a trial and error strategy. Moreover, the module-based approach in a way simplifies the issue of tracking the phylogenetic ancestry of a function or organ, as it is easier to search for similar components in other species. In this line, the studies at the time by Fuster, Goldman-Rakic and their colleagues seemed to me a promising framework to understand the origin and evolution of language circuits. I could not help but imagine similarity between the large-scale networks for visuospatial working memory depicted by Patricia Goldman-Rakic, and the Wernicke-Geschwind model of the language circuit via the arcuate fasciculus. The ventral pathway for language was not yet fully recognized.

The existence of a circuit comparable to the language network in the monkey would strongly imply evolutionary continuity between non-human primates and us. The first step in this line was to determine elements in other species homologous to Broca's region, Wernicke's region and their connections (Aboitiz 1988). But homology does not mean identical. Richard Owen, whom we met in the Chapter 1, defined homology in the mid-1800s as the "same" organ in different species, regardless of differences in form or function (Owen 1837; Rupke 1994). This means that homologous organs can display a variety of shapes and functions, like the fins of fish and the limbs of mammals. With Darwin, the concept of homology acquired a completely new historical dimension as it implied a structure present in the common ancestor of two species that diverged into different forms but is still recognizable in terms of development, inner structure or relative position. Unfortunately, there is no clear-cut criterion to determine homology, which has sometimes led to agitated controversies, as I will discuss in Chapter 9.

Fortunately, finding areas homologous to those assigned to the classical language circuits was not that difficult. In the early 1980s, Al Galaburda, working with Friedrich Sanides and Deepak Pandya, parcellated the human and macaque auditory cortices in detail, subdividing it into a mosaic of interconnected areas organized around the primary auditory regions (Brodmann's areas 41 and 42; see Chapter 2) (Galaburda and Sanides 1980; Galaburda and Pandya 1983). One of the most posterior of these areas was Tpt in the planum temporale, which we have referred to before in relation to its asymmetry in the human, and its possible correspondence to Wernicke's region. Subsequent studies by Todd Preuss and Goldman-Rakic identified area Tpt in the galago, a basal primate, indicating that this area has a long evolutionary history and predates the origin of speech (Preuss and Goldman-Rakic 1991a). What happened with area Tpt in human evolution, did it acquire a new function, associated with speech processing? Things like this may happen. An example is the visual word form area in humans, described by Stanislaas Dehaene, which decodes the visual structure of letters translating them into phonological representations (see Chapter 2) (Cohen et al. 2002). This area exists in illiterate people, but obviously does not play this function, and probably participates in a bimodal or multimodal integration network. Furthermore, the capacity for orthographic processing is present even in pigeons, showing that this ability can develop from general perceptual abilities (Scarf et al. 2016). Likewise, area Tpt is probably part of a multimodal interface in primates, and may have acquired its function in human evolution through its engagement in a novel auditory-vocal interface. Area Tpt has been described as a multisensory "hub" in which visual, auditory and somatosensory inputs from the occipital, parietal and temporal lobes converge, respectively. In this sense, it is well placed to participate in the sensorimotor transformation of vocal sounds, and to associate these sounds with other sensory modalities. As I have said, elucidating the relationship between this area and area Spt described in the previous chapter may be worth pursuing. The identification of a homologue to Broca's region was also relatively straightforward. As I described in Chapter 2, Broca's area consists at its core, but not exclusively, of cytoarchitectonic areas 44 and 45 in the ventrolateral cortex of the human brain. Preuss and Goldman Rakic identified area 45 (corresponding to anterior Broca's region, pars triangularis), but not area 44, in the macaque (Preuss and Goldman Rakic 1991b). For many researchers, areas 44, corresponding to posterior Broca's region in the human, emerged in humans as an outgrowth from the ventral premotor region that represented orofacial movements.

However, the connectivity between the presumed homologues of Broca's and Wernicke's regions provided some surprising findings. By the 1980s and 1990s there were studies on the frontal connectivity of the macaque inspired largely by the earlier work by Goldman-Rakic. The most important at that time were a series of papers published by Todd Preuss and Goldman-Rakic, and Michael Petrides and Deepak Pandya (Preuss and Goldman-Rakic 1991c; Petrides and Pandya 1984, 1988). This evidence indicated that the main input to what corresponds to Broca's area in the monkey originated in the inferior parietal lobe, traveling via the superior longitudinal fasciculus. On the other hand, the main output of the posterior auditory areas was directed to dorsal premotor regions involved in eye movement control, instead of running via the arcuate fasciculus into the ventrolateral prefrontal cortex as was supposed in humans. No strong evidence had been found of a direct connection between the homologues of Broca's and Wernicke's areas via an arcuate fasciculus. There was only one study, by Terrence Deacon indicating direct connectivity between a region lateral to area Tpt and ventral premotor areas in the monkey, which overlaps with terminations from inferior parietal regions (Deacon 1992).

In 1995, I wrote an article in a low-profile journal proposing that the language areas and their connections arose through the establishment of a robust temporoparietal-prefrontal auditory-vocal network that served as a basic working memory system for names and primitive vocal utterances (Aboitiz 1995). I speculated that the capacity to keep vocal signals in mind for some time was critical for tasks such as recalling the name of an object that was not present. Thus, an amplification of vocal working memory capacity was the basis of the origin of the language-related circuits and speech. Subsequently, Ricardo García and I proposed a more detailed scheme for the homologies and evolution of the language regions (Fig. 7.3) (Aboitiz and Garcia 1997). We depicted a three-way input to Broca's area and its corresponding region in the monkey. The evidence at that time indicated that the main projection to Broca's homologue in the monkey is not from auditory areas but from the inferior parietal lobe, particularly areas 40 and 39, together corresponding to the human supramarginal and angular gyri. We speculated that auditory projections reach the inferior parietal lobe via a projection from the superior temporal lobe. This makes an indirect projection between Wernicke and Broca's areas via the inferior parietal lobe, which we argued is also present in the human. A second input to the homologue of Broca's area consists of a direct projection from auditory regions via the arcuate fasciculus as specified by the Wernicke-Geschwind model. However, this tract was considered rudimentary in the monkey, if present at all. Finally, we proposed a third input to Broca's area or its homologue from the anterior temporal lobe, carrying complex visual information to be associated with auditory projections. This projection fits the ventral visual pathway described above, which, as we will see below, partly merges with the ventral auditory pathway.

Adding and subtracting a few elements, the network for language we proposed is essentially the same as the one that is accepted today and was depicted in Chapter 2. We hypothesized that the vocal repertoire of early humans expanded concomitant with the amplification of the arcuate fasciculus and other projections from premotor regions to the brainstem

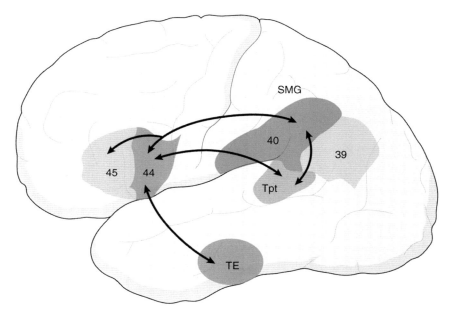

Fig. 7.3 Our original model of language connectivity. We proposed that connections between area Tpt and area 40, and between area Tpt and Broca's area (areas 44, 45) became amplified in the human lineage. Note however that area 44 had not yet been described in the monkey (Aboitiz 1997). Connections between Broca's area and the dorsolateral prefrontal cortex were also depicted in the original model (not shown). Overall, the diagram contains many of the elements shown in Fig. 2.3. AF, arcuate fasciculus; SMG, supramarginal gyrus, TE, area TE; Tpt, area Tpt

controlling vocal musculature. Together with this expansion, an increase in auditory working memory capacity was provided by the growing arcuate fasciculus and inferior parietal projections, generating an incipient phonological loop for learning increasingly complex vocal utterances. In subsequent articles, my students and I emphasized the anatomically more conservative arrangement of the ventral auditory pathway, which in monkeys may be the main circuit for auditory-vocal coordination. On the other hand, the dorsal pathway (especially the arcuate fasciculus) has undergone the greatest degree of expansion in human evolution (Aboitiz et al. 2006, 2010; Aboitiz and García 2009; Aboitiz 2012).

The Paths of Sound

A couple years after our proposal, two independent groups, one led by Liz Romanski in collaboration with Goldman-Rakic and Josef Rauschecker, and the other involving Troy Hackett and Jon Kaas, confirmed that the dorsal auditory stream in the monkey directs to dorsal prefrontal areas instead of the homologue of Broca's area. In addition, they described a robust ventral stream of auditory-prefrontal projections originating in the anterior temporal lobe, which ends principally in the anterior ventrolateral prefrontal cortex and adjacent areas (Fig. 7.2) (Romanski et al. 1999a, b, 2000; Romanski 2007; Kaas and Hackett 1999). These studies showed that the dorsal auditory pathway is associated with spatial and motion auditory processing, while the ventral pathway is more involved in identifying sounds including vocalizations and speech. Ricardo Gil-da-Costa and collaborators also showed that species-specific calls induce activation of visual and limbic areas of the inferior temporal lobe of the macaque (Gil-da-Costa et al. 2004). These notable findings were widely confirmed by a subsequent series of studies indicating a similar organization of visual and auditory projections, both subdivided in dorsal and ventral pathways.

Romanski and Goldman-Rakic also described an auditory domain in the ventrolateral prefrontal cortex (areas 12 and 45) of the monkey, with auditory neurons sensitive to conspecific vocalizations, intermingled with visual neurons sensitive to faces (Romanski and Goldman-Rakic 2002). This indicates that the ventral auditory and visual pathways converge in this region, integrating vocalizations and orofacial gestures. More recently, Romanski and collaborators showed that a population of neurons in the monkey ventrolateral prefrontal cortex responds to videos of conspecific faces, auditory vocalizations or a combination of these (Romanski and Diehl 2011; Romanski 2012; Sugihara et al. 2006). In addition, the activity of some neurons is suppressed when incongruous face-vocalization pairs are presented, which may be relevant for determining the caller's identity (Diehl and Romanski 2014). Likewise, Steffen Hage and Andreas Nieder analyzed single neurons in the macaque ventrolateral prefrontal cortex, the discharge rate of which is modulated by both vocalizations and the perception of species-specific calls (Hage and Nieder 2015). Altogether, this evidence provides an excellent starting point for the development of Broca's area in human evolution, notably receiving its main projection from the ventral auditory and visual pathways. Nonetheless, face-voice associations may not be as developed in monkeys as they are in humans. Julia Sliwa, Sylvia Wirth and collaborators recently described dissociation between facial and vocal responses in hippocampal and inferotemporal cortex neurons of monkeys, in which facial information correlated with individual recognition while voice information did not (Sliwa et al. 2016). This finding contrasts with the reports by Quian Quiroga and collaborators that hippocampal neurons in humans can multimodally represent familiar conspecifics (Quiroga 2012). Thus, associations between faces and voices in the ventral pathway may have been strengthened over the course of human evolution (Viskontas et al. 2009).

Subsequent findings in the ventrolateral prefrontal cortex of the macaque further refined the homologies with Broca's area. Michael Petrides and collaborators were the first to identify area 44 in the macaque brain, providing a complete homology between human and macaque areas 44 and 45, the core of Broca's region (Petrides et al. 2005, Frey et al. 2014). Stimulation of area 44 triggered orofacial movement and rarely hand movements, but not ocular movements, indicating that it is mainly involved in the control of vocal behavior. Eye and hand movements were elicited with stimulation in other dorsal premotor areas. Therefore, the rudiment of Broca's region in the monkey contains two components, an anterior sensory one (area 45) that receives auditory and visual input, and a posterior motor one (area 44) that controls orofacial movement. The ventral auditory and visual pathways feed into the anterior component, while the posterior component receives projections from the dorsal pathway.

Petrides and collaborators subsequently analyzed the dorsal pathway to Broca's area in the human and its homologue in the macaque (Petrides 2014). The authors depicted a nested hierarchy of connections between ventrolateral prefrontal and inferior parietal areas in which lower-order sensory and motor areas close to each other are heavily interconnected, while slightly more distant middle-order parietal and frontal areas are also interconnected. The even more distant higher order parietal and prefrontal areas also have strong connectivity between them (see Fig. 2.3 of Chapter 2). In addition, Petrides and collaborators proposed that the temporal lobe feeds multimodal input (including auditory signals) to the inferior parietal lobe, which provides a route connecting the auditory cortex, the inferior parietal lobe and Broca's area or its homologue (Petrides 2014, Yeterian et al. 2012, Petrides et al 2012). Petrides and his group also described an arcuate fasciculus in the monkey, directly connecting area Tpt and area 45, but it seems less developed than in humans. Finally, the superior temporal lobe connects with anterior Broca's area (area 45) via the ventral pathway (Frey et al. 2008; Petrides and Pandya 2009; Margulies and Petrides 2016). Although here I tried to make a simplified scheme of inferior parietal-prefrontal connections, there are still some discrepancies among authors in the details of this network, which will probably be resolved by further work and the development of more sophisticated imaging techniques (see next Chapter). In a very similar vein, Marco Catani, Dominic ffychte and Valentina Bambini depicted a quite conserved pattern of connectivity between the language-related networks and their homologue regions in the monkey brain (the SCALED model; see Chapter 2) (Catani et al. 2005; Catani and Bambini 2014; Tremblay and Dick 2016). In both species, there are profuse longitudinal tracts along the ventral pathway, but the direct connections between Wernicke's and Broca's regions via the arcuate fasciculus, and between Wernicke's area and the inferior parietal lobe are poorly developed in the monkey, as was proposed in our original scheme (Fig. 7.3).

The above model is widely accepted today as the basic network for language processing (see Chapter 2), and is consistent with our original proposal of a phylogenetically conserved tripartite input into Broca's region or its monkey homologue. In humans, the dorsal pathway processes phonological and articulatory information, and complex syntactic processes, while the ventral pathway has more to do with identification of sounds and speech, and with associating these inputs with other stimuli and long-term memories in a semantic network. Accordingly, while the more posterior part of Broca's area (area 44), which is connected to the dorsal pathway, has a role in phonological fluency and grammatical processing, the anterior Broca's region (area 45), which is more connected to the ventral pathway, is more related to associative processes and memory retrieval.

From Ape to Human

A potential weakness of the aforementioned studies is that none of them has directly compared the auditory pathways in humans and non-human primates in a single study. James Rilling and collaborators made such pioneering comparative studies using tractographic information from monkey, chimpanzee and human brains (Rilling et al. 2008). In a groundbreaking study, they reported that the arcuate fasciculus is present in monkeys, chimpanzees and humans. Nonetheless, Rilling and colleagues found a progressive expansion of the arcuate fasciculus from the macaque to chimpanzee, with maximum development in humans. Conversely, the ventral pathway has remained relatively unchanged in primates, and therefore becoming relatively smaller than the dorsal pathway as brains have increased in size. Note that the dorsal pathway visualized by Rilling and colleagues includes fibers from both inferior parietal and superior temporal areas, possibly including elements from the superior longitudinal fasciculus. As I said in Chapter 2, these fiber tracts are most likely not discrete entities but made up of a continuous plexus of longitudinal fibers covering the white matter below the posterior temporal, parietal and frontal lobes. Very recently, the group led by Kristina Simonyan found robust connectivity in humans between the area in the motor cortex representing the larynx (aptly termed the laryngeal motor cortex) and somatosensory and inferior parietal regions, much stronger than that observed in the macaque, which further highlights the relevance of inferior parietal components in controlling speech processing (Kumar et al. 2016).

Rilling and his team also found that the arcuate fasciculus proper emerges in humans both from the superior temporal sulcus and middle temporal gyrus, while in the chimp these fibers originate only in the superior temporal gyrus (Rilling et al. 2012; Rilling 2014). This implies a broader connectivity in the former, and supports the concept of a role of the dorsal pathway (including inferior parietal projections) in human language. Nonetheless, the arcuate fasciculus of the chimpanzee is larger than that of the monkey. Furthermore, in the chimpanzee the authors found asymmetry in this tract similar to that in the human, consistent with earlier reports of an asymmetric planum temporale in both species (see Chapter 4). One possibility is that the gradual amplification of the dorsal auditory pathway, compared to the conservation of the ventral pathway, is explained by the allometry of cortical expansion. In other words, there is disproportionate expansion of the posterior ventrolateral prefrontal regions and the inferior parietal lobe or posterior temporal areas (making up the dorsal pathway) compared to the more conservative growth of anterior ventrolateral prefrontal regions connected to the anterior temporal lobe. From this perspective, the arcuate fasciculus can be considered an extension of the ventral aspect of the superior longitudinal fasciculus, as there is no clear-cut separation between the two tracts. As I discussed in Chapter 3, the evidence for selective enlargement of the entire frontal lobe in primates and humans is controversial. However, the group led by Marcello Rosa (Chaplin et al. 2013) tackled this question by quantifying the differential volumetric expansion of specific cortical regions using surface models of the cortex of New World monkeys and macaques, and identified homologous regions as points of reference. They further compared these patterns with published data on the cortical expansion of the human brain. Their results show selective expansion across species of the temporoparietal junction, the ventrolateral prefrontal cortex and the dorsal cingulate cortex. Moreover, the above authors argue that these regions are among the latest to mature in the cerebral cortex, which agrees with Georg Striedter and Barbara Finlay's assertion that late developing brain components have undergone the greatest expansion during brain growth (Chapter 3). More recent reports have reached similar conclusions (Margulies et al. 2016).

Another issue is that although anatomical evidence has shown robust connectivity between the inferior parietal lobe and Broca's region or its surroundings, the function of this projection in verbal processing and working memory remains enigmatic, partly after Buchsbaum and D'Esposito's critique of these areas as representing the phonological storage of Baddeley's phonological loop (Buchsbaum and D'Esposito 2008). In the last chapter, I proposed that the inferior parietal lobe supports working memory in different ways, but at this point it may be of interest to discuss the role of these areas in the non-human primate in order to visualize an evolutionary transition to their role in human speech. In this line, Jon Kaas and collaborators have emphasized the general development of parietal-frontal connections in mammalian and primate evolution, very likely concomitant with increasing brain size, ant their role in the selection of complex ethologically relevant behavioral patterns among competing motor programs (Kaas and Stepniewska 2016). Specifically, the inferior parietal lobe represents a converging site of different sensory modalities and participates in the execution of several complex motor behaviors, including grasping behavior and object manipulation, but it also drives facial motor patterns and communicative gestures, which may have been of relevance for early human communication. Dietricht Stout and Tierry Chaminade associated these areas with tool use, particularly in the right hemisphere (see Chapter 4) (Stout and Chaminade 2012). On the other hand, Josef Rauschecker has offered an interpretation more related to vocal-auditory circuitry. He proposes that the dorsal pathway conveys a backward "efference copy" (that is, a template of ongoing motor activity) from prefrontal and motor cortices into the inferior parietal lobe to reach auditory areas in order to generate an "optimal state estimation" of vocalizations and refine the output. That is, the dorsal pathway not only works forwardly, but is also bidirectional, like most cortical pathways (Rauschecker 2012). This is complementary to Angela Friederici's proposal that the arcuate fasciculus in humans conveys a top-down influence on early speech processing areas, which originates in Broca's region (Chapter 2) (Skeide and Friederici 2016). Thus, the co-option of the inferior parietal areas to support an incipient phonological loop could have originated from a top-down control system to optimize vocalizations, which may have been increasingly relevant as our human ancestors learned to vocalize, as opposed to the stereotypical calls of other primates.

Function and Behavior

Concomitant with tract-tracing analyses, a series of comparative functional imaging studies have yielded important evidence of the activation patterns of the macaque brain in relation to heard or produced vocalizations. Most of these studies have shown striking resemblance between the areas involved in language processing in humans and those supporting conspecific vocalization processing in non-human primates. For example, some years ago Ricardo Gil-da-Costa and collaborators published a PET study with macaques in which they observed activations in the ventral premotor area, auditory area Tpt and the posterior parietal cortex after exposure to species-specific vocalizations (Gil-da-Costa et al. 2006). Notably, the activations were either bilateral or had no consistent left or right asymmetry (see Chapter 4). More recently, the group led by Christopher Petkov showed that learning a simple artificial grammar involves perisylvian regions highly similar to the language networks in both humans and monkeys (Wilson et al. 2013). They used a simple sequential pattern that had specific variants, and assessed the brain activity of consistent sequences, contrasted with violations of these sequences. The authors observed activations in monkeys associated with this contrast in brain areas comparable to those seen in relation to language tasks, particularly involving syntactic processing (perisylvian, frontal temporal and parietal areas). In a subsequent study, Petkov and colleagues examined the brain activity of monkeys during a non-word sequencing task and found activation in the ventrolateral prefrontal cortex similar to that in humans performing syntactic tasks (Wilson et al. 2015). They concluded that syntactic capacity evolved in humans from a domain general system involved in sequential processing. This evidence and that reviewed in the previous sections indicate that human speech networks can be traced to a basic circuitry involved in processing species-specific vocalizations in other primates. But the innovation in the human brain that allowed our ancestors to make the leap to speech and language is that we humans are endowed with a new functional circuit, the phonological loop, which produced a big bang in our communicative and cognitive capacities.

In addition to neuroanatomical evidence, there is functional and behavioral data supporting the emergence of the phonological loop in humans. Franz-Xaver Neubert and collaborators used a combined tractography and resting-state functional connectivity analysis of some 20 human brains and 20 macaque brains to unveil the relationships between the ventrolateral prefrontal cortex and other cortical areas (Neubert et al. 2014). They found an overall species similarity of network organization, although they described fundamental differences in the connectivity of posterior auditory areas (associated with the dorsal pathway) with prefrontal regions. In humans, there was a conspicuous interaction between posterior auditory areas and several areas in the ventrolateral prefrontal cortex, not only those traditionally involved in language, while in macaques these projections are minimal. Anterior auditory areas (the ventral pathway) evidenced similar frontal connectivity in the two species. These functional differences imply distinct behavioral capacities. Another recent report analyzed intracortical connectivity in macaques and humans, again concluding that the arcuate fasciculus enables the emergence of verbal working memory, a key capacity for language learning (Schomers et al. 2017).

Finally, Brian Scott, Mortimer Mishkin and Pingbo Yin provided behavioral support for a selective amplification of auditory working memory in our species. These authors presented an auditory delayed-match-to-sample task to macaques, and found that their working memory was seriously impaired when interfering stimuli were placed during the maintenance period, which indicates a strong instability of the short-term auditory memory trace (Scott et al. 2012). This contrasts with their performance in visual working memory, which is much more robust in these animals. In a more recent review, Scott and Mishkin presented evidence that short-term auditory memory in monkeys relies on passive sensory retention of the stimulus, while human working memory is based on phonological mechanisms activated by long-term memories (Scott and Mishkin 2016). Likewise, Amy Poremba and collaborators analyzed the response patterns of monkey neurons in the auditory cortex during a delayed match-to-sample task and observed little sustained activity during the retention interval. Most of the neurons changed activity either at the beginning or end of the interval (Bigelow et al. 2014). Furthermore, they also recorded similar short-term auditory memory cells in the anterior temporal lobe and found that this information is carried predominantly by the ventral auditory pathway.

A Key Innovation

In several articles we have proposed that the recruitment of the dorsal pathway to support both phonological articulation and working memory was a radical event in human evolution, astronomically propelling the vocal repertoire of our species (Aboitiz 1995, 2012; Aboitiz and García 1997, 2009; Aboitiz et al. 2006, 2010,). This process may have begun as early as Australopithecines, first with the transition from primitive fixed forms of vocal communication to more flexible, learned patterns that became strongly adaptive in social behavior. Learned vocal utterances may have been involved in mother-child relations, the establishment of individual alliances, facilitating group cohesion and other social functions, providing advantages for those groups with more elaborate vocal repertoires. Initially, vocal learning capacity was acquired by a series of peripheral adaptations including modifications of orofacial musculature and the oral cavity, and more refined neural control of the vocalization system based on the development of a descending cortical projection to brainstem nuclei controlling vocalizations (see Chapter 10). Suzana Herculano-Houzel has suggested that increasing cortical control of both the hand and orofacial motor systems is just a parallel consequence of increasing cortical size relative to subcortical systems, which concomitantly increased the density of descending cortical projections into the brainstem or spinal nuclei (see Chapter 3) (Herculano-Houzel et al. 2016). Thus, greater vocal plasticity could have been partly a consequence of increase in brain size, facilitating more complex vocal communication that in turn generated selective pressure for increasing brain size, and so on.

In addition, the eventual development of an incipient phonological loop that increased verbal working memory capacity was key to learning progressively complex vocal repertoires in the context of bidirectional, conversational interactions with others, establishing a rudimentary form of speech. Larger brain size in early humans provided the basic scaffolding for the development of a direct auditory-vocal interface in the cerebral cortex, producing the first impetus for the amplification of the dorsal auditory pathway. Specifically, the arcuate fasciculus and related tracts may have provided benefits for the development of an auditory-vocal sensorimotor interface, facilitating and amplifying learned oral communication. In addition, the indirect dorsal pathway, connecting the posterior temporal lobe with the inferior parietal lobe, and then with the ventrolateral prefrontal cortex (prospective Broca's area) and motor cortices, may have been recruited for vocal behavior by contributing to select appropriate motor commands to execute the learned utterances, and by providing a top-down control that served to refine output during learning. Recent evidence suggests that this articulatory system is to some extent bilateral, notwithstanding the possibility of hemispheric segregation of functions, as with speech perception (Cogan et al. 2014; see Chapter 4).

As vocalization behavior became crucial for social interactions in early humans, a selective tendency arose favoring genetic and epigenetic modifications that strengthened the functional connectivity of the incipient auditory-vocal circuits and their descending projection to vocal motor nuclei in the brainstem, inducing further lateralization of these functions. The developmental mechanisms involved in the refinement of these projections may not be particularly complex, including the modulation of connectivity by generating new connections or eliminating others, again by modifying the labels that axons use to establish synaptic contacts with their presumed targets. Additionally to this, and possibly more importantly, is the initial exuberance and the subsequent dramatic reduction of connectivity that occurs in early cortical development, where the majority of connections established in utero are lost by the first or second year of life (see Chapters 3 and 5). This process occurs in all cortical areas and subcortical connections, and has been associated to critical periods of language acquisition (see Chapters 1 and 10). Some of these early transient projections can be maintained by experimental means, avoiding their retraction and allowing them to form functional circuits in targets that otherwise would not receive such projections. As discussed in Chapter 3, the studies by Migranka Sur and Sarah Pallas have shown that experimental manipulations can stabilize the transient exuberant ectopic connections in the developing brain, generating novel functional circuits (Sur et al. 1990). This provides a mechanism by which neuronal connectivity can rapidly change in evolution, using minimal genetic modifications. In this line, many authors such as Dale Purves, have proposed that the process of axonal retraction during development can be viewed as a reservoir of connections that can be used for brain plasticity after early lesions. More relevant to this discussion, this transient axonal exuberance can also provide a supply for rapid evolutionary change in connectivity, where the balance of retraction of axons can be modulated to generate new circuits and eliminate old ones (Purves 1988).

In the next chapter, I will discuss other functions of the expanding parietal system and dorsal pathway that contributed to the development of human communication as a multimodal process involving not only vocalizations but also facial, hand and body gestures. This network provides a unifying context in which toolmaking, manual dexterity and gestuality contributed to shaping vocal language. As I have repeatedly said, human communication is an opportunistic phenomenon that takes advantage of any possible behavioral means to convey emotional or descriptive contents. It is in this context that human speech arose, where there was probably strong pressure for flexibility in communication, perhaps associated with more complex social life, including a rudimentary culture and the benefit of developing increasing emotional bonds among individuals.

References

Aboitiz F (1988) Homology: a comparative or a historical concept? Acta Biotheor 37:27–29

Aboitiz F (1995) Working memory networks and the origin of language areas in the human brain. Med Hypotheses 44:504–506

Aboitiz F (2012) Gestures, vocalizations, and memory in language origins. Front Evol Neurosci 4:2

Aboitiz F, García VR (1997) The evolutionary origin of the language areas in the human brain. A neuroanatomical perspective. Brain Res Rev 25:381–396

Aboitiz F, García R (2009) Merging of phonological and gestural circuits in early language evolution. Rev Neurosci 20:71–84

Aboitiz F, García RR, Bosman C, Brunetti E (2006) Cortical memory mechanisms and language origins. Brain Lang 98:40–56

Aboitiz F, Aboitiz S, García R (2010) The phonological loop: a key innovation in human evolution. Curr Anthropol 51:S55–S65

Arnsten AF (2013) The neurobiology of thought: the groundbreaking discoveries of Patricia Goldman-Rakic 1937–2003. Cereb Cortex 23:2269–2281

Arnsten AF, Cai JX, Murphy BL, Goldman-Rakic PS (1994) Dopamine D1 receptor mechanisms in the cognitive performance of young adult and aged monkeys. Psychopharmacology 116:143–151

Bigelow J, Rossi B, Poremba A (2014) Neural correlates of short-term memory in primate auditory cortex. Front Neurosci 8:250

Buchsbaum BR, D'Esposito M (2008) The search for the phonological store: from loop to convolution. J Cogn Neurosci 20:762–778

Catani M, Bambini V (2014) A model for Social Communication And Language Evolution and Development (SCALED). Curr Opin Neurobiol 28:165–171

Catani M, Jones DK, ffytche DH (2005) Perisylvian language networks of the human brain. Ann Neurol 57:8–16

Cavada C, Goldman-Rakic PS (1989a) Posterior parietal cortex in rhesus monkey: I. Parcellation of areas based on distinctive limbic and sensory corticocortical connections. J Comp Neurol 287:393–421

Cavada C, Goldman-Rakic PS (1989b) Posterior parietal cortex in rhesus monkey: II. Evidence for segregated corticocortical networks linking sensory and limbic areas with the frontal lobe. J Comp Neurol 287:422–445

Chaplin TA, Yu HH, Soares JG, Gattass R, Rosa MG (2013) A conserved pattern of differential expansion of cortical areas in simian primates. J Neurosci 33:15120–15125

Cogan GB, Thesen T, Carlson C, Doyle W, Devinsky O, Pesaran B (2014) Sensory-motor transformations for speech occur bilaterally. Nature 507:94–98

Cohen L, Lehéricy S, Chochon F, Lemer C, Rivaud S, Dehaene S (2002) Language-specific tuning of visual cortex? Functional properties of the Visual Word Form Area. Brain 125:1054–1069

Deacon TW (1992) Cortical connections of the inferior arcuate sulcus cortex in the macaque brain. Brain Res 573:8–26

D'Esposito M, Postle BR (2015) The cognitive neuroscience of working memory. Annu Rev Psychol 66:115–142

Diehl MM, Romanski LM (2014) Responses of prefrontal multisensory neurons to mismatching faces and vocalizations. J Neurosci 34:11233–11243

Eccles JC (1967) The inhibitory control of spinal reflex action. Electroencephalogr Clin Neurophysiol Suppl 25:20–34

Frey S, Campbell JS, Pike GB, Petrides M (2008) Dissociating the human language pathways with high angular resolution diffusion fiber tractography. J Neurosci 28:11435–1144

Frey S, Mackey S, Petrides M (2014) Cortico-cortical connections of areas 44 and 45B in the macaque monkey. Brain Lang 31:36–55

Funahashi S, Bruce CJ, Goldman-Rakic PS (1989) Mnemonic coding of visual space in the monkey's dorsolateral prefrontal cortex. J Neurophysiol 61:331–349

Funahashi S, Bruce CJ, Goldman-Rakic PS (1991) Neuronal activity related to saccadic eye movements in the monkey's dorsolateral prefrontal cortex. J Neurophysiol 65:1464–1483

Fuster JM (1995) Memory in the Cerebral Cortex. Bradford, MIT Press, Cambridge

Fuster JM (2003) Cortex and Mind. Unifying Cognition. Oxford University Press, Oxford

Fuster JM, Alexander GE (1971) Neuron activity related to short-term memory. Science 173:652–654

Galaburda AM, Pandya DN (1983) The intrinsic architectonic and connectional organization of the superior temporal region of the rhesus monkey. J Comp Neurol 221:169–184

Galaburda A, Sanides F (1980) Cytoarchitectonic organization of the human auditory cortex. J Comp Neurol 190:597–610

Gil-da-Costa R, Braun A, Lopes M, Hauser MD, Carson RE, Herscovitch P, Martin A (2004) Toward an evolutionary perspective on conceptual representation: species-specific calls activate visual and affective processing systems in the macaque. Proc Natl Acad Sci U S A 101:17516–17521

Gil-da-Costa R, Martin A, Lopes MA, Muñoz M, Fritz JB, Braun AR (2006) Species-specific calls activate homologs of Broca's and Wernicke's areas in the macaque. Nat Neurosci 9:1064–1070

Goldman PS, Nauta WJ (1977) Columnar distribution of cortico-cortical fibers in the frontal association, limbic, and motor cortex of the developing rhesus monkey. Brain Res 122:393–413

Goldman PS, Rosvold HE. (1970) Localization of function within the dorsolateral prefrontal cortex of the rhesus monkey. Exp Neurol 27:291–304

Goldman-Rakic PS (1990) Cellular and circuit basis of working memory in prefrontal cortex of nonhuman primates. Prog Brain Res 85:325–335; discussion 335–336

Goldman-Rakic PS (1995) Cellular basis of working memory. Neuron 14:477–485

Goldman-Rakic PS, Funahashi S, Bruce CJ (1999) Neocortical memory circuits. Cold Spring Harb Symp Quant Biol 55:1025–1038

Hage SR, Nieder A (2015) Audio-vocal interaction in single neurons of the monkey ventrolateral prefrontal cortex. J Neurosci 35:7030–7040

Herculano-Houzel S, Kaas JH, de Oliveira-Souza R (2016) Corticalization of motor control in humans is a consequence of brain scaling in primate evolution. J Comp Neurol 524:448–455

Hubel DH (1988) Eye, Brain and Vision. Scientific American Library, New York

Hubel DH, Wiesel TN (1977) Ferrier lecture. Functional architecture of macaque monkey visual cortex. Proc R Soc Lond B Biol Sci 198:1–59

Jacobsen CF (1938). Studies of cerebral function in primates. Comp Psychol Monogr 13:1–68

Jonides J, Smith EE, Koeppe RA, Awh E, Minoshima S, Mintun MA (1993) Spatial working memory in humans as revealed by PET. Nature 363:623–625

Kaas JH, Hackett TA (1999) "What" and "where" processing in auditory cortex. Nat Neurosci 2:1045–1047

Kaas JH, Stepniewska I (2016) Evolution of posterior parietal cortex and parietal-frontal networks for specific actions in primates. J Comp Neurol 524:595–608

Kubota K, Niki H (1971) Prefrontal cortical unit activity and delayed alternation performance in monkeys. J Neurophysiol 34:337–347

Kumar V, Croxson PL, Simonyan K (2016) Structural organization of the laryngeal motor cortical network and its implication for evolution of speech production. J Neurosci 36:4170–4181

Lettvin JY, Maturana HR, McCullough WS, Pitts WH (1968) What the frog's eye tells the frog's brain. In: Corning WC (ed), The Mind: Biological Approaches to its Functions. Martin Balaban, Boston, p 233–258.

Margulies DS, Petrides M (2016) Distinct parietal and temporal connectivity profiles of ventrolateral frontal areas involved in language production. J Neurosci 33:16846–16852

Margulies DS, Ghosh SS, Goulas A, Falkiewicz M, Huntenburg JM, Langs G, Bezgin G, Eickhoff SB, Castellanos FX, Petrides M, Jefferies E, Smallwood J (2016) Situating the default-mode network along a principal gradient of macroscale cortical organization. Proc Natl Acad Sci U S A 113:12574-12579

Maturana HR, Lettvin JY, McCulloch WS, Pitts WH (1959) Evidence that cut optic nerve fibers in a frog regenerate to their proper places in the tectum. Science 130:1709–1710

Maturana HR, Lettvin JY, McCulloch WS, Pitts WH (1960) Anatomy and physiology of vision in the frog (Rana pipiens). J Gen Physiol 43 (Suppl):129–175

Mishkin M, Pribram KH (1955) Analysis of the effects of frontal lesions in monkey. I. Variations of delayed alternation. J Comp Physiol Psychol 48:492–495

Mishkin M, Pribram KH (1956) Analysis of the effects of frontal lesions in monkey. II. Variations of delayed response. J Comp Physiol Psychol 49:36–40

Neubert FX, Mars RB, Thomas AG, Sallet J, Rushworth MF (2014) Comparison of human ventral frontal cortex areas for cognitive control and language with areas in monkey frontal cortex. Neuron 81:700–713

Owen R (1837) The Hunterian Lectures in Comparative Anatomy. University of Chicago Press, Chicago (1992)

Petrides M (2014) Neuroanatomy of Language Regions of the Human Brain. Academic Press, New York

Petrides M, Pandya DN (1984) Projections to the frontal cortex from the posterior parietal region in the rhesus monkey. J Comp Neurol 228:105–116

Petrides M, Pandya DN (1988) Association fiber pathways to the frontal cortex from the superior temporal region in the rhesus monkey. J Comp Neurol 273:52–66

Petrides M, Pandya DN (2009) Distinct parietal and temporal pathways to the homologues of Broca's area in the monkey. PloS Biol 7:e1000170

Petrides M, Cadoret G, Mackey S (2005) Orofacial somatomotor responses in the macaque monkey homologue of Broca's area. Nature 435:1235–1238

Petrides M, Tomaiuolo F, Yeterian EH, Pandya DN (2012) The prefrontal cortex: comparative architectonic organization in the human and the macaque monkey brains. Cortex 48:46–57

Preuss TM, Goldman-Rakic PS (1991a) Architectonics of the parietal and temporal association cortex in the strepsirhine primate Galago compared to the anthropoid primate Macaca. J Comp Neurol 310:475–506

Preuss TM, Goldman-Rakic PS (1991b) Myelo- and cytoarchitecture of the granular frontal cortex and surrounding regions in the strepsirhine primate Galago and the anthropoid primate Macaca. J Comp Neurol 310:429–474

Preuss TM, Goldman-Rakic PS (1991c) Ipsilateral cortical connections of granular frontal cortex in the strepsirhine primate Galago, with comparative comments on anthropoid primates. J Comp Neurol 310:507–549

Pribram KH, Mishkin M (1956) Analysis of the effects of frontal lesions in monkey. III. Object alternation. J Comp Physiol Psychol 49:41–45

Purves D (1988) Body and Brain. A Trophic Theory of Neural Connections. Harvard Press, Cambridge

Quiroga RQ (2012) Concept cells: the building blocks of declarative memory functions. Nat Rev Neurosci 13:587–597

Quiroga RQ, Reddy L, Kreiman G, Koch C, Fried I (2005) Invariant visual representation by single neurons in the human brain. Nature 435:1102–1107

Quiroga RQ, Kreiman G, Koch C, Fried I (2008) Sparse but not "grandmother-cell" coding in the medial temporal lobe. Trends Cogn Sci 12:87–91

Rauschecker JP (2012) Ventral and dorsal streams in the evolution of speech and language. Front Evol Neurosci 4:7

Rilling JK (2014) Comparative primate neurobiology and the evolution of brain language systems. Curr Opin Neurobiol 28:10–14

Rilling JK, Glasser MF, Preuss TM, Ma X, Zhao T, Hu X, Behrens TE (2008) The evolution of the arcuate fasciculus revealed with comparative DTI. Nat Neurosci 11:426–428

Rilling JK, Glasser MF, Jbabdi S, Andersson J, Preuss TM (2012) Continuity, divergence, and the evolution of brain language pathways. Front Evol Neurosci 3:11

Romanski LM (2007) Representation and integration of auditory and visual stimuli in the primate ventral lateral prefrontal cortex. Cereb Cortex 17 (Suppl 1):i61–i69

Romanski LM (2012) Integration of faces and vocalizations in ventral prefrontal cortex: implications for the evolution of audiovisual speech. Proc Natl Acad Sci U S A 109 (Suppl 1):10717–10724

Romanski LM, Diehl MM (2011) Neurons responsive to face-view in the primate ventrolateral prefrontal cortex. Neuroscience 189:223–235

Romanski LM, Goldman-Rakic PS (2002) An auditory domain in primate prefrontal cortex. Nat Neurosci 5:15–16

Romanski LM, Bates JF, Goldman-Rakic PS (1999a) Auditory belt and parabelt projections to the prefrontal cortex in the rhesus monkey. J Comp Neurol 403:141–157

Romanski LM, Tian B, Fritz J, Mishkin M, Goldman-Rakic PS, Rauschecker JP (1999b) Dual streams of auditory afferents target multiple domains in the primate prefrontal cortex. Nat Neurosci 2:1131–1136

Romanski LM, Tian B, Fritz JB, Mishkin M, Goldman-Rakic PS, Rauschecker JP (2000) Reply to "What", "where" and "how" in auditory "cortex". Nat Neurosci 3:966

Rupke N (1994) Richard Owen. Victorian Naturalist. Yale University Press, New Haven

Scarf D, Boy K, Uber Reinert A, Devine J, Güntürkün O, Colombo M (2016) Orthographic processing in pigeons (Columba livia). Proc Natl Acad Sci U S A 113:11272-11276

Schomers MR, Garagnani M, Pulvermüller F (2017) Neurocomputational Consequences of Evolutionary Connectivity Changes in Perisylvian Language Cortex. J Neurosci 37:3045-3055

Scott BH, Mishkin M (2016) Auditory short-term memory in the primate auditory cortex. Brain Res 1640:264–277

Scott BH, Mishkin M, Yin P (2012) Monkeys have a limited form of short-term memory in audition. Proc Natl Acad Sci U S A. 109:12237–12241

Singer W (1999) Neuronal synchrony: a versatile code for the definition of relations? Neuron 24: 49–65, 111–125

Skeide MA, Friederici AD (2016) The ontogeny of the cortical language network. Nat Rev Neurosci. 17:323–332

Sliwa J, Planté A, Duhamel JR, Wirth S (2016) Independent Neuronal Representation of Facial and Vocal Identity in the Monkey Hippocampus and Inferotemporal Cortex. Cereb Cortex 26:950–966

Spillmann L (2014) Receptive fields of visual neurons: the early years. Perception 43:1145–1176

Stout D, Chaminade T (2012) Stone tools, language and the brain in human evolution. Philos Trans R Soc Lond B Biol Sci 367:75–87

Sugihara T, Diltz MD, Averbeck BB, Romanski LM (2006) Integration of auditory and visual communication information in the primate ventrolateral prefrontal cortex. J Neurosci 26:11138–11147

Sur M, Pallas SL, Roe AW (1990) Cross-modal plasticity in cortical development: differentiation and specification of sensory neocortex. Trends Neurosci 13:227–233

Tremblay P, Dick AS (2016) Broca and Wernicke are dead, or moving past the classic model of language neurobiology. Brain Lang 162:60–71

Varela F, Lachaux JP, Rodriguez E, Martinerie J (2001) The brainweb: phase synchronization and large-scale integration. Nat Rev Neurosci 2:229–239

Viskontas IV, Quiroga RQ, Fried I (2009) Human medial temporal lobe neurons respond preferentially to personally relevant images. Proc Natl Acad Sci U S A 106(50):21329–21334

Wilson B, Slater H, Kikuchi Y, Milne AE, Marslen-Wilson WD, Smith K, Petkov CI (2013) Auditory artificial grammar learning in macaque and marmoset monkeys. J Neurosci 33:18825–18835

Wilson B, Kikuchi Y, Sun L, Hunter D, Dick F, Smith K, Thiele A, Griffiths TD, Marslen-Wilson WD, Petkov CI (2015) Auditory sequence processing reveals evolutionarily conserved regions of frontal cortex in macaques and humans. Nat Commun 6:8901

Yeatman JD, Weiner KS, Pestilli F, Rokem A, Mezer A, Wandell BA (2014) The vertical occipital fasciculus: a century of controversy resolved by in vivo measurements. Proc Natl Acad Sci U S A 111:E5214–E5223

Yeterian EH, Pandya DN, Tomaiuolo F, Petrides M (2012) The cortical connectivity of the prefrontal cortex in the monkey brain. Cortex 48:58–81

York GK 3rd, Steinberg DA (2011) Hughlings Jackson's neurological ideas. Brain 134:3106–3113

Zeki S (1993) A Vision of the Brain. Blackwell Press, Oxford

8

Grasping Mirrors

Among the early hypotheses for the origin of human language was that the first communicative signs were manual, and speech appeared only in later stages. The critical symbolic properties of language would have been acquired with primitive gestures, speech being a secondary addition that only elaborated on this crucial innovation. However, speech would have rapidly taken over as the main modality for communication. As Michael Corballis has said, present-day gestures represent a "behavioral fossil", just as our intestinal appendix reminds us of our vegetarian past (Gentilucci and Corballis 2006). In Chapter 4, I discussed gestural communication in relation to handedness and tool use, and in this chapter I will focus on the findings of mirror neurons and the mirror system hypothesis for language evolution, which have provided a neuroscientific perspective to the gestural theory of language. Although there is a wealth of evidence indicating an important role of gestures in human and animal communication, the gesture-first approach does not provide any specific insight into the mechanism by which we ended up communicating through speech. In addition, the hypothetical gestural stage of communication prior to speech remains speculative given there is no straightforward evidence for it.

© The Author(s) 2017   **287**
F. Aboitiz, *A Brain for Speech*,
DOI 10.1057/978-1-137-54060-7_8

Ancestral Gestures

Among the main arguments for the gestural origin of language is that vocalizations in non-human primates are largely fixed and stereotyped, while hands are under voluntary control, which makes their involvement in learned communication signals more likely. It is commonly asserted that vocalizations of non-human primates are used in situations directly related to survival, like calls of alarm, shows of dominance, courtship etc. Therefore, there would be a selective benefit in maintaining close genetic control of these signals. Alternatively, hand movements and gestures are apparently more flexible and not under such stringent selective conditions, providing a degree of freedom that can be used in more relaxed social situations, closer to those in which humans usually communicate (Arbib 2005, 2012; Arbib et al. 2008).

Monkeys and apes have been observed using hand and body gestures, usually to request things from one another, like the begging behavior of subordinate individuals, which is directed to higher ranking individuals to access food. This consists of extending the hand to the dominant subject, a sign that may be conceived as a ritualized grasping action. Begging gestures are often accompanied with facial gestures and vocalizations. Another kind of sign is arm-waving to call attention of others, elicit play, request nursing, or initiate group movement in a given direction (Liebal et al. 2004; Liebal and Call 2012; Genty and Zuberbühler 2014, 2015, Genty et al. 2014, Hobaiter and Byrne 2011, 2014). There is discussion about whether some of these gestures are learned, as only a few or one individual in a group may use them. Furthermore, such gestures are dependent on the other's position and gaze, which indicates that gestures are flexibly used and based on the other's attentional state (Kaminski et al. 2004). Captive apes raised by humans have been reported to point to food items with their open hand, which can be interpreted as a derivation of begging behavior. However, there are no reports of ape pointing for another ape. Pointing is a very basic communicative strategy that develops quite early in human infants as they rapidly understand the meaning of this gesture made by adults. On the other hand, apes are very slow in learning this gesture, and in most instances never get the intent of pointing (see below in this chapter) (Tomasello 2006). As a communication signal, pointing has to do with additional social capacities that I will discuss in more detail in Chapter 10. Overall, regarding both gestures and vocalizations in apes and other animals, Derek Bickerton claims that such signs are aimed at manipulating the other's behavior for the immediate benefit of the signer more than at communicating any kind of knowledge, a point also made by Michael Tomasello, who distinguishes instrumental from declarative communication (Tomasello and Call 1997; Bickerton 2009). More recent findings have shown some capacity for planning ahead in chimpanzees and bonobos, which I mentioned in Chapter 6. However, in no way do their natural social signals have the property of displacement that is common in human language, that is, the capacity for making reference to absent events. These also lack any combinatorial organization resembling syntax. In this sense, the manual and facial gestural communication of apes is as far from modern speech as their vocal behavior is, which is also unable to transmit any symbolic content (with the exception of enculturated apes that have learned some rudimentary form of hand signing language).

Neuronal Reflections

It is no exaggeration to say that the gestural theory of speech origins catapulted in recent years with the discovery of mirror neurons by the group led by Giacomo Rizzolatti, who developed the famous Mirror Neuron Hypothesis (Rizzolatti and Craighero 2004; Rizzolatti and Sinigaglia 2006). The central finding is that there is a subset of neurons that fire both when the monkey executes an action and when it observes another carrying out a similar action. The story began when Rizzolatti and colleagues at the University of Parma recorded single units in the lateral premotor cortex of the macaque (more specifically, area F5) that fired concomitantly with a grasping action. There were several types of these neurons associated with the different shapes of the objects being grasped. Furthermore, they found visuomotor neurons in F5 that fired when the monkey simply saw the object to be grasped (for example, a piece of food).

They demonstrated that the response was visually evoked by producing a short delay between the presentation of the object and the grasping action. Thus, the neuron activated with the visual presentation of the object before the motor command was executed. These were later called canonical visuomotor neurons. To their surprise, the experimenters observed that a group of neurons fired when a human experimenter picked up the food to start another experimental trial. Extending this observation with additional experiments, they found that these neurons fired specifically when the monkey observed a similar grasping action, such as a precision pinch rather than a power grip. Importantly, these cells coded for actions like grasping an actual object, but not when pantomiming a grasp when the object was not present (di Pellegrino et al. 1992). The term "mirror neurons" was coined to describe a special kind of visuomotor neuron that fires both when the animal performs a particular kind of grasping action and when it perceives the same or similar actions made by others. The Parma group interpreted these neurons as acting as a mirror between the internal motor program and the external observation of someone else's behavior, thus generating an internal representation, or simulation, of the other's motor command. Rizzolatti and coworkers concluded that mirror neurons were essential to understanding the goals or actions of others, by internally activating motor programs congruent with the behavior observed in others (Gallese et al. 1996; Rizzolatti et al. 1996a).

Subsequently, a series of articles appeared from this group and others confirming mirror neuron activity in the premotor area F5. Mirror neurons were classified as "strictly congruent", with activity that closely fits the action seen with the motor program they are involved in, and "broadly congruent" that activate with observation of actions more broadly related to the action they participate in. Moreover, the activity of some strictly congruent cells called "suppression" mirror neurons decreases when the animal observes actions that are only slightly similar to the one it performed. Finally, there are "logically related" mirror neurons that fire with observation of actions different from but contextually related to the grasping behavior they code, such as putting the object to be grasped on a table. Congruent mirror neurons were interpreted as directly involved in action understanding by automatically translating the observation of a specific behavior into an internal motor program (Rizzolatti and Craighero 2004; Rizzolatti and Sinigaglia 2006).

Other studies identified mirror neurons in the inferior parietal lobe, and mirror-like neurons in the superior temporal sulcus of the temporal lobe (close to Wernicke's area) that were sensitive to body and hand-directed movements (Fogassi et al. 2005). A circuit was then delineated that connected the superior temporal sulcus in the temporal lobe, the inferior parietal lobe and the ventral premotor area that was involved in programming and identifying goal-directed actions (Fig. 8.1). Mirror neuron properties were also detected in other areas like the primary motor cortex and the dorsal premotor cortex (Rizzolatti and Craighero 2004; Rizzolatti and Sinigaglia 2006). Furthermore, orofacial mirror neurons were detected in the monkey ventral premotor cortex, which fire in relation to feeding and swallowing behaviors, but also with communicative gestures like lip-smacking (a common vocal behavior of monkeys and apes), and tongue protrusion (Ferrari et al. 2003). These findings suggest that mirror neurons are involved in facial gestures and feeding behavior, providing an initial state for the evolution of speech. Other kinds of mirror neurons were found to fire with unnatural sounds associated with actions (such as tearing paper), and, after massive training, with observations of grasping actions using pliers (Kohler et al. 2002; Ferrari et al. 2005).

Human Mirrors

The mirror neuron experiments were quickly extended to humans, using different techniques to find mirror-like properties. Single unit studies are problematic with humans for ethical reasons. The only possibility is during brain surgery (usually with epileptic patients) when the surgeon places an electrode in the patient's brain to determine the location of the epileptic focus. Consequently, other approaches have been used like brain imaging and transcranial magnetic stimulation (TMS) that monitor the activity or function of large neuronal populations (see Chapters 2 and 4). However, with these techniques it is impossible to know whether

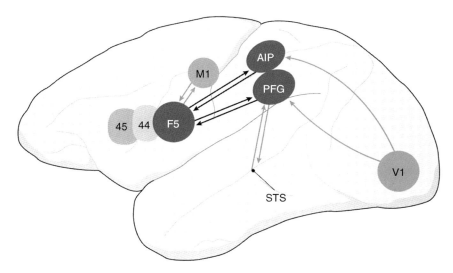

Fig. 8.1 The mirror neuron circuit in the monkey. Mirror neurons have been found in premotor area F5, in the intraparietal area AIP, and in the inferior parietal area PFG. Neurons in the superior temporal sulcus have mirror-like properties but are not mirror neurons. For reference with Brodmann's areas, area F5 corresponds to the inferior aspect of area 6; area AIP is located in Brodmann's area 7; area PFG corresponds to anterior area 39. Also shown are areas 44 and 45, corresponding to Broca's area in the human. M1, motor cortex; V1, primary visual cortex

the same neurons that are active when a subject observes an action also fire when the subject performs the same action, which is the defining criterion for mirror neurons. Thus, researchers prefer to speak of a mirror system in humans, in which there are brain regions rather than single cells that are responsive to both the observation and execution of motor actions of a specific class, like hand actions as distinct from orofacial actions. As with the monkey, the human mirror system is located in both hemispheres, and includes parietotemporal visual areas, the rostral inferior parietal lobe, and the ventrolateral prefrontal and premotor cortices (Aziz-Zadeh et al. 2002, 2006). Additional evidence for a mirror system in humans comes from studies of automatic imitation, in which observation of an action facilitates the execution of that action or interferes with the execution of a similar action. Using TMS, it was found that listening to speech increases the excitability of tongue muscles (Fadiga et al. 2002). Furthermore, disrupting activity in the inferior frontal gyrus with TMS impairs automatic imitation and blocks interference by observing related actions (Baldissera et al. 2001; Iacoboni 2009; Cross and Iacoboni 2014a, b).

While mirror neurons in macaques are restricted to grasping actions, lip movements and very constrained motor patterns, mirror activity in humans has been associated with abstract or meaningless movements, although the anatomical location of this activity does not precisely fit the macaque mirror neuron circuit. In an early study by Rizzolati's group, human subjects were exposed to videos of hand-related movements, whether grasping or pantomimic (Fadiga et al. 1995). While doing so, the hand motor area (not the premotor area, where mirror neurons are found in the monkey) was transiently stimulated using TMS, and the threshold for triggering a hand movement with this technique was lower when subjects were observing hand movements than when they were not, indicating a higher excitability of the motor cortex. Note that this effect was observed for both pantomimic and grasping hand movements that differ from monkey mirror neurons in that the latter do not respond to meaningless movements. Furthermore, the human mirror neuron system has been associated with activity in Broca's area. Reports by Rizzolatti's group published in 1996 showed that observations of the grasping actions of others increased hemodynamic activity in Broca's area and its surroundings (in addition to activity in the superior temporal lobe), compared to control situations (Grafton et al. 1996a, b; Rizzolatti et al. 1996b). A later study reported activation overlap in the observation and execution of meaningless actions (Iacoboni et al. 1999). James Kilner, Karl Friston and others used the fMRI repetition-suppression method, which consists of habituating or making less responsive the subset of Broca's area neurons involved in motor grasping through repeated execution of the behavior (Kilner et al. 2009). They showed that after having habituated the subject to perform the action, the fMRI response was also attenuated when presenting images of subjects grasping an object. This suggests that some of the neurons involved in executing the action are also involved in observing the action. However, the result was negative when analyzing cross-habituation in imitation of meaningless hand movements. Other studies showed that damage to regions including Broca's area produced deficits in pantomime recognition, suggesting that the damage to Broca's region produced a deficit in recognizing abstract movements. Direct evidence for action-observation activity at the cellular level was finally provided in patients undergoing neurosurgery for epilepsy (Mukamel et al. 2010). The authors recorded mirror neurons associated with hand grasping actions and emotional facial expressions in the supplementary motor area, hippocampus and neighboring regions, which in the monkey are devoid of mirror neurons.

It has also been proposed that the human mirror system participates in empathy, emotion recognition, and other elements related to social behavior, particularly the theory of mind. The latter concept implies that we are able to infer other people's knowledge and intentions, and assume that other people have minds like our own. Although I will deal with this issue in more detail in Chapter 11, it is useful to mention here that Simon Baron-Cohen first argued that autistic patients, whose empathy and social abilities are strongly impaired, had difficulty in understanding or inferring other people's mental sates as being different from their own (Baron-Cohen et al. 1985). This deficit was first termed mind-blindness, and was thought to be an impairment of the theory of mind. Mirror neuron theorists soon projected their interpretations to autistic symptoms, and proposed a relationship between the theory of mind and the mirror neuron system, as both involve neural systems involved in detecting complex, goal-directed actions (Rizzolatti and Craighero 2004; Rizzolatti and Sinigaglia 2006). Nonetheless, there are alternative hypotheses to explain autistic behavior, including over-reactivity (instead of indifference) to social stimuli (see Chapter 11).

Another influential proposal is that the mirror system is involved in human language, both gestural and vocal, and that it provides the neurobiological link between ancestral gestural communication and the subsequent acquisition of speech (Rizzolatti and Arbib 1998). Below, I will address some basic issues related to the development and functions of mirror neurons, and then directly address the mirror system hypothesis of language origins, mainly through Michael Arbib, who has done most of the theoretical work in this line (Arbib 2012).

Simulations, Associations or Predictions?

Rizzolatti and collaborators proposed that mirror neurons internally simulate the observed behavior of others, providing knowledge of their intentions and goals "from the inside", which facilitates predicting the behavior of others. This notion has been widely accepted among researchers and the public (Rizzolatti and Craighero 2004; Rizzolatti and Sinigaglia 2006). However, there are investigators that are skeptical about this hypothesis. The first of these is Arbib, a mirror neuron theorist, who argues that the mirror neuron system is not sufficient for understanding actions and has to interact with other systems. Arbib proposes that mirror neurons did not originally develop for social purposes, but rather to control one's behavior through mechanisms of sensorimotor learning, in which self-observation of arm movements feeds on canonical motor neurons while the animal executes these movements (Oztop and Arbib 2002). Visual feedback is in fact crucial for arm control, as it helps in predicting actions, as proposed by James Kilner and colleagues (Kilner et al. 2007). During the execution of a movement like reaching for an object, the brain has to register via the senses (proprioceptive and visual) when the arm is out of the pro-grammed trajectory, and must send a correction signal to restore the trajectory. Normally, the motor system continuously inhibits sensory feedback that would otherwise be elicited at the predicted position of the arm. Thus, if the movement is on target, there is no backward signal and everything keeps on going. But if the movement goes out of the predicted trajectory, it will trigger the activity of sensory regions that are out of the predicted goal, and therefore are not being inhibited by the motor system. A signal then comes in to restore the arm's trajectory. However, this takes time, and by the time the correction signal is executed, the arm may be in a different position than when the original error signal was sent. Thus, the motor system must predict the ongoing trajectory of the arm from the error signal, and send a correction to the predicted arm position when the signal gets to the effectors. This process has been termed predictive coding, and visuomotor mirror neurons may be an essential part of it. By the way, this mechanism has been proposed to explain why one cannot tickle oneself. As your hand approaches your own body, skin sensory receptors would become attenuated, predicting the contact and blocking part of the sensory response. Predictive coding is also observed in the auditory system, as sensory attenuation of self-generated sounds, be them speech or manually triggered sounds, has been observed in humans and mice (Curio et al. 2000; Martikainen et al. 2005; Baess et al. 2011; Rummell et al. 2016). Summarizing, the above perspective implies that the original function of mirror neurons is motor control, not action understanding. The link between internal motor programs and the observation of the behavior of others may be considered an extension of this process. In the process of complex action recognition, Arbib considers that the mirror system works in cooperation with additional, "beyond the mirror" systems involved in higher cognitive processes (Bonaiuto and Arbib 2015).

Gregory Hickok is a more radical critic of the simulation hypothesis. He has written several essays and more recently an entire book dedicated to criticizing the notion of mirror neurons, not only because of the uncritical enthusiasm for this concept in the popular literature, but also because of questions about the very nature of these neurons and their properties (Hickok 2009, 2013, 2014; Hickok and Hauser 2010). Hickok recognizes the existence of mirror neurons and considers this to be a very important finding, however, he questions one of the most fundamental interpretations, which is the simulation hypothesis, claiming that it is based on questionable assumptions, and that there is no hard evidence in its support. According to Hickok, many of the findings related to mirror neurons can be explained by associative links between contextual elements in the experimental set, rather than by a direct representation of the other's actions. This resembles again a Clever Hans phenomenon (see Chapter 1), in which animals use subtle but simple cues to solve apparently complex problems. In general terms, Hickok points out that the experimental procedures involved in recording mirror neurons include long exposure of the monkey to the experimenter's behavior, involving grasping movements and providing food items to the animal, actions that will very likely be relevant for subsequent action selection by the monkeys (i.e. grasping). Hickock asserts that through classical conditioning, motor neurons become responsive to human actions. Furthermore, an important proportion of the neurons observed in these experiments activate not by observing grasping itself, but when observing actions that predict or are preparatory to the monkey's grasping action, such as when the experimenter places food on the table so that the monkey can grasp it. These neurons are not further analyzed by the experimenters, but according to Hickok can be explained in the same terms of action selection mechanisms and classical conditioning.

Richard Cook, Cecilia Heyes and collaborators proposed a simple model for the development of mirror neurons in which higher order visual regions coding the recognition of specific actions like grasping are simultaneously activated with motor programs when infants observe themselves performing the movement (Cook et al. 2014; Catmur et al. 2007, 2009). However, simultaneous activation is not enough to produce an associative pair. This temporal coincidence has to be contingent, that is, firing of motor neurons has to be causally related to the perception of hand movement. Thus, an association between motor patterns and action perception develops that can be extended to observing the behavior of others. Like Hickok, Heyes and group claim that all kinds of mirror neurons, especially those firing with "logical" stimuli, or unnatural stimuli, can be more simply explained by associative processes rather than as instances of action recognition. In this regard, mirror neurons are viewed as part of a top-down mechanism for motor control and action selection. These circuits activate specific commands on the basis of associations with sensory cues that are contingent to the situation. The variety of such cues can be very diverse, including all kinds of visuomotor and mirror neurons. This agrees with the associative interpretations of cortical networks of earlier authors like Joaquín Fuster (see Chapter 7) and especially Norman Geschwind and his hypothesis of amplification of associative capacity in human evolution (see Chapter 2).

Copycats

Early interpretations of mirror neuron activity in the monkey proposed that they were involved in imitation, which was a straightforward interpretation, as mirror neurons associate an observed behavior with a motor program. However, some authors rapidly rejected this proposal arguing that monkeys have little or no imitation skills. About 10 years ago some of my students and I proposed that mirror neurons likely participate in imitative processes (Bosman et al. 2004; Aboitiz et al. 2005), which was rebutted by Michael Corballis (Corballis 2004). Many mirror neuron theorists think monkey mirror neurons are involved largely in object-directed actions. Imitation, particularly of complex behaviors like pantomime, is considered a high-level cognitive process acquired by humans, although it is assumed to be partly conveyed by the human mirror neuron system.

However, there is much evidence that monkeys are able to imitate. Pier Ferrari and collaborators have found evidence for imitation of several facial and hand gestures in young macaques, including lip smacking, tongue protrusion, mouth opening, hand opening, and opening and closing of eyes (Ferrari et al. 2006; Paukner et al. 2011). Simple imitation of this kind may not be cognitively complex. There are many simple reflex actions like yawning, laughter, blinking and scratching that are highly contagious. Likewise, aspects of speech like prosody are easily imitated, as anyone can testify from hearing the speech of close friends, regional accents, and other instances. Yawning is a reflex that has been well studied, and has a well-defined physiological function, contributing to the circulation of the cerebrospinal fluid in which the brain is immersed, and clearing chemicals involved in sleep induction (Walusinski 2014). Furthermore, species with larger brains tend to yawn for longer times, which might relate to the constraints for modulating fluid circulation in a larger volume (Gallup et al. 2016). Robert Provine has been studying yawning behavior in many species, and found that it has contagious properties in humans, non-human primates, and domestic and other social animals (Provine 2013, 2014). Contagious yawning is associated with empathy, and is widespread among social mammals, including domestic dogs that even respond to their owner's yawning (Joly-Mascheroni et al. 2008; Romero et al. 2013, 2014). Furthermore, yawning has an acoustic signal that elicits contagious behavior in others (Massen et al. 2015). Is this contagiousness based on a mirror system? What is its social function? Do the imitative abilities related to learning speech or early social behavior derive from these basic processes (Palagi et al. 2009; Leone et al. 2014)? This is an exciting area for future research in comparative psychology.

In any case, humans may have found imitation more useful than did other species, possibly in relation to the acquisition of toolmaking capacities and the social and cultural implications of this innovation. We start imitating others practically from when we are born, and continue doing so throughout our lives. Newborn infants have been reported to imitate facial gestures with an impressive facility, particularly tongue protrusion (a common gesture in infants, consisting of sticking the tip of one's tongue out), and other gestures like mouth opening, hand opening, finger movements, blinking and the like. This suggests to some that there is an innate capacity provided by a built-in link between actions present in the subjects' repertoire and an observational trigger. On the other hand, Cecilia Heyes asserts that our apparently prodigious imitative capacities rely on associative processes not unlike what we see in other kinds of learning, and in other animals, and that newborns and infants have enough sensory experience to shape behavior according to associative learning (Heyes 2016a, b). For example, in speech and facial gestures there is no visual input about one's performance. In infants, visual sensory feedback for facial and vocal behavior is provided by adults, who imitate the child's expressions, often in an exaggerated way. Adults reward infants for their imitative behavior, which contributes to consolidating the process in a reciprocal loop (Heyes 2016a, b). It all starts when the adult imitates the infant's facial movements, producing in the latter a nearly simultaneous activation of the perceptive and motor networks, an association that, if it involves a reward, stabilizes over time. This process may serve as the basis for the generation of a mirror system for facial gestures and vocalizations.

Perhaps both mechanisms, instinct and learning by association, participate in imitation. In ethology, an innate releasing mechanism consists of an instinctive action (say, smiling) that is elicited by a very specific stimulus (the mother's smile). In the early twentieth century Niko Tinbergen showed that adult seagulls have a bright red spot on their lower beak that acts as a triggering stimulus for beak-pecking behavior in hatchlings (Tinbergen 1951). Hatchlings peck at the red spot, which triggers a regurgitation reflex in the adult that provides food to the offspring. But this instinctive pattern may not be strictly genetic. The hatchling possibly develops an association between its own beak-pecking behavior, the mother's red spot, and the consequent delivery of food in a process called operant conditioning, but as well, this association may develop more rapidly than other associative processes. Supporting this interpretation, Peter Marler argues that the development of most instinctive behaviors is dependent on experience (Marler 2004). To become properly expressed, immature motor patterns need to be rehearsed over time, just as many birds need practice to learn to fly. But more importantly for us, these motor patterns usually need to be elicited by triggering stimuli, and the eventual association between this stimuli and behavior is dependent on the sensory experience. Consider the famous example of the geese raised by Konrad Lorenz that, inter-acted with him before they were exposed to their own mother after hatching and in the end preferred to follow him everywhere instead of members of their own species (Lorenz 1981; see also Robinson and Barron 2017 for a more recent approach). Another important example is birdsong learning, which I will discuss in the next Chapter.

The processes responsible for the consolidation of such innate released patterns depend on a critical period, not unlike that described by Hubel and Wiesel for the visual system and by others for speech acquisition (see Chapters 1 and 10), in which the subject is particularly prone to developing contingent associations among sensory stimuli, and between sensory stimuli and motor programs. There is good evidence that robust associative learning can occur with a minimum of sensory exposure. In the 1970s, John García showed that food aversion learning, in which the animal links a noxious food item with some contingent stimulus can be learned very rapidly after only one trial (García et al. 1974). Food aversion is a behavior of high selective value, as the animal's life may depend on making the right choice of food. Instances of such rapid associative capacity are called "adaptively specialized associative learning", and may be the result of selection for genes that facilitate this process. It is possible that our species is particularly endowed with these behavioral patterns, and has a genetic propensity for adaptively specialized associative learning, especially in the context of infant-adult reciprocal behavior like human imitation and speech learning. Again, this may be another of the great innovations that shaped our species and facilitated the origin of speech.

Janine Oostenbroeck and collaborators recently reported the most extensive study ever done on neonatal imitation in early infants (Oostenbroeck et al. 2016). They found that the odds of producing matching or non-matching actions in response to the presentation of adult gestures are about the same, which challenges the notion of a built-in program for copying others. Many of these behaviors, and particularly tongue protrusion, make up part of the inborn repertoire of newborn infants, and they will react with this gesture to many unrelated stimuli such as a flashlight, and even a mechanical tongue-like stimulus disembodied from a mouth. This makes this behavior strongly reminiscent of the innate-released patterns discussed above, in which innate behaviors are initially elicited by a variety of stimuli, but with experience they narrow the triggering stimulus to a very simple visual configuration, like the red spot on the gull's beak. We need more experiments to know whether a mirror system is involved in the innate imitative behavior of infants, or in the more complex imitations made by children learning to speak. My own bias is that mirror activity will be found in both instances, as in both cases there is a link between observed behavior and a motor program.

But what about subtler forms of imitation involving cognitive processes? In the 1950s, there was a study of a group of macaque monkeys on the island of Kosiva, Japan that were being fed on sweet potatoes (Fa and Lindburg 1996). As sweet potatoes were left on the sand of the riverbank where the monkeys lived, they usually tried to wipe the sand off with their hands before eating them. In one instance, a young female called Imo grasped a potato covered with sand, and washed it in the water instead of brushing it, which turned out to be a much more efficient way to clean the food. Her brothers and sisters saw her doing this, and soon began to wash their own potatoes in the river. Imo's mother also followed, and in a few years practically all macaques washed their potatoes in the water before eating them. Furthermore, at some point Imo found that washing the potatoes in seawater would make them more flavorful, a plus that also rapidly spread in the community. This has been classically considered an early forerunner of culture, that is, socially learned behavioral patterns. It is reasonable to argue that these new habits were acquired through observation and imitation, a process called observational learning. In a more controlled setup, Ralph Holloway, Herbert Terrace and collaborators taught a couple of macaques to touch a given sequence of four pictures on a screen. Each monkey learned a different sequence, and afterward the experimenters placed the two animals together, in which one macaque rehearsed its own sequence while it was observed by the other, and vice versa (Subiaul et al. 2004). The result was that both macaques learned the other's sequence simply by observation. More recently, much evidence of social imitation has been gathered from several species, including other primates (recall toolmaking in chimps), cetaceans, domesticated animals and other species, including vocal learning species, as I will show in Chapters 9 and 10 (Byrne 2009).

Cognitive imitation of tasks like food washing or cleaning sticks to extract termites has been considered to require knowledge of the goal, or the end result of an observed action, and the specific plan of action used by the agent (Tomasello 2014). It has been proposed that the capacity to infer both goals and intentions in others is necessary to respond to the observed behavior with flexibility. Simple action patterns are usually copied directly, as the observed behavior is within the animal's repertoire. But more complex actions involve knowledge of the goal to be achieved, and the animal has to generate novel behavioral sequences in order to reach the end result. If these do not work, the observer focuses on the performer's behavior to copy specific action sequences. Humans excel other animals in the capacity to use both kinds of information to copy complex behavioral patterns, which explains our rapid imitative skills. But for achieving this, motor programs must be deconstructed into components and flexibly rearranged to achieve different goals.

According to Michael Arbib and others, the imitation of novel and complex motor sequences like a pantomime or a ritual action is a fundamental step in language evolution (Arbib 2012). Particularly,

Arbib emphasizes the mimetic capacity for hand movements, to which a mirror system contributes but is not the only component as a critical stage for the origin of the language-ready brain. Arbib distinguishes what he calls "simple imitation", as the capacity for learning some motor plans after a long period of observation, like the manual signs made by enculturated apes, from learning a motor plan in just a moment, as humans do. This kind of learning is referred to as "complex imitation" and is based on the capacity to decompose the observed action and recognize each of the subcomponents in one's own motor plans. According to Arbib, the ability for complex imitation is also involved in the child's language learning capacity, and in the analysis of complex articulatory vocal patterns in the adult. Apes are quite poor at complex imitation, as opposed to humans. This capacity requires the expansion of the mirror system beyond simple imitation tasks, including additional brain systems involved in complex action recognition, such as sharing the other's attentional state to identify the goal of the object, and the details of the imitated behavior. I agree with these statements in general terms, but would add that these behaviors could largely be the result of associative phenomena, in which the individual makes a link between his/her actions, and the other's actions, possibly in the context of shared attention mechanisms. But more importantly, Arbib and others assert that speech emerged when hand motor control mechanisms broke into the orofacial sensorimotor system. On the other hand, I do not see the need for putting hands before mouth in the evolution of vocal imitation. As we will see below in this chapter, and in Chapters 9 and 10, birds and other animals learn vocal patterns quite quickly without having a hand grasping system, and apes and monkeys can indeed perform some types of orofacial imitation.

Rebirth of a Theory

One of the strongest implications of the mirror neuron hypothesis refers to the role of neurons in speech and language origins, which was first claimed in a highly influential article by Rizzolatti and Arbib (Rizzolatti and Arbib 1998). This proposal was originally based on two arguments, firstly on the assumption of homology between area F5 in the monkey premotor cortex and Broca's area in the human, which I will discuss below. Secondly, Rizzolatti considered that their findings were consistent with Alvin Liberman's motor theory of speech perception, which I mentioned in the Chapter 1 (Liberman et al. 1957, 1967; Liberman 1970). The general idea is that mirror neurons first endowed our ancestors with the capacity for hand and gestural communication, and then "colonized" vocal behavior for the acquisition of speech. In 2010, while attending a satellite meeting on the Neuroscience of Language in the context of the Society for Neuroscience, I had the opportunity to witness an interesting debate between Gregory Hickok and Luciano Fadiga, the latter representing the mirror neuron group. The discussion was agitated but respectful (and often funny). In essence, Hickok criticized motor theories of speech perception on the basis that these had been long discredited by counterfactual evidence, while Fadiga argued for a mirror neuron theory of speech perception. In the question and answer session, David Poeppel (a close friend of Hickok) naturally said that he felt Hickok had made the clearest arguments, but recognized that Fadiga made much better jokes.

Hickok's claim is partly based on evidence from brain lesion studies that challenge a critical role of motor components in speech perception (Hickok 2014; Rogalsky et al. 2011). First, deficits in speech recognition are produced by lesions in auditory, not mirror neuron areas. Broca's aphasics, whose frontal mirror neuron system should be impaired according to the theory, are reasonably able to understand speech. Hickok's second argument is based on criticism of Liberman's motor theory of speech perception. In the 1950s, Liberman noted that speech is a continuous stream in which phonemes overlap in time, such that they are never perceived in isolation (Liberman et al. 1957, 1967; Liberman 1970). Moreover, the onset time of many phonemes, such as the stop consonants, depends on the following vowel, yet they still sound the same to us. This suggested to Liberman that subjects were not just perceiving spectral stimuli, but were classifying these stimuli based on phonological motor programs, which he believed are invariant for each phonemic category. A second phenomenon that I mentioned in the Chapter 1 is categorical perception, consisting of the perception of related phonemes as discrete categories, in conditions that there is an acoustically continuous transformation from one phoneme to a related one, for example, from /b/ to /d/, or from /be/ to /de/. As I said earlier, this phenomenon was initially claimed to be unique to human speech perception until it was found that human infants and animals like the chinchilla, which are totally unable to speak, also displayed this capacity, indicating that they could not be emulating a motor speech pattern. Thus, categorical perception is probably a general acoustic process that humans may benefit from to understand other speakers.

Further evidence in favor of Liberman's theory was provided by the McGurk effect, discovered by Harry McGurk and John MacDonald (McGurk and MacDonald 1976). This takes place when a video showing someone's mouth uttering, say /ga/, is simultaneously presented with the sound of the syllable /ba/. Surprisingly, under these conditions the perceived effect is neither of the above but a third syllable, /da/, which is acoustically intermediate between /ga/ and /ba/. This evidence implies that acoustic patterns are not sufficient to enable speech perception, and that motor speech patterns have an important influence on speech perception. Dominic Massaro further investigated this effect, using this time the syllables /ba/ and /da/ (Massaro and Chen 2008). An auditory /ba/ coupled with a visual /da/ resulted in perception of the visual signal /da/. However, when it was the other way around, an auditory /da/ and a visual /ba/, subjects perceived the auditory stimulus, which is not an expected result from the perspective of the motor theory of speech perception. The point, according to Massaro, is that when sounds are very similar, visual cues help to recognize the signal; but when visually identical syllables are used like /p/ and /b/, auditory cues alone clearly distinguish them. Thus, although visual information helps in disambiguating closely similar speech signals under certain conditions, it is not mandatory for speech perception. Just as color perception depends on ambient illumination (see Chapter 7), phonemes are not just perceived on the basis of their intrinsic acoustic features, but also on comparison with contextual cues, mostly auditory, but probably also visual and motoric. The top-down modulation of other sensory and motor systems provides a contextual framework that contributes to distinguishing perceived signals. Massaro, for example, claims that larger units, like syllables, strongly shape phoneme perception. The speech signal is processed in the context of an entire syllable, and syllables in the context of even larger units, so the brain is able to reconstruct the perceived low-level items by top-down interactions (see Chapter 4).

Many authors, including Angela Friederici and Josef Rauschecker have likewise proposed a non-impositive top-down modulatory effect of motor systems on speech perception (see Chapters 2 and 7). As said, speech systems may feed back into auditory regions, participating in predictive coding mechanisms that minimize performance errors and tune speech perception (Rauschecker 2012; Moulin-Frier and Arbib 2013; Clark 2013; Pickering and Garrod 2013; Schomers and Pulvermüller 2016; Skeide and Friederici 2016; Skipper et al. 2017). Daniel Lametti and team observed that subjects that had been adapted to altered auditory feedback in a speech motor learning task displayed subtle changes in subsequent speech perception (Lametti et al. 2014). This modulatory effect can be relevant for speech learning in infancy, as 6-month-old infants were impaired in distinguishing among non-native phonemes presented to them if they were using teething toys that impeded them from moving their tongues to articulate the sounds (Bruderer et al. 2015). Another study showed that interfering with the motor cortex using TMS impaired syllable perception in general (Berent et al. 2015). However, syllables that were ill formed were the least impaired by TMS, and produced less activation of the motor area. According to the motor theory of speech perception, ill-formed syllables that are more difficult to pronounce should be more affected by this procedure. The authors concluded that although the language perception and motor systems are highly interactive, especially with learned patterns, motor systems are not causally related to speech perception. The top-down motor influence may be relevant when it comes to acquiring speech, as it may facilitate learning new phonological sequences and in particular support phonological working memory by contributing to maintaining the memory trace in presence of interfering processes. Supporting this idea, Diana Liao and collaborators used TMS to interfere with motor areas during both spatial and verbal working memory tasks. They observed impaired performance in both tasks, especially in verbal working memory when using non-words, as these stimuli put a higher load on the phonological system (Liao et al. 2014).

The Devil is in the Details

The second assumption in Rizzolatti and Arbib's article on language origins was homology between area F5 of the monkey, where mirror neurons were initially found, and Broca's region in the human (Rizzolatti and Arbib 1998). However, area F5 is part of the monkey ventral premotor cortex (area 6v in the human) and is not strictly part of the ventrolateral prefrontal cortex that makes up the restricted Broca's region in the human. Michael Petrides (Petrides et al. 2005) described areas 44 and 45, corresponding to the core of Broca's area, as distinct from area F5 (or 6v) in the monkey, as Giuseppe Luppino, a close collaborator of Rizzolatti (Belmalih et al. 2009). As mentioned in the previous chapter, Petrides and collaborators observed that stimulation of neurons in the monkey area 44 triggers orofacial movements, while oral mirror neurons that fire with the execution/observation of facial and lip-smacking movements have been located in the more lateral aspect of F5 close to area 44, but not within it. There have been no reports to date of orofacial or grasping mirror neurons in area 44 or in other regions of the ventrolateral prefrontal cortex that may contribute to an "extended Broca's area" (see Chapter 2). Another point of disagreement is that Petrides and others have described the inferior parietal connections as reaching Broca's region (areas 44 and 45) (Petrides 2014), while the group of Luppino has described these projections as terminating more posteriorly in the ventral premotor region or area F5, where mirror neurons are located (Gerbella et al. 2010).

Despite these differences in the details, the overall data points to a robust inferior parietal projection to the ventrolateral prefrontal cortex and/or the ventral premotor and motor cortices. These connections are involved in orofacial control and participate in the selection of behaviorally relevant motor patterns, as proposed by Kaas and Stepniewska (2016) and others (see previous chapter). My interpretation is that these inferior parietal regions, mainly those representing mouth and facial movements, received increasing auditory projection in human evolution (see Chapters 2 and 7). These projections contributed to auditory working memory by selecting vocal motor programs to be rehearsed in working memory processes, and by providing top-down modulations of speech perception to refine output, which is relevant for learning speech. In this way, the inferior parietal pathway began to support the phonological loop that was emerging, mainly associated with an amplification of the arcuate fasciculus. As I said above, it is expected that as part of sensorimotor circuits auditory-vocal mirror neurons are included in the circuit involved in the phonological loop (Aboitiz et al. 2005, 2010; Aboitiz 2013). Examples of these are the audiovisual and the orofacial mirror neurons described above (Kohler et al. 2002; Ferrari et al. 2003). It has been argued that audiovisual mirror neurons activate with the sound of paper being torn but not with the corresponding hand movement, and that the orofacial mirror neurons relate to ingestive movements other than those involved in phonation, which is supposedly produced by a highly rigid, non-plastic sensorimotor system. But there is no reason why auditory mirror neurons should not activate with noises made directly with the hand, and it does not seem difficult to extend ingestive-related mirror neurons to vocalization processes (see Chapter 10). Therefore, auditory-vocal mirror neurons need not derive from a hand grasping system, but may have originated directly from associative processes within the auditory modality. This is not to say that hand-based and phonological representations were totally independent; as I have previously mentioned, an increase in manual skills was also taking place at that point, allowing for the fabrication tools and weapons, which was synergistic with vocal and gestural communication (Chapter 4) (McGinn 2015; Morgan et al. 2015). Nonetheless, circuits involved in toolmaking and vocal behavior may have partially segregated to avoid interference, so it is possible that in some instances they inhibited each other.

Protosigns and Protospeech

Michael Arbib has continued updating the mirror system hypothesis for language origins, disputing the notion that mirror neurons contain a simulation of the other's behavior, and including components "beyond the mirror" to account for action understanding and complex imitation of pantomimes and hand gestures (Arbib 2005, 2009, 2012, 2013a, b, 2016a, b). He retains the key element of the original hypothesis based on an action-oriented framework that derives from manual dexterity, which is the precursor of the circuits involved in speech and language. According to Arbib, it was only through use of the hands that our ancestors were able to develop a primitive lexicon and grammar supporting a semantic network. Arbib has developed an elaborate theory of motor control and language processing, and I will only refer here to those aspects that relate directly to this book's purposes. He proposes that the mirror system for grasping was extended in early humans to facilitate imitation, which evolved from a slow "object oriented" process in non-human primates to a complex imitation system that allows rapid imitation of complex behaviors, including gestures and pantomimes that resemble animal movements or natural events (see above in this Chapter). From here, a "protosign" stage emerged, following Derek Bickerton's concept of protolanguage (see Chapter 1), which is a combinatorial open repertoire of manual gestures conveying simple meanings about objects or events. Protosigns provide neural scaffolding for the origin of a primitive vocal communication system called protospeech. In Arbib's terms, the brain was then "language-ready" but not "language-using". From then on, protosign and protospeech co-evolved in an "expanding spiral" that lasted for most of the history of our ancestors until speech became dominant. Eventually, modern language appeared, with a complex syntax and compositional semantics. Arbib also asserts that while the acquisition of the protosign and protospeech stages (i.e. the language-ready brain) was dependent on genetic mechanisms, modern language is the result of more recent cultural evolution in the history of *Homo sapiens*, rather than resulting from a genetic process. In this way, Arbib claims to depart from the classical Chomskyan approach, which states that the structure of human grammar is innately pre-specified.

Nonetheless, I see some similarity between Arbib's notion of a "language-ready" brain and Chomsky's concept of competence for language (see Chapter 1). Chomsky argues that individuals may be competent for language even if they do not express it. The innate element of Chomsky's language ability resides in the competence, not in the executed structure. In human evolution, the transition from the acquisition of competence to actual performance is very unlikely to have been instantaneous, as language only develops within a language-using community. Our ancestors probably needed a few millenniums of cultural development to actually start using language. Thus, one could say that at the protosign/protospeech stage, humans were already competent for language in Chomsky's terms. The difference between the two views seems to lie in the cognitive interpretation of language-readiness or competence, which Arbib and others claim is deeply intertwined with semantics, and Chomsky proposes is an encapsulated modular system (see Chapter 1). But if language execution is the result of cultural evolution, why do all languages share similar syntactic rules? This could be due to a single origin of all languages, or to genetic constraints in the kinds of structures that cultural learning can develop. We do not yet have a clear answer to this question. By the way, this gets to the argument of Alfred Russell Wallace, the co-discoverer of evolution by natural selection. He observed that native children from the Malay Archipelago could learn English, to read and to do arithmetic under the same conditions as those of their ancestors, who never done any of these things. Dissenting from Darwin, Wallace believed that these traits were not product of natural selection. The point is that these individuals are already language (or mathematically) competent, or have a "language-ready" brain that is an instrument for complex learning. Note however that the analogy is not perfect, as these natives did speak their own language, and had the capacity to estimate quantities based on magnitude. The point I want to make is that our brain may be equipped to do a lot more than what our cultural environment can make us express at any time in history.

Arbib hypothesizes that the last common ancestor of humans and monkeys was manually skilled, but had few imitation capacities, and communication consisted of innate, stereotyped vocal calls. More recently, the last common ancestor of humans and chimps was, in addition, capable of simple imitation of manual tasks and had a simple communicative repertoire of manual gestures, using ritualized gestures to transmit desires. Arbib considers ritualization a key element in this process, and he borrows Michael Tomasello and Josep Call's model

(Tomasello and Call 1997) for the development of ritualization. Imagine, for example, the origin of begging behavior in apes. There are two individuals, one of which (the acting one) is extending its arm to obtain food that the other (the responding one) is eating. The responding individual is able to recognize the action when it begins, so it can anticipate the response (giving some food) before the action to obtain food is totally executed. But this anticipation might not preclude the acting individual to finish extending its arm, as is proposed to happen with monkeys. With chimps however, the acting subject "anticipates the anticipation" of the responding subject, producing a ritualized begging behavior that is rapidly responded to and is subsequently conventionalized. The basic point here is that the responding individual is able to recognize the other's action in its early stages, which can make the acting individual use only the first elements of its own action chain to express its desire.

According to Arbib, the ritualization mechanism emerges when the acting individual can recognize proprioceptive signals to abort the motor program before it ends, something that is proposed to depend on the elaboration of the mirror system for motor control. Another kind of ritualization is human-assisted ritualization, in which the ape unsuccessfully attempts to perform a behavior, but sees a human being effective in this action (like grasping an object). Eventually, the ape produces a ritualized form of this behavior (for example, pointing) to get the human to perform the action for him. This mechanism, however, can be seen in domestic species like dogs and cats, and is not exclusive to primates. Some authors argue that although ritualization can be seen in captivity, there is no evidence of ritualized behavior in wild apes (Hobaiter and Byrne 2011). In any case, macaques are claimed to be unable to arrest the initiated motor program (in the example, the extension of the arm) like captive chimpanzees can do.

Continuing with Arbib's scenario, he proposes that after reaching the ritualization stage, early humans added the capacity to discern the shapes of movements and to form complex hierarchies of motor skills (Arbib 2012). This led to elaborate imitation patterns that resulted in the development of pantomime, or the imitation of actions to direct the attention of others to specific objects, places or events. For example, pantomime is used by modern humans to teach children to use tools, which may have happened with early humans as well (Arbib 2005). Protosigns emerged by conventionalizing pantomimes in the community, which made communication less energetically demanding, less ambiguous and more precise. Protosigns could then be fractionated, for example, a mimic of a flying bird could become split into two protosigns, one for "flying" and the other for "bird", which could be used to transmit novel meanings, like "bird nest". In all these stages, protohumans are supposed to have had a rudimentary capacity for vocal control and vocal learning, even if they made use of facial and vocal gestures during communication. Up to then, vocal behavior would have had little communicative influence besides grunts or noises denoting ingestive behaviors, which fits the mirror neuron evidence. Arbib and others consider that at some point, coincident with the development of a direct tract from premotor and motor cortices into the laryngeal muscles that control vocalization, the control of vocalizations became voluntary. From then on, an "expanding spiral" between gestural and vocal communication developed in which all three modalities, gestures and speech, mutually reinforced the other, until speech took over communication and hand-based signs became limited to gestures that accompany speech.

In summary, Arbib proposes a sequence of several stages in the evolution of language readiness: (1) grasping behavior in primates; (2) the development of a mirror system for grasping in the common ancestor of humans and monkeys; (3) acquisition of a simple imitation system for grasping in the common ancestor of humans and chimpanzees; (4) the development of a complex imitation system for grasping; (5) the advent of protosign, that breaks through the vocal system to produce an open repertoire; (6) protospeech, an open-ended vocal system for production and perception of vocal gestures; (7) an expanding spiral between protospeech and protogestures; and (8) recent cultural evolution generating modern language.

I have said that Arbib proposes that the neural underpinnings of language acquisition depend on the mirror neuron system, but also on its interactions with networks "beyond the mirror system". He emphasizes the organization of the visual system in the dorsal and ventral pathways described in Chapter 7, and the interaction between the two pathways. In Arbib's model, the ventral visual pathway recognizes objects in a scene, and their approximate spatial relationship. By virtue of its connectivity with the prefrontal cortex, this pathway contributes to action planning by maintaining perceptual and motor schemas that are relevant for interaction with the physical and social world. For its part, the dorsal visual system includes mirror neurons and other kinds of neurons that mediate production and recognition of actions. Using complex imitation and planning behavior, execution and observation of familiar actions can be extended to create novel actions leading to pantomimes and protosigns. During the acquisition of protospeech, the dorsal mirror system for compound actions extends in evolution to a mirror system for words, maintaining its connectivity with the ventral pathway. In this way, words can be raised to more elaborate utterances using complex imitation and planning, as happened with hand control in the protosign stage. As protospeech emerges, conveying conventionalized meanings, communicative actions acquire symbolic content and dissociate from praxic actions. The dorsal auditory pathway, mapping sound into articulatory representations, is involved in the production of words-as-actions (i.e. controlling the articulatory process), while the ventral stream that maps sound to meaning provides an interface between phonological signals and conceptual representations.

Following the above argument, Arbib sees syntax as deeply intertwined with semantics. He proposes a "visually constructed grammar" based on a hierarchical "semantic representation" of a visual scene, containing information about agents, attributes and other relevant issues, from which an algorithm operates to produce a sentence describing the event (Arbib 2012). In the process, function words that serve auxiliary grammatical roles (like "if", "the", and "or") are produced to disambiguate meanings conveyed by content words. A key property of symbolic systems is compositionality, that is, when the semantic contents of a complex expression can be fractionated in the meanings of its different components, as in the above example of "flying bird". According to Arbib, repeating this fragmentation procedure to generate longer communicative structures yields recursion as a by-product. Likewise, Friedemann Pulvermüller also argues, the hierarchical structure of an action is composed of an ordered array of action sequences and subsequences (Arbib 2012, Pulvermüller 2014). The difference is that in an action, there is sensory and contextual information at each step that helps to decide the next step, while in a sentence there is no such cue, and working memory is required to keep the sentence going on. This view has commonalities with other proposals like Ronald Langacker's cognitive model of grammar, which emphasizes the transformation of a perceptual code into a behavioral code (Langacker 2013). However, linguists like Andrea Moro remain unconvinced and insist that sensory-motor systems lack both an equivalent to function words and locality principles as found in syntax (Moro 2014a, b). Locality governs the proximity relationship between lexical items, minimizing the load on working memory and computational capacity (otherwise, there would be truly no limit to the complexity of sentences used). The controversy between traditional linguists, heirs of the Chomskyan tradition on one side, and cognitivists that try to intertwine language and semantics on the other, will probably continue for a long time. As I said in Chapter 7, I am more inclined to the notion that syntax represents an algorithm to accurately translate a sequential phonological working memory code into a visual (or visuomotor) working memory representation, minimizing computational load, and involving participation of both the dorsal and the ventral auditory and visual streams (Aboitiz et al. 2006). Thus, syntax is neither "visually constructed" or "motor constructed", nor an encapsulated module, but rather represents an interface between the phonological and sensory-motor systems (particularly vision), and as such may have elements not found in either of these.

The Chicken or the Egg?

A crucial point in Arbib's hypothesis is that visuo-manual circuits were far more developed in the last common ancestor between humans and chimps, which makes an initial gesturing stage more likely, leading to pantomime and protosign. According to Arbib, using and combining learned manual symbols in the protosign stage provided the social and cognitive context to acquire vocal control and vocal learning capacity, leading to protospeech. Songbirds and other animals are particularly good at learning complex vocal patterns by imitation, but Arbib asserts that this ability by itself cannot generate a primitive lexico-semantic system. On the other hand, the grasping mirror neuron system is directly related to praxis, and grasping actions are easier to be decomposed in smaller elements that are amenable to ritualization and can subsequently acquire symbolic properties.

The above is a plausible but speculative scenario, and there are other possibilities as well. Primates (and other mammals) have had voluntary control of their hands for quite some time, but no tendency has arisen to develop gestural symbols or pantomime in any of them. Perhaps non-human primates are stagnated in a stage comparable to that of non-human vocal learning animals. Something else is needed for the origin of semantic communication, which Arbib attributes to the advent of complex manual imitation. In my opinion, there is no reason why such complex action recognition could not develop by itself in the vocal system, by learning to articulate vocal utterances by imitation. There are many species that can perform quite complex vocal imitations and do not have a grasping apparatus. In more technical terms, there is no phylogenetic association between vocal learning capacity and grasping abilities. In other words, I see no need for proposing a protosign stage to account for the development of vocal learning and imitation. It is not whether pantomime or vocal behavior was first; the point is that it is only in the human lineage that a combination of learned gestures and vocal plasticity has taken place to develop a symbolic system, possibly fueled by increasing imitative behavior in both systems. Supporting this perspective, Stephanie King and Peter McGregor recently explained that while birdsong focuses on mate attraction and territorial defense, vocal learning in other animals like parrots and cetaceans promotes social bonds and behavioral coordination, a condition that may be closer to developing a primitive referential system (King and McGregor 2016).

Therefore, I prefer the notion that vocal plasticity is quite ancient in our lineage, probably appearing as far back as Australopithecines. In Chapter 10, we will see that some apes can in fact do vocal imitation

(Lameira et al. 2016). Our ancestors may have used learned vocalizations mainly for social purposes like bonding, group cohesion and other social functions, as songbirds and other animals do. In addition, parrots can learn to name objects, and vervet monkeys use vocal signals to signal specific predators, although the latter are largely fixed and stereotyped (see Chapters 9 and 10). If Australopithecines acquired vocal learning for social purposes, and also developed vervet-like calls, a rudimentary semantics could have emerged. Our ancestors may have had a relatively broad repertoire of calls, some of them imitating animals or events like the wind or running water. A vocal learning circuit may have been endowed with sophisticated predictive coding mechanisms and vocal mirror neurons, and may have had powerful working memory capacities, even in the absence of semantic contents (remember that verbal working memory is assessed using meaningless non-words; Chapter 6). These signals worked together with hand and body gestures to transmit simple meanings. Nonetheless, speech rapidly took over, possibly as hands were recruited for toolmaking and tool use, and because speech was energetically more efficient (Bosman 2005; Aboitiz 2013; Garcia et al. 2014).

I completely agree with Arbib in that language, and human communication are multimodal devices, and I also consider that there was a close gestural-vocal coevolution in our lineage. There is increasingly evidence that communication is multimodal in humans, apes and monkeys. Jared Taglialatela et al. (2008, 2011), working with chimpanzees, has shown activation of Broca's area homologue with the production of both manual and vocal communicative signals. Likewise, Peter Hagoort (Willems and Hagoort 2007) and others have shown a similar situation in humans. Body gesturing not only accompanies speech, it also helps communication in a similar way as prosody supports speech. There are studies that point to gestures as being more eloquent than vocal imitation in modern human communication, and perhaps it was like this for early humans as well. For example, if human subjects are prohibited from using language, they use gestures and signs better than vocal behavior for communication (Fay and Lim 2012). Furthermore, gestures are more prevalent than words for 16-month old children, while for 20-month old children words are more prevalent than gestures (Iverson et al. 1994). However, infants begin vocalizing and then babbling and using prosody at a much earlier age, which is perhaps more comparable to gestural behavior. In addition, there is no direct indication that gestural communication ever became more complex than what is observed in modern human gestuality, child or adult, in different speaking cultures. In other words, although gestures may have been present since very early in human evolution, there are no traces of the hypothetical protosign stage in modern human behavior. Arbib somehow concedes that only limited protosign was required to ground the ascending speech-gesture spiral (Arbib 2013b).

Mirror neuron theorists point to the ability of the hearing impaired to develop sign language. Sign languages are highly complex and syntactically organized, relying on a neural system that overlaps with the language network. Broca's area activates when deaf subjects use hand-signing languages, and damage to this area results in aphasic-like behavior in the deaf (Poizner et al. 1987; Xu et al. 2009; Newman et al. 2010, 2015). But these findings do not imply that this is the original function of Broca's area. Other findings indicate that the structure of sign languages develops in specific steps, starting with only dominant (usually right) hand signing, but then involves head movements, facial expression, torso movements and finally the use of the non-dominant hand (Matacic 2016). This evidence suggests to some that there was an ancestral hand-signing system that is reactivated in the hearing impaired. However, this capacity may be due to a phenomenon of brain plasticity and opportunism for using distinct sensory motor systems for communication. An example of this is the famous patient suffering cerebral palsy Christy Brown, who painted and wrote with his left foot (his story was popularized in the award-winning movie "My Left Foot", directed by Jim Sheridan and starring Daniel Day-Lewis); or the case of patients that can only communicate by moving their eyes. As communication is opportunistic and multimodal, we use any possible way to convey messages if we cannot speak. Hands come in as a first choice, but we can and will use any other means to transmit complex messages if necessary (Aboitiz 2013). Similarly, Johan Bolhuis and collaborators claim that sign languages develop in individuals with modern brains already equipped for language, including the computational systems needed to learn language, but in many cases lacking the sensory components to develop speech (Huybregts et al. 2016).

Mirror neuron theorists also maintain that in monkeys, vocalizations are largely fixed and stereotyped, while hand movement is under voluntary control. The latter is associated with strong and direct motor cortical projection to the hand motor neurons in the cervical spinal cord, which is absent for laryngeal motor neurons controlling vocalizations. However, in Chapter 10 we will see examples of apes able to voluntarily imitate the human voice (Lameira et al. 2016). Furthermore, Suzana Herculano-Houzel et al. (2016) has argued that the development of descending cortical control is mainly due to increased brain size (see Chapters 3 and 7). If this is so, there may be no need for transmission of voluntary control from hand to mouth, but only an independent growth of the innervation of the respective nuclei. This parallel increase may have had two consequences: one was facilitated vocal plasticity and learning, and the other was increased manual dexterity to be used in sign- and toolmaking. It is possible that gestural communication was arrested at early stages in human evolution, due to the involvement of hands in toolmaking and object manipulation, while the vocal system took over communicative behavior. Although I will discuss this in more detail in Chapter 10, I want to make the point that speech is the result of a history with many complex innovations, from peripheral modifications of the vocal tract to changes in innervation of the tongue and vocal cords, not to mention the development of a vocal neural circuitry at different levels, enabling learning complex vocalization sequences. Vocal learning capacity leading to speech is very unlikely to have appeared uniquely as a result of simple traits like the development of an orofacial corti-cobulbar tract, nor as consequence of a protosign communicative stage that put social and cognitive pressure on the vocal system (Aboitiz 2013). More than grasping behavior, vocal behavior is what has made our lineage different from that of other apes, and probably our vocal system underwent rapid evolution in early stages of our lineage to support social cohesion and behavioral coordination like toolmaking or foraging over long distances (see Chapter 10).

The take-home message of this Chapter is that speech has never been the only channel for communication and there are other ways to transmit complex messages when speech is not available. Furthermore, there may have been close coevolution of speech and gestures (including body, face and hands), each supporting the other from very early times of human evolution. In the following two chapters, I will discuss the evolution of speech mechanisms, showing evidence for a continuous evolution of many of the processes involved in speech, and presenting comparative evidence that gaining voluntary control of the vocal apparatus may not have been such a difficult evolutionary step. After this, and provided a hand manipulation system, the evolution of speech and language could begin.

References

Aboitiz F (2013) How did vocal behavior "take over" the gestural communication system? Lang Cognit 5:167–176

Aboitiz F, García R, Brunetti E, Bosman C (2005) Imitation and memory in language origins. Neural Netw. 18:1357

Aboitiz F, García R, Brunetti E, Bosman C (2006) The origin of Broca's area from an ancestral working memory network. In: Grodzinsky Y, Amunts K (eds), Broca's Region. Oxford, Oxford University Press, p 3–16

Aboitiz F, Aboitiz S, García R (2010) The phonological loop: a key innovation in human evolution. Curr Anthropol 51:S55–S65

Arbib MA. (2005) From monkey-like action recognition to human language: an evolutionary framework for neurolinguistics. Behav Brain Sci 28:105–124; discussion 125–167

Arbib MA (2009) Evolving the language-ready brain and the social mechanisms that support language. J Commun Disord 42:263–271

Arbib MA (2012) How The Brain Got Language. The Mirror System Hypothesis. Oxford University Press, Oxford

Arbib MA (2013a) Précis of how the brain got language. The mirror system hypothesis. Lang Cognit 5:107–131

Arbib MA (2013b) Complex Imitation and the language-ready brain. Lang Cognit 5:273–312

Arbib MA (2016a) Towards a computational comparative neuroprimatology: framing the language-ready brain. Phys Life Rev 6:1–54

Arbib MA (2016b) Toward the language-ready brain: biological evolution and primate comparisons. Psychon Bull Rev 24:142–150

Arbib MA, Liebal K, Pika S (2008) Primate vocalization, gesture, and the evolution of human language. Curr Anthropol 49:1053–1063; discussion 1063–1076

Aziz-Zadeh L, Maeda F, Zaidel E, Mazziotta J, Iacoboni M (2002) Lateralization in motor facilitation during action observation: a TMS study. Exp Brain Res 144:127–131

Aziz-Zadeh L, Koski L, Zaidel E, Mazziotta J, Iacoboni M (2006) Lateralization of the human mirror neuron system. J Neurosci 26:2964–2970

Baess P, Horváth J, Jacobsen T, Schröger E (2011) Selective suppression of self-initiated sounds in an auditory stream: an ERP study. Psychophysiology 48:1276–1283

Baldissera F, Cavallari P, Craighero L, Fadiga L (2001) Modulation of spinal excitability during observation of hand actions in humans. Eur J Neurosci 13:190–194

Baron-Cohen S, Leslie AM, Frith U. Baron-Cohen S, Leslie AM, Frith U (1985) Does the autistic child have a "theory of mind"? Cognition 21:37–46

Belmalih A, Borra E, Contini M, Gerbella M, Rozzi S, Luppino G (2009) Multimodal architectonic subdivision of the rostral part (area F5) of the macaque ventral premotor cortex. J Comp Neurol 512:183–217

Berent I, Brem AK, Zhao X, Seligson E, Pan H, Epstein J, Stern E, Galaburda AM, Pascual-Leone A (2015) Role of the motor system in language knowledge. Proc Natl Acad Sci U S A 112:1983–1988

Bickerton, D (2009) Adam's Tongue. How Humans Made Language, How Language Made Humans. Hill and Wang, New York

Bonaiuto J, Arbib MA (2015) Learning to grasp and extract affordances: the Integrated Learning of Grasps and Affordances (ILGA) model. Biol Cybern 109:639–669

Bosman C, García R, Aboitiz F (2004) FOXP2 and the language working-memory system. Trends Cogn Sci 8:251–252

Bosman C, López V, Aboitiz F (2005) Sharpening Occam's razor: is there necessity of a hand-signing stage prior to vocal communication? Commentary. Behav Brain Sci 28:128–129

Bruderer AG, Danielson DK, Kandhadai P, Werker JF (2015) Sensorimotor influences on speech perception in infancy. Proc Natl Acad Sci U S A 112:13531–13536

Byrne RW (2009) Animal imitation. Curr Biol 19:R111–R114

Catmur C, Walsh V, Heyes C (2007) Sensorimotor learning configures the human mirror system. Curr Biol 17:1527–1531

Catmur C, Walsh V, Heyes C (2009) Associative sequence learning: the role of experience in the development of imitation and the mirror system. Philos Trans R Soc Lond B Biol Sci 364:2369–2380

Clark A (2013) Whatever next? Predictive brains, situated agents, and the future of cognitive science. Behav Brain Sci 36:181–204

Cook R, Bird G, Catmur C, Press C, Heyes C (2014) Mirror neurons: from origin to function. Behav Brain Sci 37:177–192; discussion 221–241

Corballis MC (2004) FOXP2 and the mirror system. Trends Cogn Sci 8:95–96

Cross KA, Iacoboni M (2014a) Neural systems for preparatory control of imitation. Philos Trans R Soc Lond B Biol Sci 369:20130176

Cross KA, Iacoboni M (2014b) To imitate or not: avoiding imitation involves preparatory inhibition of motor resonance. Neuroimage 91:228–236

Curio G, Neuloh G, Numminen J, Jousmäki V, Hari R (2000) Speaking modifies voice-evoked activity in the human auditory cortex. Hum Brain Mapp 9:183–191

di Pellegrino G, Fadiga L, Fogassi L, Gallese V, Rizzolatti G (1992) Understanding motor events: a neurophysiological study. Exp Brain Res 91:176–180

Fa J, Lindburg D (1996) Evolution and Ecology of Macaque Societies. Cambridge University Press, New York

Fadiga L, Fogassi L, Pavesi G, Rizzolatti G (1995) Motor facilitation during action observation: a magnetic stimulation study. J Neurophysiol 73:2608–2611

Fadiga L, Craighero L, Buccino G, Rizzolatti G (2002) Speech listening specifically modulates the excitability of tongue muscles: a TMS study. Eur J Neurosci 15:399–402

Fay N, Lim S (2012) From hand to mouth: An experimental simulation of language origin. In: Smith ADM, Schouwstra M, de Boer B, Smith K (eds), The Evolution of Language. World Scientific Press, Singapore, p 401–402

Ferrari PF, Gallese V, Rizzolatti G, Fogassi L (2003) Mirror neurons responding to the observation of ingestive and communicative mouth actions in the monkey ventral premotor cortex. Eur J Neurosci 17:1703–1714

Ferrari PF, Rozzi S, Fogassi L (2005) Mirror neurons responding to observation of actions made with tools in monkey ventral premotor cortex. J Cogn Neurosci 17:212–226

Ferrari PF, Visalberghi E, Paukner A, Fogassi L, Ruggiero A, Suomi SJ (2006) Neonatal imitation in rhesus macaques. PLoS Biol 4:e302

Fogassi L, Ferrari PF, Gesierich B, Rozzi S, Chersi F, Rizzolatti G (2005) Parietal lobe: from action organization to intention understanding. Science 308:662–667

Gallese V, Fadiga L, Fogassi L, Rizzolatti G (1996) Action recognition in the premotor cortex. Brain 119:593–609

Gallup AC, Church AM, Pelegrino AJ (2016) Yawn duration predicts brain weight and cortical neuron number in mammals. Biol Lett 12, pii:20160545

Garcia J, Hankins WG, Rusiniak KW (1974) Behavioral regulation of the milieu interne in man and rat. Science 185:824–831

García RR, Zamorano F, Aboitiz F (2014) From imitation to meaning: circuit plasticity and the acquisition of a conventionalized semantics. Front Hum Neurosci 8:605

Gentilucci M, Corballis MC (2006) From manual gesture to speech: a gradual transition. Neurosci Biobehav Rev 30:949–960

Genty E, Zuberbühler K (2014) Spatial reference in a bonobo gesture. Curr Biol 24:1601–1605.

Genty E, Zuberbühler K (2015) Iconic gesturing in bonobos. Commun Integr Biol 8:e992742

Genty E, Clay Z, Hobaiter C, Zuberbühler K (2014) Multi-modal use of a socially directed call in bonobos. PLoS One 9:e84738

Gerbella M, Belmalih A, Borra E, Rozzi S, Luppino G (2010) Cortical connections of the macaque caudal ventrolateral prefrontal areas 45A and 45B. Cereb Cortex 20:141–168

Grafton ST, Arbib MA, Fadiga L, Rizzolatti G (1996a) Localization of grasp representations in humans by positron emission tomography. 2. Observation compared with imagination. Exp Brain Res 112:103–111

Grafton ST, Fagg AH, Woods RP, Arbib MA (1996b) Functional anatomy of pointing and grasping in humans. Cereb Cortex 6:226–237

Herculano-Houzel S, Kaas JH, de Oliveira-Souza R (2016) Corticalization of motor control in humans is a consequence of brain scaling in primate evolution. J Comp Neurol 524:448–455

Heyes C (2016a) Homo imitans? Seven reasons why imitation couldn't possibly be associative. Philos Trans R Soc Lond B Biol Sci 371:20150069

Heyes C (2016b) Imitation: not in our genes. Curr Biol 26:R412–R414

Hickok G (2009) Eight problems for the mirror neuron theory of action understanding in monkeys and humans. J Cogn Neurosci 21:1229–1243

Hickok G (2013) Do mirror neurons subserve action understanding? Neurosci Lett 540:56–58

Hickok G (2014) The Myth of Mirror Neurons: The Real Neuroscience of Communication And Cognition. Norton Press, New York

Hickok G, Hauser M (2010) (Mis)understanding mirror neurons. Curr Biol 20:R593–R594

Hobaiter C, Byrne RW (2011) The gestural repertoire of the wild chimpanzee. Anim Cognit 14:745–767

Hobaiter C, Byrne RW (2014) The meanings of chimpanzee gestures. Curr Biol 24:1596–1600

Huybregts MA, Berwick RC, Bolhuis JJ (2016) The language within. Science 352:1286

Iacoboni M (2009) Imitation, empathy, and mirror neurons. Annu Rev Psychol 60:653–670

Iacoboni M, Woods RP, Brass M, Bekkering H, Mazziotta JC, Rizzolatti G (1999) Cortical mechanisms of human imitation. Science 286:2526–2528

Iverson JM, Capirci O, Caselli MC (1994) From communication to language in two modalities. Cogn Devel 9:23–43

Joly-Mascheroni RM, Senju A, Shepherd AJ (2008) Dogs catch human yawns. Biol Lett 4:446–448

Kaas JH, Stepniewska I (2016) Evolution of posterior parietal cortex and parietal-frontal networks for specific actions in primates. J Comp Neurol 524:595–608

Kaminski J, Call J, Tomasello M (2004) Body orientation and face orientation: two factors controlling apes' behavior from humans. Anim Cogn 7:216–223

Kilner JM, Friston KJ, Frith CD (2007) Predictive coding: an account of the mirror neuron system. Cogn Process 8:159–166

Kilner JM, Neal A, Weiskopf N, Friston KJ, Frith CD (2009) Evidence of mirror neurons in human inferior frontal gyrus. J Neurosci 29:10153–10159

King SL, McGregor PK (2016) Vocal matching: the what, the why and the how. Biol Lett 12:20160666

Kohler E, Keysers C, Umilta MA, Fogassi L, Gallese V, Rizzolatti G (2002) Hearing sounds, understanding actions: action representation in mirror neurons. Science 297:846–848

Lameira AR, Hardus ME, Mielke A, Wich SA, Shumaker RW. (2016) Vocal fold control beyond the species-specific repertoire in an orang-utan. Sci Rep 6:30315

Lametti DR, Rochet-Capellan A, Neufeld E, Shiller DM, Ostry DJ (2014) Plasticity in the human speech motor system drives changes in speech perception. J Neurosci 34:10339–10346

Langacker RW (2013) Essentials of Cognitive Grammar. Oxford University Press, Oxford

Leone A, Ferrari PF, Palagi E (2014) Different yawns, different functions? Testing social hypotheses on spontaneous yawning in Theropithecus gelada. Sci Rep 4:4010

Liao DA, Kronemer SI, Yau JM, Desmond JE, Marvel CL (2014) Motor system contributions to verbal and non-verbal working memory. Front Hum Neurosci 8:753

Liberman AM (1970) Some characteristics of perception in the speech mode. Res Publ Assoc Res Nerv Ment Dis 48:238–254

Liberman AM, Harris KS, Hoffmann HS, Griffith BC (1957) The discrimination of speech sounds within and across phoneme boundaries. J Exp Psychol 54:358–368

Liberman AM, Cooper FS, Shankweiler DP, Studdert-Kennedy M (1967) Perception of the speech code. Psychol Rev 74:431–461

Liebal K, Call J (2012) The origins of non-human primates' manual gestures. Philos Trans R Soc Lond B Biol Sci 367:118–128

Liebal K, Call J, Tomasello M (2004) Use of gesture sequences in chimpanzees. Am J Primatol 64:377–396

Lorenz K (1981) The Foundations of Ethology. Springer Verlag, New York

Marler P (2004) Innateness and the instinct to learn. An Acad Bras Cienc 76:189–200

Martikainen MH, Kaneko K, Hari R (2005) Suppressed responses to self-triggered sounds in the human auditory cortex. Cereb Cortex 15:299–302

Massaro DW, Chen TH (2008) The motor theory of speech perception revisited. Psychon Bull Rev 15:453–457; discussion 458–462

Massen JJ, Church AM, Gallup AC (2015) Auditory contagious yawning in humans: an investigation into affiliation and status effects. Front Psychol 6:1735

Matacic C (2016) How sign languages evolve. Science 352:392–393

McGinn C (2015) Prehension: The Hand and the Emergence of Humanity. MIT Press, Cambridge

McGurk H, MacDonald J (1976) Hearing lips and seeing voices. Nature 264:746–748

Morgan TJ, Uomini NT, Rendell LE, Chouinard-Thuly L, Street SE, Lewis HM, Cross CP, Evans C, Kearney R, de la Torre I, Whiten A, Laland KN (2015) Experimental evidence for the co-evolution of hominin tool-making teaching and language. Nat Commun 6:6029

Moro A (2014a) On the similarity between syntax and actions. Trends Cogn Sci 18:109–110

Moro A (2014b) Response to Pulvermüller: the syntax of actions and other metaphors. Trends Cogn Sci 18:221

Moulin-Frier C, Arbib MA (2013)Recognizing speech in a novel accent: the motor theory of speech perception reframed. Biol Cybern 107:421–447

Mukamel R, Ekstrom AD, Kaplan J, Iacoboni M, Fried I (2010) Single-neuron responses in humans during execution and observation of actions. Curr Biol 20:750–756

Newman AJ, Supalla T, Hauser PC, Newport EL, Bavelier D (2010) Prosodic and narrative processing in American Sign Language: an fMRI study. Neuroimage 52:669–676

Newman AJ, Supalla T, Fernandez N, Newport EL, Bavelier D (2015) Neural systems supporting linguistic structure, linguistic experience, and symbolic communication in sign language and gesture. Proc Natl Acad Sci U S A 112:11684–11689

Oostenbroek J, Suddendorf T, Nielsen M, Redshaw J, Kennedy-Costantini S, Davis J, Clark S, Slaughter V (2016) Comprehensive longitudinal study challenges the existence of neonatal imitation in humans. Curr Biol 26:1334–1338

Oztop E, Arbib MA (2002) Schema design and implementation of the grasp-related mirror neuron system. Biol Cybern 87:116–140

Palagi E, Leone A, Mancini G, Ferrari PF (2009) Contagious yawning in gelada baboons as a possible expression of empathy. Proc Natl Acad Sci U S A 106:19262–19267

Paukner A, Ferrari PF, Suomi SJ (2011) Delayed imitation of lipsmacking gestures by infant rhesus macaques (Macaca mulatta). PLoS One 6:e28848

Petrides M (2014) *Neuroanatomy of Language Regions of the Human Brain.* Academic Press, New York

Petrides M, Cadoret G, Mackey S (2005) Orofacial somatomotor responses in the macaque monkey homologue of Broca's area. Nature 435:1235–1238

Pickering MJ, Garrod S (2013) An integrated theory of language production and comprehension. Behav Brain Sci 36:329–347

Poizner H, Klima ES, Bellugi U (1987) What the Hands Reveal about the Brain. MIT Press, Cambridge

Provine RR (2013) Laughing, grooming, and pub science. Trends Cogn Sci 17:9–10

Provine RR (2014) Contagious behavior: an alternative approach to mirror-like phenomena. Behav Brain Sci 37:216–217

Pulvermüller F (2014) The syntax of action. Trends Cogn Sci 18:219–220

Rauschecker JP (2012) Ventral and dorsal streams in the evolution of speech and language. Front Evol Neurosci 4:7

Rizzolatti G, Arbib MA (1998) Language within our grasp. Trends Neurosci 21:188–194

Rizzolatti G, Craighero L (2004) The mirror-neuron system. Annu Rev Neurosci 27:169–192

Rizzolatti G, Sinigaglia C (2006) Mirrors in the Brain. How Our Minds Share Actions and Emotions. Oxford University Press, Oxford

Rizzolatti G, Fadiga L, Gallese V, Fogassi L (1996a) Premotor cortex and the recognition of motor actions. Cogn Brain Res 3:131–141

Rizzolatti G, Fadiga L, Matelli M, Bettinardi V, Paulesu E, Perani D, Fazio F (1996b) Localization of grasp representations in humans by PET: 1. Observation versus execution. Exp Brain Res 111:246–252

Robinson GE, Barron AB (2017) Epigenetics and the evolution of instincts. Science 356:26–27

Rogalsky C, Love T, Driscoll D, Anderson SW, Hickok G (2011) Are mirror neurons the basis of speech perception? Evidence from five cases with damage to the purported human mirror system. Neurocase 17:178–187

Romero T, Konno A, Hasegawa T (2013) Familiarity bias and physiological responses in contagious yawning by dogs support link to empathy. PLoS One 8:e71365

Romero T, Ito M, Saito A, Hasegawa T (2014) Social modulation of contagious yawning in wolves. PLoS One 9:e105963

Rummell BP, Klee JL, Sigurdsson T (2016) Attenuation of responses to self-generated sounds in auditory cortical neurons. J Neurosci 36:12010–12026

Shomers MR, Pulvermüller F (2016) Is the sensorimotor cortex relevant for speech perception and understanding? An integrative review. Front Hum Neurosci 10:435

Skeide MA, Friederici AD (2016) The ontogeny of the cortical language network. Nat Rev Neurosci 17:323–332

Skipper JI, Devlin JT, Lametti DR (2017) The hearing ear is always found close to the speaking tongue: Review of the role of the motor system in speech perception. Brain Lang 164:77–105

Subiaul F, Cantlon JF, Holloway RL, Terrace HS (2004) Cognitive imitation in rhesus macaques. Science 305:407–410

Taglialatela JP, Russell JL, Schaeffer JA, Hopkins WD (2008) Communicative signaling activates "Broca's" homolog in chimpanzees. Curr Biol 18:343–348

Taglialatela JP, Russell JL, Schaeffer JA, Hopkins WD (2011) Chimpanzee vocal signaling points to a multimodal origin of human language. PLoS One 6:e18852

Tinbergen N (1951) The Study of Instinct. Clarendon Press, New York

Tomasello M (2006) Why don't apes point? In: Enfield NJ, Levinson SC (eds), Roots of Human Sociality: Culture, Cognition and Interaction. Berg Publishers, Oxford and New York, p 506–524

Tomasello M (2014) A Natural History of Human Thinking. Harvard University Press, Cambridge

Tomasello, M., & Call, J (1997) Primate Cognition. Oxford University Press, New York

Walusinski O (2014) How yawning switches the default-mode network to the attentional network by activating the cerebrospinal fluid flow. Clin Anat 27:201–209

Willems RM, Hagoort P (2007) Neural evidence for the interplay between language, gesture, and action: a review. Brain Lang 101:278–289

Xu J, Gannon PJ, Emmorey K, Smith JF, Braun AR (2009) Symbolic gestures and spoken language are processed by a common neural system. Proc Natl Acad Sci U S A 106:20664–20669

9

Of Birds and Men

One of Darwin's boldest assertions regarding the origins of speech was to suggest an analogy between the acquisition of songs by songbirds and the early stages of speech learning. His main argument was that like birdsong, language is an instinctive skill that nonetheless has to be learned. If not stimulated properly, neither language nor birdsong will develop normally. Eloquently, Darwin said that no child is born with an instinctive tendency to cook, bake or brew, as he or she is born with a drive to communicate with others. Like birdsong, language was probably musical in its origins, and was also a product of male competition for attracting females in a process termed sexual selection. Nonetheless, the theory of the origin of birdsong by sexual selection has been challenged in recent years as there are several songbird species in which both males and females sing (Langmore 1998; Odom et al. 2014). Instead, a broader concept called social selection has been proposed, where sexual partners compete with other couples for territory and nesting sites. With tropical songbirds, both sexes tend to sing, while with species in colder climates it is more common that only males sing, which is similar to what is found in our closer relatives, the gibbon, where both males and females sing in duet to defend their territory (see the next chapter). Furthermore,

Tecumseh Fitch claims that there is no evidence of sexual selection for human language, as both sexes are equally able to learn it and language is acquired at very early stages, as opposed to most sexually dimorphic traits that appear in adolescence (Fitch 2009).

In this chapter I will discuss the bird brain and its cognitive and communicative abilities including birdsong, always in comparison to mammals and human speech. I will attempt to illustrate the fact that despite having widely diverging evolutionary histories, birds and mammals have developed convergent solutions for many characters relevant for brain function and behavior, including vocal capacities.

Dinosaurs All Around

The common ancestor of birds and humans was a lizard-like creature that lived some 300–350 million years ago, when tetrapods (four-legged animals) were colonizing the land (Prothero 2006). This ancestor belongs to a group of tetrapods called amniotes, which gave rise to reptiles, birds and mammals. Amniote eggs were covered with a fluid-filled sac that conserved moisture that allowed these animals to lay their eggs on the land instead of in water as ancestral amphibians did. From very early, amniotes diverged into stem reptiles (sauropsids) on one side, and into mammal-like reptiles (synapsids) on the other. Initially, the synapsids were relatively successful and diversified into a series of forms, both carnivores and herbivores. But this early radiation ended abruptly 250 million years ago with what is called the great Permian extinction, one of the largest mass extinction events in the history of life (Prothero 2006). After this event, the Mesozoic era began, which lasted a little less than 200 million years. This was the reign of the dinosaurs, the "terrible lizards" that emerged from the sauropsid lineage, together with ancient crocodiles and pterodactyls. The early synapsids that had flourished earlier disappeared almost completely, leaving a lineage of small animals called cynodonts, which gave rise to the first mammals some 200–150 million years ago, in the Jurassic period. Birds emerged from a lineage of small carnivorous dinosaurs called maniraptors, at about the same time. Early birds and mammals coexisted with the non-avian dinosaurs for a very long time, and in the Cretaceous period they witnessed the proliferation of flowering plants and the associated radiation of insects, which since the Permian had been co-evolving with flowers by acting as their pollinators. This provided a rich ecological condition for small animals like early birds and mammals to diversify (Prothero 2006; Luo 2007, Brusatte and Luo 2016). The world was changing rapidly, but this was nothing compared with what was to come. We have all been told that some 66 million years ago the dinosaurs dramatically disappeared in a single event, in the last great extinction in our planet's history. In the 1980s, Luis Alvarez provided evidence for a massive asteroid impact in what is now Yucatán, Mexico, which may have triggered the extinction (Alvarez et al. 1980). But there are also records of massive volcanism at that time, which increased the effect of the impact (Cloudsley-Thompson 2001; Burgess and Bowring 2015). I am not a geologist, but it is possible that the impact itself triggered increasing geological activity that resulted in increased volcanism. In any case, the effects of these events were catastrophic, and early mammals and birds were not immune to them. The majority of these early lineages also disappeared, leaving only a few animals that made it through and colonized the new world that was to come (Brusatte et al. 2015a). Other evidence has been accumulating that dinosaurs were already on the decline when the asteroid hit the earth, which would have given these animals a *coup de grâce* to extinguish most of them (Prothero 2006; Sakamoto et al. 2016).

But did the dinosaurs really disappear? Research has shown robust evidence that characters previously believed to be privative to birds, like feathers, their respiratory system, warm-bloodedness and skeletal features were shared by maniraptors that coexisted with birds in the Cretaceous (Pickrell 2014; Brusatte 2016; Brusatte et al. 2015b). Birds are a surviving lineage of dinosaurs and have become the most successful terrestrial vertebrate, with more than 10,000 species living today (compared with 5,000 species of mammals, 8,000 reptiles and surprisingly, 6,000 species of amphibians). There are dinosaurs all around us, and many of them are singing.

Sniffing and Whisking

Birds inherited the reptile brain, which is superficially quite different from that of mammals, as it does not have a six-layered cerebral cortex as the mammalian brain does. In birds, as in other vertebrates, a significant part of visual processing begins in brainstem nuclei, and the cerebral hemispheres receive substantial input from them. On the other hand, in mammals these brainstem centers are regressive at the expense of the expansion of the cerebral cortex (Butler et al. 2011). The laminated cerebral cortex of mammals represents a diverging trend in the evolution of the amniote brain, and the evolutionary explanation for this unique organization is a major enigma. My former students Juan Montiel and Francisco Zamorano and I have proposed that the origin of the mammalian cerebral cortex is closely linked to many behavioral and physiological adaptations of early mammals (Aboitiz and Zamorano 2013, Aboitiz and Montiel 2007a, 2012, 2015). These innovations defined a new lifestyle driven by nocturnal semi-burrowing habits, and the expansion of olfactory capacity associated with a new form of respiration based on a muscular diaphragm (Gerkema et al. 2013, Kielan-Jaworowska et al. 2004, Rowe and Shepherd 2016). Furthermore, early mammals developed a secondary palate that separates the vocal and the nasal cavities, contributing to moistening the air while breathing. This was associated with three important sensory and behavioral innovations. The first was increasing olfactory capacity and sniffing behavior, which is important for behavioral exploration (Aboitiz and Montiel 2015). In this line, the mammalian olfactory receptor gene family is some 10 times as large as its reptilian and avian counterparts, giving mammals a keen olfactory discrimination capacity (Niimura 2009). Notably, Timothy Rowe and colleagues showed that there is a dramatic increase in brain size in the first mammals compared with their immediate cynodont ancestors, associated with the expansion of the olfactory bulbs in the brain, and of the internal nasal surface, indicating an expanded olfactory epithelium (Rowe et al. 2011). The second innovation was the acquisition of mastication aided by a new jaw articulation and more elaborate dentition. As a consequence, two tiny ossicles, which in reptiles provides jaw articulation, were liberated from their function and became embedded in the middle ear, making up the malleus and the incus of the ossicle ear chain, which notably increased acoustic capacity (Rowe 1996, Luo et al. 2011). Thirdly, early mammals also enhanced their tactile sense, as their skins were covered with fur rather than scales or feathers. Fur was accompanied with the development of secretory glands, with the production of milk and full homeothermy. But perhaps most important for us, most mammals have whiskers, or vibrissae around the mouth, which they use to explore the environment as they go sniffing around (Ahisar 2008; Grant et al. 2013).

In most mammals, the olfactory system is very important for behavior, and is closely connected to the hippocampus, a structure involved in spatial memory and orientation (Lynch 1986). Linda Jacobs has emphasized the role of olfactory navigation, guiding the animal toward food or mating sources (Jacobs 2012). Furthermore, the olfactory system is proposed to provide scaffolding for the cognitive orientation map that develops in the hippocampus (Fig. 9.1). There are both olfactory and visually sensitive neurons in the rodent hippocampus, which segregate in alternating bands. The group led by Howard Eichenbaum has shown that hippocampal olfactory neurons participate in associating different odors, and more importantly in associating odors with contextual information, thus extracting cues for behavioral orientation (Eichenbaum 1998, 2004, 2010, 2014; Dickerson and Eichenbaum 2010). Eichenbaum and collaborators have also described "time cells" in the hippocampus that contribute to providing a spatio-temporal representation of stimuli that provides a behaviorally relevant sequence of events (Howard and Eichenbaum 2015). Furthermore, electrophysiological studies by Cornelius Vanderwolf showed that high-frequency hippocampal oscillations (in the gamma range) are selectively associated with active sniffing. He proposed that the hippocampus is originally an olfactory-motor interface that serves to orient behavior (Vanderwolf 2001). The cognitive operations of the hippocampus, including the generation of complex spatial maps, are considered a secondary

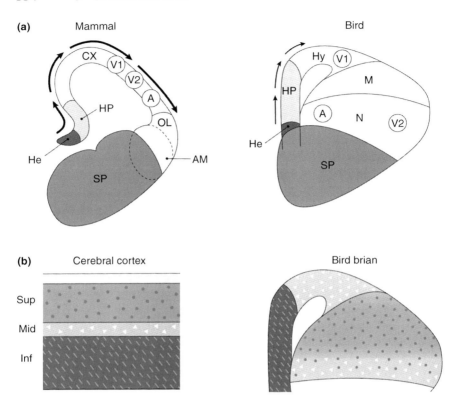

Fig. 9.1   The brains of birds and mammals. (**a**) Comparison of cross sections of the embryonic cerebral hemispheres of a mammal and a bird. All regions located above the subpallium (SP) make up the embryonic pallium. Brainstem-derived visual and auditory projections (A, auditory; V2, secondary visual) end in the cortex of mammals (CX), and in the nidopallium (N) of birds. Primary visual projections (V1) and somatosensory projections (not shown) end in the CX of mammals and in the hyperpallium (Hy) of birds. AM, amygdala complex, with pallial and subpallial components; He, cortical hem; HP, hippocampus; M, meso-pallium; OL, olfactory cortex. (**b**) Comparison of the distribution of neurochemical markers in the different layers of the mammalian cerebral cortex, and the different regions of the avian pallium.

acquisition. Likewise, recent studies have stressed the critical role of coordinated sniffing and whisking in orientation behavior, both rhythmic behaviors that are coupled to theta low-frequency oscillatory activity in hippocampal neurons (Deschênes et al. 2012; Kleinfeld et al. 2016;

Grion et al. 2016). These orienting functions may have been particularly important for the first nocturnal mammals, whose visual abilities were limited. They may also have been important for young searching for the source of milk secreted from their mothers' bellies, as is observed in newborn rabbits and kittens (Schaal et al. 2009). Notably, the most important regions of the mammalian brain in which the production of new neurons in adult life (called adult neurogenesis) has been demonstrated are the olfactory system and the dentate gyrus, an important hippocampal region that provides substantial input to the other hippocampal components (Ming and Song 2011). As we will see below, adult neurogenesis has been shown to be important for neural plasticity, and it may not be just chance that it occurs in these brain regions involved in behavioral orientation.

Another function of the hippocampus is to generate a bi-dimensional (or tridimensional) spatial map, independent of the animal's position. John O'Keefe earned the Nobel Prize for the discovery, together with his then student Jonathan Dostrovsky, of the so-called "place cells" in the hippocampus (O'Keefe and Dostrovsky 1971; O'Keefe 1979 1990, Alme et al. 2014). Place cells fire selectively when the animal is located in a specific region of a labyrinth that it has learned to travel through. Combining the activity of the different place cells, the animal is believed to generate a cognitive representation of the labyrinth. This interpretation was further supported by the discovery of "grid cells" in the entorhinal cortex by the co-winners of the Nobel Prize with O'Keefe, Edvard Moser and May-Britt Moser (Fyhn et al. 2004; Hafting et al. 2005; Moser et al. 2008). The entorhinal cortex is located adjacent to the hippocampus and provides multimodal sensory input to it. Grid cells are like place cells, but fire at multiple locations, establishing a regular bidimensional grid-like pattern that represents the entire space in which the animal is moving in a given situation. This results in a time and subject-independent map of the relevant space that involves visual, motor, somatosensory and other modalities like olfaction. Eichenbaum and O'Keefe engaged in an important controversy regarding the role of the hippocampus in behavior, as the former conceives it as a system that binds elements in time through sequential mapping, and the latter envisions it as providing a subject-independent representation of space.

In my opinion, both models can be correct, and the role in providing sequential cues for behavioral orientation may be more olfactory-based and better represent the ancestral mammalian condition. On the other hand, the generation of a multimodal Cartesian map is multimodal but strongly dependent on visual and other sensory inputs provided by the cerebral cortex. Juan Montiel and I have speculated that the earliest mammals or mammal-like cynodonts emphasized olfactory-based sequential maps as they had nocturnal habits (Aboitiz and Montiel 2015). Later, when mammals started invading diurnal niches, visual information became increasingly important for spatial orientation. We proposed that the mammalian cerebral cortex arose as an expansion of regions like the entorhinal cortex, which is comparable to a small region called the dorsal cortex in reptiles, and was probably also present in mammal-like reptiles. In early mammals, the nascent cerebral cortex inherited the laminar organization that is characteristic of the hippocampus and the olfactory system, and expanded like a two-dimensional sheet as increasing sensory input was reaching this region (Shepherd 2011; Rowe and Shepherd 2016; Kaas 2013). The expanding cerebral cortex thus provided multimodal input to the hippocampal system to participate in behavioral orientation. Reptiles and of course birds have good spatial and sequential capacities, and further studies may soon find place and grid-like neurons, as well as time cells in their brains. My point is that sequential mapping was more important than spatial mapping in early mammalian evolution, while the latter regained significance when mammals became diurnal. Historical contingency, where olfaction was a dominant sense in early mammals, had a profound impact on the anatomical organization of the growing cerebral cortex.

The Thorniest Problem of Comparative Neuroanatomy

Birds have a large brain, similar in size to that of modern mammals and larger than that of most reptiles. Although the emblematic early bird *Archaeopteryx* had a relative brain size intermediate between birds and other reptiles, a tendency toward increasing brain size was already evident in some non-avian maniraptor dinosaurs like *Troodon* (Pickrell 2014). In its internal structure, the avian brain looks like a hypertrophied reptilian brain, and its anatomy has been the subject of much debate during this and the previous century. Before we start with another anatomical puzzle, I will first mention some basic aspects of brain anatomy (see Fig. 9.1). The embryonic cerebral hemispheres are subdivided into a dorsal part called the pallium ("roof" in Latin), and a ventral part called the subpallium. In mammals, the pallium contains all cortical areas including the olfactory cortex, cerebral cortex and hippocampus; and part of the amygdala, a nuclear complex involved in emotional responses and instinctive patterns. The subpallium contains the basal ganglia, which includes the corpus striatum and the pallidum, and other structures including the remaining parts of the amygdala located in the pallial-subpallial border. However, the situation in reptiles and birds is a little more complicated. The brains of reptiles are characterized by the presence of a large structure called the dorsal ventricular ridge, which protrudes into the cerebral ventricle and receives most sensory inputs. As opposed to the laminar cerebral cortex of mammals, this is a large, non-laminated mass of cells. In birds, the dorsal ventricular ridge is highly expanded and is subdivided into several components, termed mesopallium, nidopallium, and arcopallium. Above these structures is the hyperpallium, which corresponds to the dorsal cortex of reptiles mentioned above. The brains of reptiles and birds also possess a hippocampus and a small olfactory cortex (Butler et al. 2011, Reiner et al. 2004a, b).

The dorsal ventricular ridge of reptiles and its avian equivalent (mostly the nidopallium and mesopallium) have been a source of controversy for comparative anatomists since they were first analyzed in the early twentieth century (Fig. 9.1). While these structures were first considered to be part of the subpallium (more precisely, of the corpus striatum), in the 1970s Harvey Karten showed that auditory and some visual sensory projections ascend from brainstem centers and end in the nidopallium of birds, while in mammals these projections end in the auditory and the secondary, or extrastriate visual cortex, respectively, making the avian nidopallium comparable to parts of the mammalian cerebral cortex. Other sensory inputs (visual and somatosensory) that ascend directly to the brain, bypassing brainstem centers, end instead in the avian hyperpallium (Karten 1968, 1969). In mammals, these projections arrive to the primary visual and somatosensory areas of the cerebral cortex, respectively. Thus, the nidopallium of birds receives similar sensory input as the auditory and extrastriate visual cortices of mammals. On the other hand, the avian hyperpallium receives similar inputs as the mammalian somatosensory and primary visual cortices. Kartén then proposed a dual origin of the mammalian cerebral cortex, with its lateral aspect deriving from the reptilian equivalent of the avian nidopallium (the dorsal ventricular ridge), and its medial aspect deriving from the reptilian homologue of the avian hyperpallium (the reptilian dorsal cortex) (Karten 1991, 1997, 2013). This perspective prevailed for many years, but has been challenged by more recent evidence.

As a graduate student in the 1980s, I became interested in the origin of the mammalian cerebral cortex as it appeared to be so widely different from corresponding brain structures in other vertebrates. It looked truly unique in evolution. By studying the early embryological descriptions of reptiles by Bengt Källén in the early twentieth century, I came to the conclusion that the reptilian dorsal ventricular ridge was largely separated from the reptilian dorsal cortex by the olfactory cortex, which produces discontinuity between the two structures (Källén 1951). Perhaps more importantly, the reptilian dorsal ventricular ridge and its avian equivalent are located adjacent to the pallial-subpallial border, while the mammalian cerebral cortex is separated from this boundary by the amygdala and the olfactory cortex (Aboitiz 1992, 1993, 1995). Unifying the dorsal ventricular ridge and the dorsal cortex of reptiles to generate a continuous cortical field, as Karten's hypothesis requires, implies substantial developmental rearrangement that in my view is unlikely to have occurred, given conserved topography of most brain regions across species. Karten argued that massive migration of excitatory neurons from the dorsal ventricular ridge to the dorsal cortex was a plausible mechanism for the fusion of the two structures, but to date there has been no evidence supporting this possibility. Much more likely to me is the possibility that the sensory pathways that end in the reptilian dorsal ventricular ridge deviated from their route during development, and were redirected to the rudimentary dorsal cortex of early mammals, which expanded and eventually transformed into the entire neocortex of mammals (Aboitiz et al. 2003 Aboitiz 2011). More recently, evidence has been found of the migration of inhibitory neurons, but not excitatory neurons, from the subpallium to the cerebral cortex (see Chapter 3) (Anderson et al. 1997). However, these are not the cell types Karten had in mind in his hypothesis. A more recent study described the migration of excitatory neurons from the pallial-subpallial boundary to the embryonic cerebral cortex, but all these neurons disappear shortly after birth (Teissier et al. 2010). My students and I have proposed that this migration of transient cells could be a mechanism for attracting sensory axons toward the developing cortex in mammals (Aboitiz and Zamorano 2013). Shortly after my first papers, Georg Striedter published an influential article proposing similar ideas, and adding a hypothesis of homology between the dorsal ventricular ridge and parts of the mammalian amygdala complex (Striedter 1997, 2005). Laura Bruce and Timothy Neary argued along the same line (Bruce and Neary 1995). Homology between amygdalar components and the reptilian dorsal ventricular ridge had been argued earlier by Nils Holmgren, who used the term "hypopallium" to refer to these nuclei across species, but this work was much neglected for most of the twentieth century (Holmgren 1922).

I also speculated that comparative genetics would show molecular markers evidencing different embryonic origins of the mammalian cerebral cortex, the reptilian dorsal ventricular ridge, and the avian nidopallium and mesopallium (Aboitiz 1995). By that time, evidence was emerging that suggested a conserved genetic plan in the embryos of animals as different as flies and humans, and I extrapolated this idea to the evolution of the vertebrate brain. Strong support for this view came from subsequent embryological and molecular studies, first in a report from Edoardo Boncinelli's laboratory, and later by the paramount work by Luis Puelles and his collaborators, notably Loreta Medina, who provided genetic evidence that the reptilian dorsal ventricular ridge and the avian nidopallium are embryologically more comparable to the mammalian amygdala complex, all these structures originating from an embryonic region called the ventral pallium (Smith-Fernández et al.

1998; Puelles et al. 1999, 2000; Medina and Abellán 2009). On the other hand, the cerebral cortex of mammals was found to derive from a different embryonic region, called the dorsal pallium, and equivalent to the reptilian dorsal cortex. Summarizing, the dorsal ventricular ridge of reptiles and the nidopallium/mesopallium of birds originate the embryonic ventral pallium; and the mammalian cerebral cortex develops mostly in the embryonic dorsal pallium (Fig. 9.1). This explains the different topographic positions of the two structures. This evidence provided a new frame of reference for the anatomy of the brain, which the extensive group led by Luis Puelles and John Rubenstein has elegantly extended to many vertebrate species (Rubenstein et al. 1994; Puelles and Rubenstein 2003). In 2005, Striedter published a comprehensive compilation of the above and other evidence in his book *Principles of Brain Evolution* (Striedter 2005).

However, the issue is far from settled, as there are sympathizers with Karten and Puelles', Striedter's and my views, and there is little crosstalk and strong disqualification among them. The well-known comparative neuroanatomist Glenn Northcutt even said that the issue of possible homologies between mammalian and avian brains was very likely the thorniest problem of comparative neuroscience (Northcutt 2003). In my opinion, these controversies are on their way to being resolved. In recent years, genetic evidence has unveiled deep commonalities in the developmental mechanisms at work in the avian and mammalian brains, even if the exact anatomical origin of the avian nidopallium and the mammalian cerebral cortex are not the same (Montiel and Aboitiz 2015, Aboitiz and Zamorano 2013). Several studies, including those of Zoltan Molnár, Georg Striedter and Christine Charvet have found evidence of an embryonic layer termed the subventricular zone (see Chapter 3) that contains proliferating neural precursors and participates in brain expansion in mammals and birds, indicating similar cellular mechanisms (Abdel-Mannan 2008; Striedter and Charvet 2009; Cheung et al. 2010; Molnár 2011). Furthermore, several laboratories, including those of Tadashi Nomura, Ikuo Suzuki and Federico Luzzati have found similar neurochemical types in the avian nidopallium and the superficial layers of the mammalian cerebral cortex. Notably, neurochemical markers of neurons in the deep cortical layers of mammals are comparable to those of hippocampal and amygdala neurons of birds (Fig. 9.1) (Nomura et al. 2013, 2016; Suzuki et al. 2012, Luzzati et al. 2009; Luzzati 2015; Aboitiz and Zamorano 2013).

The laminar segregation of neuronal types that is seen in the cerebral cortex of mammals is also observed across brain regions in reptiles and birds. Luzzati has argued that the cortical superficial layers are a new evolutionary acquisition (which others also affirm), and have benefited from the same developmental genetic system as the one that takes place in the amplification of the avian nidopallium, leading to similar neurochemical types. Other studies, including those of Juan Montiel and Grant Belgard in the laboratory of Zoltán Molnár have used large-scale analyses of gene expression in different brain regions of birds and mammals and have found similar patterns in the avian nidopallium and the mid-layer of the mammalian cortex, which they attribute to evolutionary convergence (Belgard et al. 2013; Montiel et al. 2016). Using similar techniques, the group led by Erich Jarvis also reported similarity in gene expression between the nidopallium and regions of the hyperpallium of birds, pointing to a common developmental pattern in different brain regions of the avian brain (Jarvis et al. 2013; Chen et al. 2013).

Attempting to make some sense of all this information, we have proposed that the genetic and developmental mechanisms for brain amplification are largely conserved in mammals and birds, although the process of amplification itself may have taken place in different embryonic brain regions in each species (Aboitiz and Zamorano 2013; Montiel and Aboitiz 2015). One of the candidate genes for participating in this conserved amplifying cascade is Pax6 (but there are many others), which promotes the proliferation of progenitor neurons during development. It is critical for the development of the embryonic subventricular zone, and is expressed embryonically both in the cerebral cortex and in the avian and reptilian pallium (Georgala et al. 2011). The proposed shared genetic cascade involved in brain expansion in both groups was likely present in the common ancestor, and is probably more ancient than this, but participated in other developmental contexts, controlling stem cell proliferation in different neural systems. In birds and mammals, this cascade was independently activated for brain amplification, possibly because it was easily recruited from other preexisting developmental processes (Aboitiz 2011; Aboitiz and Montiel 2007b).

But if developmental genetics is so conserved, why is the cerebral cortex anatomically so different from the avian nidopallium? We claim that an additional developmental process underwent significant expansion in mammals but not in birds or reptiles, providing the laminar organization and pyramidal morphology of excitatory cells that are characteristic of the mammalian cerebral cortex (Aboitiz and Zamorano 2013; Montiel and Aboitiz 2015). In all studied vertebrates, a small embryonic region called the cortical "hem" is involved in the differentiation of the hippocampus in the most medial aspect of the cerebral hemispheres (Grove et al. 1998; Rubenstein 2011) (Fig. 9.1). The influence of the cortical hem of mammals (but not in reptiles and birds) has amplified beyond the realm of the developing hippocampus, reaching more lateral regions of the brain and patterning the developing cerebral cortex (Cabrera-Socorro et al. 2007; Caronia-Brown et al. 2014). The cortical hem is also the main site of origin of a special kind of embryonic neuron called Cajal-Retzius cell that secretes a protein called reelin that participates in establishing the columnar and laminar organization of the cerebral cortex (see Chapter 3, Fig. 3.2). An additional source of Cajal-Retzius cells in mammals is the olfactory cortex in the lateral hemisphere, which as discussed above, probably played a crucial role in neocortical origins (de Frutos et al. 2016). Cajal-Retzius neurons and reelin expression are dramatically amplified in the mammalian cerebral cortex, compared with the brains of other vertebrates (Tissir and Goffinet 2003). Thus, in the embryonic mammalian cerebral cortex there is an overlap between (1) a differentiation program driven by the cortical hem and Cajal-Retzius cells, imposing a laminar organization of the cerebral cortex; and (2) a genetic cascade that amplifies in later development, increasing neuronal numbers and brain size. This cascade may be initiated by Pax6 activity, but is later executed by a complex regulatory gene network (Aboitiz and Zamorano 2013, Montiel and

Aboitiz 2015). In reptiles and birds, both differentiation cascades have less overlap, which results in a regional rather than a laminar gradient of cell differentiation, with the hem acting on more medial regions, and the Pax6-driven increase in neuronal proliferation taking place in more lateral regions of the pallium.

Thus, homology between the mammalian cerebral cortex and the avian nidopallium (and related components) may be better sought in the genetic mechanisms involved in their respective brain growth rather than in adult structures. In other words, different brain regions may have independently benefited from a common genetic mechanism, simply because there may not be many possible alternatives to increase the size of the brain (Aboitiz and Montiel 2007b). Walter Gehring introduced the concept of "deep homology" to refer to structures that have been acquired independently (i.e. are not strictly homologous), but are based on homologous, ancestral genetic mechanisms (Gehring and Ikeo 1999). The best-known example of this is the compound eyes of flies and the cup-shaped eyes of vertebrates, both depending on the gene Pax6 for their development (again!), although they clearly developed independently in evolution. Personally, I prefer the term genetic homology for these instances, because homology can be found at many different levels that do not always agree with each other (Aboitiz 1995). There can be homology of behavioral traits, of anatomical structures, of cell types, and of genetic processes, and there are known examples of homology at one level but not at others. In 1971, Sir Gavin De Beer published a brief but in my view outstanding monograph in which he described instances of homologous functions performed by non-homologous organs, and homologous adult structures generated by non-homologous developmental processes (De Beer 1971). Glenn Northcutt and Georg Striedter further built on this point, emphasizing the existence of homology at different levels (Striedter and Northcutt 1991). In my view, the evidence of a conserved developmental brain topography across species suggests no regional or embryonic homology between the avian nidopallium and the mammalian cerebral cortex, but instead the genetic evidence indicates partial homology in the molecular mechanisms involved in their amplification.

Canonical Circuits

In line with his hypothesis of homology between the avian nidopallium and the mammalian cerebral cortex, Harvey Karten proposed the equivalent cell hypothesis, depicting a microprocessing circuit in the avian brain comparable to the columnar organization of the mammalian cerebral cortex (Karten 1991, 1997, 2013). Karten visualized a specific network connecting different avian brain regions in a similar way to the interconnectivity of the different layers of the cerebral cortex. This idea was reinforced by a series of recent studies by him and several collaborators like my friend and former classmate Jorge Mpodozis, who described in fine detail the similarities between the avian and mammalian brain microcircuits, including shared molecular markers for input-receiving and output-sending neurons (Wang et al. 2010; Dugas-Ford et al. 2012; Ahumada-Galleguillos et al. 2015). Considering this evidence, some authors have asserted that birds have "columns", homologous to the mammalian cortical columns, but their cellular elements are dispersed in different brain nuclei instead of in different layers, as in the cerebral cortex. In my opinion, mammalian columns not only make up a specific microcircuit, but are also composed of clonally related neurons deriving from the same progenitor cell (see Chapter 3), which is consistent with the radial differentiation of cell types in the cortex, as opposed to the tangential differentiation gradient in birds. It is not known whether the "columns" observed in the brains of birds are also clonally related (personally, I consider it unlikely). Nonetheless, I partly agree with this statement, if we consider that a simple version of such microcircuits, also referred to as canonical microcircuits (see Chapter 2), may have been present in the brain of the common ancestor of birds and mammals.

Ancestral amniotes had a rudimentary tubular brain, resembling that of modern salamanders, with a very limited degree of neuronal proliferation and cell migration compared to mammals and birds (Aboitiz and Montiel 2007a; Kielan-Jaworowska et al. 2004). In this tiny brain, like in more evolved brains, an appropriate balance between excitation and inhibition was a cardinal character to maintain proper functions. Conrado Bosman and I have proposed that this balanced activity represents one of the basic functions of microcircuits, and must be a very ancient character required for the assembly of large-scale neuronal networks (Bosman and Aboitiz 2015). Specifically, inhibitory neurons serve to regulate the oscillatory dynamics of such reverberating microcircuits, hence a very simple circuit architecture consisting of input-receiving and output neurons, combined with some excitatory and inhibitory interneurons, may well have existed in the brains of the earliest amniotes (and possibly in the earliest vertebrates as well). In the lineages leading to mammals and birds, the complexity of these rudimentary microcircuits independently increased, always constrained by stringent physiological requirements to maintain processing capacity. Thus, although there may be an ancestral microcircuit underlying the canonical circuits of mammals and birds, the further elaboration of it was highly constrained by similar functional demands. As I mentioned in Chapter 2, language processing may also be based on the operation of these canonical microcircuits, in the same way as other cognitive processes are. Likewise, birdsong probably relies on a similar microcircuitry recruited for this function during the evolution of this group of birds.

Thus, the fine commonalities observed between avian and mammalian connectivity may reflect the fact that they are designed by natural selection to do the same thing, rather than being strict indicators of common ancestry. An eloquent example that resemblance of circuit assembly does not imply common ancestry is the retinae of mammals and insects. Santiago Ramón y Cajal noted this intriguing similarity, which in both cases consists of three vertical and two horizontal cellular layers that exert lateral inhibition. Furthermore, in both the fly and vertebrates, axons leaving the retina make synapses in a relay center before reaching the brain (protocerebrum in insects) (Ramón y Cajal and Sánchez 1915; Sanes and Zipursky 2010). A more recent study demonstrated a striking similarity in the neural mechanisms involved in motion detection in flies and vertebrates (Borst and Helmstaedter 2015). The common ancestor of flies and vertebrates was among the earliest members of urbilateria, a large-level taxon that includes all animals with bilateral symmetry, and excludes sea sponges, jellyfish and other animals. In urbilateria there are so many groups devoid of retina that it is very unlikely that the earliest ancestor had a retina like that of insects and vertebrates. Nonetheless, the gene Pax6 may have been at work, contributing to specifying photoreceptive cells (see above) (Gehring and Ikeo 1999). The most likely explanation is that the retinal circuits of insects and vertebrates arose separately, but converged in a nearly optimal design for vision.

The Raven Said, Nevermore

As an undergraduate, I got interested in literature and particularly in the so-called Damned Poets, one of my favorites being Edgar Allan Poe, whose complete works I still have on my shelves. To me, one of his best poems is "The Raven", which stylishly tells the story of a raven's visit to a young man mourning the loss of his love Lenore. The bird only repeats the word "Nevermore" while the lover falls into increasing melancholy and despair. Ravens, crows, jays, rooks and the like make up the family Corvidae, close relatives of songbirds, and legendarily known for their vocal capacities, but especially for their cleverness, which has been compared to that of apes (Clayton and Emery 2005, 2015; Emery and Clayton 2004, 2009; Güntürkün and Bugnyar 2012; Güntürkün 2016). Corvids have a very complex repertoire of calls to refer to food, danger and social instances, and are particularly good vocal imitators, including of human speech. Anecdotes about smart crows abound, with books written on their admirable behavior. There is a BBC film that shows crows leaving nuts in front of cars at a red light, then flying off and waiting for the cars to move and crush the nuts when the light turns green. With the next red light, the birds fly down and eat the cracked nuts[1]. Crows are also very good at social cognition, with anecdotes of crows purposefully deceiving others for their benefit, and even displaying a sense of humor. In her book *Crows*, Candace Savage tells a story in which a female crow watched a petal fall on her brother, who jumped in surprise. The bird then began dropping petals on her brother, presumably expecting him to jump again (Savage 2007). Working with ravens,

---

[1] https://www.youtube.com/watch?v=BGPGknpq3e0

Thomas Bugnyar observed a pair of birds collecting food from colored tubes, where in each trial a different color was the one associated with food. While one bird (the subordinate one) rapidly learned the task, the other (the dominant one) decided to wait for the subordinate bird's first choice and then robbed the food from him. But the subordinate soon started to poke tubes that he knew were empty, making the dominant approach them, and then rapidly flew to the correct ones to get his reward. He did not do this often, so that the dominant one would still follow him to the decoys (Bugnyar and Kotrschal 2004).

While many birds migrate south to warmer zones during the harsh winter of Northern Europe and North America, crows stay put throughout the year. Migrating birds have evolved very powerful flight musculature and respiratory apparatus, and a sophisticated orienting system, while non-migrating birds have on average larger brains than migrating birds, particularly in the hippocampal region, which as I have said is involved in spatial memory and orientation. In preparation for tougher times, in autumn crows cache food in different places to which they return in winter. To be able to do this impressive task, birds need powerful episodic memory, or memory of events. This is not unlike the odor-based memory of rats described above, and includes solving the three W questions: what happened at some event, where did it happen and when did it happen. Nicola Clayton and Nathan Emery have studied the impressive memory capacities of corvids for a long time (Clayton and Emery 2005, 2015). It is now known that these animals do not develop an extensive map of an entire forest to remember their cache sites, but rather use a conspicuous and stable landmark from which the position of different cache sites can be seen. In a series of clever experiments, Clayton's group has found that jays can remember the kind of food placed in a given place, and the time it has spent there. For example, peanuts last for a very long time when hidden, but wax worms degrade very quickly. The birds prefer to retrieve the wax worms first and leave the peanuts last, while avoiding sites where food is probably rotten (Clayton and Emery 2015).

Emery and Clayton have added a fourth W to episodic memory, namely "who" was watching the event (Dally et al. 2006). Jays usually re-cache their food after it has been stored, presumably to avoid it being stolen by other nearby birds. Thus, Clayton and colleagues observed the caching behavior of jays in the laboratory under three conditions: alone, with another bird that could not see the caching sites, and with a bird that witnessed all the caching behavior. After some hours, the storing birds were allowed to go back to the storing sites, and researchers observed re-caching behavior under the three conditions. Re-caching was much more frequent when there was a witnessing bird than in the other two conditions. Furthermore, they first re-cached from the sites in which they knew they had been observed by another bird. Finally, birds that had experience in stealing from other birds' cache sites were much more prone to re-cache and more sensitive to observation by others than birds with no history of stealing food. Although these findings argue for a strong episodic memory capacity in corvids, they do not necessarily imply a human-like ability to attribute intentions to the witnessing animal, such as "he/she knows what I know", and "he/she will attempt to steal the food I stored in this place, but not in that place". This would require what is known as a mind-reading ability or Theory of Mind, which is subjectively evident in we humans, but has proven elusive as a scientific concept. A simpler interpretation may be that they have associated the close presence of other birds with stealing food and acted accordingly. We have not yet designed the appropriate experiments to discriminate the subjective condition of experimental animals, and perhaps never will (see Chapter 11). In this line, Thomas Nagel 1974 wrote an influential article in the 1970s titled "What is it Like to be a Bat?" in which he asserted that it would be impossible to get into the minds of other species.

Crows vs Chimps

Crows can also be very good at manipulating objects, perhaps better than any other non-human animal. In his splendid book *Not a Chimp*, Jeremy Taylor eloquently criticizes the primatocentric view of comparative psychology, which assumes that apes represent the condition closest to ours in the elaboration of cognitive abilities (Taylor 2009). True, we are phylogenetically very close to apes (our DNA differs from theirs by only 1% or 2%), but Taylor claims this is misleading when it comes to cognitive capacity, in which very small genetic mutations may have explosive phenotypic effects, not to mention possibly substantial epigenetic modifications. Elaborate cognitive abilities perhaps more comparable to those of humans may be found in distant species like crows. In his book, Taylor makes a comparison of the cognitive capacities of chimps and crows and shows that the latter have no reason to envy apes, which I will briefly outline below. As I said above, there is a strong convergence in the evolution of the brains of birds and mammals, despite the two groups having diverging gross neuroanatomy. Onur Güntürkün and others have described an avian equivalent of the prefrontal cortex, which like that of mammals, receives strong dopaminergic innervation and is involved in executive functions like behavioral flexibility, attention, decision making and working memory (Güntürkün 2005). However, the anatomical location of this region does not fit that of mammals, because the brains of birds and mammals have very different gross morphologies. Whether the common ancestor of birds and mammals had a rudimentary region performing some prefrontal cortex-like functions is open to question.

Although showing some capacity for planning behavior (see Chapter 7), apes seem to have a very limited understanding of the physical properties of objects and how to use them for their purposes, a capacity that has been termed "folk physics". In the wild, chimps are apparently able to understand simple causal effects by making tools like little twigs to extract termites from their nest, cracking nuts with stones, using leaves as sponges to extract water and sometimes using forked branches as hooks. However, in captivity, they show very limited capacity to understand basic laws of physics, like the resistance of materials and physical causation that 4-year-old children master quite successfully. The group of David Povinelli and other teams have made important contributions to unveiling the limitations of chimpanzees to manipulate physical objects (Povinelli 2000; Penn and Povinelli 2007). For example, captive chimps can learn to use a long twig to extract a piece of food from a transparent cylinder, but they have a hard time when the twig has side branches that keep it from entering the cylinder. They fail to realize that they can remove the branches to put the twig in the cylinder, which contrasts to what is seen in the wild where chimps clean twigs to dip for termites. This indicates that in the wild they learn to use these instruments very slowly, probably by a mixture of trial and error and imitation of others.

A task amply used for testing cognitive capacity in monkeys and chimps is the trap-tube test, in which there is an opening on the bottom of a tube where food can be trapped if it falls in. Experimenters placed a peanut on one side of the trap such that to extract it had to be poked at from the opening on the other side of the trap to keep the peanut from falling in the hole. Only one monkey could do the task. But when the trap was upside down and the hole facing upward, the monkey still pushed the food from the other side even though it made no difference from which side the food was poked. Povinelli found that chimps behaved similarly to monkeys in this task. Another experiment was the trap-table problem. In this case, food had to be raked from a table either with a trap as in the trap tube problem, or with a painted rectangle of the same size as the trap. Only one of 7 chimps got the difference between the two conditions. Chimps did only marginally better in the same task, this time either with a correct rake or an inverted one that did not work, selecting in many instances the incorrect rack (Povinelli 2000; Penn and Povinelli 2007).

Povinelli then wondered whether chimps understand the concept of force transmission through contact. He and collaborators designed a string-pulling trap in which several strings were located close to a visible but inaccessible banana, but only one string was tied to the banana such that pulling the string made the banana fall. Another test was simply placing the banana on the string, so that pulling the latter moved the banana and made it fall. Chimps chose the correct string when it was tied to the banana, but not when it was simply placed under the banana. Other experiments tested more directly the ability to use and manipulate tools. Chimps were presented with an appropriate tool to retrieve an apple, straight at one end with a side bar at the other, versus a T-shaped tool that did not work for the task. Again, chimps showed only a mild preference for the appropriate tool. And when using the appropriate tool, they sometimes tried to use the incorrect end. Finally, chimps were provided with a flexible pipe that was bent by the experimenter in the chimps' presence, and the chimps had to unbend it to use it for reaching food. They also performed badly in this test (Povinelli 2000; Penn and Povinelli 2007).

These experiments indicate that chimps have some elemental understanding of physical properties and tools like appropriate size and basic configuration, but not much more than that. They seem to have very little capacity to manipulate objects, and their abilities for tool-making in the wild may be strictly based on imitation learning, following a procedure that is probably acquired very slowly. On the other hand, crows are equal or even better than apes in solving these kinds of tasks. Crows have also shown a capacity for tool-making in the wild that is comparable to or surpasses that of chimpanzees. Gavin Hunt and Russell Gray have shown that New Caledonian crows make very sophisticated tools by delicately cutting the long leaves of a shrub called *Pandalus*, making a long twig with one end much narrower than the other (Hunt 1996; Taylor et al. 2009). Moreover, the barbs at the edge of the leaf point to the wider side, which is the end that the birds hold to insert the leaf in a hole. They then use the barbs as hooks to catch insects as they pull the leaf out. Interestingly, they often use the twig on the left side of their beaks, indicating consistent lateralization in tool use. These birds deliberately make hooks by cutting a small branch from a twig near its origin, leaving the little stem pointing upward. There is circumstantial evidence, but not yet proof, that this behavior is learned and is not an inherited motor program. This is closely similar to, or even better than what wild chimpanzees do, as they have never been found to prepare the sophisticated hooks made by crows.

In the laboratory, crows and the like are also good problem solvers. Emery, Clayton, and collaborators got rooks to perform a trap-tube task similar to that presented to chimps, which they solved very well, outdoing the best chimps (Tebbich et al. 2007). Additionally, Hunt and Gray showed that crows also perform admirably well in a bird version of the trap-table test (Hunt 1996). However, they found that New Caledonian crows, with their exquisite tool-making capacity, performed no better than monkeys and chimps in the trap-tube task. Using a design similar to the rope-pulling experiment, Berndt Heinrich and his colleagues put pieces of meat and stones hanging from ropes (Heinrich and Bugnyar 2007). The ravens retrieved the food but not the stones by pulling on the strings with their beaks while holding the string with their feet to prevent it from fall again. They had to repeat this procedure several times as the string was longer than the bird's height so they could not reach the food with a single pull. They also knew from simple sight when a food item was too heavy for them to lift and did not choose these items.

To me, the most impressive demonstration of cognitive abilities was provided by the team of Alex Kacelnik who put New Caledonian crows in a task in which food was placed on a transparent tube, and birds had to select an appropriate stick out of many placed nearby to get the food out (Weir et al. 2002; Weir and Kacelnik 2006; Chappell and Kacelnik 2002). They did pretty well in the task, as monkeys and chimps have also done. They even removed leaves from branches before using them. But the most notable experiment involved a female crow called Betty, whose performance in some tasks can be found in You-tube [2]. In the first test, Betty and other crows had to retrieve food from a vertical tube, in which the only way to do this was to use a hook to lift the container inside the tube. The crows were presented with straight and hooked wires, and appropriately chose the correct tools. In one instance, when Betty had chosen the last hook that was left, a dominant male took it from her. Incredibly, and the first time this seen with an animal, Betty bent a straight wire and used it to retrieve the food. But the most impressive of Betty's performances was shortly before her death. She had to retrieve food placed deep in a long tube and had only a small stick beside the tube. There was no way she could get the food out with this tool. Nonetheless, there were other tubes nearby, and a stick long enough for the task was inside one of them. This could not be retrieved with the short stick she had available, but there were intermediate sticks in the other

---

[2] https://www.youtube.com/watch?v=ZE4BT8QSgZk; https://www.youtube.com/watch?v=UDg0AKfM8EY; https://www.youtube.com/watch?v=lcvbgq2SSyc

tubes that would serve the purpose and could be retrieved using the short stick. Impressively, Betty figured out that she had to use the short stick to get an intermediate and then use that to get the long stick and then finally retrieve the food. This is far more than anyone has been able to show at this point with non-human primates or any other species. More recently, Christian Rutz and colleagues have equipped wild New Caledonian crows with miniature video cameras to explore their natural behavior. Astonishingly, they saw birds bending collected twigs in the same way as Betty had done, indicating that this behavior is not just found in captivity (Troscianko and Rutz 2015)[3].

Why have crows developed such a complex knowledge of physics? Emery and Clayton claim that this is not strictly related to tool use capacity, but with the ability to plan behavior, which may be partly correct (Emery and Clayton 2004, 2009). Nonetheless, I believe this may also have to do with another behavior that is highly prominent in birds, which is nest building (Healy et al. 2008). Nest building is a largely innate behavior present in most birds and other species, including non-avian dinosaurs. In some birds, including Passeriformes (crows, songbirds and others), nests are made preferentially by females and are highly elaborate, consisting of small sticks intricately woven into a solid structure in which eggs are safely placed. In other bird species, males construct fancy nests to attract females, for which they collect all kinds of conspicuous and colorful objects. Unfortunately, little is known about the neural mechanisms involved in nest building. There are doubtlessly several largely inherited automatic programs controlling this behavior. But on the other hand, the bird also needs goal-directed planning for nest construction, and more importantly has to select the appropriate sticks and objects and gauge their size and flexibility. It then has to bend the sticks and interweave them to make a rigid structure. It may be that the physical knowledge of crows and other birds is partly a spin-off of this inherited motor program. Nesting behavior is sexually dimorphic in

---

[3] https://www.newscientist.com/article/2100535-genius-crows-tool-bending-behaviour-may-be-natural-to-its-kind/

several species, and therefore it might be expected that females tend to be better at these tasks than males. Furthermore, there are wide species differences in nest structure, and perhaps a correlation can be found between nest complexity and cognitive abilities across species.

Talking and Singing

Birds differ from mammals not only in their brains but also in the structure of their phonatory organs. Instead of a larynx with vocal folds as in mammals, birds have a syrinx, a membranous structure located at the base of the trachea where it divides in two bronchii. The syrinx consists of two halves, one at the base of each bronchus, and each innervated by the same side hypoglossal nerve and controlled by the ipsilateral hemisphere (Schmidt and Martin 2014). Many bird species can learn new vocalizations by imitation, like songbirds, crows, parrots and even hummingbirds. Collectively, all these species are called vocal learning birds, and are distinguished from other birds that are termed vocal non-learning birds (Petkov and Jarvis 2012). A noteworthy example of a vocal learning bird is the African forked trail drongo, a small bird that mimics the alarm calls of several other species, like meerkats, to trick them and rob their food, but also uses calls to provide genuine alarm when predators are approaching. In this way, they avoid the "boy who cried wolf" effect of habituation to the alarm signals of other species[4].

One of the most impressive cases of vocal learning in birds was an African grey parrot named Alex, who was bought at a pet store by Irene Pepperberg, a comparative psychologist interested in animal communication (Pepperberg 2008). Alex learned a sophisticated vocabulary of up to 150 words, with a capacity to understand simple syntactic rules. Pepperberg used a special procedure to teach Alex called the model/ rival technique, which is based on a human instructor presenting the model to be copied, and a "rival" human student who gives correct and incorrect responses, and competes with the animal in attracting the

---

[4] http://www.bbc.co.uk/nature/life/Drongo#p013bxk7

instructor's attention. This novel technique was so successful that it has been proposed for therapeutic use with children with language disabilities. Alex's abilities went beyond pure vocal learning, as he learned to add numbers in a way that surprised Pepperberg. She was trying to teach another parrot to count up to two clicks with the hand, and had instructed Alex to remain silent. His disobedience turned out to be a great discovery. Pepperberg had made two clicks with her hand, to which the parrot being trained did not respond. So she made another two clicks and asked him again. Then, Alex came in and said "four"! Pepperberg insisted he keep quiet, and made an additional pair of clicks, to which Alex answered "six"! Some critics have objected that Alex's case may be an instance of associative learning, as in the "clever Hans" story I mentioned in the Chapter 1. Pepperberg has responded that Alex would talk with a variety of people, not only with her, and responded correctly in the absence of anybody who knew the answer, showing sometimes a high degree of insight. Unfortunately, Alex passed away unexpectedly before more sophisticated controls could be made to test his performance.

As claimed by Stephanie King and Peter McGregor, vocal learning in parrots and crows may be used in social contexts more comparable to human speech than songbird learning (King and McGregor 2016). Unfortunately, we know very little about the neural bases of the mimicking capacity of crows and parrots, but notable advances have been made in the recent years in our understanding of the neural circuits involved in birdsong. Note, however, that although birdsong sounds very musical to us, birds may not perceive it in the same way. Working in Timothy Gentner's lab, Micah Bregman showed that as with human speech European starlings can generalize conspecific melodies based primarily on spectral envelopes rather than on pitch cues that contain the fine structure of the stimulus (Bregman et al. 2016). On the other hand, the relevant cues for music processing derive from the temporal fine structure of the signal (Shannon 2005) (see Chapter 4). Thus, birds may not communicate musically (as understood by us), but rather in a speech-like manner.

Darwin's analogy between birdsong and human speech was largely ignored during the last century despite notable advances by ethologists like Peter Marler. Marler was among the first to revive Darwin's hypothesis by conceptualizing both birdsong and human language in the ethological framework proposed by Konrad Lorenz and Niko Tinbergen (Marler 1990a, b). Marler's main point was that both language and birdsong are innate release mechanisms in which a sensory template needs to be presented early to the young. This auditory template is then gradually matched to motor output and eventually refined into adult speech or birdsong, respectively (see Chapter 8). Furthermore, the now classical experiments by Masakazu Konishi established that deaf birds developed abnormal songs, which interestingly were similar across related species, while young birds with normal hearing but without exposure to conspecific songs, developed more elaborate songs than those of the deaf birds, although still abnormal (Konishi 2004). A very recent experiment shed further light on this issue. Makoto Araki and colleagues raised young zebra finches with adult Bengalese finches, so they learned to sing using another species' model. In these conditions, the zebra finches acquired a song with mixed characters, with a morphology reminiscent of Bengalese finches, but with the temporal structure of the zebra finch song (Araki et al. 2016). These findings indicate that some of the song features are dependent to sensory feedback, while others are genetically determined.

Marler was a pioneer in the study of the ethological bases of birdsong learning, and, consistent with Darwin's ideas, described the acquisition of a "subsong" acquired in early stages of learning. The subsong is initially overly extensive in its sounds and combinations, but with exposure to adult songs it is selectively reduced to a set of combined syllables representing the adult song. Birdsong learning is highly dependent on the kind of songs that the bird listens to, such that birds learn their song from an adult "tutor", which in most cases is their own father. In this way, the bird acquires some idiosyncratic features from its father's song that are transmitted across generations. Thus, true dialects can be observed in separate populations of birds, something that was also recognized by Darwin. More recent studies led by Johan Bolhuis and collaborators have established that learning in both humans and songbirds undergoes an initial phase of perception in which the speech or song sounds are stored in memory (Bolhuis et al. 2010, Berwick et al.

2012, 2011, Beckers et al. 2014). This is followed by an execution part in which the motor systems rehearse the imprinted vocalizations. The execution stage begins with a subsong, which is a rudimentary vocal output that is successively refined to match the auditory template stored in the memory, until it crystallizes as an adult song. Similar processes have been observed in human infants that begin with a wide repertoire of vocalizations (the babbling stage, which has been compared to the bird's subsong) that becomes gradually restricted to the phonemes used in the community learning he or she is immersed in. Likewise, the infant's ability to perceive speech sounds becomes restricted to the sounds used by adults. An example of this is the difficulty to recognizing the phonemes of non-native speakers who learned another language late in life.

Fernando Nottebohm, a former student of Marler, contributed enormously to dissecting the cerebral circuits that participate in song learning and identified a group of brain nuclei involved in song learning and production (Nottebohm 1970, 2005). First, he found that song learning is strongly lateralized and restricted to only one hemisphere of the brain, preferentially the left in canaries, but the right in zebra finches. One interpretation for this arrangement is that rapid frequency movements may be more easily controlled from only one hemisphere, especially in animals like birds that lack a corpus callosum. However, song-related nuclei are present in both hemispheres, and if the singing hemisphere is damaged, the contralateral nuclei can perfectly develop song. More recent studies by Bolhuis' group have extended these findings and confirmed lateralization for both song perception and production from early stages of learning (Bolhuis and Gahr 2006; Bolhuis et al. 2010). Moreover, separate circuits for song perception and production have been identified in the songbird brain, which emulates the development of lateralized Wernicke and Broca's regions in humans (Fig. 9.2). The auditory pathway for song learning includes a nucleus called field L (equivalent, but probably not homologous to the mammalian auditory cortex), which connects with a nucleus called HVC. Both nuclei activate specifically when the bird hears song (Bolhuis et al. 2010). Erich Jarvis and his team found that this auditory pathway also exists in vocal non-learning birds, indicating that it is ancient, although in songbirds it

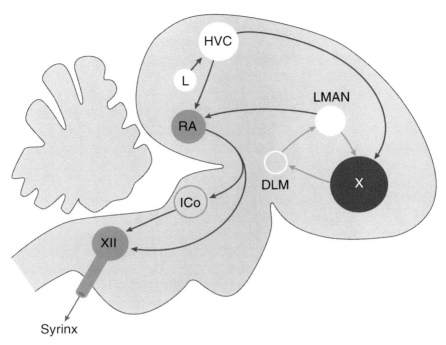

Syrinx

Fig. 9.2 The brain nuclei involved in song learning in songbirds. In black, subpallial components (area X); in white, pallial components (L, HVC and LMAN); in gray, amygdalar components (RA). ICo, nucleus intercollicularis; nXII, XII cranial nucleus. L is the analogue of the auditory cortex of mammals. A circuit including LMAN, area X and thalamic nucleus DLM is comparable to the cortico-striato-thalamic circuit for speech production in humans, while the descending projection from RA to brainstem motor nuclei parallels the projection from motor cortex to vocal motor nuclei in humans (see Chapter 10)

probably developed some specific adaptations for perceiving song stimuli (Jarvis 2004; Petkov and Jarvis 2012).

The motor pathways seem to be more complex. Put very schematically, there are two vocal pathways for song learning in birds: a posterior vocal pathway involved in song production that includes the HVC nucleus, possibly involved in song sequencing. The HVC then projects to the RA nucleus, part of the avian amygdala, which sends descending projections to brainstem vocal control nuclei.

Secondly, the anterior pathway, which is thought to participate in song acquisition and auditory-vocal feedback, includes nuclei termed LMAN, involved in song variability, area X in the basal ganglia, and the dorsal lateral nucleus of the medial thalamus (Fig. 9.2). This circuit emulates the cortico-basal ganglia-thalamus circuit involved in speech production in humans (Petkov and Jarvis 2012, 2014). Interestingly, lesions in the song learning nuclei impair learning new songs, but not the execution of songs already learned. Notably, these vocal learning motor circuits have also been found in other vocal learning birds like hummingbirds and parrots, but seem to be absent in birds with no or poor vocal learning (Jarvis et al. 2000; Liu et al. 2013). The common ancestor of parrots, hummingbirds and songbirds is very likely not to have been a vocal learner, and therefore this may be another case of evolutionary convergence. Nonetheless, the similarity of the respective circuits indicates that convergence is based on a shared and possibly ancestral system involved in motor control that differentiated independently into similar neural circuits in the three lineages of vocal learning birds. In this way, brain pathways for vocal learning probably evolved separately in different bird species, but under common constraints (Chakraborty and Jarvis 2015).

Considering this evidence, Gesa Feenders, Erich Jarvis and collaborators have proposed a motor theory for the evolutionary origin of vocal learning in birds, in which the vocal learning control system derives from a vocal control system present in vocal non-learners (Feenders et al. 2008). Notably, the vocal non-learning circuit is anatomically close to the location of vocal learning nuclei in songbirds, and is interconnected in a similar way to the vocal learning nuclei. Furthermore, this system activates during non-vocal behavior of vocal learners like limb and body movements, and during vocal behavior of vocal non-learners. In humans, learning to speak is also considered to consist principally of the development of motor control, and as I mentioned previously, vocal rehearsal is a very important element, perhaps not so much for vocal perception *per se*, but for the maintenance of phonological memory traces that are critical for speech learning. Additional studies led by Jarvis (Pfenning et al. 2014; Whitney et al. 2014) used a massive computational approach to gene expression patterns in vocal learning birds (songbirds, parrots and hummingbirds), vocal non-learning birds (quails and doves), humans and macaques. The authors observed a well-defined pattern of neural activity-induced gene expression in the different song nuclei. Furthermore, there was a significant convergence in gene expression between the avian RA and the laryngeal motor cortex in humans, and between area X in songbirds and the striatal area that activates during speech production in humans. Notably, these gene expression patterns were not found in vocal non-learning species (quail, dove and macaque).

Finally, a couple words on the cellular processes involved in song learning. There are two kinds of songbirds: some, like the zebra finch, acquire a song only once and maintain it for the rest of their lives. The songs of zebra finches are relatively simple compared to those of the second group of songbirds, including mockingbirds and canaries, which modify their songs every year in the mating season. Nottebohm found that the song nuclei of seasonal songbirds have a cyclical dynamic, growing larger during the period of song acquisition (spring) and shrinking afterward, only to grow again the next spring (Nottebohm 1989, 2004; Nottebohm and Liu 2010). It was found that the days getting longer is important in triggering the growth of these nuclei and song learning, mediated by a burst of testosterone in the male. Thus, injecting testosterone into females increased the size of their nuclei and resulted in their developing a song, while castrating males had the opposite effect, blocking song learning and nucleus growth. But the most striking finding by Nottebohm was that the growth of such nuclei was due to the production of new neurons born in the subventricular region, deep in the brain, that migrated to the respective nuclei. Furthermore, after each breeding season there is a significant loss of neurons concomitant with the partial decline in singing capacity, until the next spring when new neurons are added and the bird develops a song containing elements of the old one, but also adds new elements to it. Adult neurogenesis had been observed before in lower vertebrates, but the dogma at that time was that higher animals like birds and mammals were born with a fixed number of neurons that could only decrease with age. Nottebohms's findings were highly criticized in the beginning, but slowly they became established as a powerful scientific fact. Additional studies have shown that beside neuronal death and neurogenesis, the dendritic ramifications of the neurons that remain across breeding seasons undergo dramatic reductions in winter and expansions in spring. Recent field studies of free-living birds have revealed a more complex story, in which some species do not show significant seasonal changes in the volume of nuclei but do express seasonal differences in song structures, while others show significant seasonal differences in song structure but not in the size of song nuclei (Bolhuis and Gahr 2006).

The Grammar of Birds

Some songbirds learn complex songs, with a hierarchical organization that resembles that of speech sounds. Birdsongs usually contain a structure based on introductory single notes followed by "motifs" that are repeated and contain fixed sequences of "syllables" with one or two notes. This arrangement is however fixed, and songbirds have been considered unable to develop more complex syntactical organization like the recursive or combinatorial grammar that characterizes human language. However, a provocative article in 2006 by Timothy Gentner and his collaborators claimed that songbirds can learn simple recursive rules in artificial songs presented to them (see Chapter 1) (Gentner et al. 2006). However, other studies showed that birds cannot generalize this learning to structurally similar sequences composed of different sounds, implying that birds are not able to grasp recursion as an abstract property but store the learned sequences by memory (Berwick et al. 2011, 2012). Nonetheless, studies by Luca Bonatti, Marcela Peña and collaborators with human infants have shown that children initially use phonetic clues to recognize and memorize structural patterns that are later assimilated as abstract rules (Bonatti et al. 2005). Thus, there may be a stage in syntactic learning in which infants also use sound patterns and memory to recognize structural regularities that eventually become generalized to different settings. In other words, songbird learning might represent an early stage in grammar acquisition, which is also present in infants but develops into a truly recursive syntax only in humans. In this same line, a recent article by Dina Lipkind and collaborators compared the vocal combinatorial capacity of zebra finches, Bengalese finches and human infants, and observed a conserved stepwise pattern of vocal learning in the three species (Lipkind et al. 2013). Juvenile birds were trained to change syllable order or to insert new syllables into a learned string, in which birds gradually approximated the correct sequences by slowly developing new syllable combinations. Likewise, babbling infants developed their vocalizations in several steps, in which each new syllable type was gradually combined with different syllables, expanding the repertoire of utterances from repetitive sequences to diversified patterns of vocalizations.

There are other findings indicating grammatical complexity in bird songs and calls. Toshitaka Suzuki and collaborators have found that great tit calls can be very elaborate, combining ten different notes to produce complex vocalizations with distinct meanings (Suzuki et al. 2016). For example, they emit a three-syllable call (ABC) to signal danger, inducing other birds to scan the environment. In addition, they use a single call (D) to request approaching the caller, and the combination ABC-D signifies approaching while also scanning the surroundings. Suzuki and collaborators presented audio recordings of these syllables to wild great tits that reproduced the natural responses. However, the combination ABC-D was structure dependent, as it did not elicit any behavior when placed in the order D-ABC. The authors argue that this reflects the property of compositionality, a property of human language (particularly the lexicon) in which semantic units are combined in larger units whose meaning depends on the independent units and the structural organization of the sentence. In a related experiment, Sabrina Engesser and collaborators recognized another property of speech, called combinatoriality, which occurs, for example, in the aggregation of phonemes, meaningless by themselves, to assemble meaningful larger units (Engesser et al. 2015). The authors analyzed the calls of the chestnut-crowned babbler, a social bird from the Australian desert. They found that this bird uses two different acoustic signals (say A and B) that are arranged in different ways to convey distinct meanings (AB, promoting flight; and BAB, prompting for begging for food at the nest), and that the alteration of the call structure impairs their social significance. They suggest that this is evidence of a phonemic contrast like that found in speech, as in the case of the words "pat" and "bat". Commenting on these findings, Daniel Bowling and Tecumseh Fitch raised the point that although a very relevant finding of animal combinatoriality, the observed signals are unlike phonemes, as they are used only in specific circumstances (during flight) (Bowling and Fitch 2015). Moreover, these sounds are separated by silent gaps, and the difference between AB and BAB is the presence or absence of the initial sound B, rather than the use of similar sounds to convey different meanings, as in "pat" and "bat".

Songbirds show a wide range of song complexity across species, and Timothy Gardner and his group have detected non-adjacent correlations in the call structure of birds like the canary that develop complex songs (Markowitz et al. 2013). This points to the existence of long-term dependencies (see Chapter 6), in which the next syllable during a song depends on the current syllable but also on the history of the song up to ten seconds before. Johan Bolhuis and collaborators have also argued that increasing numbers of song elements (notes and syllables) as songs become more complex requires an expansion of working memory capacity in order to manipulate these sounds and alter preexisting sequences to generate novel ones (Bolhuis et al. 2010). This assumption implies that with increasing working memory capacity songbirds are able to remember and master longer strings of syllables that can be manipulated, altering their order and generating new songs. More generally, Erich Jarvis and Christopher Petkov propose that mastering long distance dependencies can be considered a critical evolutionary transition toward the development of complex syntax, which would require an expansion of short-term memory capacity (Jarvis 2004; Petkov and Jarvis 2012).

To test these ideas, we first need to assess auditory-vocal working memory capacity in songbirds and if a mechanism is found to increase working memory in them, perhaps by genetic manipulation, we might begin to test the possibility of inducing recursive grammar in their songs. This is almost science fiction, as no genes have yet been found that increase working memory, and the genetic manipulation of birds is still in its infancy. Another possibility is to artificially select birds with better memory capacities. In any case, the point is that working memory is proposed to have a role in the appearance of recursive grammar, as there is a mnemonic limit to the number of elements one can keep online while processing other sound elements. Thus, there is a noticeable convergence between Bolhuis and collaborators' ideas and our proposals, both involving working memory in the evolution of complex communication signals.

References and Notes

Abdel-Mannan O, Cheung AF, Molnár Z (2008) Evolution of cortical neurogenesis. Brain Res Bull 75:398–404

Aboitiz F (1992) The origin of the mammalian brain as a case of evolutionary irreversibility. Med Hypotheses 38:301–304

Aboitiz F (1993) Further comments on the evolutionary origin of the mammalian brain. Med Hypotheses 41:409–418

Aboitiz F (1995) Homology in the evolution of the cerebral hemispheres. The case of reptilian dorsal ventricular ridge and its possible correspondence with mammalian neocortex. J Hirnforsch 36:461–472

Aboitiz F (2011) Genetic and developmental homology in amniote brains. Toward conciliating radical views of brain evolution. Brain Res Bull 84:125–136

Aboitiz F, Montiel J (2007a) Origin and evolution of the vertebrate telencephalon, with special reference to the mammalian neocortex. Adv Anat Embryol Cell Biol 193:1–112

Aboitiz F, Montiel J (2007b) Co-option of signaling mechanisms from neural induction to telencephalic patterning. Rev Neurosci 18:311–342

Aboitiz F, Montiel JF (2012) From tetrapods to primates: conserved developmental mechanisms in diverging ecological adaptations. Prog Brain Res 195:3–24

Aboitiz F, Montiel JF (2015) Olfaction, navigation, and the origin of isocortex. Front Neurosci 9:402

Aboitiz F, Zamorano F (2013) Neural progenitors, patterning and ecology in neocortical origins. Front Neuroanat 7:38

Aboitiz F, Morales D, Montiel J (2003) The evolutionary origin of the mammalian isocortex: towards an integrated developmental and functional approach. Behav Brain Sci 26:535–552; discussion 552–585

Ahissar E, Knutsen PM (2008). Object localization with whiskers. Biol Cybern 98:449–458

Ahumada-Galleguillos P, Fernández M, Marin GJ, Letelier JC, Mpodozis J (2015) Anatomical organization of the visual dorsal ventricular ridge in the chick (Gallus gallus): layers and columns in the avian pallium. J Comp Neurol 523:2618–2636

Alme CB, Miao C, Jezek K, Treves A, Moser EI, Moser MB (2014) Place cells in the hippocampus: eleven maps for eleven rooms. Proc Natl Acad Sci U S A 111:18428–18435

Alvarez LW, Alvarez W, Asaro F, Michel HV (1980) Extraterrestrial cause for the cretaceous-tertiary extinction. Science 208:1095–1108

Anderson SA, Eisenstat DD, Shi L, Rubenstein JL (1997) Interneuron migration from basal forebrain to neocortex: dependence on Dlx genes. Science 278:474–476

Araki M, Bandi MM, Yazagi-Sugiyama Y (2016) Mind the gap: neural coding of species identity in birdsong prosody. Science 354:1282–1287

Beckers GJ, Berwick RC, Bolhuis JJ (2014) Comparative analyses of speech and language converge on birds. Behav Brain Sci 37:547–548

Belgard TG, Montiel JF, Wang WZ, García-Moreno F, Margulies EH, Ponting CP, Molnár Z (2013) Adult pallium transcriptomes surprise in not reflecting predicted homologies across diverse chicken and mouse pallial sectors. Proc Natl Acad Sci U S A 110:13150–13155

Berwick RC, Okanoya K, Beckers GJ, Bolhuis JJ (2011) Songs to syntax: the linguistics of birdsong. Trends Cogn Sci 15:113–121

Berwick RC, Beckers GJ, Okanoya K, Bolhuis JJ (2012) A bird's eye view of human language evolution. Front Evol Neurosci 4:5

Bolhuis JJ, Gahr M (2006) Neural mechanisms of birdsong memory. Nat Rev Neurosci 7:347–357

Bolhuis JJ, Okanoya K, Scharff C (2010) Twitter evolution: converging mechanisms in birdsong and human speech. Nat Rev Neurosci 11:747–759

Bonatti LL, Peña M, Nespor M, Mehler J (2005) Linguistic constraints on statistical computations: the role of consonants and vowels in continuous speech processing. Psychol Sci 16:451–459

Borst A, Helmstaedter M (2015) Common circuit design in fly and mammalian motion vision. Nat Neurosci 18:1067–1076

Bosman CA, Aboitiz F (2015) Functional constraints in the evolution of brain circuits. Front Neurosci 9:303

Bowling DL, Fitch WT. (2015) Do animal communication systems have phonemes? Trends Cog Sci 19:555–557

Bregman MR, Patel AD, Gentner TQ (2016) Songbirds use spectral shape, not pitch, for sound pattern recognition. Proc Natl Acad Sci U S A 113:1666–1671

Bruce LL, Neary TJ (1995) The limbic system of tetrapods: a comparative analysis of cortical and amygdalar populations. Brain Behav Evol 46:224–234

Brusatte SL (2016) How some birds survived when all other dinosaurs died. Curr Biol 26:R415–R417

Brusatte S, Luo ZX (2016) Ascent of the mammals. Sci Amer 6:28–35

Brusatte SL, Butler RJ, Barrett PM, Carrano MT, Evans DC, Lloyd GT, Mannion PD, Norell MA, Peppe DJ, Upchurch P, Williamson TE (2015a) The extinction of the dinosaurs. Biol Rev Camb Philos Soc 90:628–642

Brusatte SL, O'Connor JK, Jarvis ED (2015b) The origin and diversification of birds. Curr Biol 25:R888–R898

Bugnyar T, Kotrschal K (2004) Leading a conspecific away from food in ravens (Corvus corax)? Anim Cogn 7:69–76

Burgess SD, Bowring SA (2015) High-precision geochronology confirms voluminous magmatism before, during, and after Earth's most severe extinction. Sci Adv 1:e1500470

Butler AB, Reiner A, Karten HJ (2011) Evolution of the amniote pallium and the origins of mammalian neocortex. Ann N Y Acad Sci 1225:14–27

Cabrera-Socorro A, Hernandez-Acosta NC, Gonzalez-Gomez M, Meyer G (2007) Comparative aspects of p73 and Reelin expression in Cajal-Retzius cells and the cortical hem in lizard, mouse and human. Brain Res 1132:59–70

Caronia-Brown G, Yoshida M, Gulden F, Assimacopoulos S, Grove EA (2014) The cortical hem regulates the size and patterning of neocortex. Development 41:2855–2865

Chakraborty M, Jarvis ED (2015) Brain evolution by brain pathway duplication. Philos Trans R Soc Lond B Biol Sci 370:1684

Chappell J, Kacelnik A (2002) Tool selectivity in a non-primate, the New Caledonian crow (Corvus moneduloides). Anim Cogn 5:71–78

Chen CC, Winkler CM, Pfenning AR, Jarvis ED (2013) Molecular profiling of the developing avian telencephalon: regional timing and brain subdivision continuities. J Comp Neurol 521:3666–3701

Cheung AF, Kondo S, Abdel-Mannan O, Chodroff RA, Sirey TM, Bluy LE, Webber N, DeProto J, Karlen SJ, Krubitzer L, Stolp HB, Saunders NR,

Molnár Z (2010) The subventricular zone is the developmental milestone of a 6-layered neocortex: comparisons in metatherian and eutherian mammals. Cereb Cortex 2:1071–1081

Clayton N, Emery N (2005) Corvid cognition. Curr Biol 15:R80–R81

Clayton NS, Emery NJ (2015) Avian models of human cognitive neuroscience: a proposal. Neuron 86:1330–1342

Cloudsley-Thompson J (2001) Multiple factors in the reptile extinctions of the Cretaceous period. Biologist 48:177–181

Dally JM, Emery NJ, Clayton NS (2006) Food-caching western scrub-jays keep track of who was watching when. Science 312:1662–1665

DeBeer G (1971) Homology, an Unsolved Problem. Oxford University Press, Glasgow

de Frutos CA, Bouvier G, Arai Y, Thion MS, Lokmane L, Keita M, Garcia-Dominguez M, Charnay P, Hirata T, Riethmacher D, Grove EA, Tissir F, Casado M, Pierani A, Garel S (2016) Reallocation of olfactory Cajal-Retzius cells shapes neocortex architecture. Neuron 92:435–448

Deschênes M, Moore J, Kleinfeld D (2012) Sniffing and whisking in rodents. Curr Opin Neurobiol 22:243–250

Dickerson BC, Eichenbaum H (2010) The episodic memory system: neurocircuitry and disorders. Neuropsychopharmacology 35:86–104

Dugas-Ford J, Rowell JJ, Ragsdale CW (2012) Cell-type homologies and the origins of the neocortex. Proc Natl Acad Sci U S A 109:16974–16979

Eichenbaum H (1998) Using olfaction to study memory. Ann N Y Acad Sci 855:657–669

Eichenbaum H (2004) Hippocampus: cognitive processes and neural representations that underlie declarative memory. Neuron 44:109–120

Eichenbaum H (2010) Memory systems. Wiley Interdiscip Rev Cogn Sci 1:478–490

Eichenbaum H (2014) Time cells in the hippocampus: a new dimension for mapping memories. Nat Rev Neurosci 15:732–744

Emery NJ, Clayton NS (2004) The mentality of crows: convergent evolution of intelligence in corvids and apes. Science 306:1903–1907

Emery NJ, Clayton NS (2009) Tool use and physical cognition in birds and mammals. Curr Opin Neurobiol 19:27–33

Engesser S, Crane JM, Savage JL, Russell AF, Townsend SW (2015) Experimental evidence for phonemic contrasts in a nonhuman vocal system. PLoS Biol 13:e1002171

Feenders G, Liedvogel M, Rivas M, Zapka M, Horita H, Hara E, Wada K, Mouritsen H, Jarvis ED (2008) Molecular mapping of movement-associated areas in the avian brain: a motor theory for vocal learning origin. PLoS One 3:e1768

Fitch WT (2009) Musical protolanguage: Darwin's theory of language evolution revisited. http://languagelog.ldc.upenn.edu/nll/?p=1136

Fyhn M, Molden S, Witter MP, Moser EI, Moser MB (2004) Spatial representation in the entorhinal cortex. Science 305:1258–1264

Gehring WJ, Ikeo K (1999) Pax 6: mastering eye morphogenesis and eye evolution. Trends Genet 15:371–317

Gentner TQ, Fenn KM, Margoliash D, Nusbaum HC (2006) Recursive syntactic pattern learning by songbirds. Nature 440:1204–1207

Georgala PA, Carr CB, Price DJ (2011) The role of Pax6 in forebrain development. Dev Neurobiol 71:690–709

Gerkema MP, Davies WI, Foster RG, Menaker M, Hut RA (2013) The nocturnal bottleneck and the evolution of activity patterns in mammals. Proc Biol Sci 280:20130508

Grant RA, Haidarliu S, Kennerley NJ, Prescott TJ (2013) The evolution of active vibrissal sensing in mammals: evidence from vibrissal musculature and function in the marsupial opossum Monodelphis domestica. J Exp Biol 216:3483–3494

Grion N, Akrami A, Zuo Y, Stella F, Diamond ME (2016) Coherence between rat sensorimotor system and hippocampus is enhanced during tactile discrimination. PLoS Biol 14:e1002384

Grove EA, Tole S, Limon J, Yip L, Ragsdale CW (1998) The hem of the embryonic cerebral cortex is defined by the expression of multiple Wnt genes and is compromised in Gli3-deficient mice. Development 125:2315–2325

Güntürkün O (2005) The avian "prefrontal cortex" and cognition. Curr Opin Neurobiol 15:686–693

Güntürkün O (2012) The convergent evolution of neural substrates for cognition. Psychol Res 76:212–219

Güntürkün O, Bugnyar T (2016) Cognition without Cortex. Trends Cogn Sci 20:291–303

Hafting T, Fyhn M, Molden S, Moser MB, Moser EI (2005) Microstructure of a spatial map in the entorhinal cortex. Nature 436:801–806

Healy S, Walsh P, Hansell M (2008) Nest building by birds. Curr Biol 18: R271–R273

Heinrich B, Bugnyar T (2007) Just how smart are ravens? Sci Amer 4:64–71

Howard MW, Eichenbaum H (2015) Time and space in the hippocampus. Brain Res 1621:345–354

Holmgren N (1922) Points of view concerning forebrain morphology in lower vertebrates. J Comp Neurol 34:391–459

Hunt GR. (1996) Manufacture and use of hook-tools by New Caledonian crows. Nature 379:249–251

Jacobs LF (2012) From chemotaxis to the cognitive map: the function of olfaction. Proc Natl Acad Sci U S A 109(Suppl. 1):10693–10700

Jarvis ED (2004) Learned birdsong and the neurobiology of human language. Ann N Y Acad Sci 1016:749–777

Jarvis ED, Ribeiro S, da Silva ML, Ventura D, Vielliard J, Mello CV (2000) Behaviourally driven gene expression reveals song nuclei in hummingbird brain. Nature 406:628–632

Jarvis ED, Yu J, Rivas MV, Horita H, Feenders G, Whitney O, Jarvis SC, Jarvis ER, Kubikova L, Puck AE, Siang-Bakshi C, Martin S, McElroy M, Hara E, Howard J, Pfenning A, Mouritsen H, Chen CC, Wada K (2013) Global view of the functional molecular organization of the avian cerebrum: mirror images and functional columns. J Comp Neurol 521:3614–3665

Kaas JH (2013) The evolution of brains from early mammals to humans. Wiley Interdiscip Rev Cogn Sci 4:33–45

Källén B (1951) On the ontogeny of the reptilian forebrain. Nuclear structures and ventricular sulci. J Comp Neurol 95:307–347

Karten HJ (1968) The ascending auditory pathway in the pigeon (Columba livia). II. Telencephalic projections of the nucleus ovoidalis thalami. Brain Res 11:134–153

Karten HJ (1969) The organization of the avian telencephalon and some speculations on the phylogeny of the amniote telencephalon. Ann New York Acad Sci 167:164–179

Karten HJ (1991) Homology and the evolutionary origins of the "neocortex". Brain Behav Evol 38:264–272

Karten HJ (1997) Evolutionary developmental biology meets the brain: the origins of mammalian neocortex. Proc Natl Acad Sci U S A 94:2800–28004

Karten HJ (2013) Neocortical evolution: neuronal circuits arise independently of lamination. Curr Biol 23:R12–R15

Kielan-Jaworowska Z, Cifelli R, Luo ZX (2004) Mammals from the Age of Dinosaurs. Columbia University Press, New York

King SL, McGregor PK (2016) Vocal matching: the what, the why and the how. Biol Lett 12:20160666

Kleinfeld D, Deschênes M, Ulanovsky N (2016) Whisking, sniffing, and the hippocampal θ-Rhythm: a tale of two oscillators. PLoS Biol 14: e1002385

Konishi M (2004) The role of auditory feedback in birdsong. Ann N Y Acad Sci 1016:463–475

Langmore NE (1998) Functions of duet and solo songs of female birds. Trends Ecol Evol 13:136–140

Lipkind D, Marcus GF, Bemis DK, Sasahara K, Jacoby N, Takahasi M, Suzuki K, Feher O, Ravbar P, Okanoya K, Tchernichovski O (2013) Stepwise acquisition of vocal combinatorial capacity in songbirds and human infants. Nature 498:104–108

Liu WC, Wada K, Jarvis ED, Nottebohm F (2013) Rudimentary substrates for vocal learning in a suboscine. Nat Commun 4:2082

Luo ZX (2007) Transformation and diversification in early mammal evolution. Nature. 450:1011–1019

Luo ZX, Ruf I, Schultz JA, Martin T (2011) Fossil evidence on evolution of inner ear cochlea in Jurassic mammals. Proc Biol Sci 278:28–34

Luzzati F (2015) A hypothesis for the evolution of the upper layers of the neocortex through co-option of the olfactory cortex developmental program. Front Neurosci 9:162

Luzzati F, Bonfanti L, Fasolo A, Peretto P (2009) DCX and PSA-NCAM expression identifies a population of neurons preferentially distributed in associative areas of different pallial derivatives and vertebrate species. Cereb Cortex 19:1028–1041

Lynch G (1986) Synapses, Circuits, and the Beginnings of Memory. MIT Press, Cambridge

Markowitz JE, Ivie E, Kligler L, Gardner TJ (2013) Long-range order in canary song. PLoS Comput Biol 9:e1003052

Marler P (1990a) Innate learning preferences: signals for communication. Dev Psychobiol 23:557–568

Marler P (1990b) Song learning: the interface between behaviour and neuroethology. Philos Trans R Soc Lond B Biol Sci 329:109–114

Medina L, Abellán A (2009) Development and evolution of the pallium. Semin Cell Dev Biol 20:698–711

Ming GL, Song H (2011) Adult neurogenesis in the mammalian brain: significant answers and significant questions. Neuron 70:687–702

Molnár Z (2011) Evolution of cerebral cortical development. Brain Behav Evol 78:94–107

Montiel JF, Aboitiz F (2015) Pallial patterning and the origin of the isocortex. Front Neurosci 9:377

Montiel JF, Vasistha NA, Garcia-Moreno F, Molnár Z (2016) From sauropsids to mammals and back: new approaches to comparative cortical development. J Comp Neurol 524:630–645

Moser EI, Kropff E, Moser MB (2008) Place cells, grid cells, and the brain's spatial representation system. Annu Rev Neurosci 31:69–89

Nagel T (1974) What is it like to be a bat? Philos Rev 83:435–450

Niimura Y (2009) On the origin and evolution of vertebrate olfactory receptor genes: comparative genome analysis among 23 chordate species. Genome Biol Evol 1:34–44

Nomura T, Gotoh H, Ono K (2013) Changes in the regulation of cortical neurogenesis contribute to encephalization during amniote brain evolution. Nat Commun 4:2206

Nomura T, Ohtaka-Maruyama C, Yamashita W, Wakamatsu Y, Murakami Y, Calegari F, Suzuki K, Gotoh H, Ono K (2016) The evolution of basal progenitors in the developing non-mammalian brain. Development 143:66–74

Northcutt RG (2003) The Use and abuse of developmental data. Behav Brain Sci 26:565–566

Nottebohm F (1970) Ontogeny of bird song. Science 167:950–956

Nottebohm F (1989) From bird song to neurogenesis. Sci Am 2:74–79

Nottebohm F (2004) The road we travelled: discovery, choreography, and significance of brain replaceable neurons. Ann N Y Acad Sci 1016:628–658

Nottebohm F (2005) The neural basis of birdsong. PLoS Biol 3:e164

Nottebohm F, Liu WC (2010) The origins of vocal learning: New sounds, new circuits, new cells. Brain Lang 115:3–17

Odom KJ, Hall ML, Riebel K, Omland KE, Langmore NE (2014) Female song is widespread and ancestral in songbirds. Nat Commun 5:3379

O'Keefe J (1979) A review of the hippocampal place cells. Prog Neurobiol 13:419–439

O'Keefe J (1990) A computational theory of the hippocampal cognitive map. Prog Brain Res 83:301–312

O'Keefe J, Dostrovsky J (1971) The hippocampus as a spatial map. Preliminary evidence from unit activity in the freely-moving rat. Brain Res 34:171–175

Penn DC, Povinelli DJ (2007) Causal cognition in human and nonhuman animals: a comparative, critical review. Annu Rev Psychol 58:97–118

Pepperberg I (2008) Alex & Me. How a Scientist and a Parrot discovered a Hidden World of Intelligence – and Formed a Deep Bond in the Process. Harper Collins, New York

Petkov CI, Jarvis ED (2012) Birds, primates, and spoken language origins: behavioral phenotypes and neurobiological substrates. Front Evol Neurosci 4:12

Petkov CI, Jarvis ED (2014) The basal ganglia within a cognitive system in birds and mammals. Behav Brain Sci 37:568–569; discussion 577–604

Pfenning AR, Hara E, Whitney O, Rivas MV, Wang R, Roulhac PL, Howard JT, Wirthlin M, Lovell PV, Ganapathy G, Mouncastle J, Moseley MA, Thompson JW, Soderblom EJ, Iriki A, Kato M, Gilbert MT, Zhang G, Bakken T, Bongaarts A, Bernard A, Lein E, Mello CV, Hartemink AJ, Jarvis ED (2014) Convergent transcriptional specializations in the brains of humans and song-learning birds. Science 346:1256846

Pickrell J (2014) Flying Dinosaurs. How Fearsome Reptiles Became Birds. NewSouth Publishers, Sydney

Povinelli DJ (2000) Folk Physics for Apes. Oxford University Press, Oxford

Prothero DR (2006) After the Dinosaurs. The Age of Mammals. Indiana Press, Bloomington

Puelles L, Rubenstein JL (2003) Forebrain gene expression domains and the evolving prosomeric model. Trends Neurosci 26:469–476

Puelles L, Kuwana E, Puelles E, Rubenstein JL (1999) Comparison of the mammalian and avian telencephalon from the perspective of gene expression data. Eur J Morphol 37:139–150

Puelles L, Kuwana E, Puelles E, Bulfone A, Shimamura K, Keleher J, Smiga S, Rubenstein JL(2000) Pallial and subpallial derivatives in the embryonic chick and mouse telencephalon, traced by the expression of the genes Dlx-2, Emx-1, Nkx-2.1, Pax-6, and Tbr-1. J Comp Neurol 424:409–438

Ramón y Cajal Y, Sánchez D (1915) Contribución al conocimiento de los centros nerviosos de los insectos. Parte I Retina y centros ópticos. Trab Lab Invest Biol Univ Madrid 13:1–168

Reiner A, Perkel DJ, Bruce LL, Butler AB, Csillag A, Kuenzel W, Medina L, Paxinos G, Shimizu T, Striedter G, Wild M, Ball GF, Durand S, Gütürkün O, Lee DW, Mello CV, Powers A, White SA, Hough G, Kubikova L, Smulders TV, Wada K, Dugas-Ford J, Husband S, Yamamoto K, Yu J, Siang C, Jarvis ED (2004a) The avian brain nomenclature forum:

terminology for a new century in comparative neuroanatomy. J Comp Neurol 473:E1–E6

Reiner A, Perkel DJ, Mello CV, Jarvis ED (2004b) Songbirds and the revised avian brain nomenclature. Ann N Y Acad Sci 1016:77–108

Rowe T (1996) Coevolution of the mammalian middle ear and neocortex. Science 273:651–654

Rowe TB, Shepherd GM (2016) Role of ortho-retronasal olfaction in mammalian cortical evolution. J Comp Neurol 524:471–495

Rowe TB, Macrini TE, Luo ZX (2011) Fossil evidence on origin of the mammalian brain. Science 332:955–957

Rubenstein JL (2011) Development of the cerebral cortex: implications for neurodevelopmental disorders. J Child Psychol Psychiatr 52:339–355

Rubenstein JL, Martinez S, Shimamura K, Puelles L (1994) The embryonic vertebrate forebrain: the prosomeric model. Science 266:578–580

Sakamoto M, Benton MJ, Venditti C (2016) Dinosaurs in decline tens of millions of years before their final extinction. Proc Natl Acad Sci U S A 113:5036–5040

Sanes JR, Zipursky SL (2010) Design principles of insect and vertebrate visual systems. Neuron 66:15–36

Savage C (2007) Crows. Encounters with the Wise Guys of the Avian World. Douglas & McIntyre, London

Schaal B, Coureaud G, Doucet S, Delaunay-El Allam M, Moncomble AS, Montigny D, Patris B, Holley A (2009) Mammary olfactory signalisation in females and odor processing in neonates: ways evolved by rabbits and humans. Behav Brain Res 200:346–358

Schmidt MF, Martin Wild J (2014) The respiratory-vocal system of songbirds: anatomy, physiology, and neural control. Prog Brain Res 212:297–335

Shannon RV (2005) Speech and music have different requirements for spectral resolution. Int Rev Neurobiol 70:121–134

Shepherd GM (2011) The microcircuit concept applied to cortical evolution: from three-layer to six-layer cortex. Front Neuroanat 5:30

Smith-Fernández A, Pieau C, Repérant J, Boncinelli E, Wassef M (1998) Expression of the Emx-1 and Dlx-1 homeobox genes define three molecularly distinct domains in the telencephalon of mouse, chick, turtle and frog embryos: implications for the evolution of telencephalic subdivisions in amniotes. Development 125:2099–2111

Striedter GF (1997) The telencephalon of tetrapods in evolution. Brain Behav Evol 49:179–213

Striedter GF (2005) Principles of Brain Evolution. Sinauer Associates, Sunderland

Striedter GF, Charvet CJ (2009) Telencephalon enlargement by the convergent evolution of expanded subventricular zones. Biol Lett 5:134–137

Striedter GF, Northcutt RG (1991) Biological hierarchies and the concept of homology. Brain Behav Evol 38:177–189

Suzuki IK, Kawasaki T, Gojobori T, Hirata T (2012) The temporal sequence of the mammalian neocortical neurogenetic program drives mediolateral pattern in the chick pallium. Dev Cell 22:863–870

Suzuki TN, Wheatcroft D, Griesser M (2016) Experimental evidence for compositional syntax in bird calls. Nat Commun 7:10986

Taylor J (2009) *Not a Chimp*: The Hunt to Find the Genes that Make us Human. Oxford University Press, Oxford

Taylor AH, Hunt GR, Medina FS, Gray RD (2009) Do new caledonian crows solve physical problems through causal reasoning? Proc Biol Sci 276:247–254

Tebbich S, Seed AM, Emery NJ, Clayton NS (2007) Non-tool-using rooks, Corvus frugilegus, solve the trap-tube problem. Anim Cogn 10:225–231

Teissier A, Griveau A, Vigier L, Piolot T, Borello U, Pierani A (2010) A novel transient glutamatergic population migrating from the pallial-subpallial boundary contributes to neocortical development. J Neurosci 30:10563–10574

Tissir F, Goffinet AM (2003) Reelin and brain development. Nat Rev Neurosci 4:496–505

Troscianko J, Rutz C (2015) Activity profiles and hook-tool use of New Caledonian crows recorded by bird-borne video cameras. Biol Lett 11:20150777

Vanderwolf CH (2001) The hippocampus as an olfacto-motor mechanism: were the classical anatomists right after all? Behav Brain Res 127:25–47

Wang Y, Brzozowska-Prechtl A, Karten HJ (2010) Laminar and columnar auditory cortex in avian brain. Proc Natl Acad Sci U S A 107:12676–12681

Weir AA, Kacelnik A (2006) A New Caledonian crow (Corvus moneduloides) creatively re-designs tools by bending or unbending aluminium strips. Anim Cogn 9:317–334

Weir AA, Chappell J, Kacelnik A (2002) Shaping of hooks in New Caledonian crows. Science 297:981

Whitney O, Pfenning AR, Howard JT, Blatti CA, Liu F, Ward JM, Wang R, Audet JN, Kellis M, Mukherjee S, Sinha S, Hartemink AJ, West AE, Jarvis ED (2014) Core and region-enriched networks of behaviorally regulated genes and the singing genome. Science 346:1256780

10

Talking Heads

We saw that songbirds and other vocal learning birds can serve as very interesting models for the acquisition of human speech. However, because not only their brains but also their peripheral phonatory systems have different evolutionary histories from those of humans, they provide only limited insight into the specific origin of speech. For this, we have to turn our attention to vocalizing mammals that at least share a cerebral cortex, homologous brainstem nuclei and vocal tract, vocal folds and larynx, as well as to human infants and children acquiring speech. Non-human primate calls, like those of other mammals, convey information to their conspecifics about the individual's social status, sex, age and identity. The transition from such stereotyped vocalizations to vocal learning and then to speech has become a major issue in the study of language evolution. In this chapter I will argue that speech is a complex behavior, in which historical continuity between monkeys, apes and humans can be found in the peripheral organs involved in speech, in their neural control, and in the cerebral networks involved in speech processing. The gradual evolution of these systems was a requisite for the acquisition of the phonological loop, and the origin of modern speech.

© The Author(s) 2017
F. Aboitiz, *A Brain for Speech*,
DOI 10.1057/978-1-137-54060-7_10

Vocal Beasts

There are well-known examples of domestic dogs and other animals that can learn, often quickly, the meanings of many words and even phrases uttered by humans (Kaminski et al. 2004; Andics et al. 2016). However, the evolution of vocal learning is driven by modifications of the motor rather than the auditory system, which is more conserved across species, and relies on general-purpose mechanisms (see Chapter 9) (Feenders et al. 2008). While vocal learning is present in only a few species, the capacity for auditory learning is widespread in vertebrates.

Some species display voluntary use of vocalizations depending on the context, as some animals can learn to vocalize only in specific circumstances, and can modulate the intensity or duration of their calls in different settings. However, these vocalizations remain stereotyped in structure. This is seen in apes and monkeys, domestic animals and many other species (Hauser 1996). What is more interesting to us is the capacity to learn new sounds by imitation and to develop novel strings with different combinations of sounds. Although we seem to be alone among primates in our vocal abilities, other mammalian species have shown a sometimes impressive capacity to imitate, not only sounds made by conspecifics, but also physical phenomena and even the human voice. Vocal imitation is observed in seals, toothed whales and elephants, while the ability to generate new sequences of sounds generating a rudimentary syntax is much less common. Furthermore, the capacity for vocal learning is not strictly a gift given to some animals, but there are different levels of vocal learning abilities in different species. Christopher Petkov and Erich Jarvis categorized species on the basis of their vocal learning capacities, where animals like monkeys display a limited learning capacity, songbirds and parrots are relatively complex vocal learners and our species apparently exceeds all the others in the voluntary and fine control of phonation (Petkov and Jarvis 2012).

Echolocating species like bats and cetaceans are good vocal learners. These animals have developed several anatomical and biochemical hearing and vocal specializations that allow them to hear and emit a much wider range of sound frequencies (into the ultrasonic range) than can humans. Particularly, the protein prestin, which is expressed in external ciliary cells of the cochlea (they are only found in mammals), provides motility to the receptors, dramatically increasing their sensitivity. Notably, convergent mutations have been reported in this protein in echolocating bats and cetaceans that enhance their ultrasonic hearing range (Caspermeyer 2014). Furthermore, work in Nobuo Suga's laboratory has shown that the auditory cortex of some bats is proportionally quite large, and is subdivided into several highly specialized areas (Suga 1989). There is an area that processes frequency modulated signals (called FM-FM area), with neurons sensitive to the time delay of the echo, providing information about the distance to a target. Neurons in another area (called CF-CF area) process a constant frequency (around 30 Hz, the frequency of the echolocating call) and its harmonics, which is used to calculate changes in echo frequencies produced by the bat's velocity relative to a target (the Doppler effect). A third component is the DSCF area, which represents the frequency range of maximal sensitivity (an acoustic fovea), matching the echo call frequency. Bats in enclosed environments rely more on the FM signal, while bats in open environments use the CF signal more. It is not yet clear whether these auditory specializations are restricted to echolocation or if they also participate in vocal learning mechanisms. If this is so, it would be an exception to Erich Jarvis' claim that the evolution of vocal learning is mainly dependent on motor adaptations. Finally, there is significant asymmetry in the acoustic properties of the FM-FM and the DSCF areas of the bat auditory cortex, with the left hemisphere more sensitive to echo time delays, while the right specializes in frequency analysis (Washington and Tillinghast 2015).

Bats not only use their calls for echolocation but also sing intensely when landing on their roosts (and sometimes also when flying), producing songs that are sometimes as complex as those of highly specialized songbirds (Bradbury and Emmons 1974). As with bird songs, there is a tremendous variety of "bat songs" across species (Knörnschild et al. 2010; Morell 2014), some of which are simple and involve the rhythmical repetition of one variable note, while the songs of other species are hierarchically organized but also highly flexible, with structures that change according to circumstances, such as the appearance of males nearby. In species of the genus *Pipistrellus*, songs are formed by a sequence of phrases that signal the animal's species, the individual's identity, group information, and a landing site signal.

Like many songbirds, male bats are usually the ones that sing, both to signal territory and to attract mates. Some bats use the same song for both functions, but others have different songs for territorial disputes and courtship. Furthermore, bats do not sing when they are alone, and do not sing only in the mating season. Bats learn their songs by babbling and imitating, like songbirds and humans. The learning process may extend to the echolocation call, as young horseshoe bats adapt their echolocating call to that of their mother, and in many species pup calls have individual signatures that distinguish them from those of other pups in the colony.

Harbor seals, belugas and elephants have been reported to imitate human speech, while some whales display very long complex songs that change with time in synchrony with other members of the group (Ridgway et al. 2012; Stoeger et al. 2012; Reichmuth and Casey 2014; Janik 2009). As with bats, whale songs have repetitions of elements that can be organized into syntax-like structures similar to those of songbirds (Janik 2013, 2014; Janik and Sayigh 2013, King and Janik 2013). The nasal cavities of dolphins are rather complex, with two phonic lips and two air sacs that enable them to control the vibration of air before it comes out through the blowhole at the top of the head. The emitted sound is transmitted and radiated through the melon, a fatty deposit in the front of the head. Dolphins use vocalizations ("nasalizations" would apply better in this case) to localize prey and to explore their surroundings. As mentioned by Stephanie King and Peter McGregor cetacean vocalizations facilitate social bonding and group synchrony, which makes it perhaps more comparable to early human communication than birdsong (see Chapters 8 and 9) (King and McGregor 2016). Vincent Janik and collaborators observed that each individual dolphin produces a learned but individually specific signature call that allows them to recognize one other. However, this signature call is not categorically different from other calls shared by all members of the group, but is rather a variant of these. Recent research suggests that dolphin mothers start singing to their babies before they are born, apparently teaching them their signature whistle, a process that continues over the first weeks after birth (King et al. 2016)[1]. The signature call of

---

[1] http://www.livescience.com/55699-mother-dolphins-teach-babies-signature-whistle.html

dolphins serves to maintain group cohesion, as individuals separated from the group emit their signature whistles while the others respond with their own signatures until they come together again.

Although mice have traditionally been ignored in vocal learning studies, more recent studies by Julia Fischer and by Erich Jarvis and Gustavo Arriaga have focused on mouse ultrasonic vocalizations, which are remarkably song-like and produced by males to attract females (Fischer and Hammerschmidt 2011; Hammerschmidt et al. 2009, 2012; Arriaga et al. 2012; Arriaga and Jarvis 2013). Adult male mice produce sonic vocalizations by vibrating their vocal folds, and ultrasonic vocalizations by expiring air while maintaining the vocal folds tight and forcing the air to pass through a rigid slit. Male mice use and modulate ultrasonic vocalizations in different social contexts such as in the presence of other males. Deafening mice early in life affects the syllabic structure of the animal's calls, which suggests that mice song learning is partly a sensory-driven learning process, although it is not yet clear whether the songs develop through a babbling-like stage as in humans and songbirds. A laryngeal motor cortex-like region was recently described by Arriaga and Jarvis, which is active during vocalizations and makes a direct although faint projection into the nucleus ambiguus (Arriaga et al. 2012).

Noisy Primates

Although our primate cousins are highly vocal species, little vocal learning capacity has been observed in them, which is another argument for how unusual we are in our evolutionary family. But this is not to say that non-human primates have absolutely no voluntary control over their vocalizations. For example, the Indri, a social lemur from Madagascar, develops long cries that are synchronized along the group, but the song varies in structure according to social condition (Gamba et al. 2016). Monkeys and apes can choose when and what to vocalize depending on contextual cues, and there is evidence of voluntary control over the upper vocal tract, including lip musculature (Hage et al. 2013, 2016). Early studies showed that socially isolated and deafened monkeys display somewhat abnormal vocalizations (Newman and Symmes 1974; Talmage-Riggs et al. 1972; Egnor et al. 2006). South American tamarin monkeys are highly loquacious, and there are call differences among subspecies. Some individuals develop mixed calls, but these could be hybrids among subspecies (Bradley and McClung 2015). There are some indications that marmosets modify their calls and vocalizations depending on the presence of other individuals, but these consist of modulations of pitch and other acoustic features, and no evidence has yet been found of learning new vocalizations (Miller et al. 2003; Bezerra et al. 2009; Seyfarth and Cheney 2010). Nonetheless, Asif Ghazanfar and associates recently reported that the development of marmoset vocalizations, as in songbirds and humans, proceeds from an initial stage of highly variable sounds that become clustered in acoustical properties as individuals mature (Takahashi et al. 2015). But perhaps more interestingly, parental vocal feedback is a key variable in the maturation of vocalizations of marmosets, songbirds and humans, which indicates a common substrate for early vocal learning across species.

There is some evidence of vocal plasticity in old world monkeys, possibly because they have been heavily studied (Hage and Nieder 2013). The calls of rhesus monkeys display troop differences, and cross-fostered individuals develop the typical call of the group they belong to (Owren et al. 1993). Studies in the late twentieth century showed that these animals can be trained to modulate the amplitude and duration of their calls to match them with playbacks presented to them, but again these modifications are only in the length and strength of the expiration phase (Hauser 1996, 1998). Likewise, guenon monkeys have been observed to use specific combinations of calls in specific circumstances, like initiating group movements (Candiotti et al. 2012; Arnold and Zuberbühler 2012). In this context, David Reby and colleagues described a noticeable parallel between human and ape vocalizations, reporting that both species voluntarily modulate the fundamental frequency of speech, increasing or decreasing pitch in different contexts, as when one talks to a man, woman, or infant, or when tries to impose authority (Pisanski et al. 2016). These basic control mechanisms are shared with other mammals, especially primates, and are proposed to represent a starting point from which voluntary vocal control evolved in our species.

Some primates are characterized by their long complex calls that can be heard from very far away. One of these is the howler monkey in South America, which has been little studied, and the others are the gibbon and siamang of South Asia. Gibbons are relatively close to us, as we both belong to the hominoidea superfamily of Old World monkeys, commonly called "apes", which separated from other monkeys about 18–20 million years ago. Gibbons are arguably the most elaborate vocalizers among non-human primates (Clarke et al. 2006). They live in stable couples and both sexes sing to defend their territory, similar to tropical songbirds discussed in the previous chapter. Like some song-birds, male and female gibbons usually sing in coordinated duets where the female leads (Geissmann 2002). However, gibbon songs are highly stereotyped and show little geographic variation, and hybrids between two species develop a mixed call between the two parent species (Brockelman and Schilling 1984). Furthermore, phylogenetic trees have been established based on the divergence of song patterns of different species that match genetically based trees (Thinh et al. 2011). There is a role for learning in the gibbon song, which has mainly to do with coordinating vocalizations while making the male and female duet, although some evidence suggests that there is a maternal role in the maturation of the song's structure (Koda et al. 2013). It has been reported that gibbons can also modulate and change the organization of their songs in the presence of predators, but this needs to be con-firmed. In summary, our primate lineage has been characterized by a limited vocal learning capacity. Even our closest relatives, chimpanzees and bonobos, have demonstrated little ability to imitate and combine vocal utterances, aside from the voluntary control of lip movements and facial gestures.

As they have limited respiratory control, many non-human primates, especially highly vocal ones like gibbons, some apes and howler mon-keys, have developed laryngeal sacs, which are extensions of the vocal tract cavity principally in the laryngeal region (Hewitt et al. 2002). One interpretation is that the sacs serve as a reservoir of air that allows for producing longer and more rapid calls, or to provide an additional sound source without the risk of hyperventilating. There is some support for this hypothesis as vocalizations of primates with air sacs are free from body size constraints that apply to primates without air sacs, which limit respiratory frequency and call duration. According to another view, air sacs increase resonance to amplify vocalizations, or to provide the impression of being produced by a larger individual. It has been claimed that there is evidence of vestigial air sacs in humans, but this is controversial. As well, speech may not be as energy demanding as the calls of gibbons and other species. We will see below that early humans took another route to generate complex vocalizations, based on restructuring the laryngeal cavity.

Chimpanzees have been reported to elicit referential food calls that provide information about food quality to the group (Lalamn and Boesch 2013). The acoustic structure of such food calls was reported to adapt to that of a different group when an outsider joined it (Watson et al. 2015). However, these findings have been contested on the grounds that these calls and their modulation were likely driven by emotional arousal rather than directly signaling food quality (Wheeler and Fischer 2012; Fischer et al. 2015). Evidence for vocal modulation has also come from gorillas. After an extensive analysis of recorded videos, Markus Perlman and Nat Clark recently concluded that Koko, the gorilla raised by Francine Patterson (see Chapter 1), was able to modulate breathing-related vocalizations with tongue and lip movements (Perlman and Clark 2015). Furthermore, this was done in the context of manual actions and gestures. More recently, a study reported food-associated "songs" of gorillas, but it is still unclear whether these are actually learned (Luef et al. 2016). Finally, orangutans have been reported to imitate the human voice[2] (Lameira et al. 2015, 2016; Wich et al. 2009). Although not our immediate ancestor like the chimpanzee, this species can provide a useful model for acquisition of an open-ended vocal repertoire (see below).

---

[2] https://www.youtube.com/watch?v=0zr2eunVDxw

Neanderthal Throats

To begin with the ancestry of human speech, it is important first to depict the structure of our phonatory organs. These can be divided into a deep component that generates the vocal sounds, consisting of the larynx and the vocal folds. Vocal folds are two membranous infoldings that make up a vibrating groove in the upper larynx that generates a variety of acoustically complex sounds, depending on their vibration rate. The folds are controlled by the nucleus ambiguus of the brainstem, via the vagus nerve. In turn, the nucleus ambiguus receives input from the vocal motor cortex, providing voluntary control of the vocal folds. Some authors have equated cortical control of vocal fold motoneurons to the capacity for vocal learning, but we will see that there is more to tell about this. The sound generated by the vocal folds resonates in the oral cavity until it is expelled and radiates outwardly at the lips. The other component of the speech apparatus is provided by superior or supralaryngeal organs including the oral and nasal cavities, which provide a sound filter that modulates the air column; and the tongue and the lips, which control airflow and are critical for the production of most consonants.

In the late 1960s and early 1970s, Philip Lieberman observed that the human vocal tract was longer, and the larynx in a lower position than in other primates (Fig. 10.1) (Lieberman 1968, 1979, 1984). This results in an additional cavity, the pharyngeal, located between the larynx and the oral cavity that increases resonance in the air column. According to Lieberman, this makes it possible to produce a diversity of vowel types, but has the drawback of increasing the risk of choking while ingesting food, as the larynx remains open while swallowing. This impedes us from breathing and swallowing at the same time. Interestingly, human babies are born with a high-positioned larynx, which enables them to swallow and breathe simultaneously. With age, the position of the larynx descends to its adult position. Thus, our larynx diverges from that of other primates, but in the infant it is similar to that of non-human primates, presumably to avoid choking in the young. This apparently contrasts with the widespread notion, championed by the late Stephen Jay Gould, and mentioned earlier in this book, that we are juvenilized

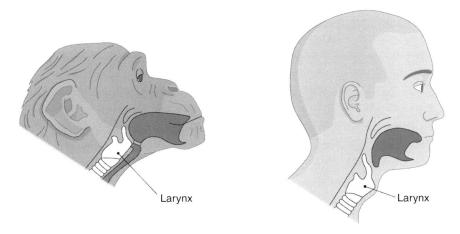

Fig. 10.1   The position of the larynx in the chimpanzee and in the human

apes that have retained infant-like features into adulthood (see also Chapter 11). Nonetheless, another possible explanation is that the shortening of the human face and jaw, a juvenilized character as we discussed above, forced the movement of the larynx in order to maintain the length of the vocal tract to permit adequate breathing and swallowing (Coquerelle et al. 2013).

Lieberman and his collaborators went further in their analyses into the structure and position of the hyoid bone in Neanderthals. Lieberman concluded that the larynx of this species was in an upward position relative to that of humans; hence they were limited in the vowels they could produce. This sparked intense debate about Neanderthal speech, which was not really evidence-based as the vocal tract and larynx are largely formed of soft tissue that does not fossilize, and inferring the position of the hyoid bone under these conditions is very questionable. Furthermore, biomechanical analysis of the Neanderthal hyoid suggests that Neanderthals were able to pronounce vowels as well as we do (D'Anastasio et al. 2013). Finally, the descended larynx is not uniquely human, being present at least in deer. Tecumseh Fitch noted that while at rest, the deer larynx has a position similar to that of the human larynx, while when deer roar the larynx descends, even reaching the sternum (Fitch and Reby 2001). According to Fitch, the descended larynx contributes to decreasing resonant frequencies and exaggerates perceived body size, a feature of sexual selection. This is because larger animals with larger vocal tracts tend to generate lower frequency vocalizations than smaller animals, all else being equal. This interpretation has also been invoked for the lower voice tone acquired by men compared to women after puberty. In any case, whatever the reason for the origin of the descent of the larynx and its status in Neanderthals, our ancestors may have taken advantage of it to produce a more diverse vocal repertoire.

Read My Lips

"Read my lips: no new taxes", said US presidential candidate George H. W. Bush in 1988, a promise that although probably key to his winning the election, remained unfulfilled during his term, and was an important reason for his losing the next election to Bill Clinton. The deaf and some hearing people are usually able to understand speech just by looking at lip movements. In fact, speech is a lot more than just the larynx and vocal folds. The word "language" itself derives from the Latin "lingua", which means "tongue". Most research on vocal communication in primates and other mammals has focused on the larynx and vocal folds, and dismissed the crucial role of the upper vocal tract. While we have gathered some evidence on the neural processes involved in controlling the larynx, comparative studies on the generation of lip and tongue movements are only beginning. The human tongue and lips are highly movable and allow us to modulate the air column to produce different types of sounds that are essential for speech and for phoneme production. The lips are innervated by the facial nerve and nucleus, like other muscles for facial expression, and the tongue is innervated by the hypoglossal cranial nucleus. Both structures are under voluntary control in monkeys and in humans, although non-human primates seem to have finer control of lip than of tongue movements. A recent study showed that the hypoglossal nucleus in monkeys is directly innervated by the motor and premotor cortices in addition to other regions like the insula and the anterior cingulate gyrus (Morecraft et al. 2014).

While the vocal folds are mostly involved in vowel production, the lips and tongue participate in both vowel and consonant production. Furthermore, consonants are made largely by rapid movements of the tongue and lips, most of them not requiring vocal fold vibrations to be produced. Consonants outnumber vowels in practically all human languages, there being overall some 600 while there are only about 200 vowels in all known languages. In this line, Adriano Lameira and collaborators called attention to supralaryngeal control in the evolution of speech, arguing that while the separation between vocal learners and vocal non-learners is rather clear in primates, a continuum can be observed between humans and other primates in the control of voiceless calls involving the lips, tongue and jaws (Lameira et al. 2014). There are a variety of such calls in apes, including "clicks", "smacks" (I referred to lip smacks in Chapter 8), "kissing sounds" and "whistles". In contrast to their voiced calls, the voiceless calls of apes are apparently influenced by social learning and fine-tuned with experience. There is also evidence of imitation of voiceless calls like lip vibrations by chimpanzees. Lameira and collaborators mention the case of Viki, the vocally trained chimp, who learned to say words like "mama", "papa" or "cup", by using only the supralaryngeal tract (see Chapter 1) (Hayes and Hayes 1951). But orangutans seem to be vocally more gifted than chimps, being able to mimic not only the human voice (see above), but also voiceless sounds like whistles (Lameira et al. 2013, 2015). Dialect-like vocal variability has been observed in different orangutan populations, some using "raspberry calls" during nest building, while others use lip smacks, and still others are silent for the same behavior; although it still needs to be shown that these differences are the product of learning. Lameira and colleagues claim that a first stage in the evolution of speech was represented by control of the supralaryngeal tract, which was then followed by voluntary modulation of the vocal folds (Lameira et al. 2014). The tongue and lips are also fundamental for the production of vowels. The vertical and horizontal positions of the tongue largely determine the type of vowel that is being produced, as their combinations define two axes that determine what is called the vowel diagram: closed vs. open vowels (e.g. /i/and /u/vs. /ae/, respectively), and front vs. back vowels (e.g. /i/ and /ae/vs. /u/and /o/). Thus, the production of both vowels and consonants depends perhaps more on the upper rather than the lower vocal tract.

Finally, in a very recent study, Tecumseh Fitch and Asif Ghazanfar analyzed with X-ray videos the jaw movements of a macaque while it ate, drank, yawned, vocalized and made lip smacking movements, and compared these movements with the oral movements involved in human speech. Notably, they observed that all oral movements required for speech are within the macaque's repertoire. Furthermore, the researchers were even able to generate a computerized simulation of the monkey's vocal tract, uttering sentences like "will you marry me?". The result was that the simulation was perfectly able to generate these movements, producing an acoustically intelligible sentence. To the authors, this implies that the vocal tract of macaques is already equipped for speech. The difference, the authors say, must rely on the neuronal control of these movements (Price 2016). An additional study reported that monkeys emit vowel-like sounds in their daily behavior (Boë et al. 2017). Despite this evidence, it is yet possible that further modifications of the upper vocal tract, like lowering the larynx, may have contributed to optimize vocal production in our recent ancestors.

The Origin of Rhythm

The rhythmic movements of voice and lips are an essential component of speech, and are marked by the duration of vowels, and the variability of consonant intervals. Speech rhythm is determined by changes in intensity, duration and pitch, in a complex hierarchy that ranges from phonemes to higher order linguistic units, and is considered to be fundamental in infant language learning. Notably, the rhythmic characteristics of a language determine some of its fundamental grammatical structure, as in object-verb languages and verb-object languages. Furthermore, speech rhythm is perceived multimodally, using both acoustic and visual cues, from observing lip movements (Peña et al. 2016). In humans, the perception of rhythm has been associated with activation of dorsal premotor areas, the basal ganglia, and auditory regions, showing some overlap with language networks, particularly as auditory-prefrontal connectivity is apparently mediated by the parietal lobe.

The analysis of lip movements of monkeys has provided a new and interesting perspective that may provide a plausible scenario of speech origins. Tecumseh Fitch, Asif Ghazanfar and collaborators found that lip smacking movements in monkeys are dissociated from throat movements and have a frequency of close to 5 cycles per second, which is similar to the frequency of lip movements during human speech and much more rapid than chewing (Ghazanfar et al. 2012). Like human lip movements, monkey lip smacking gradually changes during development from variable and slow movements to rapid and stereotyped movements (Morrill et al. 2012). Jaw, lip, tongue and hyoid bone (to which laryngeal muscles are attached) movements are coordinated during speech and chewing. However, these movements are more closely tuned for chewing than either speech or lip-smacking. David Poeppel and collaborators have shown that during speech perception, the human auditory cortex displays oscillations at about the same frequency as lip smacking movements (see Chapter 2) (Chait et al. 2015; Ding et al. 2016).

Our faces also move concomitantly with speech, making both speech-induced and indirectly related emotional expressions that are processed multimodally in the ventrolateral prefrontal cortex (including Broca's area). In human speech, facial movements (particularly those of the mouth) are finely coordinated at specific rhythms with the emitted sounds. However, monkey vocalizations dissociate from gestures, and rhythmicity takes place only in the acoustic dimension. Ghazanfar and collaborators proposed that vocalizations in the human lineage synchronized with lip-smacking, which in a first instance would have involved babbling-like expressions that evolved into speech-like behavior (Ghazanfar and Takahashi 2014a, b). Notably, primates use lip-smacking as an approaching signal or during close contact like grooming and face-to-face interactions. An instance of lip-vocal synchronization has been observed in male geladas (a large baboon-like monkey), which make a sound called a "wobble" to approach females. In another study, Morgan Gustison and colleagues found that as in human speech, gelada vocalizations include shorter segments as the vocalization they make is more complex, which follows Menzerath's law that longer words tend to have shorter syllables (Gustison et al. 2016). This may make the gelada a particularly good model to study speech origins.

Since rhythmic behavior may be a key element in the evolution of speech, researchers have investigated whether non-human animals are able to perceive rhythmic sequences. Monkeys and apes display very limited capacity for rhythmic beat, while vocal learning birds like parrots can synchronize to rhythmic beats, but not as well as humans do. Considering this evidence, Anhiruddh Patel proposed the "vocal learning and rhythmic synchronization hypothesis" that vocal learning is required for the capacity to synchronize motor outputs with a musical beat (Patel et al. 2009). Likewise, Ghazanfar proposed that the perception of rhythm partly depends on synchronization between the upper and lower vocal tracts (Ghazanfar and Takahashi 2014a, b). However, Peter Cook and colleagues, and others more recently showed that the California sea lion, whose vocal plasticity is supposedly below that of typical vocal learners, is able to follow acoustic rhythms by head bobbing (Cook et al. 2013, Ravignani et al. 2016, Rouse et al. 2016). More studies are needed to determine the vocal imitation capacities of these animals. In any case, if the ability to learn rhythmic beats is only present in vocal learning animals, then the capacity to perform rhythmic movements with the hands, as in tool making, might be a derivative of vocal learning capacity rather than the other way around, hand skills inducing vocal rhythmic capacity, as the gestural theory of language origins may suggest.

Ghazanfar and colleagues also addressed another key aspect of speech, which is the production of conversational vocal exchanges between people, with distinct gaps of silence between each turn (Takahashi et al. 2013, 2015, 2016). The capacity for reciprocal conversation is a universal character of speech, and is seen even in babbling children. Conversations may not have been produced originally to convey meaning, but rather as a bonding mechanism. We saw that gibbons engage in such vocal turn-taking behavior. In addition, Takahashi, Ghazanfar and collaborators have analyzed in more detail the turn-taking behavior of the marmoset monkey, whose vocalizations are more variable than those of gibbons. Marmosets are highly social and cooperative, showing biparental or multiparental care of their young. These monkeys communicate vocally, with few manual gestures, and engage in vocal exchanges where both individuals take turns. Marmoset conversations may take up to 30 minutes, with a turn-taking frequency that is not unlike that of human conversations. Another conversing animal seems to be dolphins, which can match each other's vocalizations in the wild, alternating their respective emissions.

The Melodic Ape

Music is acquired in a similar way as is speech. It is learned quite early in life, as studies suggest that 1- or 2-year-old babies already have a capacity to follow music by vocalizing and moving their limbs. As with speech learning, babies memorize melodies in terms of sequences that are more likely to occur than others, which then generate expectations of the notes that will follow in a given melody (Patel 2008). The brain regions involved in musical perception include the auditory cortex, premotor cortex, intraparietal sulcus, and other emotion-related regions like the anterior insula and the anterior cingulate cortex, the latter also involved in the control of innate vocalizations in both humans and monkeys (Patel 2008). Music has an intricate and recursive structure that has often been compared to that of language. Notably, important researchers in the neuroscience of music like Robert Zatorre and Anhiruddh Patel emphasize that the capacity to store sequences of notes in working memory is critical for learning and anticipating melodies (see Chapter 6) (Patel 2008; Grimault et al. 2009; Peretz and Zatorre 2005; Zatorre 2003; Zatorre and Salimpoor 2013). This is subserved by strong loops connecting frontal and temporal cortices, using both the dorsal (conveying time and sequence information) and ventral auditory pathways (conveying signals like pitch and emotion).

Darwin proposed that speech could have first evolved as primitive melodies that are controlled by the vocal folds rather than the lips and tongue, which seem to be more related to rhythm. This is partly supported by comparative evidence showing that vocal learners are usually melodic, and that melodic-like vocalizations can be found in many species including our relative the gibbon. However, as Timothy Gentner's group recently argued, the acoustically relevant cues of these "songs" may be more speech-like than melodic (see Chapter 9) (Bregman et al. 2016).

Another defender of a musical origin of speech is Tecumseh Fitch, who proposes the existence of a "musical protolanguage", the central aspects of which were prosodic and phonological, and from which a hierarchic syntax-like organization emerged (Fitch 2009, 2010). Fitch argues that as with songbirds this melodic protolanguage characteristically lacked a rhythmic component. However, if we accept that superior vocal tract-based consonants are more related to rhythm, and that these may have been under voluntary control before the control of exhalative vocalizations, it seems more likely that this musical protolanguage contained both melodies and rhythmic components. From this initial condition, vocal communication may have diverged into songs on the one hand, and semantically based speech on the other.

There are some disorders of music perception and production, one of which is called amusia. Studies by Patel have revealed that congenital amusia implies speech impairments, particularly in the capacity to perceive intonation and emotion, and in the capacity to maintain auditory patterns in working memory (Liu et al. 2015). Moreover, Maija Hausen and her collaborators assessed the perception of music and speech prosody in healthy adults, evidencing an association between the two capacities but not with visual perception (Hausen et al. 2013). Another similarity between prosodic and musical processing was reported by Anastasia Glushko and collaborators, who evidenced that the closure positive shift, a specific event-related potential associated with prosodic phrase boundaries, is also observed at the onset of musical phrase boundaries (Glushko et al. 2016). Like prosody, harmony perception in untrained individuals tends to be right-lateralized (rhythm is left-lateralized), although trained musicians use their left hemisphere to process musical information (Springer and Deutsch 1981; Patel 2008). Thus, (proto-)music and (proto-)speech may be separated concomitant with enhancement of a rudimentary level of brain lateralization, music to the right and speech to the left. Subsequently, with the appearance of more complex musical aspects that require syntactic processing in trained musicians, the left hemisphere becomes dominant again.

From Meaning to Grammar

It was probably semantics that separated speech and song. But how did semantics appear? How did social-bonding vocalizations begin to represent events in the world around us? There are examples of semantic vocal communication in mammals like vervet monkeys, baboons and suricates. Some years ago, Robert Seyfarth, Dorothy Cheney and Peter Marler observed that vervet monkeys make different alarm calls when they spot a leopard, eagle or snake, each eliciting distinct escape behaviors (Seyfarth et al. 1980). For example, after an eagle alarm call, animals on the ground run to a bush, while after a snake alarm call they disperse. This selectivity is learned, as vervet infants often use predator alarms in response to harmless species. When they hear false alarms, adults usually look up but do not respond, but when the alarm is correct they repeat it. This provides feedback to the young that permits them to gradually refine their calls (Seyfarth and Cheney 2003a, b). However, alarm calls are triggered by a reflex pattern and are not necessarily goal-directed behavior in which there is a pursued outcome. On the other hand, symbolic reference depends on learned associative relations between different kinds of stimuli, say visual and auditory. According to Steffen Hage and Andreas Nieder, a precursor of semantic associations can be observed in neurons of the monkey ventrolateral prefrontal cortex, where single neurons associate arbitrary visual signs with numerical stimuli that are presented contingently (Diester and Nieder 2007; Hage and Nieder 2016). This mechanism probably depends on interactions with hippocampal and medial temporal lobe structures.

As I said in Chapter 8, early meanings based on vocal mimicry and gestural pantomimes may have been the first instances of a primitive semantic system. Moreover, a factor that may have been relevant for the evolution of conventionalized meaning is the capacity to share an attentional state between two individuals. Converging attention may be directed to an external object within sight, or more abstractly, to internal meaning like the concept of an absent object, where both subjects generate similar representations of the referred object (Garcia 2014). Thus, the capacity to direct the other's attention is a critical step for the acquisition of meanings. Children use at least two mechanisms to direct the attention of adults to specific objects. One is finger-pointing and gaze direction, and the other is vocal behavior. Vocalizations and other gestures are more generic and do not convey spatial information. In the monkey, vocalizations are associated with an innate circuit that includes the cingulate gyrus in the frontal cortex (described in the next section). This region signals the occurrence of contextually incongruent or unpre-dicted events, and triggers activation of executive brain systems in the dorsolateral prefrontal cortex that engage in resolving the conflict or incongruence. Thus, the cingulate cortex signals behaviorally relevant events that are transmitted to others by vocalizations (Paus 2001; Roelofs and Hagoort 2002). One possibility is that vocalizations and non-pointing gestures served to attract the other's attention to the respective individual, and then gaze direction and pointing served to direct attention to a given position in space. These steps, I believe, might represent a missing link between predominantly emotional communica-tion and a primitive referential system based on vocal mimicry and pantomimic sounds.

In a further step, imitation of animals or physical events, be they vocal, gestural, or both, may have represented an early instance of symbolic reference (see Chapter 8). But how did we go from simple meanings like those conveyed in vocal imitation and pantomime to more complex meanings involving phrases depicting actions? Hage and Nieder argue that complex behaviors like sequence planning, behavioral sequences and strategy changes are encoded by monkey lateral prefrontal cortex neurons, which may be considered a precursor of syntactic structure (Hage and Nieder 2016, Fujii and Graybiel 2003, Wallis et al. 2001). Likewise, fMRI studies suggest that complex, nested motor plans including speech could be processed by Broca's area (Koechlin and Jubault 2006). On the other hand, the insula and other speech-related areas may rather control the precise timing of complex motor acts.

More into behavior, Bickerton proposes that words began to be combined in different ways to achieve increasingly complex meanings, first in random order (as in Creole languages; see the Chapter 1), but then using short words like prepositions and other elements as links between them (Bickerton 2009). For Bickerton, the lexical properties of words determine the linguistic elements that can be bound to them, and syntax emerges from these binding rules. Others like Otto Jespersen, and Tecumseh Fitch after him have argued that propositional utterances originally consisted of entire sung phrases, which had a kind of holistic or contextual meaning, perhaps more like vervet monkey calls. In a subsequent stage, this continuous message was decomposed into several mobile "chunks", or primitive words that combined with others, which is similar to what Michael Arbib proposed (see Chapter 8) (Jespersen 1922; Fitch 2009, 2010; Arbib 2012). This is compatible with the notion that vocalizations were originally used for play and other apparently non-utilitarian behaviors rather than for directly transmitting relevant information about the environment. Similarly, Simon Townsend and collaborators have argued that syntactically ordered messages appeared early in human vocal evolution, and that a phonologically organized system of words was a late acquisition (Collier et al. 2014). In any of these cases, the learning, processing and combination of words probably put a much heavier load on working memory capacity, and it is tempting to propose that the origin of syntax was associated with a significant amplification of the phonological loop.

My own perspective is that the two kinds of signaling had different uses. The primitive speech of our ancestors may have contained both long structured vocal strings signaling identity, group membership and other social signals; and short primitive word-like utterances and gestures used to call the attention of others and to direct their attention to specific objects or events. Playful behavior and learned emotional signals like vocalizations and gestures may have been important to generate cohesive behavior and generate dyads, not only between mother and child, but also among allies within a group. In addition, the capacity to use word-like utterances like onomatopoeias and conventionalized vocalizations to address simple meanings generated primitive semantics. In this context, Damián Blasi and collaborators found a strong statistical relationship between speech sounds and word meanings, as in /t/ for "tongue" and /n/ for nose, across about two-thirds of the world's languages (Blasi et al. 2016), which is in line with the onomatopoeia hypothesis of speech origins. If I had to guess, I would bet that early *Homo,* and even Australopithecines communicated extensively through learned vocalizations, which developed from a condition similar to the babbling of human infants. This type of vocalization developed a primitive syntactic organization, as in songbirds. From this behavior, a "lexical component" emerged, signaling events that may have been relevant for group behavior, such as recruiting individuals to obtain a distant food source. Another possibility for the emergence of a lexical component is tool-making (see Chapters 4 and 8). These two components, lexical and syntactical, coalesced in later stages, possibly in very recent times, to produce the first forms of speech as we know it. This may have taken place concomitant with the origin of modern humans, and the associated Cultural Revolution that took place at that time. In this line, Vitor Nóbrega and Shigeru Miyagawa proposed that there are two key formal elements in language structure, the expressive and the lexical (Nóbrega and Miyagawa 2015). The expressive system is related to intentionality and is hierarchically organized but limited (finite) in its possible structures, while the lexical system conveys semantic content but does not admit structural organization. There are examples of expressive communication among non-human animals such songbirds, and of lexical communication as in vervet monkeys, but the two never occur together. The two communication domains fused only in human language. We may never know when this happened in human evolution, giving rise to modern speech. It may have been gradual, starting concomitantly with the incipient phonological loop, perhaps already in Australopithecines, but it may have been fully expressed much later, as human culture became increasingly complex. This perspective differs from the notions of protospeech and protosign of Derek Bickerton and Mike Arbib, respectively, in that early human communication took place in two different domains, not just conveying signals about external events, but also a rudimentary phonology in which preverbal strings were used for socializing.

Down from the Cortex

The above is a plausible, but admittedly very speculative scenario of speech origins. Now I will turn to harder evidence of the neural mechanisms involved in vocalizations. The rhythmic organization of vocalizations, together with other orofacial movements like breathing, licking, chewing, and swallowing, depend on brainstem sensorimotor circuits that control the precise coordination of many muscles involved in generating and regulating subtly different movements of the respiratory muscles, nose, lips, tongue and throat. Feeding behaviors like eating, drinking and swallowing require the coordinated action of some 26 muscles and five brainstem motor nuclei to be correctly executed. All these behaviors have to be strictly timed with breathing, which is essential to staying alive. These processes are coordinated by small brainstem circuits called central pattern generators, which in some cases are synchronized by upstream central rhythmic generators. Jaw movements are controlled in the brainstem by the trigeminal motor nucleus; tongue movements by the hypoglossal nucleus, lip and nose movements by the facial nucleus, and finally swallowing and vocalization by the nucleus ambiguus. The close neural relationship in mammals between the control of swallowing and vocalization suggests to many that primitive vocalizations originated from modulations of ingestive behaviors, which is supported by the findings of mirror neurons involved in swallowing that I mentioned in Chapter 8, and may relate to the recently reported "food songs" of gorillas (see above). Likewise, the production of speech requires elaborate neural control of the phonatory system at different levels. For example, we need close regulation of thoracic musculature during exhalation when we speak because air has to be expelled much more slowly and in bursts than during normal respiration. Furthermore, there have to be very rapid inspirations as we run out of air while speaking. This pattern contrasts with the inhalation-exhalation patterns observed during vocalization by non-human primates, who alternate inspirations and expirations much more regularly during long vocalizations, putting a limit on the duration and rate of their calls. Asif Ghazanfar and others have argued that the thoracic vertebral canal, housing the thoracic spinal cord that innervates breathing muscles, is larger in modern humans and Neanderthals than in non-human primates and other fossil hominids (Ghazanfar and Rendell 2008). However, whether larger size indicates increased motor control has not been demonstrated.

Some vocalizations made by non-human primates and other mammals during play are reminiscent of human laughter. Robert Provine has studied laughter in non-human primates and has observed that with chimpanzees, such vocalizations are accompanied by a "play face" that allows us to recognize this as a form of laughter (Provine 2013, 2016). While human laughter sounds like "ha-ha-ha", chimp laughter sounds like "ah-ah-ah", and sounds more like panting. This is because humans can parse the exhalation into a sequence of several vowel-like sounds, while chimps produce one laughing sound per respiratory cycle. This is proposed to result from a tight coupling of the respiratory cycle to locomotion that is observed in four-legged animals, and remains in most apes even if they walk bipedally. According to Provine, full bipedality in humans released this constraint, and provided the necessary flexibility of the respiratory system for the emergence of speech. Interestingly, Provine also notes that there are plenty of laughter during normal speech, which normally intercalates with it between phrases, not interfering with syntactical structure. Provine calls this the punctuation effect, which serves to provide emphasis to speech, and probably co-evolved with speech in a similar way to hand gestures and other behaviors. Finally in this line, I have always been intrigued by the variety of laughs different people have. One can quickly tell whether a friend is in a place or not just by hearing his or her laughter. Perhaps laughter partly evolved as an individual signature like what is seen in dolphins and other species, which favored group cohesion.

Descending control for speech originates in different brain centers and establishes the patterns of the activity of brainstem and spinal motor neurons in organized sequences. There are two basic circuits that control vocal behavior in humans. The first and more ancient is shared with monkeys and other mammals, and participates in reflex and emotionally triggered vocalizations like laughing and crying, as well as in monkey vocalizations. Recently reviewed by Gert Holstege and Hari Subramanian, this circuit encompasses the anterior cingulate cortex, orbitofrontal cortex, insula and amygdala, with projections to a brain-stem region called the periaqueductal gray (Fig. 10.2). From there, projections reach the reticular formation and are then directed to the ambiguus nucleus (more specifically for vocalizations, the nucleus retro-ambiguus). This nucleus controls the soft palate, pharynx, larynx and respiratory muscles (Holstege and Subramanian 2016). In turn, these muscles control the air pressure in the respiratory tract, which is needed for proper vocalization. Activation of this circuit may partly explain the unimpaired speech of stutterers when they sing or swear. Perhaps related to these functions is Marco Catani's frontal aslant tract (see Chapter 2), running down from the dorsomedial prefrontal cortex to Broca's area, which is involved in motivational aspects of speech (Catani et al. 2013).

The second descending circuit is associated with Broca's region and related cortical areas that connect with the premotor and motor cortices and the basal ganglia, thalamus and the cerebellum. Originating from the laryngeal cortex in the primary motor cortex, axons reach the brainstem reticular formation, and directly innervate the ambiguus nucleus containing the motor neurons that control the laryngeal muscles for vocalization. The cortical- ambiguus projection is specific to humans among primates, and is thought to participate in learned vocalizations including speech (see Chapter 8), and has been compared to the descending projection to vocal brainstem nuclei in songbirds (Chapter 9). Electrophysiological stimulation of the human larynx area (usually the left) of the ventral motor cortex triggers vocalizations and oral movements, while activation of regions related to Broca's area can elicit more complex, speech-like behavior (see Chapter 2).

In the monkey primary motor cortex there is also a larynx representation that Kristina Simonyan and Uwe Jürgens have exhaustively characterized (Simonyan and Jürgens 2003; Simonyan et al. 2016). Axons from the monkey laryngeal motor cortex reach brainstem reticular neurons, which in turn connect with ambiguus motor neurons. However, some axons are found in the periphery of the nucleus ambiguus, which implies that the purported differences from humans in motor innervation of the nucleus ambiguus are of degree rather than kind. Furthermore, the group of Leonardo Fogassi reported the existence of ventral premotor neurons in the macaque that activate specifically with voluntary vocalizations, and a ventral premotor region that produces simple mouth movements and contraction of laryngeal muscles but not vocalizations when stimulated, while lesions in this region have no effect on spontaneous vocalizations (Coudé et al. 2011). Likewise, Steffen Hage and Andreas Nieder evidenced call-related neurons in the ventrolateral prefrontal cortex that predict pre-paration for voluntary vocalizations (Hage and Nieder 2013). In addition, Simonyan and collaborators recently reported a substantial increase from

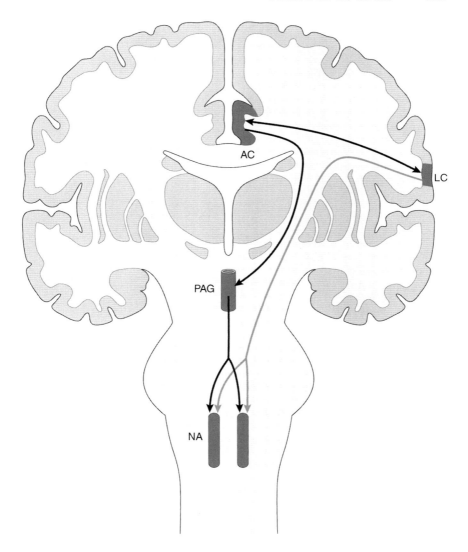

Fig. 10.2   The cortical pathways for vocal control in the human. Black arrows show the pathway that is shared with other primates and mammals. Gray arrows show a tract that is more developed in our species. AC, anterior cingulate; LC, laryngeal cortex; PAG, periaqueductal gray; NA, nucleus accumbens

monkey to human in the connectivity of the laryngeal motor cortex with somatosensory and inferior parietal cortex, which indicates greater sensory and cognitive control of this region (see Chapter 7) (Kumar et al. 2016).

Hage and Nieder have recently summarized this evidence, describing two neural circuits controlling speech (Hage and Nieder 2016). The first is a volitional motor network dependent on the prefrontal cortex, centered in Broca's area, and a phylogenetically older vocal motor network that depends on limbic areas (involved in the initiation of vocalizations) and brainstem systems (controlling the motor output). Hage and Nieder argue that the volitional network is present in monkeys, but its link with the vocal motor network is weak, only allowing to control the initiation of stereotyped vocal output. In human evolution, the volitional network has progressively gained control over the vocal motor network, mainly through inhibitory interactions. This is coupled with two other major innovations, the reinforcement of direct descending projections from the motor cortex to the brainstem, and the amplification of auditory projections to the frontal executive network (contributing to the phonological loop). In summary, rudimentary motor cortical control of the orofacial region already existed in non-human primates, from which voluntary control of speech may have emerged at some point.

Look Who's Talking

Another approach to the study of speech origins is infant vocal and speech development. Kimborough Oller and collaborators have found notable flexibility in early infants' affective vocalizations (squeals, vowel-like sounds, and growls), denoting positive, neutral or negative emotions depending on the context (Oller et al. 2013). These vocalizations contrast with the innately specified cry and laughter, which always denote negative and positive effects, respectively, and can be compared to the vocalizations of non-human primates. Flexibility of the former calls may have been important for subsequent acquisition of vocal learning in early humans, contributing to the emotional meaning of speech.

Consistent with the notion of the origin of the phonological loop as a key innovation in speech origins, the anatomical development of the language network fits the trajectory of speech acquisition in infants. Michael Skeide and Angela Friederici recently summarized the chronology of speech development in infants, correlating it with the maturation of the dorsal and ventral auditory pathways (Skeide and Friederici 2016). Firstly, bottom-up mechanisms in the ventral auditory stream develop in the first year of life, generating the capacity to segment phonological information into distinct word forms, and after 12 months lexical items and lexico-semantic information is already being processed in the superior temporal lobe. By the time the baby is 2 years of age, morphosyntactic processing and grammatical categorization have matured, mostly involving the ventrolateral prefrontal cortex. Finally, at around 4 years of age, the child starts developing top down processing mechanisms through the dorsal pathway, and the neural systems involved in syntactic and semantic processing begin to diverge into distinct but overlapping networks. This process ends when children reach the age of ten, when adult-like syntactic and semantic networks are evident. Friederici's group and others have recently observed that the maturation of the arcuate fasciculus correlates with both the maturation of hemodynamic responses during sentence comprehension, and with the subject's behavioral performance in the task (Skeide et al. 2016; Yeatman et al. 2011). The group led by Ghislaine Dehaene-Lambertz showed that the ventral language pathway matures earlier, while the dorsal pathway (including the arcuate fasciculus) is slower to mature but catches up in the first months after birth, which they suggest relates to the development of combinatorial speech processing (Dubois et al. 2016). Likewise, Pascale Tremblay and collaborators have recently found that the length of the frontal aslant tract in the left hemisphere predicts the receptive language development of 5-to-8-year-old children, a period characterized by improvements in language and communication (Broce et al. 2015).

In addition, an intense research agenda has focused on the mechanisms of speech perception in infants. Nonetheless, these studies have failed to show a language-specific mechanism for the early processing of speech. Take the example of categorical perception described in the Chapters 1 and 8. In early language learning, infants need to weigh the fact that different speakers generate different acoustic patterns for the same linguistic sound, for which they cluster each speaker's sounds into discrete categories, which are normalized for the general population, such as the sound of the letter /a/ is classified as the same regardless of the speaker. However, this capacity has been observed in other species as well. Furthermore, when infants are exposed to language, they are said to commit their brains to the sound patterns that are specific to the particular language they use, while blocking the capacity to distinguish the sound patterns of other languages (Kuhl 2004). Commitment to one language is believed to occur during a critical or sensitive period, where from the 800 or so sounds that are present in all languages, the child becomes sensitive to some 40 elements that are characteristic of the mother's language. Children who acquire an additional language after this critical period develop the typical foreign accent most of us have in our second languages. Again, this process is consistent with general mechanisms of brain development. Giorgio Innocenti has suggested that the processes of axonal pruning and connectional rearrangement that take place during normal development may be particularly relevant during critical periods, including those instances of sensory deprivation during early language acquisition. In this case, the consequences may range from minor ones like the lack of exposure to phonemic boundaries in some languages, to more severe consequences among socially deprived individuals. Innocenti speculates that the process of terminal retraction may be stunted in these cases (Innocenti 2007). A recent report by Jacques Mehler, Marina Nespor and collaborators concluded that there are innate preferences of infants for syllable types. Using a non-invasive technique called near infrared spectroscopy, which can measure brain oxygen supply on the surface of the infant's skull, these authors found that syllable structures that are common in many languages elicited a specific response in language-related regions of the left hemisphere of 2-5-day old infants, as opposed to uncommon syllable structures (Gómez et al. 2014). However, this assumes that newborns have had no exposure to speech before they were born, which may not be totally correct. Babies may start hearing their mother's voice when they are still in the womb.

Once infants recognize the sounds of a language, they begin to break it down into words. Separating the verbal string into its constituent words is a difficult task, as any one knows who has been exposed to an unknown language. The groups led by Jenny Saffran, Patricia Kuhl and Jacques Mehler have made outstanding contributions to this problem, evidencing that infants perform a statistical analysis of the frequencies of syllable transitions during speech, and detect unlikely transitions as candidates for word separations (Saffran et al. 1996; Kuhl 2004; Peña et al. 2002). This capacity requires maintaining the syllable string in the memory. Children can detect word candidates after only two minutes of exposure to continuous syllable strings when they hear an artificial language for the first time consisting of syllable sequence patterns. This process may also contribute to extract structural regularities of the speech string, which can be generalized to novel inputs, contributing to the acquisition of certain grammatical rules. Not only infants, but also children and adults can perform well in tasks requiring statistical learning of syllables. Furthermore, Lucca Bonatti, Marcela Peña, and collaborators have disclosed different roles for consonants and vowels in language learning (Bonatti et al. 2007). As in working memory studies, consonants have been associated with lexical structure, while vowels are linked to grammatical order (see Chapter 6). Manuel Carreiras has further shown that vowels put processing demands on prosody, while as expected, consonants are related to lexical and semantic analysis (Carreiras and Price 2008). The arcuate fasciculus is still immature in infants and Broca's and motor areas are still incapable of programming accurate articulatory mechanics, which makes unlikely that infants are using adult-like verbal working memory circuits to understand speech (Skeide et al. 2016). Nonetheless, the auditory system seems to be sufficiently mature to perform these tasks, and probably contains the critical elements of sensory processing that will be later used in working memory networks. Note however that statistical learning is not exclusive to speech learning and can also be observed in sequences of tones and melodies. It is not exclusively human either as it has been observed in non-human primates and even rats (Toro and Trobalón 2005).

Many regular associations in language are distantly related to each other, with intervening elements located between them. These are the long distance dependencies discussed in Chapter 6, a feature that has been considered a central aspect of language structure. Elissa Newport and Richard Aslin showed that adults had difficulty learning syllable transitions when a pair of critical syllables that are normally together in words are separated by an intermediate syllable (e.g. /ba/-/di/-/te/; /ba/-/ku/-/te/; /ba/-/to/-/te/). However, the same subjects had no problem learning pairs of non-adjacent letters, be they two vowels separated by a variable consonant, or two consonants separated by a variable vowel (Newport and Aslin 2004). It is possible that tracking non-adjacent syllables puts a computationally intractable load on the memory system. In a second study, Newport and Aslin joined the ethologist Marc Hauser and trained tamarin monkeys in these tasks, who were able to learn non-adjacent relationships between vowels but not between consonants (Newport et al. 2004). Like human adults, monkeys were unable to detect distant regularities between syllables, but performed well in the case of letters. Notably, human infants were unable to learn any of these non-adjacent dependencies made by syllables or letters. Tracking non-adjacent dependencies in music is also possible depending on the context. For example, Ansgar Endress showed that adult humans have less difficulty doing these tasks using tonal melodies (as opposed to random melodies), indicating the role of higher-level processes in this type of learning (Endress 2010). Summarizing this evidence, the known perceptual strategies that infants use for recognizing speech, like categorical perception or statistical learning, are not uniquely human or speech-specific, which again reinforces the notion that the perceptual mechanisms involved in speech recognition are domain general processes underlying neural plasticity in many systems.

Infants use not only the complicated strategies described above to recognize and separate words, but also other social signals, like prosody, semantics and pragmatics. For example, mothers and adults in all cultures speak to their infants in what is called baby talk, or motherese, in which adults modulate some aspects of prosody like slowing rhythm, exaggerating pitch differences and stretching vowel sounds, to which infants have been found to benefit in discriminating speech sounds. Infants are not only aroused by their parents' intonation patterns, but also use prosodic cues to extract lexical and grammatical information. Furthermore, it is known that actual face to face and even physical contact with adults are highly important for language learning, as well as for song learning in songbirds. In addition, the pragmatics of language, which settles the behavioral context in which this takes place, is a critical aspect of language development, as it consists of the association of words and sentences with current and previous situations, and with the mother and child's ongoing behavior and intentions. All of this contextual information is required to make reference to external events and associate specific strings with different behavioral situations (Skeide and Friederici 2016). The relative contribution of statistical processing and behavioral cues for learning words remains to be determined, but I would predict that the latter make at least a robust contribution to this process.

Gene Tracks

The last, but in no way the least aspect of speech origins that I will discuss in this chapter is genetics. In Chapter 9, I mentioned the notable parallelism in patterns of gene expression between language-related areas in humans, and regions involved in vocal learning in songbirds (Pfenning et al. 2014). Another approach has been the study of inherited speech disorders. As with other human traits, there are many conditions that affect the development of speech and language, which have been collectively termed as specific language impairment to distinguish them from language disorders that are secondary to other conditions like autism or hearing impairments (see Chapter 6). However, this clinical category is far from homogeneous, there being dysfunctions in expressive language, in both expressive and receptive language, phonological disorders, stuttering and non-specified communication disorders. Furthermore, clinicians usually separate speech disorders like stuttering and phonological disorders from language disorders that are more profound and affect morphology (formation of words), grammar, and in some cases semantics and pragmatics. Despite the attempts to separate and categorize these alleged subgroups, there is a noticeable overlap among these conditions, and few children fit neatly into any of these subgroups (van der Lely and Pinker 2014).

In many cases, genetic factors contribute to susceptibility of language and speech disorders, as these conditions usually run in families, and have shown a strong heritability: monozygotic twins show a stronger concordance for language disorders than dizygotic twins. However, pinpointing genes specifically affecting the development of speech and language is difficult. The first gene to be associated with language, and possibly the one we now know most about is FOXP2, first identified in the analysis what is called the KE family. Some of the members of this family have impaired control of orofacial musculature, resulting in interrupted speech and the incapacity to articulate words fluently and intelligibly, a condition termed verbal dyspraxia. This condition resembles the deficits observed in acquired Broca's aphasia, showing deficits in grammatical competence, especially with past tenses in irregular verbs, and in word formation. Notably, the affected subjects have no deficits in manual praxis and are usually taught sign language to supplement their communication difficulties. It is however not clear if learning highly skilled manual operations like playing musical instruments would be deficitary in these subjects.

In 1995, Fanareh Vargha-Khadem and collaborators published an influential article showing that the inherited disorder of the KE family is not language-specific, including not only deficits in articulated speech and syntactic operations, but also in general orofacial functions and intellectual capacity (verbal and non-verbal IQ) (Vargha-Khadem et al. 1995, 2005). Affected members of the KE family vary in the severity of this condition, some having relatively mild deficits while others show profound intellectual and communicative impairment. Three years later, Vargha-Khadem and collaborators located an alteration in a specific region in chromosome 7 strongly associated with the condition (Fischer et al. 1998). In a subsequent paper in 2001, the gene in chromosome 7 was identified as coding for a regulatory gene called FOXP2 (Lai et al. 2001).

Neuroanatomical observations of the affected family members point to a significant reduction of cerebellar regions and the caudate nucleus (a component of the basal ganglia), and underactivation of the basal ganglia during speech production. Broca's area and related regions connected to the basal ganglia have less gray matter in affected individuals than in normal subjects, and show lower than normal activation during speech. Conversely, in posterior regions, Wernike's area, the superior temporal sulcus and the putamen showed an increased level of gray matter compared to the normal condition (Vargha-Khadem et al. 1998). In normal postmortem subjects, FOXP2 was found to be active in several brain regions, including the cerebral cortex, limbic regions, and especially the basal ganglia and the thalamus (Vargha-Khadem et al. 2005; Fisher 2009). All together, these findings suggest that FOXP2 is important for the development of motor neural circuits involving the cerebral cortex, the basal ganglia and the cerebellum, which participate in learning an planning skilled motor movements. These movements are principally orofacial but could involve manual skills as well. Further research has found another gene, CNTNAP2 that codes for a protein involved in cell adhesion and neuronal recognition, to which the FOXP2 protein binds (Newbury et al. 2010). Variants of this gene have been associated with cases of specific language impairment. In addition, human mutations in FOXP1, a gene closely related to FOXP2, produce language disorders and other symptoms like developmental delay, dropping eyelids and hand and foot contractions. Other speech-related candidate genes have appeared recently, but there is still much research to be done.

Notably, FOXP2 is found in most studied non-human species, many of which are vocal non-learners, and in these the gene expression profile is similar to that in humans. Moreover, the gene structure is highly conserved and is identical among primates like macaques, gorillas and chimpanzees (Enard et al. 2002). Human FOXP2 differs in two amino acids from that of other primates, while the mouse FOXP2 differs from primate FOXP2 in only one amino acid. Recall that mice are vocal learners and develop ultrasonic "songs". Mutations characterizing human FOXP2 are claimed to date from about 200,000 years ago. Notably, DNA sequences from our Neanderthal cousins suggest that they had already acquired these two mutations (Krause et al. 2007). However, the common ancestor of modern humans and Neanderthals is believed to have existed some 300,000 years ago (Johansson 2014). Clearly more studies are needed to settle the chronology of these events in human evolution.

Mice are an excellent animal model for many genetic conditions, as so-called knock-out mutants can be produced in which a specific gene is suppressed, for example, by inserting a non-functional copy of the gene that replaces the normal one in the single cell embryo (Enard et al. 2002, 2009; Hammerschmidt et al. 2015). Several mutants for FOXP2 have been produced, which show a general developmental delay and usually die 3 or 4 weeks after birth, possibly because of respiratory impairment. Since FOXP2 mutants live for a short time, research has focused on the largely innate ultrasonic vocalizations of young pups, which they usually emit when separated from their mother. The evidence from different mutants indicates that inactivation of FOXP2, or associated genes like SRPX2, results in the absence or reduction of isolation calls and other mild behavioral deficits, but in more stringent conditions they do emit these vocalizations, with a generally conserved acoustic structure. Reviewing this evidence, Simon Fisher and Constance Scharff concluded that the evidence does not yet support a parallel between the development of mouse vocalizations and that of human speech, nor in the role of FOXP2 in vocalizations of the two species (Fisher 2009). However, new findings using heterozygous FOXP2 mutant mice, who live until adulthood, have found that in these animals the songs are altered in syllable structure and rhythmicity, and develop abnormally in relation to wild type mice (Castelucci 2016; Chabout et al. 2016). Other interesting animals in which to assess FOXP2 functions are songbirds, which express this gene in the corpus striatum, cerebellum and other brain regions. FOXP2 is upregulated in the striatal area X during song learning and is higher when adult males sing to females than when they sing alone (White et al. 2006). In another study, the group of Constance Scharff showed that after interfering with FOXP2 gene expression by means of a directed viral infection in area X of the zebrafinch, young birds were impaired in their song learning abilities, copying some notes but not others from the exposed songs (Haesler et al. 2007). Furthermore, even imitated notes were not accurate, which was interpreted as a deficit in sensorimotor coordination, FOXP2 mediating the proper synaptic activity of two main neurotransmitters in the basal ganglia: glutamate and dopamine.

It has been proposed that FOXP2 participates in the development of the neural networks that make up the frontal cortex, corpus striatum and cerebellum, involved in sensorimotor integration and particularly in motor skill learning (Schreiweis et al. 2014; Groszer et al. 2008). This evidence in part has prompted authors like Constance Scharff and Johan Bolhuis to suggest that FOXP2 was recruited in several instances (songbirds, humans and possibly bats) to assist vocal learning capacities (Bolhuis et al. 2010; Scharff and Petri 2011). This may be another case of "deep homology" (in my opinion, a better term is genetic homology), like the one I described in Chapter 9, where the gene Pax6 was recruited for the development of eyes in widely different animal lineages, presumably because it originally served some role in the specification of phototransducing receptors.

Beyond Genetics

I have argued throughout this book that the acquisition of the phonological loop was a key evolutionary innovation, in which an auditory-motor interface provided by the development of the dorsal pathway supported vocal learning. These anatomical features are likely to have been associated with increasing brain size, showing a gradation from early *Homo*, with a brain volume of some 500 cc., to the large 1,500 cc. brains of modern humans that appear about 300 thousand years ago. Nonetheless, since we achieved our large brains, a very long time passed before the critical transition some 40,000 to 50,000 years ago that marked the emergence of more sophisticated cultures. Richard Wrangham and others attribute this cultural explosion to the process of self-domestication, in which we adapted ourselves to live in community by inhibiting aggressive behavior and other traits (I will go further on this in the next chapter) (Wrangham 2003, Hare et al. 2012). As I said above, modern speech combining the lexico-semantic and the phonological-syntactic components could have appeared slowly, from an initial stage in which phonological sequences were used for social bonding and lexical-semantic items were used for contingent behavioral coordination. These two domains may have been progressively mixed, until a stage at which it triggered major cultural innovations. Some authors, like Michael Arbib, consider that the acquisition of modern speech was very recent and a largely cultural event, with few genetic changes, in which individuals learned new behaviors, first through imitation of others and subsequently by instruction (Chapter 8). This may be partly correct, as we are born to learn from others, an evolutionary tendency that probably began before we acquired speech. Nevertheless, were there genetic changes associated with this transition that were favored by natural selection (see the next chapter). Paradoxically, apart from FOXP2 and a couple other genes, there has not been a great deal of success in finding a genetic blueprint for language evolution. Of course one possibility is that we still have not found the relevant genes for this development and further research into the genetic foundations of language is certainly worth pursuing.

Another emerging possibility is the epigenetic action of proteins like histones and other chemicals like methyl groups and the small RNAs that surround the DNA molecule and participate in gene expression regulation. Epigenetic processes are normally involved in cell differentiation during development, in which many genes are repressed while others are activated, generating different cellular phenotypes. There has been an explosion of studies analyzing the effects of epigenetic modifications, some of which have been contentiously reported to be transmitted across generations. Michael Skinner is one of the defenders of this process as an important evolutionary mechanism (Skinner 2014). Despite all the criticism and controversy his work has received, Skinner claims that this may be one of the biggest scientific paradigm shifts of the century. Epigenetic changes in development have been linked to several clinical conditions, particularly stress response and developmental disorders like autism and attention deficit hyperactivity disorder.

Epigenetic processes may have also been involved in human brain evolution. Working with Svante Pääbo and a team of other researchers, Liran Carmel mapped the methylation patterns of modern humans and compared these with genomes extracted from ancient human, Neanderthal and Denisovan fossils (Gokhman et al. 2014). They used a sophisticated computational approach to infer the original methylation pattern in the highly distorted DNA of ancient humans. Although this is an indirect measure, it has provided intriguing results that still need to be confirmed by other methods. The genetic difference between modern and ancient humans is minimal (fewer than 100 genes), but they found important differences in DNA methylation patterns, particularly in disease-related genes, and about one third of these were in genes associated with neuropsychiatric disorders. On the other hand, another recent study shows that regions in the genome that underwent most accelerated evolution in the human lineage are associated with risk of cognitive and social disorders like autism (Doan et al. 2016). Thus, it is possible that both, rapid genetic evolution and epigenetic modifications have contributed to the origin of the human mind and its diseases.

This evidence points to the intriguing possibility that epigenetic mechanisms had a profound effect on the evolution of language-related circuits. Is the acquisition of the phonological loop related to such changes? This remains an enigmatic question that fortunately can be addressed by future studies. Evidence indicates that epigenetic mechanisms were involved in the domestication of the silkworm and the chicken, as reported by the group of Per Jensen (Jensen 2014). If the proposal of Wrangham is correct and our species experienced a domestication-like process in the last 50,000 years, it may be that epigenetics played a role in the evolution of our sociality, and perhaps in the acquisition of critical traits like the phonological loop (Wrangham 2003). In the last chapter of this book, I will refer to the contextual and social circumstances in which speech may have emerged, as it is not an isolated achievement but is interwoven with several other behavioral innovations.

References and Notes

Arbib MA (2012) How the Brain Got Language. The Mirror System Hypothesis. Oxford University Press, Oxford

Andics A, Gábor A, Gácsi M, Faragó T, Szabó D, Miklósi Á (2016) Neural mechanisms for lexical processing in dogs. Science 353:1030–1032

Arriaga G, Jarvis ED (2013) Mouse vocal communication system: are ultrasounds learned or innate? Brain Lang 124:96–116

Arriaga G, Zhou EP, Jarvis ED (2012) Of mice, birds, and men: the mouse ultrasonic song system has some features similar to humans and song-learning birds. PLoS One 7:e46610

Arnold K, Zuberbühler K (2012) Call combinations in monkeys: compositional or idiomatic expressions? Brain Lang 120:303–309

Bezerra BM, Souto Ada S, de Oliveira MA, Halsey LG (2009) Vocalisations of wild common marmosets are influenced by diurnal and ontogenetic factors. Primates 50:231–237

Bickerton D (2009) Adam's Tongue. How Humans Made Language, How Language Made Humans. Hill and Wang, New York

Blasi DE, Wichmann S, Hammarström H, Stadler PF, Christiansen MH (2016) Sound-meaning association biases across thousands of languages. Proc Natl Acad Sci U S A 113:10818–10823

Boë LJ, Berthommier F, Legou T, Captier G, Kemp C, Sawallis TR, Becker Y, Rey A, Fagot J (2017) Evidence of a Vocalic Proto-System in the Baboon (Papio papio) Suggests Pre-Hominin Speech Precursors. PLoS One 12(1): e0169321

Bolhuis JJ, Okanoya K, Scharff C (2010) Twitter evolution: converging mechanisms in birdsong and human speech. Nat Rev Neurosci 11:747–759

Bonatti LL, Peña M, Nespor M, Mehler J (2007) On consonants, vowels, chickens, and eggs. Psychol Sci 8:924–925

Bradbury JW, Emmons LH (1974) Social organization of some trinidad bats I. Emballonuridae. Z Tierpsychol 36:137–183

Bradley CE, McClung MR (2015) Vocal divergence and discrimination of long calls in tamarins: A comparison of allopatric populations of Saguinus fuscicollis nigrifrons and S. f. lagonotus. Am J Primatol 77:679–687

Bregman MR, Patel AD, Gentner TQ (2016) Songbirds use spectral shape, not pitch, for sound pattern recognition. Proc Natl Acad Sci U S A 113:1666–1671

Broce I, Bernal B, Altman N, Tremblay P, Dick AS (2015) Fiber tracking of the frontal aslant tract and subcomponents of the arcuate fasciculus in 5-8-year-olds: Relation to speech and language function. Brain Lang 149:66–76

Brockelman WY, Schilling D (1984) Inheritance of stereotyped gibbon calls. Nature 312:634–636

Candiotti A, Zuberbühler K, Lemasson A (2012) Context-related call combinations in female Diana monkeys. Anim Cogn 15:327–339

Carreiras M, Price CJ (2008) Brain activation for consonants and vowels. Cereb Cortex 18:1727–1735

Caspermeyer J (2014) For bats and dolphins, hearing gene prestin adapted for echolocation. Mol Biol Evol 31:2552

Castellucci GA, McGinley MJ, McCormick DA (2016) Knockout of Foxp2 disrupts vocal development in mice. Sci Rep 6:23305.

Catani M, Mesulam MM, Jakobsen E, Malik F, Martersteck A, Wieneke C, Thompson CK, Thiebaut de Schotten M, Dell'Acqua F, Weintraub S, Rogalski E (2013) A novel frontal pathway underlies verbal fluency in primary progressive aphasia. Brain 136:2619–2628

Chabout J, Sarkar A, Patel SR, Radden T, Dunson DB, Fisher SE, Jarvis ED (2016) A FOXP2 mutation implicated in human speech deficits alters sequencing vocalizations in adult male mice. Front Behav Neurosci 10:197

Chait M, Greenberg S, Arai T, Simon JZ, Poeppel D (2015) Multi-time resolution analysis of speech: evidence from psychophysics. Front Neurosci 9:214

Clarke E, Reichard UH, Zuberbühler K (2006) The syntax and meaning of wild gibbon songs. PLoS One 1:e73

Collier K, Bickel B, van Schaik CP, Manser MB, Townsend SW (2014) Language evolution: syntax before phonology? Proc Biol Sci 281:20140263

Cook P, Rouse A, Wilson M, Reichmuth C (2013) A California sea lion (Zalophus californianus) can keep the beat: motor entrainment to rhythmic auditory stimuli in a non vocal mimic. J Comp Psychol 127:412–427

Coquerelle M, Prados-Frutos JC, Rojo R, Mitteroecker P, Bastir M (2013) Short faces, big tongues: developmental origin of the human chin. PLoS One 8:e81287

Coudé G, Ferrari PF, Rodà F, Maranesi M, Borelli E, Veroni V, Monti F, Rozzi S, Fogassi L (2011) Neurons controlling voluntary vocalization in the macaque ventral premotor cortex. PLoS One 6:e26822

D'Anastasio R, Wroe S, Tuniz C, Mancini L, Cesana DT, Dreossi D, Ravichandiran M, Attard M, Parr WC, Agur A, Capasso L (2013) Micro-biomechanics of the Kebara 2 hyoid and its implications for speech in Neanderthals. PLoS One 8:e82261

Ding N, Melloni L, Zhang H, Tian X, Poeppel D (2016) Cortical tracking of hierarchical linguistic structures in connected speech. Nat Neurosci 19:158–164

Diester I. Nieder A (2007) Semantic associations between signs and numerical categories in the prefrontal cortex. PLoS Biol 5:e294

Doan RN, Bae BI, Cubelos B, Chang C, Hossain AA, Al-Saad S, Mukaddes NM, Oner O, Al-Saffar M, Balkhy S, Gascon GG; Homozygosity Mapping Consortium for Autism., Nieto M, Walsh CA (2016) Mutations in Human

Accelerated Regions Disrupt Cognition and Social Behavior. Cell 167:341–354

Dubois J, Poupon C, Thirion B, Simonnet H, Kulikova S, Leroy F, Hertz-Pannier L, Dehaene-Lambertz G (2016) Exploring the Early Organization and Maturation of Linguistic Pathways in the Human Infant Brain. Cereb Cortex 26:2283–2298

Egnor SE, Iguina CG, Hauser MD (2006) Perturbation of auditory feedback causes systematic perturbation in vocal structure in adult cotton-top tamarins. J Exp Biol 209:3652–3663

Enard W, Przeworski M, Fisher SE, Lai CS, Wiebe V, Kitano T, Monaco AP, Pääbo S (2002) Molecular evolution of FOXP2, a gene involved in speech and language. Nature 418:869–872

Enard W, Gehre S, Hammerschmidt K, Hölter SM, Blass T, Somel M, Brückner MK, Schreiweis C, Winter C, Sohr R, Becker L, Wiebe V, Nickel B, Giger T, Müller U, Groszer M, Adler T, Aguilar A, Bolle I, Calzada-Wack J, Dalke C, Ehrhardt N, Favor J, Fuchs H, Gailus-Durner V, Hans W, Hölzlwimmer G, Javaheri A, Kalaydjiev S, Kallnik M, Kling E, Kunder S, Mossbrugger I, Naton B, Racz I, Rathkolb B, Rozman J, Schrewe A, Busch DH, Graw J, Ivandic B, Klingenspor M, Klopstock T, Ollert M, Quintanilla-Martinez L, Schulz H, Wolf E, Wurst W, Zimmer A, Fisher SE, Morgenstern R, Arendt T, de Angelis MH, Fischer J, Schwarz J, Pääbo S (2009) A humanized version of Foxp2 affects cortico-basal ganglia circuits in mice. Cell 137:961–971

Endress AD (2010) Learning melodies from non-adjacent tones. Acta Psychol 135:182–190

Feenders G, Liedvogel M, Rivas M, Zapka M, Horita H, Hara E, Wada K, Mouritsen H, Jarvis ED (2008) Molecular mapping of movement-associated areas in the avian brain: a motor theory for vocal learning origin. PLoS One 3:e1768

Fischer J, Hammerschmidt K (2011) Ultrasonic vocalizations in mouse models for speech and socio-cognitive disorders: insights into the evolution of vocal communication. Genes Brain Behav 10:17–27

Fischer J, Wheeler BC, Higham JP (2015) Is there any evidence for vocal learning in chimpanzee food calls? Curr Biol 25:R1028–1029

Fisher SE, Scharff C (2009) FOXP2 as a molecular window into speech and language. Trends Genet 25:166–177

Fisher SE, Vargha-Khadem F, Watkins KE, Monaco AP, Pembrey ME (1998) Localisation of a gene implicated in a severe speech and language disorder. Nat Genet 18:168–170

Fitch WT (2009) Musical protolanguage: Darwin's theory of language evolution revisited. http://languagelog.ldc.upenn.edu/nll/?p=1136

Fitch WT (2010) The Evolution of Language. Cambridge University Press,
Cambridge.

Fitch WT, Reby D (2001) The descended larynx is not uniquely human. Proc
Biol Sci 268:1669–1675

Fujii N, Graybiel AM (2003) Representation of action sequence boundaries by
macaque prefrontal cortical neurons. Science 301:1246–1249

Gamba M, Torti V, Estienne V, Randrianarison RM, Valente D, Rovara P,
Bonadonna G, Friard O, Giacoma C (2016) The Indris Have Got Rhythm!
Timing and Pitch Variation of a Primate Song Examined between Sexes and
Age Classes. Front Neurosci 10:249

García RR, Zamorano F, Aboitiz F (2014) From imitation to meaning: circuit
plasticity and the acquisition of a conventionalized semantics. Front Hum
Neurosci 8:605

Geissmann T (2002) Duet-splitting and the evolution of gibbon songs. Biol
Rev Camb Philos Soc 77:57–76

Ghazanfar AA, Rendall D (2008) Evolution of human vocal production. Curr
Biol 18:R457–R460

Ghazanfar AA, Takahashi DY (2014a) The evolution of speech: vision, rhythm,
cooperation. Trends Cogn Sci 18:543–553

Ghazanfar AA, Takahashi DY (2014b) Facial expressions and the evolution of
the speech rhythm. J Cogn Neurosci 26:1196–1207

Ghazanfar AA, Takahashi DY, Mathur N, Fitch WT (2012) Cineradiography
of monkey lip-smacking reveals putative precursors of speech dynamics.
Curr Biol 22:1176–1182

Glushko A, Steinhauer K, DePriest J, Koelsch S (2016) Neurophysiological
Correlates of Musical and Prosodic Phrasing: Shared Processing
Mechanisms and Effects of Musical Expertise. PLoS One 11:e0155300

Gokhman D, Lavi E, Prüfer K, Fraga MF, Riancho JA, Kelso J, Pääbo S,
Meshorer E, Carmel L (2014) Reconstructing the DNA methylation maps
of the Neandertal and the Denisovan. Science 344:523–527

Gómez DM, Berent I, Benavides-Varela S, Bion RA, Cattarossi L, Nespor M,
Mehler J (2014) Language universals at birth. Proc Natl Acad Sci U S A
111:5837–5841

Grimault S, Lefebvre C, Vachon F, Peretz I, Zatorre R, Robitaille N, Jolicoeur P
(2009) Load-dependent brain activity related to acoustic short-term memory for
pitch: magnetoencephalography and fMRI. Ann N Y Acad Sci 1169:273–277

Groszer M, Keays DA, Deacon RM, de Bono JP, Prasad-Mulcare S, Gaub S, Baum MG, French CA, Nicod J, Coventry JA, Enard W, Fray M, Brown SD, Nolan PM, Pääbo S, Channon KM, Costa RM, Eilers J, Ehret G, Rawlins JN, Fisher SE (2008) Impaired synaptic plasticity and motor learning in mice with a point mutation implicated in human speech deficits. Curr Biol 18:354–362

Gustison ML, Semple S, Ferrer-I-Cancho R, Bergman TJ (2016) Gelada vocal sequences follow Menzerath's linguistic law. Proc Natl Acad Sci U S A 113: E2750–E2758

Haesler S, Rochefort C, Georgi B, Licznerski P, Osten P, Scharff C (2007) Incomplete and inaccurate vocal imitation after knockdown of FoxP2 in songbird basal ganglia nucleus Area X. PLoS Biol 5:e321

Hage SR, Nieder A (2013) Single neurons in monkey prefrontal cortex encode volitional initiation of vocalizations. Nat Commun 4:2409

Hage SR, Nieder A (2016) Dual Neural Network Model for the Evolution of Speech and Language. Trends Neurosci 39:813–829

Hage SR, Gavrilov N, Nieder A (2013) Cognitive control of distinct vocalizations in rhesus monkeys. J Cogn Neurosci 25:1692–1701

Hage SR, Gavrilov N, Nieder A (2016) Developmental changes of cognitive vocal control in monkeys. J Exp Biol 219:1744–1749

Hammerschmidt K, Radyushkin K, Ehrenreich H, Fischer J (2009) Female mice respond to male ultrasonic "songs" with approach behaviour. Biol Lett 5:589–592

Hammerschmidt K, Reisinger E, Westekemper K, Ehrenreich L, Strenzke N, Fischer J (2012) Mice do not require auditory input for the normal development of their ultrasonic vocalizations. BMC Neurosci 13:40

Hammerschmidt K, Schreiweis C, Minge C, Pääbo S, Fischer J, Enard W (2015) A humanized version of Foxp2 does not affect ultrasonic vocalization in adult mice. Genes Brain Behav 14:583–590

Hare B, Wobber V, Wrangham R (2012) The self-domestication hypothesis: evolution of bonobo psychology is due to selection against aggression. Anim Behav 83:573–585

Hausen M, Torppa R, Salmela VR, Vainio M, Särkämö T (2013) Music and speech prosody: a common rhythm. Front Psychol 4:566

Hauser M (1996) The Evolution of Communication. MIT Press, Cambridge

Hauser MD (1998) Functional referents and acoustic similarity: field playback experiments with rhesus monkeys. Anim Behav 55:1647–1658

Hayes KJ, Hayes C (1951) The intellectual development of a home-raised chimpanzee. Proc Am Philos Soc 95:105–109

Hewitt G, MacLarnon A, Jones KE (2002) The functions of laryngeal air sacs in primates: a new hypothesis. Folia Primatol 73:70–94

Holstege G, Subramanian HH (2016) Two different motor systems are needed to generate human speech. J Comp Neurol 524:1558–1577

Innocenti GM (2007) Subcortical regulation of cortical development: some effects of early, selective deprivations. Prog Brain Res 164:23–37

Janik VM (2009) Whale song. Curr Biol 19:R109–R111

Janik VM (2013) Cognitive skills in bottlenose dolphin communication. Trends Cogn Sci 17:157–159

Janik VM (2014) Cetacean vocal learning and communication. Curr Opin Neurobiol 28:60–65

Janik VM, Sayigh LS (2013) Communication in bottlenose dolphins: 50 years of signature whistle research. J Comp Physiol A Neuroethol Sens Neural Behav Physiol 199:479–489

Jensen P. (2014) Behavior genetics and the domestication of animals. Annu Rev Anim Biosci 2:85–104

Jespersen O (1922) Language: Its Nature, Development and Origin. W W Norton & Company, New York

Johansson S (2014) Neanderthals did speak, but FOXP2 doesn't prove it. Behav Brain Sci 37:558–559

Kaminski J, Call J, Fischer J (2004) Word learning in a domestic dog: Evidence for "fast mapping". Science 304:1682–1683

King SL, Janik VM (2013) Bottlenose dolphins can use learned vocal labels to address each other. Proc Natl Acad Sci U S A 110:13216–13221

King SL, McGregor PK (2016) Vocal matching: the what, the why and the how. Biol Lett 12:20160666

King SL, Guarino E, Keaton L, Erb L, Jaakkola K (2016) Maternal signature whistle use aids mother-calf reunions in a bottlenose dolphin, Tursiops truncatus. Behav Processes 126:64–70

Knörnschild M, Nagy M, Metz M, Mayer F, von Helversen O (2010) Complex vocal imitation during ontogeny in a bat. Biol Lett 6:156–159

Koda H, Lemasson A, Oyakawa C, Rizaldi, Pamungkas J, Masataka N (2013) Possible role of mother-daughter vocal interactions on the development of species-specific song in gibbons. PLoS One 8:e71432

Koechlin E, Jubault T (2006) Broca's area and the hierar-chical organization of human behavior. Neuron 50:963–974

Krause J, Lalueza-Fox C, Orlando L, Enard W, Green RE, Burbano HA, Hublin JJ, Hänni C, Fortea J, de la Rasilla M, Bertranpetit J, Rosas A, Pääbo S (2007) The derived FOXP2 variant of modern humans was shared with Neandertals. Curr Biol 17:1908–1912

Kuhl PK (2004) Early language acquisition: cracking the speech code. Nat Rev Neurosci 5:831–843

Kumar V, Croxson PL, Simonyan K (2016) Structural organization of the laryngeal motor cortical network and its implication for evolution of speech production. J Neurosci 36:4170–4181

Lai CS, Fisher SE, Hurst JA, Vargha-Khadem F, Monaco AP (2001) A fork-head-domain gene is mutated in a severe speech and language disorder. Nature 413:519–523

Lalamn A, Boesch C (2013) Do wild chimpanzees have functionally referential food calls? Folia Primatol 84:290

Lameira AR, Hardus ME, Kowalsky B, de Vries H, Spruijt BM, Sterck EH, Shumaker RW, Wich SA (2013) Orangutan (Pongo spp.) whistling and implications for the emergence of an open-ended call repertoire: a replication and extension. J Acoust Soc Am 134:2326–2335

Lameira AR, Maddieson I, Zuberbühler K (2014) Primate feedstock for the evolution of consonants. Trends Cogn Sci 18:60–62

Lameira AR, Hardus ME, Bartlett AM, Shumaker RW, Wich SA, Menken SB (2015) Speech-like rhythm in a voiced and voiceless orangutan call. PLoS One 10:e116136

Lameira AR, Hardus ME, Mielke A, Wich SA, Shumaker RW (2016) Vocal fold control beyond the species-specific repertoire in an orangutan. Sci Rep 6:30315

Lieberman P (1968) Primate vocalizations and human linguistic ability. J Acoust Soc Am 44:1574–1584

Lieberman P (1979) Hominid evolution, supralaryngeal vocal tract physiology, and the fossil evidence for reconstructions. Brain Lang 7:101–126

Lieberman P (1984) The Biology and Evolution of Language. Harvard Univeristy Press, Harvard

Liu F, Jiang C, Wang B, Xu Y, Patel AD (2015) A music perception disorder (congenital amusia) influences speech comprehension. Neuropsychologia 66:111–118

Luef EM, Breuer T, Pika S (2016) Food-associated calling in Gorillas (Gorilla g. gorilla) in the Wild. PLoS One 11:e0144197

Miller CT, Flusberg S, Hauser MD (2003) Interruptibility of long call production in tamarins: implications for vocal control. J Exp Biol 206:2629–2639

Morell V. (2014) When the bat sings. Science 344:1334–1337

Morecraft RJ, Stilwell-Morecraft KS, Solon-Cline KM, Ge J, Darling WG (2014) Cortical innervation of the hypoglossal nucleus in the non-human primate (Macaca mulatta). J Comp Neurol 522:3456–3484

Morrill RJ, Paukner A, Ferrari PF, Ghazanfar AA (2012) Monkey lipsmacking develops like the human speech rhythm. Dev Sci 15:557–568

Newbury DF, Fisher SE, Monaco AP (2010) Recent advances in the genetics of language impairment. Genome Med 2:6

Newman JD, Symmes D (1974) Vocal pathology in socially deprived monkeys. Dev Psychobiol 17:351–358

Newport EL, Aslin RN (2004) Learning at a distance I. Statistical learning of non-adjacent dependencies. Cogn Psychol 48:127–162

Newport EL, Hauser MD, Spaepen G, Aslin RN (2004) Learning at a distance II. Statistical learning of non-adjacent dependencies in a non-human primate. Cogn Psychol 49:85–117

Nóbrega VA, Miyagawa S (2015) The precedence of syntax in the rapid emergence of human language in evolution as defined by the integration hypothesis. Front Psychol 6:271

Oller DK, Buder EH, Ramsdell HL, Warlaumont AS, Chorna L, Bakeman R (2013) Functional flexibility of infant vocalization and the emergence of language. Proc Natl Acad Sci U S A 110:6318–6323

Owren MJ, Dieter JA, Seyfarth RM, Cheney DL (1993) Vocalizations of rhesus (Macaca mulatta) and Japanese (M. fuscata) macaques cross-fostered between species show evidence of only limited modification. Dev Psychobiol 26:389–406

Patel AD (2008) Music, Language and the Brain. Oxford University Press, Oxford

Patel AD, Iversen JR, Bregman MR, Schulz I (2009) Studying synchronization to a musical beat in nonhuman animals. Ann N Y Acad Sci 1169:459–469

Paus T (2001) Primate anterior cingulate cortex: where motor control, drive and cognition interface. Nat Rev Neurosci 2:417–424

Peña M, Bonatti LL, Nespor M, Mehler J (2002) Signal-driven computations in speech processing. Science 298:604–607

Peña M, Langus A, Gutiérrez C, Huepe-Artigas D, Nespor M (2016) Rhythm on your lips. Front. Psychol 7:1708

Peretz I, Zatorre RJ (2005) Brain organization for music processing. Annu Rev Psychol 56:89–114

Perlman M, Clark N (2015) Learned vocal and breathing behavior in an enculturated gorilla. Anim Cogn 18:1165–1179

Petkov CI, Jarvis ED (2012) Birds, primates, and spoken language origins: behavioral phenotypes and neurobiological substrates. Front Evol Neurosci 4:12

Pfenning AR, Hara E, Whitney O, Rivas MV, Wang R, Roulhac PL, Howard JT, Wirthlin M, Lovell PV, Ganapathy G, Mouncastle J, Moseley MA, Thompson JW, Soderblom EJ, Iriki A, Kato M, Gilbert MT, Zhang G, Bakken T, Bongaarts A, Bernard A, Lein E, Mello CV, Hartemink AJ, Jarvis ED (2014) Convergent transcriptional specializations in the brains of humans and song-learning birds. Science 346:1256846

Pisanski K, Cartei V, McGettigan C, Raine J, Reby D (2016) Voice modulation: a window into the origins of human vocal control? Trends Cogn Sci 20:304–318

Price M (2016) Why monkeys can't talk—and what they would sound like if they could. Science Magazine online, Dec. 9. http://www.sciencemag.org/news/2016/12/why-monkeys-can-t-talk-and-what-they-would-sound-if-they-could

Provine RR (2013) Laughing, grooming, and pub science. Trends Cogn Sci 17:9–10

Provine RR (2016) Laughter as a scientific problem: an adventure in sidewalk neuroscience. J Comp Neurol 524:1532–1539

Ravignani A, Fitch WT, Hanke FD, Heinrich T, Hurgitsch B, Kotz SA, Scharff C, Stoeger AS, de Boer B (2016) What pinnipeds have to say about human speech, music, and the evolution of rhythm. Front Neurosci 10:274

Reichmuth C, Casey C (2014) Vocal learning in seals, sea lions, and walruses. Curr Opin Neurobiol 28:66–71

Ridgway S, Carder D, Jeffries M, Todd M (2012) Spontaneous human speech mimicry by a cetacean. Curr Biol 22:R860–R861

Roelofs A, Hagoort P (2002) Control of language use: cognitive modeling of the hemodynamics of Stroop task performance. Cogn Brain Res 15:85–97

Rouse AA, Cook PF, Large EW, Reichmuth C (2016) Beat keeping in a Sea Lion as coupled oscillation: implications for comparative understanding of human rhythm. Front Neurosci 10:257

Saffran JR, Aslin RN, Newport EL (1996) Statistical learning by 8-month-old infants. Science 274:1926–1928

Scharff C, Petri J (2011) Evo-devo, deep homology and FoxP2: implications for the evolution of speech and language. Philos Trans R Soc Lond B Biol Sci 366:2124–2140

Schreiweis C, Bornschein U, Burguière E, Kerimoglu C, Schreiter S, Dannemann M, Goyal S, Rea E, French CA, Puliyadi R, Groszer M, Fisher SE, Mundry R, Winter C, Hevers W, Pääbo S, Enard W, Graybiel AM (2014) Humanized Foxp2 accelerates learning by enhancing transitions from declarative to procedural performance. Proc Natl Acad Sci U S A 111:14253–14258

Seyfarth RM, Cheney DL (2003a) Signalers and receivers in animal communication. Annu Rev Psychol 54:145–173

Seyfarth RM, Cheney DL (2003b) Meaning and emotion in animal vocalizations. Ann N Y Acad Sci 1000:32–55

Seyfarth RM, Cheney DL (2010) Production, usage, and comprehension in animal vocalizations. Brain Lang 115:92–100

Seyfarth RM, Cheney DL, Marler P (1980) Monkey responses to three different alarm calls: evidence of predator classification and semantic communication. Science 210:801–803

Simonyan K, Jürgens U (2003) Efferent subcortical projections of the laryngeal motorcortex in the rhesus monkey. Brain Res 974:43–59

Simonyan K, Ackermann H, Chang EF, Greenlee JD (2016) New developments in understanding the complexity of human speech production. J Neurosci 36:11440–11448

Skeide MA, Friederici AD (2016) The ontogeny of the cortical language network. Nat Rev Neurosci 17:323–332

Skeide MA, Brauer J, Friederici AD (2016) Brain functional and structural predictors of language performance. Cereb Cortex 26:2127–2139

Skinner MK (2014) Environment, epigenetics and reproduction. Mol Cell Endocrinol 398:1–3

Springer SP, Deutsch G (1981) Left Brain, Right Brain. WH Freeman & Company, New York

Stoeger AS, Mietchen D, Oh S, de Silva S, Herbst CT, Kwon S, Fitch WT (2012) An Asian elephant imitates human speech. Curr Biol 22:2144–2148

Suga N (1989) Principles of auditory information-processing derived from neuroethology. J Exp Biol 146:277–286

Takahashi DY, Narayanan DZ, Ghazanfar AA (2013) Coupled oscillator dynamics of vocal turn-taking in monkeys. Curr Biol 23:2162–2168

Takahashi DY, Fenley AR, Teramoto Y, Narayanan DZ, Borjon JI, Holmes P, Ghazanfar AA (2015) The developmental dynamics of marmoset monkey vocal production. Science 349:734–738

Takahashi DY, Fenley AR, Ghazanfar AA (2016) Early development of turn-taking with parents shapes vocal acoustics in infant marmoset monkeys. Philos Trans R Soc Lond B Biol Sci 371:1693

Talmage-Riggs G, Winter P, Ploog D, Mayer W (1972) Effect of deafening on the vocal behavior of the squirrel monkey (Saimiri sciureus). Folia Primatol 17:404–420

Thinh VN, Hallam C, Roos C, Hammerschmidt K (2011) Concordance between vocal and genetic diversity in crested gibbons. BMC Evol Biol 11:36

Toro JM, Trobalón JB (2005) Statistical computations over a speech stream in a rodent. Percept Psychophys 67:867–875

van der Lely HK, Pinker S (2014) The biological basis of language: insight from developmental grammatical impairments. Trends Cogn Sci 18:586–595

Vargha-Khadem F, Watkins K, Alcock K, Fletcher P, Passingham R (1995) Praxic and nonverbal cognitive deficits in a large family with a genetically transmitted speech and language disorder. Proc Natl Acad Sci U S A 92:930–933

Vargha-Khadem F, Watkins KE, Price CJ, Ashburner J, Alcock KJ, Connelly A, Frackowiak RS, Friston KJ, Pembrey ME, Mishkin M, Gadian DG, Passingham RE (1998) Neural basis of an inherited speech and language disorder. Proc Natl Acad Sci U S A 95:12695–12700

Vargha-Khadem F, Gadian DG, Copp A, Mishkin M (2005) FOXP2 and the neuroanatomy of speech and language. Nat Rev Neurosci 6:131–138

Wallis JD, Anderson KC, Miller EK (2001) Single neurons in prefrontal cortex encode abstract rules. Nature 411:953–956

Washington SD, Tillinghast JS (2015) Conjugating time and frequency: hemispheric specialization, acoustic uncertainty, and the mustached bat. Front Neurosci 9:143

Watson SK, Townsend SW, Schel AM, Wilke C, Wallace EK, Cheng L, West V, Slocombe KE (2015) Vocal learning in the functionally referential food grunts of chimpanzees. Curr Biol 25:495–499

Wheeler BC, Fischer J (2012) Functionally referential signals: a promising paradigm whose time has passed. Evol Anthropol 21:195–205

White SA, Fisher SE, Geschwind DH, Scharff C, Holy TE (2006) Singing mice, songbirds, and more: models for FOXP2 function and dysfunction in human speech and language. J Neurosci 26:10376–10379

Wich SA, Swartz KB, Hardus ME, Lameira AR, Stromberg E, Shumaker RW (2009) A case of spontaneous acquisition of a human sound by an orangutan. Primates 50:56–64

Wrangham R (2003) The Evolution of Cooking. In: Brockman J (ed), The New Humanists: Science at the Edge. Sterling Publishing, New Dehli, p 108–109

Yeatman JD, Dougherty RF, Rykhlevskaia E, Sherbondy AJ, Deutsch GK, Wandell BA, Ben-Shachar M (2011) Anatomical properties of the arcuate fasciculus predict phonological and reading skills in children. J Cogn Neurosci 23:3304–3317

Zatorre RJ (2003) Music and the brain. Ann N Y Acad Sci 999:4–14

Zatorre RJ, Salimpoor VN (2013) From perception to pleasure: music and its neural substrates. Proc Natl Acad Sci U S A 110 (Suppl 2):10430–10437

11

Taming Ourselves

In the preceding chapters, I have argued that speech and language originated due to the acquisition of the phonological loop, a species-specific auditory-vocal cortical network. This circuit is coupled with additional elements like the basal ganglia, thalamus and cerebellum, and via the motor cortex it sends a descending projection to brainstem nuclei controlling vocal and oral musculature. The phonological loop endowed our ancestors with a powerful auditory working memory capacity, which was a keystone in the evolution of prehuman communication, allowing us to learn and articulate complex vocal messages. Eventually, this memory boost helped transform sequential vocal information into complex meaningful events in space and time, represented in visuospatial working memory. This ability results from an interface between the auditory-vocal networks and other networks involved in perception-action cycles, and depends on the integration between auditory-vocal, visual-gestural, and visuomotor circuits in which the mirror neuron system probably played an important role.

Nonetheless, the question that is perhaps the most fundamental of all remains open. Charles Darwin said that we are gifted with an instinctive

© The Author(s) 2017
F. Aboitiz, *A Brain for Speech*,
DOI 10.1057/978-1-137-54060-7_11

tendency to acquire an "art" (language), which may be more generally expressed as an innate drive to communicate with others (Darwin 1887). Without this, speech and language would never have evolved. Probably no other animal depends as much as we do on social life, especially in our early years. Many studies with primates and other animals have shown the effects of early social deprivation, but it may not be an exaggeration to say that in humans these effects are far more devastating, largely because we live immersed in a culture where even the most basic objectives, like eating and mating, are achieved by social learning. The case of feral children (see Chapter 1) shows the tremendous effects that early social deprivation can have on human behavior, in which these girls and boys may be unable to speak or even walk upright, much less socialize. In this last chapter, I will attempt to provide a social and ecological scenario in which the development of iterated reciprocal interactions between individuals resulted in a great benefit for them, channeling evolution to the development of increasingly early social attachments and communication. It is in this context that the emergence of the phonological loop may have been a critical inflection point for social behavior and for the evolution of our species.

The Brain in Society

There is a well conserved subcortical network that regulates the social behavior of all vertebrates, which includes limbic components like the amygdala, deep forebrain nuclei involved in reward processing, the hypothalamus regulating the internal milieu and controlling hormonal levels, and brainstem nuclei controlling arousal and emotional behavior (Syal and Finlay 2011). This network is involved in the control of aggressive, sexual and parental behavior and other social activities. But our brains are different in the sense that we rely, perhaps more than any other species, on attachment to others to find reward. Onto this basic scaffolding, primates, and especially humans have built a complex network that has permitted the development of a new form of social behavior, based on learning and cooperation, not denying the intense competition among groups and individuals. As early *Homo* developed the ability to cooperate and learn from others, individuals increased their capacity and intention to establish reciprocal interactions like trading, or conversational situations in which two individuals mutually engaged in gestural and vocal interactions, just for the sake of it. There has to be pleasure in this for it to be an important motivation, just as we look for pleasure in food and sex. For some reason, our ancestors greatly enjoyed being together, perhaps much more than do our close primate relatives. This is not to say that there are no signs of attachment or empathy in non-human primates or in other mammals, which of course there are. It is just that this behavior became uniquely prominent in early humans. Neither does it mean that primitive societies were all love, as there was strong competition and rivalry both within and among groups. Some authors, in particular Robin Dunbar, have claimed that living in a social group in which the balance between competition and cooperation is critical, was a main motor for our unique cognitive capacities (Dunbar and Shultz 2007).

The establishment of close individual attachments, including strong kinship bonds emerging from mother-infant communication contributed to establishing group identity and to maintaining strategic alliances in a context of competition within and among groups. The increasing dependence of newborns on their mothers is partly a consequence of humans being born at a much earlier developmental stage than other primates. As we saw earlier in this book, human babies are born premature for two possible reasons, one is that development is slowed down allowing an extended period for neurogenesis, and the other is that a big brain (or a big head) is difficult to pass through the pelvic canal, which thus favored earlier birth to avoid delivery complications. Another, not alternative, possibility is that the metabolic costs of developing a large brain are ameliorated by slowing down development and completing it after birth.

As children grew up in these early societies, they were endowed with a still maturing brain that was molded by the different circumstances they had to face, from cooperation to empathy to aggression and outright violence. Thus, the young early human had to adapt to this increasingly complex social life in which appropriate behavior became progressively dependent on learning social skills and practical abilities like tool-making. Efficient neural networks involved in planning, behavioral control, emotional perception and anticipation were selected in order to behave appropriately and obtain food and sex. Following Dunbar's idea, Daniel Kennedy and Ralph Adolphs have proposed that the neural systems involved in social behavior encompass at least four broad networks related to empathy (cingulate gyrus and anterior insula), emotion regulation (amygdala and inferior temporal, ventromedial prefrontal and orbitofrontal cortices), a mirror system for understanding intentions and actions (parietal cortex and ventrolateral prefrontal cortex); and the capacity to mentalize, that is, to infer the mental states of other people (anterior temporal lobe, superior temporal sulcus, and midline regions in the prefrontal cortex and the retrosplenial and posterior cingulate cortices) (Fig. 11.1) (Kennedy and Adolphs 2012). This capacity is often referred to as having a theory of mind of others, a subject I introduced in Chapter 8. The network involved in inferring the other's mental state overlaps with Marcus Raichle's default or resting state network, which I described in Chapter 2. A significant portion of our social lives may depend on the operation of the default network, from imagining situations, engaging in daily conversations, sharing laughs and other things that make our lives enjoyable. According to Kennedy and Adolphs, malfunction in any of these networks due to localized brain lesions results in deficits in social behavior. Moreover, the symptoms of conditions like autism, attention deficit and hyperactivity disorder, depression and schizophrenia have been interpreted as associated with deregulation of these networks.

Nonetheless, the above neural systems are not exclusive to humans, as we share these brain components with other primates. How do we explain our intense sociality when the respective networks seem to be so conserved? Are these regions just working differently in humans? The expansion of our brain, although following primate trends as we discussed in Chapter 3, involves more intense amplification of many of the areas that are involved in social behavior. Were these differences sufficient to develop our social behavior? It is likely that, as with the language networks, circuits involved in social behavior were co-opted from other networks performing more basic functions.

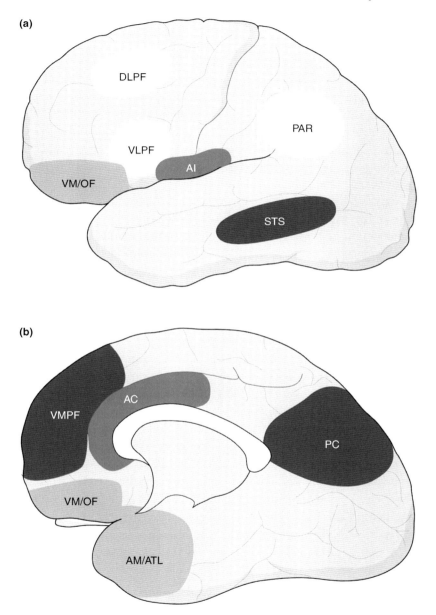

Fig. 11.1   Regions involved in the social brain. A, lateral view; B, medial view. AC, anterior cingulate cortex; AI, anterior insula; AM/ATL, amygdala and

Mind Readers

For example, let us consider some simple abilities like following another person's gaze or looking where someone points, which I discussed in Chapters 8 and 10. The neural networks involved in shared attention (when two subjects agree to focus on the same event), as well as in mental state attribution, depend on midline regions of the frontal cortex, which indicates a broad neurological overlap among these capacities (Shteynberg 2015). Pointing and gaze following can be seen as requisites for both shared attention, and the onset of a primitive learned semantics (see Chapter 8). As we became able to share knowledge about the world by developing rudimentary semantics, we also slowly became aware that the other might know the same as what we know. A complication of this knowledge is when we realize that the other might not know all that we know, or know things we don't know. More complicated is the knowledge that others may believe things that are incorrect. This process gradually develops in the child as the semantic space and the world we share becomes increasingly complex.

It has been said that science is just common sense formalized, as opposed to metaphysics, which goes beyond common sense. This is why, for example, scientists' concept of causality sometimes seems too basic for philosophers. Working with children, Alison Gopnik has found that they start to reason about the world very early, by making hypotheses that are empirically put to the test by letting objects fall, hiding them, or hiding themselves, breaking toys apart and other manipulations they make (Gopnik and Meltzoff 1984; Gopnik 2012). In this way, they develop folk physics, in which they understand basic causality, mechanical interactions and transformations in time and space (see Chapter 9). In parallel to this development, normal children acquire full-blown mind-reading abilities by the age of four, which is evidenced by highly

Fig.11.1 (Continued)
anterior temporal lobe; DLPF, dorsolateral prefrontal cortex; MPF, medial prefrontal cortex; PAR, parietal lobe; PC, posterior cingulate cortex; STS, superior temporal sulcus; VLPF, ventrolateral prefrontal cortex; VM/OF, ventromedial and orbitofrontal cortices

standardized neuropsychological tests. Gopnik and others have shown that children recognize human faces, facial expressions and the human voice by the age of one and are able to imitate some facial gestures practically as soon as they are born (see Chapter 8). They are able to follow pointing gestures by 1 year of age, and start pointing to objects soon after this. Gopnik says that children understand their own mental states at this point, but are able to infer these states in other people only by the time they are four. However, the capacity to detect intentions or preferences in other people arises much earlier. Gopnik has shown that when offering food that children like, together with other food they dislike, they will naturally prefer the one they like. If the experimenter says that he or she prefers the food the child dislikes, and then asks the child to offer him or her one of the two types of food, children under 18 months will offer the one they like themselves, but over 18 months they understand that the experimenter has different taste from theirs, and offer him or her the food they dislike. As noted before, the capacity to infer knowledge in other people is more complex. If 3-year olds are shown an open candy box that contains something totally different (say buttons), and are asked what another child believes is inside the box (now closed), a child under four assumes the other child knows there are buttons in it, but children over four say that the other child wrongly believes there are candies in the box (Gopnik and Schulz 2004; Gopnik 2012; Meltzoff et al. 2012; Sobel et al. 2007; Waismeyer et al. 2015).

In a now classic article, David Premack and Guy Woodruff asked whether chimpanzees had a theory of mind, that is, are they able to infer the mental states and intentions of others or assume that others have minds like theirs (Premack and Woodruff 1978). This article sparked an intense debate and research programs to determine whether apes are able to read minds as we can. In particular, Michael Tomasello, Josep Call and Brian Hare made important contributions to this research, which initially produced no evidence of mind reading by captive chimps. Later findings made these investigators doubt that the ability to read minds was an all-or-nothing capacity but rather a gradually evolving ability, much more akin to what Darwin would have proposed (Tomasello et al. 1998, 2003a, b, Call et al. 1998 and Hare et al. 2000, 2001). For example, baby apes and monkeys may be able to deceive others by crying when a larger individual has food they want, thus inducing their mother to attack the latter, who then flees and releases the food. Another instance of deception is when subordinate males court or copulate with females out of sight from the dominant male. A subtler example is an ape fixing its gaze on some point to distract others and then grabbing their food (Hare et al. 2000, 2001). Do these behaviors imply that chimpanzees and other apes can read minds? Do they have any knowledge of their own mental states? Do they avoid the dominant male´s sight only because they won't feel his presence, or do they really know that the other is ignorant of what they are doing?

In order to determine whether or not chimpanzees have a theory of others' minds, Tomasello, Call, Hare and their collaborators have conducted an enormous number of experiments with chimps, that were interpreted as showing at the best a limited capacity to understand others' knowledge of the world. It is now well known that apes are very good at following the others' gaze. For example, Tomasello and collaborators showed that if a chimpanzee is sitting in front of an experimenter but separated by a barrier that prevents the chimp from seeing the experimenter's arms, the ape is able to follow the experimenter's gaze to locate an object that he moved with his hands (Call et al. 1998). However, this does not necessarily mean that they understand that the other has any knowledge of what he or she is seeing. For example, David Povinelli and collaborators observed that when chimps beg food from experimenters, they seem not to care whether or not the experimenter is looking at them (he or she may even be wearing a bucket over his head or is evidently blindfolded), as long as the experimenter is standing in front of the chimp (Povinelli 2000; Penn and Povinelli 2007). They can learn to beg food only with experimenters directly looking at them, but after a couple years after doing the task they have forgotten the trick completely and have to start from zero. However, in the 2000s Brian Hare devised an experiment that suggested some capacity for mind reading in apes (Hare et al. 2000, 2001). Two chimps, one dominant and the other subordinate, were placed in front of each other. Food was placed where both could see it, and other food where only the subordinate could see it. Subordinates preferred to direct themselves to the food only they were able to see. Additional experiments involved misinforming the dominant about the location of food (in which case the subordinate looks for places where the dominant believes there is no food), and switching dominants so that the second dominant had not seen where food had been located (in this case subordinates collect more food than in the former situation).

Tomasello, Call and Hare's position now is that chimps are stuck in a stage comparable or slightly inferior to that of 2- or 3-year-old children, where they can follow gazes and understand perspective taking, all of this slowly moving in the direction of a theory of mind in children, but never reaching this stage (Tomasello et al. 2003a, b; Hermann et al. 2007). More recently, Tomasello proposed that apes are noticeably human-like in their ability for abstract thought, using inferences about things, understanding the other's goals and planning for the future, as seen in tool retaining behavior (see Chapters 4, 6 and 9) (Tomasello 2014). He envisions two critical steps in the evolution of human behavior; the first taking place some 400,000 years ago, when early *Homo* started to develop complex cooperative and reciprocal behaviors based on mind reading capacities. From there a protolanguage developed, first based on manual gestures and only later speech became the main communication system (but see Chapter 8). The second stage does not have a clear starting date, but is marked by the acquisition of shared conventions that specify behavioral norms, permitting further organization of social behavior and catapulting cultural complexity. Moreover, Tomasello views grammar as a secondary elaboration of the incorporation of conventionalized rules of behavior, rather than as an innately driven capacity. More generally, his perspective is that what is different about us from our ape cousins is the innate predisposition to cooperate with each other.

Other researchers, like Cecilia Heyes and David Povinelli have criticized Tomasello, Call and Hare's interpretations, essentially by arguing that none of their experiments demonstrate that chimps have any knowledge of others' mental states, and that there are lower-level explanations based on associative behavior that can account for these findings (Heyes 1998; Povinelli 2000; Povinelli and Vonk 2003, Penn and Povinelli

2007). The above disagreement is clearly illustrated by the interpretations of an experiment by Fumihiro Kano and Christopher Krupenye. These authors recently recorded the eye movements of bonobos while they watched a video in which a researcher wearing a "King Kong" suit pretended to attack a human and then hid behind a bale. In one version of the movie, King Kong moved to another bale in front of the human, who then left the scene and came back with a stick to attack the presumed ape. In the second version, the human left and went for the stick first, and while he was away, King Kong moved to the other hiding place and then left the scene. So, when the human character came back, he is supposed to believe that the beast was still hiding in the first place. In this second version of the movie, Bonobos predicted the behavior of the human character and consistently looked at the first hiding place when the actor came back, which was interpreted as proof of mind reading in apes, that is, they apparently knew that the human had a false belief about King Kong's location (Krupenye et al. 2016). Another experiment in the same line was very recently performed by the same group (Buttelmann et al. 2017). Regarding the first experiment, researchers like Carla Krachun and Robert Lurz claim that bonobos just remember the place where the human last saw King Kong as an efficient predictive rule, without any knowledge about the agent's beliefs (Caruso 2016). Likewise, Cecilia Heyes refers to this ability as "submentalization", indicating that it relies on anticipatory cues rather than true mind reading (Heyes 2017). This controversy continues and in my opinion it will be very hard to demonstrate that the animals are in fact inferring the other's mental state. Once again, we could be in a "Clever Hans" situation, as in the Mirror Neuron foundational experiments, where clever but relatively simple associative mechanisms, instead of inner simulations of others, account for these findings.

I agree with Tomasello that social skills were gradually acquired over human evolution and that there may have been different stages in the development of these skills. Nonetheless, social behavior may have evolved through the use of increasingly sensitive cues to predict the other's behavior, and not necessarily by reading the other's mind. Moreover, we ourselves may be unconsciously or semi-consciously using such cues every day, and only *a posteriori* making inferences about the other's mind. As I said before, believing that others have minds may be related to the acquisition of a learned semantics around language, so that we share the world with others; a capacity that may be necessary and useful for living together.

How do we come to attribute consciousness to other beings? Alan Turing, a brilliant mathematician who contributed significantly to the Allies winning World War II by deciphering enemy codes, and who is also known as the father of artificial intelligence, asked this question from a computational perspective. Very sadly, as Turing was homosexual and the British government could not tolerate that a person with his inclinations be considered a war hero, they submitted him to aggressive hormonal treatment that practically destroyed him. His dramatic life was recently popularized in the 2014 Oscar winning movie "The Imitation Game", directed by Morten Tyldum and starring Benedict Cumberbatch and Keira Knightley. Turing reasoned that the attribution of consciousness was due to the establishment of reciprocal or conversational interactions with others, in which we share semantic knowledge about the world or about ourselves. In these conversations, the other expresses his or her non-trivial knowledge of what we are expressing, and both share a mental state. Furthermore, through conversation we also soon learn that others may not know the same as we do. As I have mentioned in previous chapters, the capacity to engage in reciprocal conversations may have been facilitated by the acquisition of vocal learning and the subsequent expansion of the phonological loop, which allowed us not only to learn more complex utterances, but also to rapidly articulate responses in order to engage in, and enjoy these reciprocal interchanges.

Turing asked himself, how we could know if a computer were conscious? He then conceived of the Turing test[1], which consists of a computer placed out of sight that interacts verbally with a human. If the human cannot tell whether he is talking to another person or to a computer, the computer has passed the test. A trick favoring the computer is that it elaborates grammatically correct sentences based on the phrases spoken by the human. The computer responds very much as a psychoanalyst does during a therapy session, using elements of the phrases to

---

[1] http://www.psych.utoronto.ca/users/reingold/courses/ai/turing.html

construct others that keep the conversation going. In this way, humans tend to automatically believe they are speaking with a conscious person. Some have even joked with the idea of selling psychoanalytic software in which you receive therapy without the need to talk to a real person. Then, perhaps people would feel less inhibited and would address deeper issues that may be difficult to discuss with a human therapist. The point is that we are indeed endowed with a cognitive mechanism that allows us to extrapolate our own thoughts and intentions to others around us, and I believe this mechanism is deeply intertwined with the development of a shared semantics through language. Going further with this argument, religion is an expression of this cognitive bias, when humans attribute intentions to natural processes.

The Pleasure of Being Together

We interpret the minds of others in the context of an intense social life to which we are instinctively driven because we need others to be happy. How did we amplify our social capacity to this extent? I believe the answer is related to the unique evolutionary history and ecology of our species, to which I will come to below. However, before delving into this issue, I will emphasize the rewarding aspects of social life, and how these may have influenced the development of our language capacity. A lot of recent research has focused on the hormonal regulation of the social behavior of animals. One of the most notable findings comes not from primates but from rodents, particularly the well-known vole, of which there are some 150 species. Researchers like Elizabeth Hammock and Larry Young have observed striking differences in family behavior in different vole populations (Hammock and Young 2006). While prairie voles are monogamic and males help care for the young, meadow voles do not establish stable couples and males are not interested in their offspring. This differential behavior is due to genetic differences in the regulatory region of genes coding for receptors of the closely related hormones vasopressin and oxytocin. Vasopressin was discovered long ago as a mediator of hydric balance but more recent evidence indicates that it also promotes social behavior. Increasing activity of this hormone (or of its receptors) may promote pair bonding and parental behavior, but only in males. Notably, this gene has been found to be mutated in some cases of autism, and in chimpanzees the same gene lacks a base pair in the same place as the deletion associated with autism (Hammock and Young 2006). In humans, several studies including those by Rachel Bachner-Melman and Richard Ebstein, and by Hasse Walum and collaborators have associated variants of this receptor's genes with cooperative behavior, creative dance and marital stability (Bachner-Melman and Ebstein 2014; Walum et al. 2008). Oxytocin is a related hormone associated with reproduction, serving physiological roles like facilitating delivery and lactation. More recent studies have found that oxytocin also participates in sexual behavior and in promoting social recognition, parental bonding, and traits like generosity and attachment in animals and humans (Gao et al. 2016). Several findings with voles suggest that oxytocin promotes within-group bonding but aggression and rejection of outsiders (Bachner-Melman and Ebstein 2014). As cute as these animals look, they can be quite nasty when attacking competitors. Notably, a recent study showed that in humans playing a bargaining game, the sex hormone testosterone promotes both aggressive and prosocial behaviors, producing stronger punishments when receiving unfair offers, and stronger rewards when receiving fair offers when compared to control subjects. This suggests that testosterone has a similar role as oxytocin in the regulation of social behavior (Dreher et al. 2016).

In addition to these hormones, some neurotransmitters like dopamine (of which I will speak later) and serotonin have been shown to influence social behavior (Crockett and Fehr 2014; Skuse and Gallagher 2009, 2011). Serotonin is a neurotransmitter that has been associated with mood disorders, and many pharmaceutical products target serotoninergic signaling as therapeutic agents. One component of this signaling process is the serotonin transporter that regulates the amount of extracellular serotonin. The gene that codes for this protein comes in at least two flavors, depending on the length of its regulatory region. The short repeat variant produces less protein than the long repeat variant, therefore allowing more circulating serotonin in the extracellular space and increasing its activity in relation to the long-repeat one. Subjects with the short-repeat version of the gene are more likely to develop mood disorders, are more reactive to fear stimuli, and tend to have a decreased functional connectivity between the anterior cingulate and the amygdala. In social contexts, it has been shown that increasing serotonin levels is related to submissiveness and decreased aggressiveness, favoring associative behavior. Below we will see that important changes in serotoninergic activity have taken place in recent human evolution that may be related to increasing sociability in humans and other animals.

   Speech is no exception to the drive to be with others, as it develops in the context of intensely rewarding social contact. Supriya Syal and Barbara Finlay appropriately claim that language learning results not only from a powerful cortico-striatal learning system, but also from its obligatory coupling to a subcortical socio-motivational circuitry regulating the rewarding aspects of social life (Syal and Finlay 2011). In fact, the relevance of direct social contact is very clear to anyone who has tried to learn a second language just by watching TV. Patricia Kuhl and her colleagues showed that English speaking children that directly interacted with native Mandarin speakers learned to discriminate some phonetic contrasts not present in English much better than did children that were exposed to the same speech signals audiovisually through television or only via audiotaped speakers (Kuhl et al. 2003). The latter group performed the same as children exposed only to English speakers, that is, they had learned practically nothing. This is partly because during direct social interaction adults refer to contingent situations by using shared attention, which gives pragmatic clues about meanings, but also because there is an intrinsic reward in social interactions. Normal children enjoy hearing speech and being physically close to someone. This is a main driver for human sociality and of course for language learning. Furthermore, speech itself is a source of reward, at least for children. Leslie Seltzer and collaborators worked with mother-child dyads in which the children had been mildly stressed, and then allowed to get in contact with their mothers, in three conditions: (i) complete mother-child contact, (ii) speech-only contact, and (iii) no contact (Seltzer et al. 2010). Afterward, blood samples from the children were tested. Children who had complete contact or only speech contact had higher levels of oxytocin and lower levels of the hormone cortisol, a stress indicator, than children in the group with no contact.

The known cases of socially deprived children have shown the fundamental relevance of early contact with caregivers in both the evolution of social skills and language learning. Kuhl claims that infants and children are able to appreciate the communicative intent of others, and in early stages develop eye-to-eye contact, together with imitating sounds and gestures, and developing shared attention (Kuhl 2004; Kuhl and Rivera-Gaxiola 2008). Surprisingly, there has been very little research on the rewarding aspects of speech and communication. Clinically, we know that social reward is therapeutically critical in children with specific language impairment, and in schizophrenics, stutterers, autistics and other patients. In the previous chapter we discussed the relevance of exaggerating prosody in Motherese in mother-infant dyadic communication. This may serve not only to help infants to discriminate the sounds of language, but also to provide them with strong emotional feedback during communication.

Pascal Belin and collaborators have been studying the emotional components of speech processing in adults. They designed morphed prosodic and visual face expression stimuli that vary continuously from angry to happy expressions, which were presented to human subjects undergoing fMRI imaging. They identified two levels of emotional speech processing: a low- level circuit including auditory regions and the amygdala, which codes for emotion-related acoustic information, and a higher-level circuit involving the anterior insula and the prefrontal cortex, which codes the abstract, cognitive representations of social affect (Bestelmeyer et al. 2014). Working with normal subjects, Diana Tamir and Jason Mitchell recently reported that we love to speak about ourselves. According to them 30% or 40% of our speech consists of informing others about our own mental state (Tamir and Mitchell 2012). Furthermore, they found that self-disclosure during speech is associated with activation of reward related regions like the ventral striatum and the dopaminergic nucleus called the ventral tegmental area, which participate in reward processing. This may be partly the reason psychotherapy is so successful. Furthermore, we spend a lot of time gossiping about others rather than talking about external events.

According to Robin Dunbar, gossip is a highly rewarding behavior that served as social glue in our ancestors, and was critical in language evolution (Dunbar 2004). In a similar line, Dean Falk has claimed that early *Homo* mothers delivered increasingly immature babies that needed constant emotional support. Furthermore, our hairless skin and the weakness of the newborns did not permit babies to cling to their mothers' bodies while they moved, as other primate babies do. Thus, mother-child vocal communication facilitated emotional attachment between both, especially when the mother was foraging and away from her baby (Falk 2004).

Rewarding Circuits

In the last 50 years, we have learned quite a lot about the neural circuits and neurochemical regulation of rewarded behavior. Early studies in the 1950s, that have now become classic, showed that rats that could self-stimulate by pressing a lever that activated an electrode implanted in regions of their brains continued doing so and preferred to do this rather than eat, which was interpreted as a highly rewarding behavior for the rat (Jacques 1979). Consequently, these places were termed "pleasure centers" as they were believed to signal hedonic value. One such center is the ventral striatum (more precisely, a region called nucleus accumbens), which receives strong dopaminergic innervation. Later studies revealed that dopamine signaling mediates the rewarding effects in this nucleus, and that practically all addictive drugs, by different mechanisms, in the end have the common effect of boosting dopaminergic activity in the nucleus accumbens (Haber 2011).

It was later found that dopaminergic activity not only signals pleasure but also has a more profound role in classical conditioning (Schultz 2007). Large amounts of dopamine are released with unexpected pleasurable events (unconditioned stimulus), but when the event is predicted, it does not induce an increase in dopaminergic activity, even if it may seem highly rewarding. Nonetheless, dopamine signals stimuli that predict the subsequent appearance of reward, as, for example, a light that precedes the delivery of food (the conditioning stimulus). Firstly, when the animal does not know the light-reward association, dopamine is released upon the presence of reward but not the light. However, as the animal develops an association between these two events, dopaminergic firing begins to be induced by the light at the same time that its release by the reward itself becomes progressively weaker, until the light produces a strong response while the reward does not change dopaminergic activity at all. However, if we provide no reward after the light to an animal that has learned this task, it experiences dopaminergic depression. On the other hand, if we deliver the reward before it is expected, there is a very strong dopaminergic response. According to Wolfram Schultz and several other researchers, dopamine signals a prediction error in the appearance of reward, that is, it activates most strongly with unexpected rewards or events associated with rewards rather than with the reward itself (Schultz 2016). Moreover, and perhaps more importantly, Peter Redgrave and Kevin Gurney have proposed that dopaminergic activity participates in generating an associative network between the unexpected reward and other stimuli that occur prior to or simultaneously with it (Redgrave and Gurney 2006). This is critical for the animal to make the link between the preceding light and the reward, or between its own behavior and a rewarding outcome, for example, by accidentally pressing a lever that delivers food. Additional studies have revealed a role of dopamine in signaling negative as well as positive rewards, which is consistent with its role in conditioned learning (Matsumoto and Hikosaka 2009).

Associations have been reported between dopamine and emotional processing during speech. Patients with Parkinson's disease, in whom there is substantial dopaminergic depletion in the basal ganglia, have been repeatedly reported to show, among other symptoms, flat prosody and lack of emotional tone in their speech. Mark Pell and Silke Paulmann have done several studies of the role of the striatum, a component of the basal ganglia, in emotional speech processing (Paulmann et al. 2008). They have observed, for example, that Parkinson patients and patients with focalized basal ganglia lesions show a specific impairment in recognizing the emotional content of prosody, although their capacity for emotional processing is otherwise intact (Garrido-Vasquez et al. 2013). Likewise, when imaging radioactive dopaminergic ligands with PET, Kristina Simonyan observed that dopamine is released in the striatum during the execution of speech in normal subjects (Simonyan et al. 2013).

A fundamental aspect of music is its deep link to emotion. In his autobiography Charles Darwin recognized that the absence of music results in less happiness (F. Darwin 1887). Music serves to communicate emotion and may have been important in human evolution, to generate empathy and form group alliances. Robert Zatorre and his collaborators have been researching the pleasurable aspects of music in different people, and have found a strong, positive relationship between subjective pleasure induced by music, and autonomic responses reflected in electrical skin conduction, heart rate and other variables (Zatorre and Salimpoor 2013; Zatorre 2015). Using fMRI, they found activation of the ventral striatum. When subjects listened to new melodies, the ventral striatum showed stronger coactivation with the auditory cortex in response to melodies that subjects considered more rewarding. Using PET, Zatorre's group observed that this activation was associated with the release of dopamine (Salimpoor et al. 2011, 2015). On the other hand, monkeys have little ability to discriminate melodies or consonant versus dissonant sequences. Thus, beside speech, humans may be unique among primates in that they can recognize, learn and enjoy musical melodies.

Unfortunately, very few studies have focused on the rewarding aspects of vocalizations in mammals. The group led by Marcus Wöhr and Ingo Willuhn has found that rats emit two types of ultrasonic vocalizations, low frequency ones that occur in aversive situations and high-frequency ones associated with appetitive situations (Willuhn et al. 2014). The former induces freezing behavior, a conduct associated with fear, while the latter induces social approach behavior. Only the social-promoting high frequency vocalizations induce activation of reward related areas like the nucleus accumbens, by triggering the release of dopamine bursts in this nucleus. More detailed research with songbirds on the role of reward during song production and song learning may illuminate the importance of the social context in the acquisition of speech and language. Lubica Kubikova and Lubor Kostal have developed an elaborate argument for the role of dopamine in motivation, reward and monitoring errors in reward prediction that leads to learning in birdsong (Kubikova and Kostál 2010). The group of Constance Scharff reported that the presentation of noxious food stimuli elicited expression of genetic markers of neural activity in only some song-related nuclei (notably HVC and RA) (Tokarev et al. 2011). According to Scharff and coworkers, this indicates that as well as song learning, these nuclei participate in non-vocal behavior, especially food-related. This finding also suggests that these nuclei participate in reward and motivational mechanisms. Collaborating with Richard Mooney, Scharff found that decreasing expression of the language-related gene FOXP2 interferes with dopaminergic signaling in the striatum, and disrupts developmental and social modulation of song variability, which points to a role in reinforcement mechanisms during song learning (Murugan et al. 2013). In addition, Yoshimasa Seki and other researchers have found that neural activity and dopamine signaling in the striatal, song related area X are modulated by reward signals including song and food (Seki et al. 2014). Sarah Earp and Donna Manney found activation of dopamine-related mesolimbic components in female white-throated sparrows exposed to male songs during breeding season, in a pattern similar to what was reported when humans listen to pleasurable music (Earp 2012); and Yael Mandelblat-Cerf and collaborators showed that the intermediate ventral arcopallium, a reward related region of the birdsong forebrain, receives auditory inputs and is sensitive to distortions of the auditory feedback during song production (Mandelblat-Cerf et al. 2014). Moreover, lesions of this nucleus impair vocal learning in these birds. Kristina Simonyan and Erich Jarvis have proposed a model for reward during birdsong, in which a specific type of dopaminergic receptor called D1 signals auditory feedback errors in the learning phase, when the bird attempts to match its song to an auditory template that was acquired by listening to the songs of other adults (Simonyan et al. 2012). Similarly, Vikram Gadagkar and collaborators produced auditory interference to young zebra finches while they were singing, such that they heard a distorted output (Gadagkar et al. 2016). These "errors" were signaled by activity bursts of the dopaminergic projection to area X, indicating that these animals have an internal goal for their song that is continuously checked by output (an instance of predictive coding; see Chapter 8). Furthermore, this can be a mechanism by which the young birds correct their errors while learning the song from adults.

Finally, studies with singing birds have also focused on the influence of social context on reward. In an early study, Erich Jarvis and colleagues reported that dopaminergic activity in area X is higher in the context of directed singing (to attract a mate) than undirected singing (Sasaki et al. 2006). Subsequently, Lauren Riters and collaborators designed a conditioned learning experiment in which birds associated undirected singing with a specific place and acquired preference for this place (Riters 2012). The birds did not develop preference for a specific place when they directed their song to a potential mate, but acquired aversion to the place if they were unsuccessful at attracting the female. The authors concluded that undirected song is driven by intrinsic reward while female directed song is reinforced by social interactions. However, this also points to undirected song as a site-specific behavior that may serve to maintain territory in the wild, while failure to attract a mate in a specific place makes the bird look for another place to attract mates. Riters also found that dopamine and particularly opioids mediate social feedback signals in directed song, as well as the intrinsic reward in undirected song. Extending these findings to human speech, reward mechanisms may have been fundamental in the acquisition of speech and the early evolution and social significance of vocal behavior.

Autism or Liking Versus Wanting

Autism refers to a diverse group of conditions that have in common deficient social skills, restricted interests and repetitive behaviors. Affected subjects may show evidence of impaired capacity to interact with others as early as 2 or 3 years of age. Although autism is usually diagnosed by the age of three, it can show evident signs after the first year. Notably, Warner Jones and Ami Klin reported that infants that were later diagnosed with autism showed significant impairment in visual fixation, especially with fixation to visual facial stimuli (Jones and Klin 2013). Simon Baron-Cohen proposed that autistic subjects are unable to infer the mental states of others, as he puts it, they are "mentally blind" (Baron-Cohen et al. 1985). In later writings, Baron-Cohen presented an even more controversial interpretation in which he refers to autistic subjects as having extremely masculine brains, as males are considered to be more narrowly focused and less empathic than females (Baron-Cohen 2002). Another perspective, led by Coralie Chevallier and collaborators, emphasizes motivational dysfunction in autism, in which affected subjects are considered to experience no pleasure or reward in social interaction (Chevallier et al. 2012). Mirror neuron researchers have proposed a different perspective on autism, which is that the mirror neuron system of these subjects is dysfunctional in that it impedes them from empathizing with others (Williams et al. 2001; Gallese 2006).

Autistic subjects have been repeatedly reported to avoid direct eye contact (depending on the severity of symptoms), and display abnormal activation of the amygdala and other emotion-related brain regions during face processing. Elisabeth von dem Hagen, teaming with Baron-Cohen and collaborators, reported that in the context of eye contact autistic subjects display atypical activation of emotion-related and theory-of-mind related brain regions (von dem Hagen et al. 2014). Activation was higher for autistic subjects with averted gaze than direct gaze, while the opposite was the case for controls. The authors hypothesized that with normal subjects direct gaze triggers automatic attributions of mental states to the other, while this is not the case with autistic subjects and there is no interest in the stimulus. This and other studies have also shown reduced connectivity between areas related to social behavior and areas relevant to social interaction like the face-selective region of the fusiform area in the temporal lobe. Daniel Abrams and colleagues have given support to the motivational theory of autism, reporting less connectivity between the left posterior superior temporal sulcus and the nucleus accumbens (Abrams et al. 2013a, b). Autistic children also showed decreased connectivity between the right superior temporal sulcus, which processes speech prosody, and reward-related regions. Furthermore, reduced connectivity correlated with deficits in communicative abilities but not specifically with the formal language abilities of autistic patients.

An opposing perspective, supported by Gregory Hickok, considers that autistic subjects do develop emotional responses from social contact, but these are simply so intense that they cannot bear them (Hickok 2014). In other words, instead of being unreactive, they are over-reactive to social stimuli. Therefore, they avoid establishing close interactions because it makes them too uncomfortable. For example, Sylvie Tordjman and collaborators observed that while autistic subjects showed fewer behavioral responses to painful stimuli, their physiological indicators of stress under these conditions (heart rate and production of stress-related hormones) were higher than those of normal subjects (Tordjman et al. 2009). Psychologists like Antonia Hamilton and Ann Gernsbacher have shown evidence that autistic patients have no problem in imitating object-directed behaviors or in understanding other people's intentions (Gernsbacher and Frymiare 2005; Hamilton et al. 2007). Gernsbacher and collaborators further argue that the deficits in Theory of Mind tests observed in autistic patients stem from their impairment in communicative ability rather than damage to a specific brain module involved in inferring the mental states of others. Furthermore, Cecilia Heyes and collaborators have shown that autistic subjects can perform tasks perfectly that involve spontaneous imitation. The authors claim that the inability of some autistic subjects to imitate pantomimic actions stems from the cognitive complexity of these tasks rather than from a specific deficit in imitation (Heyes 1998; Leighton et al. 2008). These diverging interpretations were the focus of a forum in which Vittorio Gallese, Gernsbacher, Heyes, Hickok and Marco Iacoboni participated and presented their respective views (Gallese et al. 2011). In addition, Rebecca Brewer and collaborators have conducted several studies comparing autistic and alexithymia subjects (Brewer et al. 2015; Brewer and Murphy 2016, Cook et al. 2013). Alexithymia consists of impairment to recognizing one's own and others' emotions, but these patients do feel signs of distress, sometimes more strongly than normal, when witnessing someone in pain. Brewer has confirmed that autism and alexithymia are dissociated conditions, but they overlap significantly. Furthermore, these researchers found that the inability to recognize facial emotions originates in alexythimic symptoms rather than in the autistic condition per se (Cook et al. 2013). In the autistic spectrum, there may be such heterogeneity in both symptomatology and etiology that many more cognitive, neuroscientific and genetic studies are needed before we know whether in fact we are dealing with a single condition or with a group of apparently similar disorders.

Subjects diagnosed with autism or belonging to the autistic disorder spectrum group have significantly altered electrophysiological responses to speech as well as an apparent lack of interest in speech signals, with a preference for non-speech sounds over speech sounds. Nonetheless, many autistic children are able to speak, although their speech is usually uncommon in terms of vocabulary, syntactic forms and prosody, showing stereotyped and repetitive use of language forms. Their main deficit lies in what is called the pragmatics of speech, which consists of relating language or speech to a social context in order to interpret social situations or disambiguate meanings (Sterponi et al. 2015; Baird and Norbury 2016). Elizabeth Carter and team evaluated judgments of a social situation (in which a child was behaving well or badly) and a physical situation (in which a child could be indoors or outdoors) (Carter et al. 2012). Typically developing children made use of brain regions associated with language and mentalization to solve the social task, while autistic children showed less activation of these areas during this task. Nonetheless, autistic children were equally able as controls to solve the task, which suggests to the authors that autistic children have difficulty using language to explain social situations, even if they are able to understand them. Likewise, the group led by Stefan Sunaert compared the language deficits of children diagnosed with specific language impairment to those of autistic children (Verhoeven et al. 2012). The main difference between the two clinical groups is that patients with specific language disorder are otherwise relatively normal, while autistic patients show a wide array of social and cognitive impairments, even if they are of normal or above-average intelligence. Using tractographic techniques, Sunaert and colleagues found alterations in white matter in the superior longitudinal fasciculus in the specific language impairment group but not in the autistic group, even if the two groups overlapped in linguistic receptive-expressive impairments. In a subsequent study in autistic subjects, the same group found normal functional connectivity between Broca's and Wernicke's areas, but abnormal functional connectivity between the language areas and other brain regions (Verly et al.2014).

Overall, the evidence suggests that autistic subjects have difficulty with using language rather than with its structure or articulation. They are able to produce and understand language at relatively complex syntactical and semantic levels. However, they have problems with some verbal tenses and use a generally less complex grammar than normal children. Ken Wexler and team reported that autistic children have difficulty in understanding reflexive pronouns like "himself"- as opposed to "him", as in the sentence "Tim's brother pointed to himself", where normal speakers understand that "himself" refers to Tim's brother and not to Tim (Perovic et al. 2013). However, others have argued that this could arise from difficulty with the concept of self rather than being a specifically syntactic problem. In any event, if autistic children have grammatical impairments, these are relatively mild and do not stand out as principal features of the syndrome. This supports the notion that individual development of language capacity does not rely on appropriate social interactions, or alternatively that autistic children are socially impaired but not totally incompetent, and may be able to extract clues from speakers to develop language. Coralie Chevallier indeed argues along this line (Chevallier et al. 2012).

According to behavioral neuroscientists, two different processes take place in reward-seeking behavior that can be dissociated. One is wanting, which is expressed as a motivational drive to reach a goal; and the other is liking, or the pleasure that consumption of reward produces (Pool et al. 2016). Autistic children might not be motivated to interact socially or try to avoid it, but they may nonetheless enjoy this interaction when it takes place. This view is supported by studies by Line Gebauer and collaborators, in which autistic subjects had to rate melodies on a scale from happy to sad (Gebauer et al. 2014). The patients rated the emotional content of music similarly to normal controls, but showed more activation in regions like the prefrontal cortex and anterior insula, suggesting that they may even be overreactive to the emotional content of music. This is further evidence supporting the hypothesis of hyper-reactive emotionality in autism.

The idea that autistic patients enjoy social contact even if they avoid it is consistent with a role of reward in speech learning. Nevertheless, innatists may have a point in that we are very fast learners when it comes to speech acquisition. In my view, this may be reflection of accelerated development of language and speech-related neural networks relative to others, as there was a benefit for our ancestors in being able to speak as soon as possible. This is partly because social interactions and abilities build up from earlier social experiences, and there may have been a selective value in developing these basic capacities in early life, where neural plasticity is higher. To use an extreme example, this may be like birds learning to fly. In most species, except for highly specialized species like swifts, birds require practice to fly, although they are instinctively driven to do it. The main motivation for young birds to learn how to fly is food, and at some age parents gradually begin leaving food at some distance from the nest, forcing the baby bird to leave the nest, then jumping to nearby branches and so on. There are many trials and errors, and some young birds fall to the ground and die, but most end up learning to fly. Furthermore, and what is important to this argument, the earliest flying birds probably did not learn to fly when they were young, as they started trying to flap their wings or to glide as adults. The developmental acceleration of the neural networks that were being acquired by adult practice allowed young birds to learn to fly much earlier and with less practice than their ancestors required.

The Prince and the Fox

"I am looking for friends. What does that mean – tame?"
"It is an act too often neglected," said the fox. "It means to establish ties."

"To establish ties?"

"Just that," said the fox. "To me, you are still nothing more than a little boy who is just like a hundred thousand other little boys. And I have no need of you. And you, on your part, have no need of me. To you I am nothing more than a fox like a hundred thousand other foxes. But if you tame me, then we shall need each other. To me, you will be unique in all the world. To you, I shall be unique in all the world . . . ."

Antoine de Saint-Exupéry, The Little Prince (1956), p. 71–72.
English translation.

A large part of our uniqueness relates to our being an extremely social species, a condition that provided the adequate setting for language to evolve. But how did this hyper-sociality evolve? Those who had a stronger motivation to make bonds with others and to establish cooperative behaviors were more likely to survive. We know of instances of close cooperation among species like insects, where we assume there is little emotional attachment as their interactions are largely genetically determined. But when it comes to learned cooperation, there has to be some previous emotional engagement among participants, there has to be some trust and acceptance of the other's intentions. In this section I propose a broader evolutionary and ecological context to account for our intense sociality, gathering evidence from an unexpected source that has been available for a long time, but has only received attention in recent years. This begins with Charles Darwin's original example of domesticated species as a model for natural selection, which has turned on its head by recognizing that domestication is not a special condition but rather is a powerful motor for the evolution of human social behavior.

Common chimpanzees show signs of cooperative behavior, but their social life is riddled with aggressive encounters among members of the same group and between groups, which has been popularized with images of members of one group brutally killing isolated members of other groups, and has been thoroughly described in Richard Wrangham and Dale Peterson's book *Demonic Males* (Wrangham and Peterson 1997; Wrangham et al. 1999; Wrangham 2003; Hare et al. 2012). On the other hand, the lives of the Bonobo, or pygmy chimpanzee, are totally different from that of the common chimpanzee. They are smaller, have a juvenilized appearance, and live in a much gentler society, with intense heterosexual and homosexual sexual activity. One ecological explanation for this difference is that bonobo groups are much larger than those of the chimpanzees. Groups of wild chimpanzees are composed of not more than ten individuals, while bonobos live in groups of no fewer than fifteen individuals and often many more than this. According to Wrangham, a factor influencing group size is diet. Bonobos feed on fruit and leaves that provide sufficient food for a large group, while chimps live alongside of gorillas that dominate the ground and take the major share of herbs and shoots, obliging chimps to rely more on less accessible fruit in the trees, and other food sources like monkey meat. Which of these species best represents our ancestor's behavior? Some authors like Frans de Waal have claimed that the social structure of bonobos has important things in common with that of early humans (de Waal 2005). This may be partly correct, but again we must not forget the intense competition and aggression that drives our own social behavior (Gómez et al. 2016).

As I said before, among our ancestors there were significant benefits for those that could engage in stable reciprocal relationships. We began to adapt to live with others, establishing close family ties and friendship-like alliances as well as sexual bonding. This involved an intense selection process in which the environment to which we were adapting was not just the outside world, but also our social world. Charles Darwin used the term "artificial selection" to refer to the process in which humans iterate the selection of some attributes of domestic species to maximize their usefulness, as an example to illustrate the power of restricting the reproductive resources to only some, based on the possession of specific traits. He then proposed the term "natural selection" to refer to a similar process occurring in the wild, without an operator behind it, but based solely on the differential reproduction of some lineages at the expense of others (Darwin 1871).

Technically, domestication can be defined as the process of controlling the reproduction of another species. We have been using artificial selection to "improve" the quality of species according to our needs. Using this procedure, humans have domesticated hundreds of species, from wheat to cattle, in effect everything we see in the supermarket and much more, including dogs and cats. The dog is the earliest species we tamed (or, as in Saint-Exupéry's story, we tamed each other), some 15,000 years ago (Shannon et al. 2015), although some argue it was even earlier. Recent studies suggest two sites, in Eastern and Western Asia, for the origin of the dog from two separate wolf populations (Frantz et al. 2016). Domestication of grains like maize began some 9,000 years ago in the Fertile Crescent, imposing strong selective pressure on these species to increase their nutritive capacity (Hufford et al. 2012). With domestication of plants and animals, came conditions like periodontal disease, and many mutations were selected in humans that allowed their digestive system and metabolism to adapt to increasingly starch-rich and milk-rich diets (Tishkoff et al. 2007). But not only genes involved in metabolism show a signature of intense selection, there are also genes coding for neuronal signaling pathways like the gene that codes for the short version of the serotonin transporter, whose modulation is related to mood disorders and control of aggressiveness (Chiao and Blizinsky 2010). In addition, a type of dopamine receptor, D4, has recently acquired polymorphisms that are related to risk-taking behavior, attention deficit hyperactivity disorder, and other neuropsychiatric conditions (Ding et al. 2002). After analyzing the variability of human genomes, Robert Moyzis and colleagues have come to the conclusion that our species has undergone an intense selective process, at least in the last 40,000 years, not unlike that observed in domesticated species like maize or cattle (Hawks et al. 2007; Voight et al. 2006; Wang et al. 2006).

As we domesticated other species, we adapted ourselves to the process of domestication, forming an evolutionary circle that maintained our genetic evolution and drags other species with it. Richard Wrangham argues that we humans not only domesticated other species, but that our own evolutionary history is one of self-domestication, where we adapted to the needs of our own social group, changing social dynamics that in turn put new demands on our behavior in an ongoing cyclic process (Wrangham 2003). This partly contradicts the now fashionable trend of evolutionary psychology, interpreting human behavior as the result of adaptations that occurred a long time ago, which are assumed to have been unchanged genetically since then. The field of evolutionary psychology has been abundantly criticized for its *post hoc* interpretations, which are quite difficult to disprove. On the other hand, the evolutionary interpretation of our recent history is backed by genetic and archaeological evidence. Wrangham and others have argued that there were two main inflection points in the evolution of society (Wrangham and Peterson 1997; Wrangham et al. 1999). The first stage relates to the origin of *Homo erectus* some 1.8 million years ago, who begins to control fire and starts eating cooked food, providing the energy requirements to build a large brain. From then on, brains slowly increased in size until some 300,000 years ago, with the origin of Neanderthals and modern humans, a period when our current brain size was acquired. This period was marked by several cultural innovations, including more sophisticated tools and ornaments. Another critical event took place much more recently, some 40,000 to 50,000 years ago, which coincided with the intensification of genetic selection in our species, at the time modern humans colonized the planet and began what anthropologists call the "great leap forward". Here, technology underwent a dramatic explosion, marked by the appearance of tools associated with clothing and jewelry, arrow making and cave painting among other innovations. According to Wrangham, from then until now, the self-domestication process has accelerated tremendously, which is consistent with the evidence of intense genetic selection shown above.

I am again indebted to Jeremy Taylor for calling my attention to the experiments made in the 1950s by the late Russian geneticist Dimitri Belyaev, and afterward by his colleague Lyudmila Trut, on the process of domestication and artificial selection of wild Arctic foxes (Trut 1999; Taylor 2009). Belyaev started with a population of 130 wild foxes that were held captive and allowed to reproduce. He began an intense selection process, offering food to the pups with one hand while attempting to handle them with the other. After repeating this procedure for several months, Belyaev separated the foxes into three groups, those that never approached, those that fondly accepted food, and an intermediate group. Notably, those that accepted food also wagged their tails while approaching, and these were the only ones allowed to reproduce later on. After six generations, animals had become so docile that they behaved like pets. Moreover, beside their tameness and lack of aggressiveness, these animals evidenced many other changes like precocious sensorial and vocal development, delayed appearance of the fear response, retarded developmental release of the stress hormone corticosterone, diminished adrenal gland activity and increased blood serotonin levels. There were also morphological changes, diminishing the sexual dimorphism of the skull, making it more female-like (or juvenilized) in males. Furthermore, Brian Hare experimented with the social behavior of these animals, showing that they were just as good as domesticated dogs and children at following human cues like pointing or gazing, and notably better than wild animals and even than wild non-human primates (Hare et al. 2005). More recently, Adam Wilkins, together with Richard Wrangham and Tecumseh Fitch proposed the existence of a "domestication syndrome" in several domestic animal species that includes many phenotypical features like docility, depigmentation, floppy ears, shorter muzzles, smaller brains, more frequent reproductive cycles and neotenic characters (Wilkins et al. 2014). Furthermore, they advanced the bold hypothesis that underlying many of these characters is a mild but generalized defect in an embryonic structure called the neural crest, responsible for, among other things, the development of pigmentation, the cranial skeleton and the autonomic and adrenal systems that mediate stress response and the fight-or-flight reaction. In this context, some years ago the group led by Nicole Le Douarin transplanted cranial neural crest cells from chicks to quails, which among other things resulted in chimeric hatchlings that produce intermediate chick/quail vocalizations (Le Douarin 1980). This implies that neural crest tissue is important in the generation of structures involved in vocalizations, and that its modification during self-domestication contributed to the development of vocal learning and speech.

The dog is our closest friend, not only because of its loyalty but also because dogs show clear signs of empathy, display eye-to-eye contact and are probable the most sociable of domestic animals. Unlike the domestication of cattle or grain, the ancestors of carnivorous domestic animals, like the wolf and the wild Egyptian cat probably approached humans looking for food rather than being chosen by humans for domestication. Ray and Lorna Coppinger (Coppinger and Coppinger 2002) and others have advanced this argument. According to this hypothesis, wolves and cats entered a domestication process on their own, first wolves by approaching encampments and looking for leftovers, and much later on, cats by chasing the rodents that fed on grain stocks. Step by step, humans became familiar with the most daring animals, which for their part restrained their aggressiveness to profit more from their incursions. Humans also benefited from this alliance, as wolves helped to protect human groups and provided clues about food, even helping to hunt. Cats reduced the number of mice and rats in food stocks. However, humans may have not been so passive in receiving dogs and cats. It has been reported that young adult male baboons kidnap female baboon infants from other groups to start their own harem. There are some controversial videos in YouTube suggesting that baboons also kidnap feral dog cubs, which grow to adulthood as members of the baboon troop, helping them to maintain territory and guarding against predators or rival groups[2]. Although the veracity of these videos has been questioned, similar behavior could have taken place among early modern humans. Thus, in the process of becoming more sociable, we have included other species, some for their own sake and others that were manipulated by humans from the beginning. What I am pointing to here is that the evolution of human social life is highly complex, encompassing many other species in a profound evolutionary process that goes far beyond just us. In a way, the evolution of social life and of domestication can be seen as one overarching evolutionary process, perhaps one of the most radical we have seen in the history of the Earth.

Our brains may have been subject to the same kind of selective process as other parts of the body, increasing our social dependence, decreasing intra-group aggressiveness and facilitating mutual exchanges of gestures and vocalizations as a sort of "social glue" that promoted bonding and attachment between family members and neighbors. Personally, I think this may partly be the case. As I discussed in the previous chapter, there is growing likelihood that other phenomena involving epigenetic processes rather than genetic mutation played an important role in recent and not so recent human evolution. This process has probably been taking place since long before the origin of modern humans, and may have been responsible for our physical evolution, including the acquisition of large brains, the shortening of the face, our upright posture and many other characters.

---

[2] https://www.youtube.com/watch?v=U2lSZPTa3hohttps://www.youtube.com/watch?v=QlwOViUzv10

The Peter Pan Syndrome

Domestication is associated with the maintenance of juvenile characters, a phenomenon that in the 1970s the late Stephen Jay Gould brilliantly called attention to as an important mechanism for evolutionary change, particularly in the evolution of our species (Gould 1977). Timing is of the essence in embryonic development, and modulation of the rates and duration of distinct growth patterns may be responsible for much of the morphological evolution of animals. Changes in developmental timing are collectively termed heterochronies, and as Gould proposed, these can be paedomorphic, in which juvenile traits are maintained in the adult, or recapitulatory, in which development follows a sequence dictated by evolutionary history. Paedomorphic characters can occur by truncation of the latest developmental stages (which is called progenesis), or by retardation of the developmental pace, which is called neoteny (I talked about the latter phenomenon in the Chapters 1 and 3). On the other hand, recapitulation takes place by hypermorphosis, in which new stages are added at the end of development. In recapitulation there is a general acceleration of earlier stages, thus condensing them in early development due to a sort of "pressure" produced as new structures keep adding in later developmental stages. Gould and others argued that we humans are neotenic apes, in which our development has slowed down, prolonging childhood and retarding maturity. This is evidenced in features like a flattened and broadened face, a large brain in relation to body size, small teeth and jaws, thin skull bones, large eyes, and other characters. Something similar has been proposed to occur in the evolution of speech capacities. During development, juvenile monkeys progressively lose the capacity to vocalize on instructed command as they become adults. This feature is specific to voluntary vocal production, because spontaneous vocalizations, as well as responses to other instructed motor commands like hand movements, continued into adulthood. Steffan Hage and Andreas Nieder argue that humans may represent a neotenic condition in this respect, in which the juvenile voluntary control of vocalizations extends into adulthood (Hage et al. 2016). This is consistent with evidence showing a maintained expression of genes involved in synapse formation in humans (Somel et al. 2013).

However, some authors like Michael McKinney and Kenneth McNamara have criticized the neotenic hypothesis of human evolution (McKinney and McNamara 1991). These authors make the argument that much of human brain heterochrony is in fact a case of hypermorphosis, in which both behavior and brain development go beyond the stages achieved by other primates, acquiring more capacities and brain complexity than our primate ancestors as new circuits and behaviors are built based on previous ones. As I said above, the early and rapid development of some human speech capacities may be an example of developmental acceleration, like the development of flight in birds. It may be that neoteny accounts for some of our traits, like skeletal characters, hair loss, etc., that maintain an immature condition in the adult stage. On the other hand, human brain development does not result in an immature brain but in a much larger and more complex brain because the rates of growth, neuronal proliferation and establishment of connectivity are maintained for a longer time (see Chapter 3). In my view, the situation is a combination of events in which the prolongation of development resulted in increasing plasticity to generate evolutionary novelty but also permitted brain development beyond the stages reached by other primates.

In contrast to humans, a typical feature of domesticated species is that their brain size is smaller than that of their counterparts in the wild, a character that is retained generations after returning to the wild (Kruska 2005). What makes this difference if we were both subjected to the domestication process? One possibility is that domestication is not exactly the same for the dominant and subordinate species. The subordinate species must inhibit aggressive behaviors much more than the dominant one, and there is a price for members of the dominant species that develop novel behavioral strategies. Furthermore, members of the dominant species still have to compete for mates, while those of subordinate species are by definition not able to choose mates. Thus, while some human characters indeed showed a relaxation of selection, and a positive selection for decreased aggressiveness and greater tameness that are consistent with neoteny, some other traits display intense selection for increasing behavioral complexity beyond that achieved by other primates during human evolution.

In this chapter we have seen that the process of domestication, including of ourselves as products of this behavioral and cultural innovation, is one of the main events in our recent history. We achieved this after a very long and slow history in which our ancestors initiated a rudimentary culture of stone artifacts. This primitive culture remained quite stable over time and changed only recently, first with the origin of Neanderthals and Denisovans, and then with the appearance of modern humans. The last step is believed to have occurred very recently, about 50,000 years ago, marked by the advent of domestication practices that led to agriculture, sophisticated art and a technological explosion that is still taking place. Derek Bickerton has argued that a pre-lexical system may have been at use as far back as Australopithecines, which developed into modern speech much later, producing a rapid increase in brain size and then giving rise to a Cultural Revolution (Bickerton 2014). I claim instead that the protospeech stage described by Bickerton was accompanied (and very likely preceded) by a rich vocal repertoire used for social bonding. These two elements gradually fused by inserting elements that permitted connecting words in strings, until modern speech appeared. The phonological loop probably evolved gradually along this process, but may have acquired its maximal expression with the origin of modern speech. The increasing sociality of early humans, possibly triggered by the ecological conditions in which they had to live, was slowly molding our ancestors' brains in a way that made having more communicative abilities highly beneficial. Thus, large brain networks were recruited for social behavior, in concordance with the evolution and activation of the phonological loop. Perhaps full-blown speech was acquired very recently, and may be partly dependent on cultural and epigenetic mechanisms.

References and Notes

Abrams DA, Lynch CJ, Cheng KM, Phillips J, Supekar K, Ryali S, Uddin LQ, Menon V (2013a) Underconnectivity between voice-selective cortex and reward circuitry in children with autism. Proc Natl Acad Sci U S A 110:12060–12065

Abrams DA, Uddin LQ, Menon V (2013b) Reply to Brock: Renewed focus on the voice and social reward in children with autism. Proc Natl Acad Sci U S A 110:E3974

Bachner-Melman R, Ebstein RP (2014) The role of oxytocin and vasopressin in emotional and social behaviors. Handb Clin Neurol 124:53–68

Baird G, Norbury CF (2016) Social (pragmatic) communication disorders and autism spectrum disorder. Arch Dis Child 101:745–751

Baron-Cohen S (2002) The extreme male brain theory of autism. Trends Cogn Sci 6:248–254

Baron-Cohen S, Leslie AM, Frith U. Baron-Cohen S, Leslie AM, Frith U (1985) Does the autistic child have a "theory of mind"? Cognition 21:37–46

Bestelmeyer PE, Maurage P, Rouger J, Latinus M, Belin P (2014) Adaptation to vocal expressions reveals multistep perception of auditory emotion. J Neurosci 34:8098–8105

Bickerton D (2014) More Than Nature Needs. Language, Mind, and Evolution. Harvard University Press, Cambridge

Brewer R, Murphy J (2016) People with autism can feel emotions, feel empathy. Sci Amer. Spectrum http://www.scientificamerican.com/article/people-with-autism-can-read-emotions-feel-empathy/

Brewer R, Happé F, Cook R, Bird G (2015) Commentary on "Autism, oxytocin and interoception": Alexithymia, not Autism Spectrum Disorders, is the consequence of interoceptive failure. Neurosci Biobehav Rev 56:348–353

Buttelmann D, Buttelman F, Carpenter M, Call J, Tomasello M (2017) Great apes distinguish true from false beliefs in an interactive helping task. PLoS One 12:e0173793

Call J, Hare BA, Tomasello M (1998) Chimpanzee gaze following in an object-choice task. Anim Cogn 11:89–99

Carter EJ, Williams DL, Minshew NJ, Lehman JF (2012) Is he being bad? Social and language brain networks during social judgment in children with autism. PLoS One 7:e47241

Caruso C (2016) Chimps may be capable of comprehending the minds of others. Sci Am 10: 16–17

Chevallier C, Kohls G, Troiani V, Brodkin ES, Schultz RT (2012) The social motivation theory of autism. Trends Cogn Sci 16:231–239

Chiao JY, Blizinsky KD (2010) Culture-gene coevolution of individualism-collectivism and the serotonin transporter gene. Proc Biol Sci 277:529–537

Cook R, Brewer R, Shah P, Bird G (2013) Alexithymia, not autism, predicts poor recognition of emotional facial expressions. Psychol Sci 24:723–732

Coppinger R, Coppinger L (2002) Dogs: A New Understanding of canine Origin, Behavior and Evolution. University of Chicago Press, Chicago

Crockett MJ, Fehr E (2014) Social brains on drugs: tools for neuromodulation in social neuroscience. Soc Cogn Affect Neurosci 9:250–254

Darwin C (1871) The Descent of Man, and Selection in Relation to Sex. Murray, London

Darwin F (1887) The Life and Letters of Charles Darwin, Including and Autobiographical Chapter. 3 vols. Murray, London.

De Saint-Exupéry A (1956) Le Petit Prince. Éditions Gallimard, Paris p 71–72 (1999)

De Waal F (2005) Our Inner Ape. Granta Books, London

Ding YC, Chi HC, Grady DL, Morishima A, Kidd JR, Kidd KK, Flodman P, Spence MA, Schuck S, Swanson JM, Zhang YP, Moyzis RK (2002) Evidence of positive selection acting at the human dopamine receptor D4 gene locus. Proc Natl Acad Sci U S A 99:309–314

Dreher JC, Dunne S, Pazderska A, Frodl T, Nolan JJ, O'Doherty JP (2016) Testosterone causes both prosocial and antisocial status-enhancing behaviors in human males. Proc Natl Acad Sci U S A 113:11633–11638

Dunbar RI (2004) Gossip in evolutionary perspective. Rev Gen Psychol 8:11–110

Dunbar RI, Shultz S (2007) Evolution in the social brain. Science 317:1344–1347

Earp SE, Maney DL (2012) Birdsong: is it music to their ears? Front Evol Neurosci 4:14

Falk D (2004) Prelinguistic evolution in early hominins: whence motherese? Behav Brain Sci 27:491–503; discussion 503–583

Frantz LA, Mullin VE, Pionnier-Capitan M, Lebrasseur O, Ollivier M, Perri A, Linderholm A, Mattiangeli V, Teasdale MD, Dimopoulos EA, Tresset A, Duffraisse M, McCormick F, Bartosiewicz L, Gál E, Nyerges ÉA, Sablin MV, Bréhard S, Mashkour M, Bălăşescu A, Gillet B, Hughes S, Chassaing O, Hitte C, Vigne JD, Dobney K, Hänni C, Bradley DG, Larson G (2016) Genomic and archaeological evidence suggest a dual origin of domestic dogs. Science 352:1228–1231

Gadagkar V, Puzerey PA, Chen R, Baird-Daniel E, Fargang AR, Goldberg JH (2016) Dopamine neurons encode performance error in singing birds. Science 354:1278–1281

Gallese V (2006) Intentional attunement: a neurophysiological perspective on social cognition and its disruption in autism. Brain Res 1079:15–24

Gallese V, Gernsbacher MA, Heyes C, Hickok G, Iacoboni M (2011) Mirror Neuron Forum. Perspect Psychol Sci 6:369–407.

Gao S, Becker B, Luo L, Geng Y, Zhao W, Yin Y, Hu J, Gao Z, Gong Q, Hurlemann R, Yao D, Kendrick KM (2016) Oxytocin, the peptide that bonds the sexes also divides them. Proc Natl Acad Sci U S A 113:7650–7654

Garrido-Vásquez P, Pell MD, Paulmann S, Strecker K, Schwarz J, Kotz SA (2013) An ERP study of vocal emotion processing in asymmetric Parkinson's disease. Soc Cogn Affect Neurosci 8:918–927

Gebauer L, Skewes J, Westphael G, Heaton P, Vuust P (2014) Intact brain processing of musical emotions in autism spectrum disorder, but more cognitive load and arousal in happy vs. sad music. Front Neurosci 8:192

Gernsbacher MA, Frymiare JL (2005) Does the Autistic Brain Lack Core Modules? J Dev Learn Disord 9:3–16

Gómez JM, Verdú M, González-Megías A, Méndez M (2016) The phylogenetic roots of human lethal violence. Nature 538:233–237

Gopnik A (2012) Scientific thinking in young children: theoretical advances, empirical research, and policy implications. Science 337:1623–1627

Gopnik A, Meltzoff AN (1984) Semantic and cognitive development in 15- to 21-month-old children. J Child Lang 11:495–513

Gopnik A, Schulz L (2004) Mechanisms of theory formation in young children. Trends Cogn Sci 8:371–377

Gould SJ (1977) Ontogeny and Phylogeny. Belknap Press, Harvard, Cambridge

Haber SN. (2011) Neuroanatomy of Reward: A View from the Ventral Striatum. In: Gottfried JA (ed), Neurobiology of Sensation and Reward. CRC Press/Taylor & Francis, Boca Raton, p 123–161

Hage SR, Gavrilov N, Nieder A (2016) Developmental changes of cognitive vocal control in monkeys. J Exp Biol 219:1744–1749

Hamilton AF, Brindley RM, Frith U (2007) Imitation and action understanding in autistic spectrum disorders: how valid is the hypothesis of a deficit in the mirror neuron system? Neuropsychologia 45:1859–1868

Hammock EA, Young LJ (2006) Oxytocin, vasopressin and pair bonding: implications for autism. Philos Trans R Soc Lond B Biol Sci 361:2187–2198

Hare B, Call J, Agnetta B, Tomasello M (2000) Chimpanzees know what conspecifics do and do not see. Anim Behav 59:771–785

Hare B, Call J, Tomasello M (2001) Do chimpanzees know what conspecifics know? Anim Behav 61:139–151

Hare B, Plyusnina I, Ignacio N, Schepina O, Stepika A, Wrangham R, Trut L (2005) Social cognitive evolution in captive foxes is a correlated by-product of experimental domestication. Curr Biol 15:226–230

Hare B, Wobber B, Wrangham R (2012) The self-domestication hypothesis: evolution of bonobo psychology is due to selection against aggression. Anim Behav 83:573–585

Hawks J, Wang ET, Cochran GM, Harpending HC, Moyzis RK (2007) Recent acceleration of human adaptive evolution. Proc Natl Acad Sci U S A 104:20753–20758

Herrmann E, Call J, Hernàndez-Lloreda MV, Hare B, Tomasello M (2007) Humans have evolved specialized skills of social cognition: the cultural intelligence hypothesis. Science 317:1360–1366

Heyes CM (1998) Theory of mind in nonhuman primates. Behav Brain Sci 21:101–114; discussion 115–148

Heyes CM (2017) Apes submentalise. Trends Cogn Sci 21:1–2

Hickok G (2014) The Myth of Mirror Neurons: The Real Neuroscience of Communication And Cognition. Norton Press, New York

Hufford MB, Xu X, van Heerwaarden J, Pyhäjärvi T, Chia JM, Cartwright RA, Elshire RJ, Glaubitz JC, Guill KE, Kaeppler SM, Lai J, Morrell PL, Shannon LM, Song C, Springer NM, Swanson-Wagner RA, Tiffin P, Wang J, Zhang G, Doebley J, McMullen MD, Ware D, Buckler ES, Yang S, Ross-Ibarra J (2012) Comparative population genomics of maize domestication and improvement. Nat Genet 44:808–811

Jacques S (1979) Brain stimulation and reward: "pleasure centers" after twenty-five years. Neurosurgery 5:277–283

Jones W, Klin A (2013) Attention to eyes is present but in decline in 2-6-month-old infants later diagnosed with autism. Nature 504:427–431

Kennedy DP, Adolphs R (2012) The social brain in psychiatric and neurological disorders. Trends Cogn Sci 16:559–572

Krupenye C. Kano F, Hirata S, Call J, Tomasello M (2016) Great apes anticipate that other individuals will act according to false beliefs. Science 354:110–114

Kruska DC (2005) On the evolutionary significance of encephalization in some eutherian mammals: effects of adaptive radiation, domestication, and feralization. Brain Behav Evol 65:73–108

Kubikova L, Kostál L (2010) Dopaminergic system in birdsong learning and maintenance. J Chem Neuroanat 39:112–123

Kuhl PK (2004) Early language acquisition: cracking the speech code. Nat Rev Neurosci 5:831–843

Kuhl P, Rivera-Gaxiola M (2008) Neural substrates of language acquisition. Annu Rev Neurosci 31:511–534

Kuhl PK, Tsao FM, Liu HM (2003) Foreign-language experience in infancy: effects of short-term exposure and social interaction on phonetic learning. Proc Natl Acad Sci U S A 100:9096–9101

Le Douarin NM (1980) The ontogeny of the neural crest in avian embryo chimaeras. Nature 286:663–669

Leighton J, Bird G, Charman T, Heyes C (2008) Weak imitative performance is not due to a functional "mirroring" deficit in adults with Autism Spectrum Disorders. Neuropsychologia 46:1041–1049

Mandelblat-Cerf Y, Las L, Denisenko N, Fee MS (2014) A role for descending auditory cortical projections in songbird vocal learning. Elife doi: 10.7554/eLife.02152

Matsumoto M, Hikosaka O (2009) Two types of dopamine neuron distinctly convey positive and negative motivation signals. Nature 459:837–841

McKinney ML, McNamara KJ (1991) Heterochrony. The Evolution of Ontogeny. Plenum Press, New York

Meltzoff AN, Waismeyer A, Gopnik A (2012) Learning about causes from people: observational causal learning in 24-month-old infants. Dev Psychol 48:1215–1228

Murugan M, Harward S, Scharff C, Mooney R (2013) Diminished FoxP2 levels affect dopaminergic modulation of corticostriatal signaling important to song variability. Neuron 80:1464–1476

Paulmann S, Pell MD, Kotz SA (2008) Functional contributions of the basal ganglia to emotional prosody: evidence from ERPs. Brain Res 1217:171–178

Penn DC, Povinelli DJ (2007) On the lack of evidence that non-human animals possess anything remotely resembling a "Theory of Mind". Phil Trans Roy Soc Lond B doi:10.1098/rstb.2006.2023

Perovic A, Modyanova N, Wexler K (2013) Comprehension of reflexive and personal pronouns in children with autism: A syntactic or pragmatic deficit? Appl Psycholing 34:813–835

Pool E, Sennwald V, Delplanque S, Brosch T, Sander D (2016) Measuring wanting and liking from animals to humans: A systematic review. Neurosci Biobehav Rev 263:124–142

Povinelli DJ (2000) Folk Physics for Apes. Oxford University Press, New York

Povinelli DJ, Vonk J (2003) Chimpanzee minds: suspiciously human? Trends Cogn Sci 7:157–160

Premack D, Woodruff G (1978) Chimpanzee problem-solving: a test for comprehension. Science 202:532–535

Redgrave P, Gurney K (2006) The short-latency dopamine signal: a role in discovering novel actions? Nat Rev Neurosci 7:967–975

Riters LV (2012) The role of motivation and reward neural systems in vocal communication in songbirds. Front Neuroendocrinol 33:194–209

Salimpoor VN, Benovoy M, Larcher K, Dagher A, Zatorre RJ (2011) Anatomically distinct dopamine release during anticipation and experience of peak emotion to music. Nat Neurosci 14:257–262

Salimpoor VN, Zald DH, Zatorre RJ, Dagher A, McIntosh AR (2015) Predictions and the brain: how musical sounds become rewarding. Trends Cogn Sci 19:86–91

Sasaki A, Sotnikova TD, Gainetdinov RR, Jarvis ED (2006) Social context-dependent singing-regulated dopamine. J Neurosci 26:9010–9014

Seki Y, Hessler NA, Xie K, Okanoya K (2014) Food rewards modulate the activity of song neurons in Bengalese finches. Eur J Neurosci 39:975–983

Schultz W (2007) Behavioral dopamine signals. Trends Neurosci 30:203–210

Schultz W (2016) Dopamine reward prediction-error signalling: a two-component response. Nat Rev Neurosci 17:183–195

Seltzer LJ, Ziegler TE, Pollak SD (2010) Social vocalizations can release oxytocin in humans. Proc Biol Sci 277:2661–2666

Shannon LM, Boyko RH, Castelhano M, Corey E, Hayward JJ, McLean C, White ME, Abi Said M, Anita BA, Bondjengo NI, Calero J, Galov A, Hedimbi M, Imam B, Khalap R, Lally D, Masta A, Oliveira KC, Pérez L, Randall J, Tam NM, Trujillo-Cornejo FJ, Valeriano C, Sutter NB, Todhunter RJ, Bustamante CD, Boyko AR (2015) Genetic structure in village dogs reveals a Central Asian domestication origin. Proc Natl Acad Sci U S A 112:13639–13644

Shteynberg G (2015) Shared Attention. Perspect Psychol Sci 10:579–590

Simonyan K, Horwitz B, Jarvis ED (2012) Dopamine regulation of human speech and bird song: a critical review. Brain Lang 122:142–150

Simonyan K, Herscovitch P, Horwitz B (2013) Speech-induced striatal dopamine release is left lateralized and coupled to functional striatal circuits in healthy humans: a combined PET, fMRI and DTI study. Neuroimage 70:21–32

Skuse DH, Gallagher L (2009) Dopaminergic-neuropeptide interactions in the social brain. Trends Cogn Sci 13:27–35

Skuse DH, Gallagher L (2011) Genetic influences on social cognition. Pediatr Res 69:85R–91R

Sobel DM, Yoachim CM, Gopnik A, Meltzoff AN, Blumenthal EJ (2007) The blicket within: preschoolers' inferences about insides and causes. J Cogn Dev 8:159–182

Somel M, Liu X, Khaitovich P (2013) Human brain evolution: transcripts, metabolites and their regulators. Nat Rev Neurosci 14:112–127

Sterponi L, de Kirby K, Shankey J (2015) Rethinking language in autism. Autism 19:517–526

Syal S, Finlay BL (2011) Thinking outside the cortex: social motivation in the evolution and development of language. Dev Sci 14:417–430

Tamir DI, Mitchell JP (2012) Disclosing information about the self is intrinsically rewarding. Proc Natl Acad Sci U S A 109:8038–8043

Taylor J (2009) *Not a Chimp*: The Hunt to Find the Genes that Make us Human. Oxford University Press, Oxford

Tishkoff SA, Reed FA, Ranciaro A, Voight BF, Babbitt CC, Silverman JS, Powell K, Mortensen HM, Hirbo JB, Osman M, Ibrahim M, Omar SA, Lema G, Nyambo TB, Ghori J, Bumpstead S, Pritchard JK, Wray GA, Deloukas P (2007) Convergent adaptation of human lactase persistence in Africa and Europe. Nat Genet 39:31–40

Tokarev K, Tiunova A, Scharff C, Anokhin K (2011) Food for song: expression of c-Fos and ZENK in the zebra finch song nuclei during food aversion learning. PLoS One 6:e21157

Tomasello M (2014) A Natural History of Human Thinking. Harvard University Press, Cambridge

Tomasello M, Call J, Hare B (1998) Five primate species follow the visual gaze of conspecifics. Anim Behav 55:1063–1069

Tomasello M, Call J, Hare B (2003a) Chimpanzees versus humans: it's not that simple. Trends Cogn Sci 7:239–240

Tomasello M, Call J, Hare B (2003b) Chimpanzees understand psychological states - the question is which ones and to what extent. Trends Cogn Sci 7:153–156

Tordjman S, Anderson GM, Botbol M, Brailly-Tabard S, Perez-Diaz F, Graignic R, Carlier M, Schmit G, Rolland AC, Bonnot O, Trabado S, Roubertoux P, Bronsard G (2009) Pain reactivity and plasma beta-endorphin in children and adolescents with autistic disorder. PLoS One 4:e5289

Trut LN (1999) Early canid domestication: the farm-fox experiment. Amer Sci 87:160–169

Verhoeven JS, Rommel N, Prodi E, Leemans A, Zink I, Vandewalle E, Noens I, Wagemans J, Steyaert J, Boets B, Van de Winckel A, De Cock P, Lagae L, Sunaert S (2012) Is there a common neuroanatomical substrate of language deficit between autism spectrum disorder and specific language impairment? Cereb Cortex 22:2263–2271

Verly M, Verhoeven J, Zink I, Mantini D, Peeters R, Deprez S, Emsell L, Boets B, Noens I, Steyaert J, Lagae L, De Cock P, Rommel N, Sunaert S (2014) Altered functional connectivity of the language network in ASD: role of classical language areas and cerebellum. Neuroimage Clin 4:374–382

Voight BF, Kudaravalli S, Wen X, Pritchard JK (2006) A map of recent positive selection in the human genome. PLoS Biol 4: e72. Erratum in: PLoS Biol. 2007 5:e147. PLoS Biol. 2006 4:e154

von dem Hagen EA, Stoyanova RS, Rowe JB, Baron-Cohen S, Calder AJ (2014) Direct gaze elicits atypical activation of the theory-of-mind network in autism spectrum conditions. Cereb Cortex 24:1485–1492

Waismeyer A, Meltzoff AN, Gopnik A (2015) Causal learning from probabilistic events in 24-month-olds: an action measure. Dev Sci 18:175–182

Walum H, Westberg L, Henningsson S, Neiderhiser JM, Reiss D, Igl W, Ganiban JM, Spotts EL, Pedersen NL, Eriksson E, Lichtenstein P (2008) Genetic variation in the vasopressin receptor 1a gene (AVPR1A) associates with pair-bonding behavior in humans. Proc Natl Acad Sci U S A 105:14153–14156

Wang ET, Kodama G, Baldi P, Moyzis RK (2006) Global landscape of recent inferred Darwinian selection for Homo sapiens. Proc Natl Acad Sci U S A 103:135–140

Wilkins AS, Wrangham RW, Fitch WT (2014) The "domestication syndrome" in mammals: a unified explanation based on neural crest cell behavior and genetics. Genetics 197:795–808

Williams JH, Whiten A, Suddendorf T, Perrett DI (2001) Imitation, mirror neurons and autism. Neurosci Biobehav Rev 25:287–295

Willuhn I, Tose A, Wanat MJ, Hart AS, Hollon NG, Phillips PE, Schwarting RK, Wöhr M (2014) Phasic dopamine release in the nucleus accumbens in response to pro-social 50 kHz ultrasonic vocalizations in rats. J Neurosci 34:10616–10623

Wrangham R (2003) The Evolution of Cooking. In: Brockman J (ed), The New Humanists: Science at the Edge. Sterling Publishing, Dubai, p 108–109

Wrangham R, Peterson D (1997) Demonic Males: Apes and the Origin of Human Violence. Mariner Books, San Diego

Wrangham RW, Jones JH, Laden G, Pilbeam D, Conklin-Brittain N (1999) The raw and the stolen. Cooking and the ecology of human origins. Curr Anthropol 40:567–594

Zatorre RJ (2015) Musical pleasure and reward: mechanisms and dysfunction. Ann N Y Acad Sci 1337:202–211

Zatorre RJ, Salimpoor VN (2013) From perception to pleasure: music and its neural substrates. Proc Natl Acad Sci U S A 110 (Suppl 2):10430–10437

12

Epilogue

This book has focused on a specific aspect of the evolution of our species, which are the neurobiological innovations that took place to allow us to communicate through a syntactically and semantically structured language that uses speech as its main communicative channel. Our brain is special for several reasons, most of them related to our capacity for speech and language, like its large size housing a great number of neurons, and the lateralization of its functions that puts stringent demands on interhemispheric connectivity. Our memory capacity, particularly in the form of working memory (especially auditory), is also unique among primates. This led me some years ago to think that the expansion of working memory capacity, particularly through the development of the phonological loop and its neuronal underpinnings, was a particularly relevant acquisition for the evolution of speech. Recognizing that the evolution of speech must have been an extremely complex process, my proposal has focused on identifying specific inflection points that may have significantly changed or accelerated the evolutionary trajectory of our species. In my view, this is a useful and recommended strategy to unveil the different variables involved in complex phenomena. In this direction, I have aimed to specify circumscribed neural

© The Author(s) 2017
F. Aboitiz, *A Brain for Speech*,
DOI 10.1057/978-1-137-54060-7_12

circuits that may be necessary for speech development and may have been critical in its evolution. Furthermore, I have looked for possible homologous circuits in non-human primates (possibly serving a quite different function), in order to establish an evolutionary continuity with our recent ancestors.

Throughout this book, I have discussed alternative perspectives for the origin of speech, like the gestural origin of language and the mirror neuron hypothesis, with which I partly agree, in the sense that human communication is an opportunistic, multimodal behavior that uses any means possible to transmit information, be it gestural, vocal, or otherwise. Nonetheless, none of these perspectives has really addressed the key issue of how speech became the dominant communication modality, and what were the neural and biological processes involved in this transformation. Furthermore, in my opinion, the idea that there was a primitive gesture-dominant stage that served as scaffolding for subsequent speech origins is speculative and backed by little evidence. On the other hand, I have reviewed comparative evidence from birds and mammals, including primates, to illustrate that vocal learning capacity – a critical requisite for speech evolution – occurs in several animal species. Primates may not be particularly good at vocal learning, as they have little voluntary control over the vocal folds, but their voluntary control of the upper vocal tract, particularly the lips, is related to social behavior and its motor coordination is not unlike that in humans.

The book's central argument is that at a more central level, the acquisition of the phonological loop was a key element in the acquisition of speech, as a circuit connecting the ventral motor cortex with auditory areas via the arcuate fasciculus (supported by inferior parietal and anterior temporal projections to the emerging Broca's region), and with brainstem nuclei controlling phonation. It is very likely that at least part of the circuitry involved in the phonological loop, including a rudimentary arcuate fasciculus, was already present in the common ancestor with the chimpanzee, but did not necessarily participate in vocal behavior. At some unknown point in evolution (perhaps in Australopithecines), this temporoparietal circuit was co-opted to participate in learned vocal behavior, slowly giving rise to a primitive proto-speech-like stage, marked by song-like sequences and "proto-lexical" items signaling objects or events. This resulted in behavioral changes associated with a gradual increase in brain size in early *Homo*. But the full functional expansion of this incipient phonological loop is probably a more recent event, concomitant with the development of semantics, syntax, and the development of a theory of mind, which are essential events in the cultural and genetic revolution that started with archaic *Homo sapiens* and exploded some 50,000 years ago. The acquisition of modern language, largely mediated by speech, had vast consequences for human behavior, engaging us in a large-scale evolutionary process that includes not only us but also many other species. This is perhaps one of the most radical events we have seen in the history of the Earth and is not without consequences, as we are probably on the verge of causing the sixth mass extinction of the planet. Eloquently, Brian Cox asserts, "The idea that a civilization may destroy itself is both ludicrous and likely. We are pathetically inadequate at long term planning, idiotically primitive in our destructive urges and pathologically incapable of simply getting along" (Cox 2014 p 45). But speech has also endowed us with the power to establish conversations and listen to others, and with a powerful ability to foresee outcomes that are distant in time. It therefore depends on our capacity to converse again to secure the fate of our species and our world.

Reference

Cox B (2014) Human Universe. William Collins, London

Author Index

© The Author(s) 2017
F. Aboitiz, *A Brain for Speech*,
DOI 10.1057/978-1-137-54060-7

Subject Index

© The Author(s) 2017
F. Aboitiz, *A Brain for Speech*,
DOI 10.1057/978-1-137-54060-7

fMRI repetition suppression method, 293
Folding, cortical, 94–96
Folk physics, 349, 430
Food calls, 382
Food songs, 396
Food stimuli, noxious, 443
Food storing birds, 108
Foreign accent, 402
FOXP1, 407
FOXP2, 2, 26, 161, 406–410, 443
lateralization, 161
Fractional anisotropy, 182, 190
Freezing behavior, 442
Frog, 132, 250–251
Frontal aslant tract, 70, 398, 401
Frontal cortex, 68, 110, 115–116, 227, 229, 256, 259, 393, 409, 430
frontal lobe, 115–116
Frontal lobe, 43, 116, 147–148, 151, 259, 272
Frontal vision, binocular vision, 114
Frontal vision callosal fibers, 194
Fronto-parietal networks, 144, 228
Frontoparietal segment, superior longitudinal fasciculus/arcuate fasciculus, 54
Fronto-temporal segment, arcuate fasciculus, 54
Frugivory, 108–109
Functional connectivity, 63, 64, 144, 176–177, 234, 274, 277, 438, 447
Function words, 313–314
Fundamental frequency, speech, 380
Fusiform gyrus, 56

G

Gamma interhemispheric synchrony, 198–199, 200
Gamma oscillations, 74
Gamma oscillations, interhemispheric delay, 198–199
Gamma Rhythm, 74, 75
Gamma sampling, 142
Ganglion cells, 253
Gastrointestinal tract, 93
Gaze following, 430
Gaze, gaze direction, 393
Geladas, 388
Gene, 14, 26, 45, 104, 105, 113, 114, 161–163, 332, 341–343, 346, 360, 405–410, 437, 438, 443, 452
Gene expression, 161, 341, 360, 405, 407, 408, 410
Generosity, 437
Genetic homology, 343, 409
Geniculate nucleus, lateral, 251, 253
Genu, callosum, 175, 181
Geschwind's area, 56, 202
Gestural theory of language origins, 389
Gestural-vocal coevolution, 316
Gestures, 1, 4, 6, 25, 33, 115, 152–155, 268, 273, 278, 287–289, 291, 298, 299, 301, 309, 310, 312, 315–317, 319, 381, 382, 388, 389, 393, 394, 397, 431, 433, 439, 455, 468
Gestures, communication, primates, 115, 273, 288
Gibbons, 381–382, 389
Glia, glial cells, 94, 96, 100, 101, 104

9781137540591

Printed in Japan

J0045684003